THE
THISTLETHWAITE
FAMILY.

A STUDY IN GENEALOGY.

BY

BERNARD THISTLETHWAITE.

Vol. I.

PRINTED FOR PRIVATE CIRCULATION BY
HEADLEY BROTHERS, BISHOPSGATE, LONDON, E.C.
1910.

1164915

But you are lovely Leaves, where we
    May read how soon things have
     Their end, though ne'r so brave:
And after they have shown their pride,
    Like you a while: they glide
       Into the Grave.

                   ROBERT HERRICK,
                      1591-1674.

Earth yields the milk, but all her mind
Is vowed to thresh for stouter stock.
Her passion for old giantkind,
That scaled the mount, uphurled the rock,
Devolves on them who read aright
Her meaning and devoutly serve.

                 GEORGE MEREDITH,
                      1828-1909.

NTS.

2 Jan 1910

Dear Sir,

I am enclosing you a circular describing my Thistlethwaite Family History. Although you are not a direct descendant, yet a very large part of the people described in my book are descended from Hunters & so related to you. You are therefore at liberty to subscribe. Should you ...

; do so. Love you my
thanks for much matter of
interest supplied relative to the
Hunter family. I have since
increased my knowledge considera
from several sources, & besides
the letter press, I shall show
two Intermarriage Charts
between Hunters & Thistlethwaite:
To haste I am —

yours faithfully

Bernard Thistlethwaite

SUMMARY OF CONTENTS.

INTERMARRIAGE CHARTS.

PREFACE.

OBSESSED by the Conventions, I almost penned a conventional preface. But the spirit of perversity, which has descended upon me from so many Quaker ancestors, reasserted itself with customary unwisdom on this occasion also, and I intend to write as I wish rather than by precedent.

One is familiar with the attitude of the tradesman to whom profit-making is the cause for disposing of his wares; and with that of the benevolent lady who conversely, in the tracts which she distributes, studies her own inclinations rather than those of the recipients. While I have no wish to depreciate my Nietzschean convictions by the suggestion that I am ever likely to distribute tracts, I would in this case ally my attitude with that of the benevolent lady.

I therefore make no apology for the existence of this volume. I am very well aware that it is not in any sense perfect. One never contemplates the production of a family history which shall approach at all nearly to perfection, and the compilation of this work has seen many quarrels unexpected between desirability and practicability, to the overthrow of the former. But if there were no excuse for family histories other than the vast influence which a knowledge of their heredity should have over the individual lives of all who dwell in this our world, I should still issue this book, knowing myself well justified.

That statements intentional and errors unintentional will produce dislike, is probable. My aim throughout has been to write truth. In this respect with regret, many omissions have been made in view of a somewhat wide circulation; for instance, insanity is not mentioned, although not every descendant has escaped unscathed. But there remain a few matters which I could not omit without implying a serious untruth. *Veritas prævalebit.*

The actual words of my correspondents have frequently been employed, as a paraphrase may so easily convey a different meaning.   I have continuously sought to outroot ambiguity.   It is needless to add that the consideration of literary style has been shunned as leading to this.   In proof, the manuscript from which the printers have produced this book is my first draft, built up from letters, charts, and note-books.

I have attempted to record within this volume every descendant of William Thistlethwaite, of Harborgill*, by his wife Alice Mason, whom he married in 1705.   I have traced considerably more than 1800† of these blood-descendants by name, and know that there must be several hundreds whom I have not yet discovered.   Of each I have tried to obtain the place, day, month, and year, of birth, of marriage, and of death.   The occupation of males and certain other matters are included when obtainable, but for obvious reasons little attempt has been made to describe personal characteristics, although with regret.   The length of each description is not to be taken as an indication of the relative importance of the person described.   It is chiefly attributable to the relative accessibility of particulars.   I shall be glad to include in my second volume any interesting facts herein omitted through ignorance.

I entrust this history to its subscribers with the definite understanding that no one uses for advertisement purposes, or for annoying those who may be distantly akin, the names and addresses given here. Let me appeal to the honour of my kinsfolk in this matter.   For myself, I make it a rule never to write a second time to a person until he has answered my first letter.

* The name is now spelled " Harbergill."   I know nothing of its etymology, but I have preferred to use the spelling " Harborgill," which was probably the most common form until recent years.

† Although the actual numbering only reaches 1791, many previously unknown descendants have been added as this book was going through the press, and have been numbered alphabetically, *e.g.*, (2044a), (2044b), etc.   I estimate that over 4,000 different persons are mentioned in this book altogether.

In most cases I have indicated those educated at Bootham and the Mount Schools, York, at Leighton Park, Reading, and at Polam Hall, Darlington. So many descendants have imbibed for more or less lengthy periods the spirit of those great ones which hovers between the cupolas of Ackworth School, that practicability—wrecker of so many wishes—has silenced the name herein.

Avoidance of the conceits of genealogy has been striven for. We are certainly an " old " family : I imagine that all families must be so of necessity unless their critics admit a recent spontaneous generation. But if "an old family " signifies by convention a family which amassed ,wealth previous to the last three generations, then I protest that we are still in the fœtal stage. I have not yet proved the right of our male line to use the crest and coat of arms registered to the Thistlethwayte Family of Southwick Park, Hampshire ; and in fact think the possibility of doing so remote. We are egregiously middle-class.

It is true that during the sixteenth century—so long ago that we may call it, in mixed but conforming metaphor, the zenith of a previous incarnation—our Thistlethwayte forebears had considerable transactions in real estate situated in Dent and Sedbergh. Of their land, their charities, and their progeny, I hope to write in the not distant future.*

The History of Pedigree-making would form an interesting socio-logical study. Those with decades more experience have repeatedly expressed to me a complete incapacity to understand my reasons for tracing any but direct male descent—" for when a woman changes her name, she and her descendants no longer form part of her father's family,

---

* It is my intention to issue a second volume of the Thistlethwaite Family History in the course of a year of two. This will include (a) The Wensleydale Thistlethwaite descendants, introducing branches of the Crosfield, Wallis, Fothergill, Cadbury, etc., families, and certain Seventeenth Century Quaker Sufferings, (b) A full account of the ancestors and remote relatives of the Dent Dale, Wensleydale, and Hampshire families, back to the time of Henry VII., (c) Incidental, but consider-able and interesting, particulars which I have accumulated, concerning allied families, such as those of Fothergill, Harrison, Capstick, Hunter, Mason, etc., (d) Photographs and further descriptions of Harborgill, Hudshouse, Carr End, Spicegill, Eugalas, and other family houses, (e) Corrections and additions to this First Volume, (f) An Essay on Heredity and Eugenics, (g) a complete index to both volumes. (I shall be glad of corrections, additions, and suggestions.)

but belong to the pedigree of her husband." Pedigrees were formerly made to show descent of land and titles, which usually passed to the heir male. And in truth the entail of land was an excellent method for preserving the small land-owner, and thus retaining the interest of the middle class in rural matters ; in our day an unwise wish for impartiality to offspring causes a division of real estate only possible by conversion.

But the vast science of physical and mental heredity has now aroused us with its enormous importance, and without our pedigree we cannot understand either ourselves or our children. This is the reason why a family without land or title should possess its family history, and this is the reason for tracing descent through women equally with men. Indeed if my conservative friends had buried themselves a little deeper in the past, they would have discovered sometime in the existence of every race the custom of Mother-right, that of tracing descent only through female lines. " The result of anthropological investigations during the past half-century has been to show that mother-right everywhere preceded father-right, and the reckoning of descent in the modern civilized fashion through both parents." * This last is of course the correct method. On the average our parents supply us equally with our characteristics. †

" A knowledge of the importance of heredity, instead of weakening the sense of responsibility, shows how much wider and deeper our responsibility is than had been suspected. We come to understand that on our personal and collective action depend not only the present environment of the people, but also the innate qualities of future generations. Blind

* " Primitive Paternity " (1909), by E. S. Hartland, page 256.

† The following extract from " The Family and the Nation," (1909), by W. C. D. Whetham, F.R.S. (page 22), may further prove my point : " There is some evidence to indicate that the germ cells of the female are of two kinds, while those of the male are all similar. If so, a female carries both male and female characters, while a male is exclusively male. The sex of any one offspring is determined solely by the chance whether one of the germ cells of the male meets a male or female germ cell of the female." Whetham's book is an excellent statement of the main facts of heredity and eugenics.

acquiescence in evil, ignorance of the issues at stake, may result in irremediable injury to unborn millions." * And in fact statistics show conclusively that our race is degenerating, on account of the much reduced rate of reproduction among the middle classes, during the last generation, without a relative decrease in the birth-rate of the lower classes. We are breeding the majority of the future population of this country from our worst stocks. While a knowledge of this all-important state of affairs must remould our social and political principles, it may be well here to indicate its individual influence, as suggested by one of our greatest biometricians.

" The unthrifty increase and multiply and make the struggle harder for the thrifty, the conscientious, and the able, who have to provide not only for their own offspring, but for the offspring of the unfit in the next generation.

" I would therefore emphasise the view that much of the current feeling with regard to early marriage and good-sized families is demonstrably immoral, and is opposed to social welfare in that it must lead to the degeneration of the society in which it is current.

" Our present knowledge of heredity shows us that the average man is a product of his ancestors in health, in intellect, and in honesty. Hence all social conduct should be directed on this point, to insuring that the minority, who in any case provide the next generation, is formed from the best stock in the community. The fertility of the unhealthy, of the mentally defective, of the dishonest, should be checked by custom and legislation in every way ; while that of the healthy, sane, and conscientious should, on the other hand, be in every way encouraged.

" If we consider first individual conduct, we see need for a revision of current social feeling with regard to ancestral history. Both man and woman ought to know the tale of their past ; the faults, physical and mental, of ancestors and other relations ought not to be hidden away ; and the need of a new and rational pride in ancestry should be inculcated.

" The celibacy of the individual who comes of faulty stock should be

* " The Family and the Nation," page 6.

recognised in social conduct, and social condemnation should follow marriage into a tainted stock or the marriage of any members of such stock.   But such restraint of bad stock must also be accompanied among the educated by a change of feeling as to the conduct of the healthy, able, and generally fit stock.

" We require, indeed, what it may be difficult to create—a strong social feeling against that celibacy which flows from the desire for the increased powers of enjoyment resulting when no hostages have been given to fortune." *

When one first considers the established facts of heredity, " a feeling of despair is apt to arise at the inevitableness of the succession of good or evil.   It seems of little use to fight against fate.   But in reality, for most people, there is no cause for such despondence.   As usual, a knowledge of the natural laws governing a subject leads to greater freedom, if also to increased responsibility.   We learn the exact limits of our liberty, the precise nature of our fetters.   We know partially the extent to which we are masters of fate when we realise the probable character of the abilities that are latent within us.

" Certainly, in problems connected with the education and the choice of professions for children, nothing can be more helpful than to have some idea of the directions in which they are likely to succeed, the duties and responsibilities that probably may be best undertaken by them. Similarly the time-honoured petition ' lead us not into temptation ' gains new force and meaning if we understand the nature of the temptations which are likely most to affect us.   It becomes also much more possible to remove danger from each person, or to warn and fortify him against forms of evil which have already proved fatal to others of the same stock.

" By the study of heredity, we may gain an insight into the qualities that are entrusted to each individual to develop for the advantage of himself, his family, and the community, and learn to recognise the

* " National Life from the Standpoint of Science," (1905), by Karl Pearson, F.R.S. (pages 102-103).

various failings specially to be watched and guarded against. The whole subject is fraught at once with the greatest spiritual dignity and the utmost social importance." *

Although true wisdom would have included in this history, as Professor Pearson suggests, an account of the mental and physical characteristics and diseases of each descendant, I frankly admit that I dare not so far defy the opinions of my possible subscribers. I was, therefore, glad of the excellent excuse that no one person could do this with any degree of satisfaction, and yet complete the work within any short period. This book, then, is less a family history than a basis for one.

I suggest that each descendant who is interested in this matter should devote his energies to his own branch, and work it out in detail. No more vitally important family document could exist, and the author's name and good work would live for centuries in his posterity. †

But in order that every reader and possible amplifier may understand how this foundation has been built, it will be wise to discuss it in more detail. Roughly speaking, the whole of this pedigree has been derived from Quaker records and from correspondence. Its faults must all be laid at my door, for I have myself built the whole structure within these last three years. Two large but bare beams have been given me : they have been useful, but I have probed every inch before I trusted them. I refer to the Chart of the Fothergill Family (drawn up by Watson Fothergill, Esq., of Nottingham, and lent me by Gerald Fothergill, Esq., of New Wandsworth), and to the Thompson-Thistlethwaite Chart (drawn up by Mrs. F. I. Reckitt, of Hull, and lent me by Mrs. W. J. Cudworth, of York). These were, I believe, the only two existing pedigrees in the family when I began my research three years ago. ‡

---

* " The Family and the Nation " (1909), by W. C. D. Whetham, F.R.S. (pages 120-121).

† I shall be glad to correspond with, or assist, any person who attempts to do this ; its statistical value alone would be of considerable importance. I shall also be glad to reply to any particular questions respecting any part of the family history if my correspondents will be good enough to enclose a stamped addressed envelope.

‡ I regret that I have not been in a position to burden anyone but myself with the proof-correcting. It is difficult to discover one's own errors.

Let every one who appreciates this family history render thanks to the memory of my late grandfather, Jeremiah Thistlethwaite : to his unfailing encouragement and to his excellent memory my perseverance in the task is largely due. He often expressed to me his wish that he might see the history in print. But the meting of days is not in our hands,

" And when the Angel with his darker Draught
Draws up to thee—take that and do not shrink."

He was buried in our quiet old graveyard on the twentieth of April. He had read the proof of my circular, and by a curious accident it bore this same date.

My method of arrangement is best described by reference to the explanatory charts following this. Our common ancestors, William and Alice Thistlethwaite, had nine children, eight of whom married and had issue. The descendants of each of these eight are described respectively in the eight parts into which this book is divided. Every direct descendant of our common ancestors bears a distinctive number in brackets after his name. Thus the relationship existing between any numbered persons is in very few cases more remote than fifth cousin. Those in the same part are of course more closely related than those in different parts. A line between two sub-sections denotes that the persons described in the sub-sections so divided do not bear the relationship of parent and child to one another. The order followed is that of age, without distinction of sex.

I regret extremely that neither index nor tabular pedigree accompanies this book. Until lately I thought them practicable. I prepared a section of the tabular pedigree and calculated by proportion that the whole would measure about eighty yards. The index would have increased the cost, and delayed the publication several months. I therefore decided that the history without them was better than no history.

I have printed a few more copies of this book than were actually subscribed for, and these may be obtained on application to myself.

I have refrained from praising our dalesman stock. By its progeny set forth herein shall it be judged. And if this preface should appear to the reader as a sickly gleam of facetiousness finally overcome by dreary clouds of admonition, I would ask him to blame an unfortunate literary style. Had I been offered a seat among the immortals, I would have preferred to receive it for the ponderous wisdom of a Spencer than for the unstable beauty of a Swinburne. May this book give joy in recollection ; and may it incite forward. May it help us to that wise pride and to that discerning egoism which are primary and essential virtues.

Great Ayton, Yorkshire,

June, 1910.

Name of Subscriber_____

You may be interested in referring to ~~page~~_____

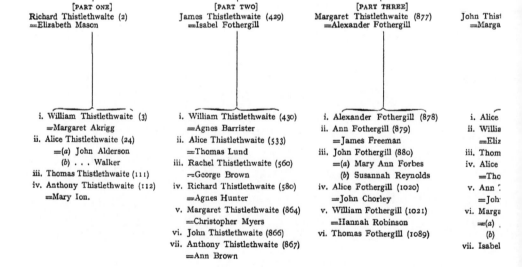

[PART ONE]
Richard Thistlethwaite (2)
=Elizabeth Mason

[PART TWO]
James Thistlethwaite (429)
=Isabel Fothergill

[PART THREE]
Margaret Thistlethwaite (877)
=Alexander Fothergill

John Thist
=Marga

i. William Thistlethwaite (3)
   =Margaret Akrigg
ii. Alice Thistlethwaite (24)
   =(a) John Alderson
     (b) . . . Walker
iii. Thomas Thistlethwaite (111)
iv. Anthony Thistlethwaite (112)
   =Mary Ion.

i. William Thistlethwaite (430)
   =Agnes Barrister
ii. Alice Thistlethwaite (533)
   =Thomas Lund
iii. Rachel Thistlethwaite (560)
   =George Brown
iv. Richard Thistlethwaite (580)
   =Agnes Hunter
v. Margaret Thistlethwaite (864)
   =Christopher Myers
vi. John Thistlethwaite (866)
vii. Anthony Thistlethwaite (867)
   =Ann Brown

i. Alexander Fothergill (878)
ii. Ann Fothergill (879)
   =James Freeman
iii. John Fothergill (880)
   =(a) Mary Ann Forbes
     (b) Susannah Reynolds
iv. Alice Fothergill (1020)
   =John Chorley
v. William Fothergill (1021)
   =Hannah Robinson
vi. Thomas Fothergill (1089)

i. Alice
ii. Willia
   =Eliz
iii. Thom
iv. Alice
   =Tho
v. Ann
   =Joh
vi. Marga
   =(a)
     (b)
vii. Isabel

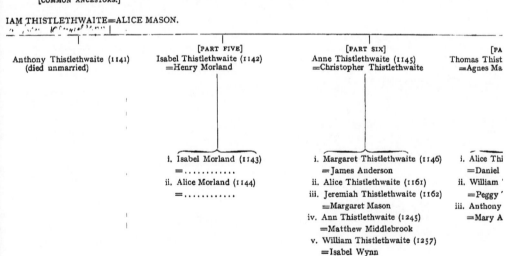

IAM THISTLETHWAITE=ALICE MASON.

Anthony Thistlethwaite (1141) (died unmarried)	[PART FIVE] Isabel Thistlethwaite (1142) =Henry Morland	[PART SIX] Anne Thistlethwaite (1145) =Christopher Thistlethwaite	[PA Thomas Thist =Agnes Ma
	i. Isabel Morland (1143) =............ ii. Alice Morland (1144) =............	i. Margaret Thistlethwaite (1146) =James Anderson ii. Alice Thistlethwaite (1161) iii. Jeremiah Thistlethwaite (1162) =Margaret Mason iv. Ann Thistlethwaite (1245) =Matthew Middlebrook v. William Thistlethwaite (1257) =Isabel Wynn	i. Alice Thi =Daniel ii. William =Peggy iii. Anthony =Mary A

PART ONE.

RICHARD THISTLETHWAITE (2)＝ELIZABETH MASON.

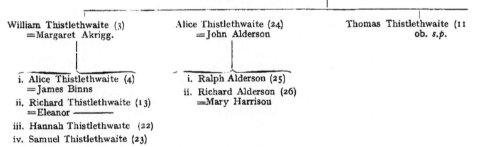

William Thistlethwaite (3)
　＝Margaret Akrigg.

　　i. Alice Thistlethwaite (4)
　　　＝James Binns
　ii. Richard Thistlethwaite (13)
　　　＝Eleanor ————
　iii. Hannah Thistlethwaite (22)
　iv. Samuel Thistlethwaite (23)

Alice Thistlethwaite (24)
　＝John Alderson

　　i. Ralph Alderson (25)
　ii. Richard Alderson (26)
　　　＝Mary Harrison

Thomas Thistlethwaite (11
　　　ob. *s.p.*

John Thistlethwaite (866)   Anthony Thistlethwaite (867)
                             =Ann Brown

i. James Thistlethwaite (868)
ii. John Thistlethwaite (869)
iii. Richard Thistlethwaite (870)
iv. Isabel Thistlethwaite (871)
v. William Thistlethwaite (872)
   =Martha ————
vi. Ann Thistlethwaite (874)
vii. Rachel Thistlethwaite (875)
viii. Anthony Thistlethwaite (876)

PART TWO

JAMES THISTLETHWAITE (429)=ISABEL FOTHERGILL

William Thistlethwaite (430) Agnes Banister	Alice Thistlethwaite (533) =Thomas Lund	Rachel Thistlethwaite (560) =George Brown	Richard Thistlethwaite (580) =Agnes Hunter	Margaret Thistlethwaite (864) =Christopher Myers
i. James Thistlethwaite (431) =Jane —	i. Elizabeth Lund (534) =William Thistlethwaite (1092)	i. Margaret Brown (561)	i. James Thistlethwaite (581)	i. Isabel Myers (865)
ii. Edmund Thistlethwaite (434) =Susannah Lister	ii. Samuel Lund (535)	ii. Isabel Brown (562)	ii. John Thistlethwaite (582) =(1) Sarah M. Smith =(2) Elizabeth Routh	
iii. Isabella Thistlethwaite (435) =Thomas Guy	iii. Isabella Lund (536) =William Walton	iii. William Brown (563)	iii. Isabel Thistlethwaite (583) =John Wetherald	
iv. John Thistlethwaite (475) =(1) Isabel Ion =(2) Esther Eliza Dickinson	iv James Lund (559)	iv. James Brown (564)	iv. Jane Thistlethwaite (759) =John Thompson	
		v. George Brown (565)	v. Anthony Thistlethwaite (841)	
		vi. Alice Brown (566) =John Burton	vi. Rachel Thistlethwaite (842) =John Webster	
		vii. John Brown (572)	vii. William Thistlethwaite (862)	
		viii. Rachel Brown (573) =Samuel Fielden	viii. Richard Thistlethwaite (863) =Sarah Yearldey	
		ix. George Brown (576)		
		x. Christopher Brown (577)		
		xi. Anthony Brown (578)		
		xii. Hannah Brown (579)		

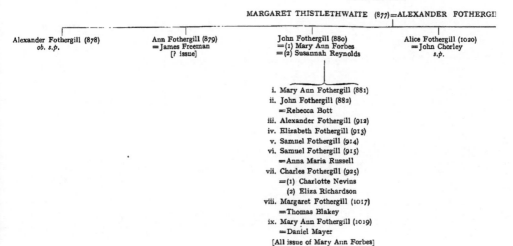

PART THREE.

MARGARET THISTLETHWAITE (877)=ALEXANDER FOTHERGI

| Alexander Fothergill (878) *ob. s.p.* | Ann Fothergill (879) =James Freeman [? issue] | John Fothergill (880) =(1) Mary Ann Forbes =(2) Susannah Reynolds | Alice Fothergill (1020) =John Chorley *s.p.* |

i. Mary Ann Fothergill (881)
ii. John Fothergill (882)
 =Rebecca Bott
iii. Alexander Fothergill (912)
iv. Elizabeth Fothergill (913)
v. Samuel Fothergill (914)
vi. Samuel Fothergill (915)
 =Anna Maria Russell
vii. Charles Fothergill (925)
 =(1) Charlotte Nevins
 (2) Eliza Richardson
viii. Margaret Fothergill (1017)
 =Thomas Blakey
ix. Mary Ann Fothergill (1019)
 =Daniel Mayer
[All issue of Mary Ann Forbes]

Margaret Thistlethwaite (1139)
=(1) John Bezzon
=(2) John Kershaw
s.p.

Isabel Thistlethwaite (1140)
ob. s.p.

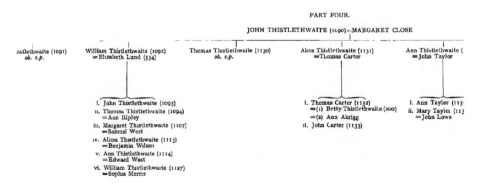

PART FOUR.

JOHN THISTLETHWAITE (1090)=MARGARET CLOSE

istlethwaite (1091)
ob. s.p.

William Thistlethwaite (1092)
=Elizabeth Lund (534)

Thomas Thistlethwaite (1130)
ob. s.p.

Alice Thistlethwaite (1131)
=Thomas Carter

Ann Thistlethwaite (
=John Taylor

i. John Thistlethwaite (1093)
ii. Thomas Thistlethwaite (1094)
=Ann Ripley
iii. Margaret Thistlethwaite (1107)
=Samuel West
iv. Alicia Thistlethwaite (1113)
=Benjamin Wilson
v. Ann Thistlethwaite (1114)
=Edward West
vi. William Thistlethwaite (1127)
=Sophia Morris

i. Thomas Carter (1132)
=(1) Betty Thistlethwaite (200)
=(2) Ann Akrigg
ii. John Carter (1133)

i. Ann Taylor (113
ii. Mary Taylor (113
=John Lowe

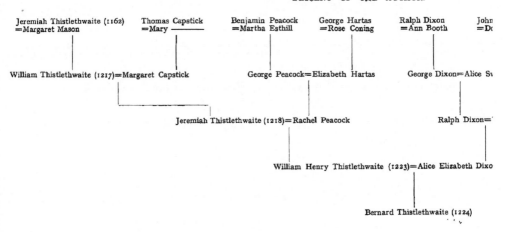

DESCENT OF THE AUTHOR.

Jeremiah Thistlethwaite (1162)   Thomas Capstick   Benjamin Peacock   George Hartas   Ralph Dixon   John
=Margaret Mason   =Mary ———   =Martha Esthill   =Rose Coning   =Ann Booth   =D

William Thistlethwaite (1217)=Margaret Capstick   George Peacock=Elizabeth Hartas   George Dixon=Alice S

Jeremiah Thistlethwaite (1218)=Rachel Peacock   Ralph Dixon=

William Henry Thistlethwaite (1223)=Alice Elizabeth Dixo

Bernard Thistlethwaite (1224)

ANNE THISTLETHWAITE (1145)=CHRISTOPHER THISTLETHWAITE

Margaret Thistlethwaite (1146) =James Anderson	Alice Thistlethwaite (1161) *ob. s.p.*	Jeremiah Thistlethwaite (1162) =Margaret Mason	Ann Thistleth =Matthew Mid

i. Michael Anderson (1147)
ii. Ann Anderson (1148)
=Thomas Thwaite
iii. Christian Anderson (1157)
=Joseph Binns
iv. Christopher Anderson (1159)
v. Margaret Anderson (1160)

i. Christopher Thistlethwaite (1163)
ii. Anthony Thistlethwaite (1164)
=Mary Hedley
iii. William Thistlethwaite (1217)
=Margaret Capstick

i. Christopher M
= Margaret –
ii. Matthew Mid
iii. Margaret Mid
iv. William Mid
v. John Middlel
vi. Ann Middleb
vii. Alice Middlet

PART SEVEN.

THOMAS THISTLETHWAITE (1260)＝AGNES MASOI

Alice Thistlethwaite (1261)
＝Daniel Harrison

William Thistlethwaite (1263)
＝Peggy Thomasson

A

i. Alice Harrison (1262)

i. Thomas Thistlethwaite (1264)

ii. Agnes Thistlethwaite (1265)

iii. Margaret Thistlethwaite (1266)

iv. Christopher Thistlethwaite (1267)

v. Alice Thistlethwaite (1268)

vi. John Thistlethwaite (1269)
＝Alice ———

vii. William Thistlethwaite (1272)
＝ Elizabeth ———

viii. Joseph Thistlethwaite (1275)

ix. Anthony Thistlethwaite (1276)

x. Isabel Thistlethwaite (1277)

xi. Mary Thistlethwaite (1278)

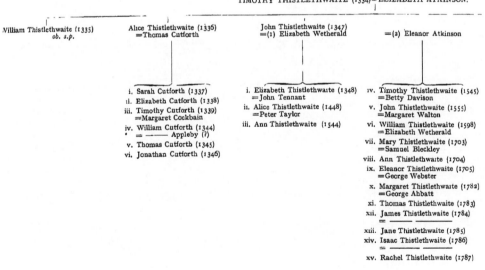

PART EIGHT.

TIMOTHY THISTLETHWAITE (1334) = ELIZABETH ATKINSON.

William Thistlethwaite (1335)
ob. s.p.

Alice Thistlethwaite (1336)
= Thomas Cutforth

John Thistlethwaite (1347)
= (1) Elizabeth Wetherald

= (2) Eleanor Atkinson

i. Sarah Cutforth (1337)
ii. Elizabeth Cutforth (1338)
iii. Timothy Cutforth (1339)
   = Margaret Cockbain
iv. William Cutforth (1344)
   • = ——— Appleby (?)
v. Thomas Cutforth (1345)
vi. Jonathan Cutforth (1346)

i. Elizabeth Thistlethwaite (1348)
   = John Tennant
ii. Alice Thistlethwaite (1448)
   = Peter Taylor
iii. Ann Thistlethwaite (1544)

iv. Timothy Thistlethwaite (1545)
   = Betty Davison
v. John Thistlethwaite (1555)
   = Margaret Walton
vi. William Thistlethwaite (1598)
   = Elizabeth Wetherald
vii. Mary Thistlethwaite (1703)
   = Samuel Bleckley
viii. Ann Thistlethwaite (1704)
ix. Eleanor Thistlethwaite (1705)
   = George Webster
x. Margaret Thistlethwaite (1782)
   = George Abbatt
xi. Thomas Thistlethwaite (1783)
xii. James Thistlethwaite (1784)
   = ———
xiii. Jane Thistlethwaite (1785)
xiv. Isaac Thistlethwaite (1786)
   = ———
xv. Rachel Thistlethwaite (1787)

William and Alice Thistlethwaite

OF HARBORGILL:

COMMON ANCESTORS

TO EVERY NUMBERED PERSON WHO FOLLOWS IN THIS VOLUME.

COMMON ANCESTORS.

William Thistlethwaite (1), was baptised 10 March, 1677, in Dent Dale, being born almost certainly at Harborgill, his father's farm. The entry in the parish register reads, "Willyam sonne of Richard Thistlethwayte, March ye 10th, 1677." The burial entry in the parish register of Dent, for his father, reads, "Richard Thystlethwayte of Harbourgill, November ye 6th, 1686." *

It therefore appears that William Thistlethwaite's father was never a Quaker, and that William Thistlethwaite was not born a Quaker. The latter's mother, Margaret Thistlethwaite, widow, of Harborgill, was married 4th May, 1688, at Sedbergh Meeting House, to Samuel Wynn, of Grisdale. Both Margaret Thistlethwaite and Samuel Wynn must have been Members of the Society of Friends before their marriage. It seems probable that Margaret Thistlethwaite and her young children joined the Society of Friends some time between her husband's death in 1686, and her second marriage in 1688. Possibly her children did not become members until later.

William Thistlethwaite (1) appears to have partially rebuilt, or repaired, Harborgill in 1700, as that date and his initials are placed over the porch, in witness of which see the frontispiece to this book. In about 1902, the year after the photograph was taken from which the frontispiece is reproduced, the windows of Harborgill were enlarged and modernised.

At the age of twenty-eight, William Thistlethwaite (1) was married, 3rd August, 1705, to Alice Mason, of Hudshouse, in Dent Dale. In

* My thanks are due to the Rev. E. S. Curwen, Vicar of Dent, for providing these two extracts from the Parish Registers. I have made several strenuous efforts to examine personally the Dent Registers, but accident has prevented up to the present. Except in quotations I have used continuously throughout this book the modern spelling " Thistlethwaite." Dent is in the extreme north-west of Yorkshire.

January, 1752, at the age of seventy-four, he had a terrible experience in escaping from his home at Harborgill during the famous Dent " gill-brach," which is described in the account of his son, Thomas Thistlethwaite (1260).   He died in Dent Dale, 12th July, 1766, aged eighty-nine years.

When at Kendal a few years ago, I spent some little time reading through the Dent Preparative Meeting Minute Book of the Society of Friends for the years 1708 to 1724.   A minute of the Preparative Meeting held at Leayat Meeting House 23rd of 2nd month, 1708, reads, " John Greenwood and Wm. Thistlethwayte is ap^{td} to attend next monthly meeting."   In the years which follow, William Thistlethwaite is frequently appointed to duties of importance under the Meeting.   For instance, in the meeting at Loaning, in Dent, held 22nd 12 mo. 1709, " Willyam Thistlethwayte is desired by this meeting to speak to Peter Chapman, to call all his creditors and offer all his goods to satisfaction."   In the meeting at Leayat in Dent, held 28th 8 mo. 1711, " William Thistle-thwayte is appointed to draw up sufferings and friends is desired to give him account thereof before our next."   In the meeting held at Leayat, 24th 8mo, 1714,* " it is agreed by this meeting that all the books that belongs to this meeting shall henceforth be lodged in William Thistle-thwayte's hand, and that all friends of this meeting shall have recourse thereunto at their request and that a catalogue thereof shall be kept in our Preparative Meeting Book."   In the meeting at Loaning, 22nd 4 mo., 1718, " agreed by this meeting that a new stable be built adjoining to the east end of the Meeting House at Leayet.   William Thistlethwayte and John Burton are appointed to see to it."

The Thistlethwaite family was one of the oldest of the " statesman " or yeoman families in Dent Dale, and William Thistlethwaite (1), as head of his family, would become a man of considerable local importance. Professor Adam Sedgwick, F.R.S., the eminent geologist, himself a native and a loyal child of Dent Dale, wrote, " Many of the old statesmen in the higher parts of Kirthwaite were numbered in the Society of Friends.

* In the meeting held at Loaning, 22nd 12 mo., 1713, it was " also agreed that friends leave that needless custom of carrying away bread and cheese at burialls, but eat and drink what we have occation for at that time, but carry not away."

Excellent men they were, and well informed in matters of common life ; lovers of religious liberty ; of great practical benevolence, and of pure moral conduct ; and they were among the foremost in all good measures of rural administration." *

The Professor, when aged eighty-four, wrote an interesting letter to a recent Thistlethwaite descendant, which may be wisely quoted here :

" The Close, Norwich,

" August 21, 1869.

" My dear Friend and brother Dalesman,

" Your letter did not require any apology, and I read it with much interest. For I do feel an emotion of brotherly love towards all the inhabitants of my native Dales, and you are one of the living represen-tatives of an ancient family of *Statesmen,* from some of whom I experienced much kindness in my boyhood. I several times was permitted to shoot rooks at Harbergill before the last representative of your name sold it and emigrated with his wife and family, I think, to Pennsylvania.

" He was a tall, good-looking man, and I also remember in my childhood, his father—a man of cheerful temper and Herculean strength, who was one of my honoured Father's dear old Friends. These are among the remembrances of my boyhood, which are still precious to me.

" My principal home still is at Cambridge, where I last year gave my *51st Annual Course of Geological Lectures.* Ought I not to thank my *Maker* with uplifted heart, when I tell you that this long score of years is counted without one single interruption of my Annual task ? It is my hope to give my 52nd and last course of University Lectures during the coming Michaelmas Term.

" Two or three months of each year, since 1834, I have had a home also at Norwich, where I have duties to perform as one of the Canons of the Cathedral. I am now, in regular course, endeavouring to perform

* An extract from " A Memorial by the Trustees of Cowgill Chapel, with a preface and appendix on the climate, history, and dialects of Dent," by Adam Sedgwick, LL.D., 8vo, Cambridge, 1868. Privately printed. Page vi. Sedgwick was born at Dent Vicarage, 22nd March, 1785, and died at Cambridge, January, 1873, unmarried. The Rev. C. A. Carter (227), then an undergraduate at St. John's, had an honourable place at his funeral.

those duties.   The infirmities of old age are gradually bringing me to the ground : I am very deaf—my eyes fail me much ; and they are so liable to inflammation that my Oculist orders me to write no long letters.   Am I not breaking his orders this moment ?   I have a niece and three great nieces with me, to cheer me, another reason for thankfulness.

" Very few copies of my pamphlet* are left.   I have three copies here, and I do not think that there is one left in the store room of the University Press at Cambridge.   But you have a positive claim upon me ; and I will send you one of the remaining copies.   The little book has produced an unexpected result.   I should never have thought of sending such a humble Pamphlet to the Queen.   But Lady Augusta Stanley, the wife of my dear friend Arthur Stanley, Dean of Westminster, begged a copy of me.   She took it with her to Windsor Castle, and read some of it to the Queen.   Then came a request (in Court language, I ought to say a command), for a copy to be sent to H.M.   Of course, I sent it joyfully.   Then came a request that a copy should be sent to Mr. Gladstone, which was, of course, also done.   He read the Pamphlet, and sent me a favourable and very amusing acknowledgment.   Our honoured Queen, after reading the Pamphlet carefully, said that she disapproved of any irregular changes of old names, and that injustice had been done. And she most kindly and condescendingly offered to hold a new Council to restore the name of Cogill Chapel.   But there was a legal difficulty in this.   So she moved the Archbishop of York to bring in a Bill before the House of Lords, which should provide for the restoration of the old name to the Incumbency of Cogill (now by a New Act of Parliament to be called the Vicarage of Cogill).   The Bill passed the Lords without opposition ; and it was carried through the House of Commons by the support of the Queen's Ministers, and so became law.

" Is not this an odd episode in the history of Dent ?

" I remain in Christian goodwill,

" Your honest friend and Dalesman,

" ADAM SEDGWICK."

* *i.e.*, the above-mentioned " Memorial."

William Thistlethwaite (1) was married to Alice Mason, of Hudshouse in Dent Dale. She was born about 1680, and was probably daughter of James and Isabel Mason. She died 7th January, 1750 or 1751, aged seventy years; a "public" Friend, *i.e.*, a religious preacher among the Quakers. She had been a minister about fifty years. In 1737 she paid religious visits in Cumberland and Northumberland, and in 1742 she visited, with Agnes Mason, in Yorkshire, Lancashire and Cheshire. She visited Cumberland in 1744, and three years later, with Agnes Mason, in East Yorkshire. In 1749, aged nearly seventy years, Alice Thistlethwaite visited the South of England with Agnes Mason. I have no descriptive records of these long and difficult journeys taken by our ancestors, under a strong sense of duty, but we may, I think, justly suppose that they met with adventures and found themselves amid circumstances which would be extraordinary and interesting to us, their twentieth century descendants. Unfortunately the contemporary Quaker Journals are apt to be uninteresting, unless one can see the humour hidden among so serious an atmosphere, and can supply in imagination the disregarded inconveniences and difficulties of travelling as Quakers in eighteenth century country districts, and of daring the dreary voyages to America and to Ireland.*

Their granddaughter gives the following personal account of William Thistlethwaite (1) and his wife :—" The father of Alice Thistlethwaite lived on his own estate at Hudsfoss House in the Dale called Dent, situated in the North West of Yorkshire. He was a very respectable character in his time, remarkably hospitable to strangers whom he entertained at his house, particularly those of the Society of Friends, of whose principles he became convinced towards the latter part of his life. In his earlier days he was so compassionate to travellers that he set apart for the reception of the poorer class of them a sort of hay loft, where he provided beds for their repose. His house, and that of his son-in-law, William Thistlethwaite (married to his daughter Alice), called Harbourgill, were

---

* I shall be most glad to correspond with anyone possessing journals or old letters of any person mentioned in this family history, in view of a future volume.

the most considerable in that part of Dent. William Thistlethwaite was a handsome man of middle stature, of friendly genteel manners, his disposition somewhat reserved, and his words few.   His wife Alice was tall, good-looking, but not handsome : her manners and temper were very firm : she was distinguished by her charity, which led her to administer not only to the corporeal necessities of her fellow creatures, but also to their mental distresses, especially of the sick and dying, endeavouring to alleviate them by all the means in her power, and her abilities in this way were enlarged by the gift of gospel ministry entrusted to her charge. Her sons were all brought up to husbandry, and all except James (who early removed into Wensleydale) settled in Dent on small estates given to them by their father." *

William Thistlethwaite (1) and Alice Mason, his wife, had nine children, as follows :—

- i.   Richard Thistlethwaite (2), see Part One.
- ii.   James Thistlethwaite (429), see Part Two.
- iii. Margaret Thistlethwaite (877), see Part Three.
- iv.   John Thistlethwaite (1090), see Part Four.
- v.   Anthony Thistlethwaite (1141), born at Harborgill, 12th December, 1714-5 ; died 18th November, 1740, unmarried, in his 26th year.
- vi.   Isabel Thistlethwaite (1142), see Part Five.
- vii. Anne Thistlethwaite (1145), see Part Six.
- viii. Thomas Thistlethwaite (1260), see Part Seven.
- ix.   Timothy Thistlethwaite (1334), see Part Eight.

---

* " The original of this paper was written at Tottenham, Middlesex in 1795 by Elizabeth Fothergill (913), from the mouth of her aunt Alice Chorley (1020), who is named in the pedigree, and who died, aged eighty-two, at that village, 1828."   I am much indebted to Watson Fothergill (887), of Nottingham, for the loan of this interesting document, a number of extracts from which will be found in different parts of this family history. One must, however, remember that Alice Chorley spoke only from memory.

PART ONE.

DESCENDANTS OF

RICHARD THISTLETHWAITE (2),

ELDEST CHILD OF

WILLIAM THISTLETHWAITE (1), OF HARBORGILL.

PART ONE.

Richard Thistlethwaite, (2) born, presumably at Harborgill, 4th July, 1706; died there 15th January, 1793, aged eighty-seven. "A man of comely, fine person, who marrying before the age of twenty-one a beautiful heiress, to whom he was tenderly attached, resided on her inheritance called Spicegill, in the same dale, until the death of his father, when he removed to Harbourgill, and Spicegill became the residence of Anthony, his third son."* He married Elizabeth Mason at Leayat Meeting House, 4th August, 1727, who died in Dent Dale, 30th April, 1762. She was born at Stonehouse in Dent Dale 24th October, 1707, daughter of Thomas and Elizabeth Mason. Thomas Mason, of Stonehouse, married Elizabeth Clerkson at Anthony Robinson's house in Ravenstondale, 4th October, 1705.

- i. William Thistlethwaite (3), whom see.
- ii. Alice Thistlethwaite (24), whom see.
- iii. Thomas Thistlethwaite (111), born at Spicegill, 8th February, 1734, "died single, of an asthma." Died at Harborgill, 1st April, 1778.
- iv. Anthony Thistlethwaite (112), whom see.

William Thistlethwaite (3), born at Spicegill, 10th December, 1728, died at Harborgill 7th May, 1801, aged seventy-two. "William, the eldest grandson of William and Alice, is now living at Hollow Mill in Dent: he is particularly fond of shooting moor game and other wild fowl which abound in that part of England."* He was "a man of cheer-

* Alice Chorley's Record.

ful temper and herculean strength," and an intimate friend of the father
of Adam Sedgwick, the geologist. He lived at Stonehouse 1781, and
at Hollow Mill 1788. He married Margaret Akrigg, probably at Leayat
Meeting House, 6th December, 1773, who died at Harborgill, 21st March,
1828, aged eighty-one.

    i.   Alice Thistlethwaite (4), whom see.

   ii.   Richard Thistlethwaite (13), whom see.

  iii.   Hannah Thistlethwaite (22), born at Stonehouse, 14th or 21st
        December, 1781, died unmarried.

  iv.   Samuel Thistlethwaite (23), born at Hollow Mill, 8th March,
        1788, died there 21st June, 1789, aged one-and-a-quarter
        years.

Alice Thistlethwaite (4), born, probably at Stonehouse, 11th
December, 1774, married from Harborgill, 30th March, 1796, to James
Binns, of Cononley Woodside, parish of Kildwick, Yorkshire, within
Knaresborough Monthly Meeting, son of John and Sarah Binns. He
is described as " Clogmaker," 1797-1808, and " Farmer " 1810-1818.
Although I can trace no farther than their children, they probably have
many descendants.

    i.   Sarah Binns (5), born at Cononley Woodside, 23rd March,
        1797.

   ii.   Margaret Binns (6), born at Cononley Woodside, 27th July,
        1800.

  iii.   William Binns (7), born at Cononley Woodside, 26th March,
        1803.

  iv.   Daniel Binns (8), born at Cononley Woodside, 11th April,
        1806.

   v.   John Binns (9), born at Cononley Woodside, 22nd August,
        1808.

  vi.   Joseph Binns (10), born at Cononley Woodside, 6th December,
        1810.

vii. Wilson Binns (11), born at Cononley Woodside, 9th June, 1815.

viii. Hannah Binns (12), born at Cononley Woodside, 15th February, 1818.

Richard Thistlethwaite (13), born, probably at Stonehouse, 31st January, 1776. He married Eleanor ———, and is said to have sold Harborgill, and to have emigrated to America, where there are probably many descendants.

    i. Alice Thistlethwaite (14), born at Harborgill, 24th October, 1804. She appears to have left an only son named
        i. Clarke V. Day (15), living in America in 1908.

    ii. William Thistlethwaite (16), born at Harborgill, 3rd September, 1806.

    iii. Thomas Thistlethwaite (17), born at Harborgill, 27th May, 1809.

    iv. Timothy Thistlethwaite (18), born at Harborgill, 22nd November, 1811.

    v. Agnes Thistlethwaite (19), born at Harborgill, 15th March, 1814.

    vi. Samuel Thistlethwaite (20), born at Harborgill, 14th September, 1816.

    vii. Margaret Thistlethwaite (21), born at Harborgill, 14th May, 1819.

Alice Thistlethwaite (24), born at Spicegill, 24th May, 1731, married 7th May, 1760, to John Alderson, of Ravenstondale.

John Alderson was born in Ravenstondale, 22nd August, 1721, the younger child of Ralph Alderson by his wife Alice Burton, whom he married 8th March, 1717. Alice Alderson, *née* Burton, was an important "public" or ministering Friend (*i.e.* Quaker). She travelled widely in the Quaker Ministry, visiting Scotland in 1713 and the South of England

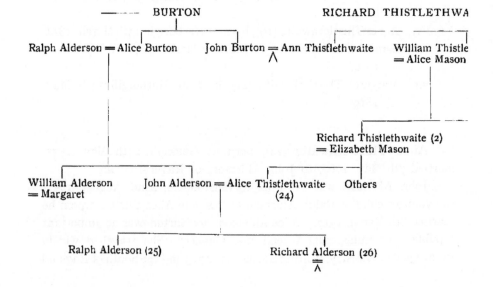

vii. Wilson Binns (11), born at Cononley Woodside, 9th June,
       1815.

viii. Hannah Binns (12), born at Cononley Woodside, 15th February,
       1818.

Richard Thistlethwaite (13), born, probably at Stonehouse,
31st January, 1776. He married Eleanor ——, and is said to have sold
Harborgill, and to have emigrated to America, where there are probably
many descendants.

 i. Alice Thistlethwaite (14), born at Harborgill, 24th October,
   1804. She appears to have left an only son named
    i. Clarke V. Day (15), living in America in 1908.

 ii. William Thistlethwaite (16), born at Harborgill, 3rd September,
   1806.

 iii. Thomas Thistlethwaite (17), born at Harborgill, 27th May,
   1809.

 iv. Timothy Thistlethwaite (18), born at Harborgill, 22nd November, 1811.

 v. Agnes Thistlethwaite (19), born at Harborgill, 15th March, 1814.

 vi. Samuel Thistlethwaite (20), born at Harborgill, 14th September,
   1816.

 vii. Margaret Thistlethwaite (21), born at Harborgill, 14th May,
   1819.

Alice Thistlethwaite (24), born at Spicegill, 24th May, 1731,
married 7th May, 1760, to John Alderson, of Ravenstondale.

John Alderson was born in Ravenstondale, 22nd August, 1721,
the younger child of Ralph Alderson by his wife Alice Burton, whom he
married 8th March, 1717. Alice Alderson, *née* Burton, was an important
" public " or ministering Friend (*i.e.* Quaker). She travelled widely
in the Quaker Ministry, visiting Scotland in 1713 and the South of England

three years later.   Her elder child, William, was born in Ravenstondale, 23rd June, 1719, and the following year she visited Ireland.   In 1722 she visited Cumberland, and ten years later crossed to America.   Her brother, John Burton, whose ministry began in 1707 in Cumberland, visited America in 1733, and " The Bishoprick " (or Durham) in 1735, accompanied by Thomas Burton.   In 1736, four years after going to America, Alice Alderson attended the half year's meeting at Dublin, and later travelled in Yorkshire and Lincolnshire.   The next year she visited Northumberland and the Bishoprick, 1740 Cumberland, 1741 Lancashire and East and South Yorkshire, 1743 Ireland, 1745 Yorkshire, and 1748 Cheshire and Derbyshire.   She died in 1765 or 1766.

Her said brother, John Burton, of Scalegillfoot, married 1st September, 1709, Ann Thistlethwaite, of Harborgill, sister of William Thistlethwaite (1).   They had at least six children, but their descendants do not affect this present volume.   In 1752, John Burton visited the South of England with his sister's son, John Alderson, who married, eight years later, a great-niece of John Burton's wife (see above).

William Burton, perhaps a brother of John Burton, married 4th August, 1704, Isabel Thistlethwaite, another sister of William Thistlethwaite (1).   They had at least two children.   Isabel Thistlewaite had a minister's certificate in 1703, and died as Isabel Burton in 1754, a " public " Friend.

Both of Ralph and Alice Alderson's children became Quaker ministers. The elder, William Alderson, and his wife Margaret (also a minister) died in 1758.

In 1754, John Alderson visited the West and South of England in company with Anthony Mason, whose two daughters married Thomas Thistlethwaite (1260) and Jeremiah Thistlethwaite (1162) respectively. Two years later John Alderson visited Scotland, Northumberland, Cumberland, Yorkshire and the Bishoprick, and the next year he visited Cumberland and Ireland.   In 1759, John Alderson visited Yorkshire, and the South as far as London ; then Cumberland and Northumberland.   The next year, at the age of thirty-nine, he married Alice

Thistlethwaite. In 1762 he visited Cumberland and Northumberland, and in 1763, again in company with Anthony Mason, he visited " in and about London and the South and West of England," and died 1764, in London, aged forty-three years. His wife was left with two young children. She married secondly —— Walker.

    i.   Ralph Alderson (25), born in Ravenstondale, 1st September, 1761, and probably died without issue.

    ii. Richard Alderson (26), whom see.

Richard Alderson (26), born in Ravenstondale, 24th September, 1763. At the time of his marriage in 1786 he was living at Leayat in Dent, but the next year he is described as " husbandman of Stonehouse." At the birth of his son in 1800 he is first styled " manufacturer," and he is thus described until 1806. His youngest child was born in 1808, at Westhouse, in Dent, her father being then described as " yeoman." He died in 1811. The designation " manufacturer " refers to the fact that he cut and polished the encrinitic and black marble which is found in Dent Dale. This trade was carried on for over a hundred years at Stonehouse, foreign marble also being polished there. Owing to a dispute as to rent, the trade ceased two years ago.

He married 10th May, 1786, at Countersett Meeting House, Mary, fourth daughter of Reuben and Hannah Harrison, who was born 13th November, 1765, at Countersett. For the many Harrison-Thistlethwaite intermarriages the reader must be content in this volume to refer to Chart II.

    i.   John Alderson (27), whom see.

    ii. Alice Alderson (41), born at Stonehouse in Dent, 17th October, 1788, married Richard (or William) Mason, and has numerous descendants in America.

    iii. Daniel Alderson (42), whom see.

    iv. Hannah Alderson (44), whom see.

    v. Margaret Alderson (78), born at Stonehouse, 2nd June, 1794, died before 1806.

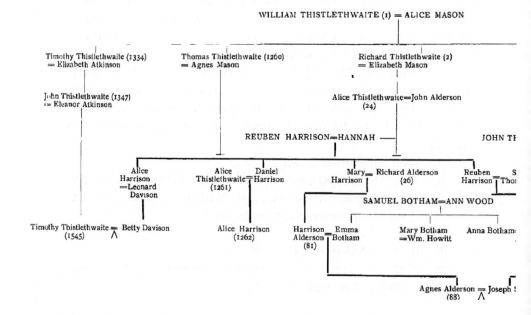

WILLIAM THISTLETHWAITE (1) = ALICE MASON

Timothy Thistlethwaite (1334)
= Elizabeth Atkinson

Thomas Thistlethwaite (1260)
= Agnes Mason

Richard Thistlethwaite (2)
= Elizabeth Mason

John Thistlethwaite (1347)
= Eleanor Atkinson

Alice Thistlethwaite=John Alderson
(24)

REUBEN HARRISON=HANNAH ——

JOHN TH

Alice
Harrison
=Leonard
Davison

Alice
Thistlethwaite=Harrison
(1261)

Daniel
Harrison

Mary=Richard Alderson
Harrison   (26)

Reuben   S
Harrison=Tho

SAMUEL BOTHAM=ANN WOOD

Timothy Thistlethwaite = Betty Davison
(1545)

Alice Harrison
(1262)

Harrison=Emma
Alderson=Botham
(81)

Mary Botham
=Wm. Howitt

Anna Botham

Agnes Alderson = Joseph S
(88)

Thistlethwaite. In 1762 he visited Cumberland and Northumberland, and in 1763, again in company with Anthony Mason, he visited "in and about London and the South and West of England," and died 1764, in London, aged forty-three years. His wife was left with two young children. She married secondly —— Walker.

    i.   Ralph Alderson (25), born in Ravenstondale, 1st September, 1761, and probably died without issue.

   ii.   Richard Alderson (26), whom see.

Richard Alderson (26), born in Ravenstondale, 24th September, 1763. At the time of his marriage in 1786 he was living at Leayat in Dent, but the next year he is described as "husbandman of Stonehouse." At the birth of his son in 1800 he is first styled "manufacturer," and he is thus described until 1806. His youngest child was born in 1808, at Westhouse, in Dent, her father being then described as "yeoman." He died in 1811. The designation "manufacturer" refers to the fact that he cut and polished the encrinitic and black marble which is found in Dent Dale. This trade was carried on for over a hundred years at Stonehouse, foreign marble also being polished there. Owing to a dispute as to rent, the trade ceased two years ago.

He married 10th May, 1786, at Countersett Meeting House, Mary, fourth daughter of Reuben and Hannah Harrison, who was born 13th November, 1765, at Countersett. For the many Harrison-Thistlethwaite intermarriages the reader must be content in this volume to refer to Chart II.

    i.   John Alderson (27), whom see.

   ii.   Alice Alderson (41), born at Stonehouse in Dent, 17th October, 1788, married Richard (or William) Mason, and has numerous descendants in America.

  iii.   Daniel Alderson (42), whom see.

  iv.   Hannah Alderson (44), whom see.

   v.   Margaret Alderson (78), born at Stonehouse, 2nd June, 1794, died before 1806.

vi.   Ralph Alderson (79), born at Stonehouse 16th October, 1796,
       a physician in Newcastle, had a "disappointment," and
       emigrated to America, where he died in middle life. He
       was unmarried when he left England.

vii.   Mary Alderson (80), born at Stonehouse, 27th October, 1798 ;
       married Joseph Nixon, of Dent, and emigrated to America,
       where she was poisoned by accident, leaving descendants.

viii. Harrison Alderson (81), whom see.

ix.   Agnes Alderson (104), born 25th May, 1802, at Stonehouse ;
       died unmarried 1828, at Blackburn.

x.   William Alderson (105), born 11th June, 1804, at Stonehouse ;
       died at Westminster, London, 1834, aged twenty-nine
       years, unmarried. An architect.

xi.   Margaret Alderson (106), whom see.

xii.   Elizabeth Alderson (110), born at Westhouse, in Dent Dale,
       24th May, 1808, and died 1853, unmarried, at Burnley,
       aged forty-six years.

John Alderson (27), born 10th March, 1787, at Stonehouse, in
Dent ; died at Broadmire in Dent in 1855, aged sixty-eight years, buried
at Leayat : for many years a schoolmaster at Leayat, in Dent Dale. He
married Alice Hunter, daughter of John Hunter, of Hebblethwaite
Hall, near Sedbergh (who died at Narthwaite in 1840, aged ninety-two
years) by his wife Ann Middlebrook, "public" Friend, daughter of
James Middlebrook, of Lowblean, yeoman. Alice Alderson, *née* Hunter,
died at Dent in the year 1868, aged eighty.

i.   Ann Alderson (28), born and died in Dent, buried at Leayat,
       s.p.

ii.   Jane Alderson (29), born and died in Dent, buried at Leayat,
       s.p.

iii.   Mary Alderson (30), born and died in Dent, buried at Leayat,
       s.p.

iv.   Alice Alderson (31), whom see.

v.   Hannah Alderson (35), born and died in Dent, buried at Leayat,
     s.p.

vi. Margaret Alderson (36), born in Dent, died and buried at
     Bentham, *sine prole*. She married Thomas Edmondson
     as his second wife.

vii. Agnes Alderson (37), born in Dent, died of smallpox, at Kendal,
     aged nineteen, *s.p.*

viii. John Alderson (38), born in Dent, died there, and buried at
      Leayat, *s.p.*

ix. Richard Alderson (39), born and died in Dent, buried at
     Leayat, *s.p.*

x.   Daniel Harrison Alderson (40), born in Dent, died at Chapel-
     le-Dale, buried at Bentham, *s.p.*

Alice Alderson (31), born at Lambparrock, in Dent, 28th November, 1818 ; died at East Ardsley, near Wakefield, 13th July, 1858. Married at Leayat Meeting House 23rd October, 1840, to James Airay, then houseman at Ackworth School near Pontefract, she being dairymaid there at the time.

James Airay was son of James Airay, of Huddersfield, labourer, and Mary, *née* Hudson, his wife, deceased. He was later a grocer of Batley and East Ardsley, and died at York. He married secondly Sarah Priest, whose brother, John Priest, married Hannah Peacock, sister of Rachel Peacock, who married Jeremiah Thistlethwaite, of Great Ayton.

The witnesses who signed Alice Alderson's (31) marriage certificate are worth quoting, as fairly representative of the Quakers in Dent in 1840.

John Alderson	Thomas Carter
Alice Alderson	Ann Carter
Ann Alderson	Agnes Ion
Harrison Alderson	Anthony Carter
Thomas Handley	John Johnson
Oswald Baynes, Jun.	William Thistlethwaite

Jane Baynes

Thomas Thistlethwaite

William Hunter,

Margaret Thistlethwaite

William Middlebrook

Mary Ann Thistlethwaite

John Middlebrook

Horatio Turner

Ann Middlebrook, Jun.

Myles Baynes

Margaret Middlebrook

William Chapman

Margaret Thistlethwaite

Thomas Harker (Cowgill)

Alice Hunter,

Alice Harker

Ann Hunter

Mary Davis

Alice Thistlethwaite

Elizabeth Davis.

James and Alice Airay had three children, as follows :—

i.   John Airay (32), born at Ackworth, 28th October, 1842; apprenticed to David Baker, grocer, of Guisboro', and died at East
Ardsley, near Wakefield, 3rd July, 1864, unmarried.

ii. Mary Agnes Airay (33), born at Batley, 7th July, 1845 ; married
at Wakefield Friends' Meeting House, 7th April, 1868, to
John Edmondson, son of her aunt's husband, Thomas
Edmondson, by his first wife. John and Mary Agnes
Edmondson live at Woodburn, Ilkley, in 1909. The latter
visits much in the Quaker ministry, as did so many of her
ancestors mentioned above. She is *sine prole*.

iii. Alice Ann Airay (34), born at East Ardsley, 3rd June, 1850 ;
died there 31st March, 1852.

Daniel Alderson (42), born 21st September, 1790, at Stonehouse,
in Dent. He married Peggy ——, and kept the " Sun Inn " in Dent's
Town. He appears to have died young, leaving at least one son. His
widow, Peggy Alderson, " was quite a character, and the old-fashioned
hostel a great attraction to the statesmen of Dent, especially in the
evenings."

i.   Richard Alderson (43), who probably has descendants living in
the neighbourhood of Dent.

Hannah Alderson (44), born 6th July, 1792, at Stonehouse, in Dent, and died at Holme, 3rd October, 1865. She married at Newcastle, 1816, John Hogarth, a brilliant schoolmaster, who was born at Firbank, near Kendal, and died at Manchester, 13th December, 1874.

    i. Charlotte Hogarth (45), whom see.

    ii. Isabella Hogarth (65), whom see.

    iii. Agnes Hogarth (71), whom see.

Charlotte Hogarth (45), born May, 1823, at Ruthin, in Wales ; married 1849, at Burnley, Lancashire, to Robert Nicholl, a cabinet maker. She died 23rd November, 1862.

    i. Emma Hogarth (46), whom see.

    ii. Hannah Mary Nicholl (54), whom see.

    iii Elizabeth Nicholl (59), born August, 1851 ; died January, 1866, *s.p.*

    iv. Margaret Alice Nicholl (60), born at Burnley, October, 1853 ; married 1881, John Pither, of Bray Villa, Sunningdale, near Ascot, and died at the birth of her only child.

        i. Margaret Alice Pither (61), born September, 1882.

    v. Martha Jane Nicholl (62), born at Wilmslow, Cheshire, 1855 ; died November, 1880, at Holme, unmarried.

    vi. Charlotte Agnes Nicholl (63), born at Wilmslow, December, 1857 ; married Thomas Cookson, and was living in 1909 at 20, Merton Street, Harpurbey, Manchester.

        i. Charlotte Elizabeth Cookson (64), born 25th October, 1888, at Manchester, unmarried.

Emma Hogarth (46), born 1846, natural child of Charlotte Hogarth (45), by her future husband Robert Nicholl. Married Charles Bracewell, at Clitheroe, 1869, and died April, 1907. Charles Bracewell was living in 1909, at 125, Tithebarn Road, Southport.

    i. Arthur Bracewell (47), born May, 1870, unmarried.

    ii. Henry Hogarth Bracewell (48), born March, 1873, unmarried.

    iii. Bertram Ernest Bracewell (49), whom see.

Bertram Ernest Bracewell (49), born June, 1877, married, and has issue.

    i.   Ernest Hogarth Bracewell (50), born July, 1897.

    ii. George Crombleholme Bracewell (51), born December, 1898.

    iii. Emmie Winifred Bracewell (52), born January, 1900.

    iv. ⸙Eugene Harold Bracewell (53), born May, 1903.

Hannah Mary Nicholl (54), born June, 1850, at Blackpool, died August, 1900.   Married John Jones, a clerk, and had issue.

    i.   Florence Mary Jones (55), born 14th September, 1878, died 6th January, 1895.

    ii. William Henry Jones (56), born August, 1880, unmarried.

    iii. Helena Alice Jones (57), born April, 1883, unmarried ; living in 1909 at 58, Cholmley Street, Boulevard, Hull.

    iv. Lilian Martha Jones (58), born January, 1891, unmarried ; living in 1909, at 1, Westcliffe Road, Birkdale, Southport.

Isabella Hogarth (65), born 23rd March, 1826, at Darlington ; married 6th April, 1849, at Burnley, Lancashire, to John Faulkner, schoolmaster, who died at Holme on Spalding Moor, 15th June, 1882. She died 25th November, 1909, while living with her daughter, Mrs. W. H. Richardson.

    i.   John Hogarth Faulkner (66), born at Woolfold, 17th May, 1850, unmarried.   Professor of Short-hand in America, if living.

    ii. George William Faulkner (67), born at Patricroft, 10th January, 1856, unmarried.   A retired tailor, living with his sister.

    iii. Mary Isabella Faulkner (68), born at Patricroft, 26th March ; died at Keighley, 15th June, 1904.   Married at Leeds, 1st March, 1888, Thomas Kettlewell, draper, of Keighley.

         i. Harold Faulkner Kettlewell (69), born at Keighley, 29th June, 1889, now musician, of Keighley.

iv. Charlotte Agnes Faulkner (70), born at Holme on Spalding
Moor, 6th February 1863. Married at Leeds, 10th
September, 1895, to William Henry Richardson, Manu-
facturing Chemist, of Park Terrace, Horsforth, Leeds. She
had one child, deceased.

Agnes Hogarth (71), born 1828, at Darlington, probably in the
month of August. She was married, 1850, at Burnley, to John Milburn,
an ironmonger. They emigrated to America, and she died 9th July,
1867, at Hamilton. I have been unable to trace the present whereabouts
of her descendants.

i. William Milburn (72), deceased 1909.
ii. John Milburn (73).
iii. George Milburn (74), deceased 1909.
iv. James Milburn (75).
v. Charles Milburn (76).
vi. Henry Milburn (77). He and all his brothers were born in
America.

Harrison Alderson (81), born 9th August, 1800, at Stonehouse, in
Dent Dale, sixth child of Richard and Mary Alderson. Died 27th July,
1871, aged seventy-one, at the residence of his son-in-law, Joseph Simpson,
Mayfield Cottage, near Ashbourne, Derbyshire, and was interred at
Uttoxeter.

His father died when Harrison was eleven years old. The latter left
Ackworth when he was fourteen, and became apprenticed to William
Satterthwaite, at Lancaster. When twenty-one years of age, he entered
into business at Blackburn ; married in 1833, and removed with his
family to America in 1842, where he settled near the infant city of
Cincinnati, Ohio. In 1851, four years after his wife's death, he gave up
the home at " Cedar Lodge," sent his children to Boarding School, and

visited England. He returned to America in the summer of 1853, and soon afterwards purchased " The Cedars," near Burlington, which continued to be his home until the spring of 1871, when he crossed to England for the last time. A Quaker minister of Burlington Monthly Meeting, New Jersey, U.S.A.

He married at Liverpool in 1833, Emma Botham, youngest daughter of Samuel and Ann Botham, of Uttoxeter, Staffordshire, born there 4th September, 1809, died at Cedar Lodge, Cincinnati, 17th December, 1847. During the last year of her life she wrote " Our Cousins in Ohio," describing a year of home life at " Cedar Lodge." Her sister Mary Howitt, the authoress, had it published the following year.

Emma Botham's mother was born Ann Wood, whose great-grandfather was William Wood, the discoverer of platinum, and the object of Swift's fierce attack in " The Drapier Letters." He was descended from a brother of the infamous Cardinal Du Bois, who had fled to England on the Revocation of the Edict of Nantes, and had anglicised his name to " Wood " in order to hide his connection with the cardinal. Emma Botham's father was so strict a Quaker, that he would not let the nurse take his children into certain streets lest they should hear an organ playing.

Her sister, Mary Botham, married William Howitt, of Heanor, in Derbyshire, the well-known author and topographer, and was herself an authoress of some repute, writing, among other things, a story named " Hope on, Hope ever, or a Peep into Dent," which should be read by everyone interested in the people and district of Dent Dale. The eldest sister, Anna Botham, married in 1823, Daniel Harrison, a first cousin of her future brother-in-law, Harrison Alderson (see Chart II.).

    i.   Mary Ann Alderson (82) died in infancy.

   ii.   William Charles Alderson (83), whom see.

  iii.   Agnes Alderson (88), whom see.

  iv.   Anna Mary Alderson (98), whom see.

    v.   Alice Ann Alderson (102) died young.

  vi.   Samuel Harrison Alderson (103) died in infancy.

William Charles Alderson (83), born 5th November, 1837, probably at Blackburn. Married 1st June, 1870, to Eleanor Tyson Yarnall, who was born 12th December, 1840. He resides at 228, South 3rd Street, Philadelphia, Pa., but in June, 1910, was visiting England.

 i. Eleanor C. Alderson (84), born 23rd February, 1877, married, in September, 1898, to Dr. Theodore Janeway, of New York. Their children are,

  i. Eleanor Janeway (85).

  ii. Charles Edward Janeway (86).

  iii. Agnes Janeway (87).

Agnes Alderson (88), born 2nd November, 1839, probably at Blackburn. Married 15th September, 1870, to Joseph Simpson, of Mayfield, mill-owner, who was born 8th September, 1835, and died 2nd October, 1901, aged sixty-six years. He was a son of George Simpson by his wife Sarah, daughter of Reuben and Sarah Harrison, therefore he was a second cousin of his wife Agnes Alderson (88) (see Chart II.), who is still residing at Sunnyside, Mayfield, Staffordshire.

 i. Agnes Simpson (89), born 18th November, 1871.

 ii. Harrison Alderson Simpson (90), born 11th April, 1873.

 iii. Sarah Mildred Simpson (91), born 25th May, 1874.

 iv. Joseph Simpson (92), born 13th September 1875 ; married 5th August, 1903, to Dorothea Maw, who was born 1st August, 1874. They live at Shrewsbury, and have two children.

  i. Agnes Dorothea Grace Simpson (93).

  ii. Josephine Mary Simpson (94).

 v. Emma Beatrice Simpson (95), born 8th September, 1876.

 vi. Arthur Simpson (96), born 27th December, 1877.

 vii. Annie Wilberforce Simpson (97), born 20th September, 1881.

Anna Mary Alderson (98), born 28th November, 1841, probably at Blackburn. As her parents removed to America in 1842, I suppose that her younger sister and brother were born near Cincinnati, U.S.A. She was married 15th October, 1863, at Charlestown, to William Wilberforce Wistar, an American doctor, who died 24th May, 1866, leaving one child. He was related to the American anatomist, Caspar Wistar (1761-1818), after whom the magnificent climbing plant, Wistaria, is named.

    i.   Emma Alderson Wistar (99), born 2nd September, 1865, and died 19th August, 1898. She married John Shaw, of Derby, 23rd April, 1888, and had two children,

        i.   Mary Violet Shaw (100), born 9th April, 1890.
        ii.   John Valentine Wistar Shaw (101), born 14th February, 1894.

Margaret Alderson (106), born 28th March, 1806, at Stonehouse, in Dent Dale. At the age of seventeen she was married at Gretna Green, to James Eastham, an ironmonger, of Burnley, Lancashire. He was very successful in business and lived for several years at Ayton House, Great Ayton, Yorkshire. They adopted a girl, but many years after marriage they had three children of their own.

    i.   Richard Eastham (107), who was a magistrate, and died unmarried.
    ii.   John Eastham (108), a major in the army, and died unmarried.
    iii.   Emma Eastham (109) died unmarried. On account of each child dying without issue, the family money is said to have passed into the hands of some relatives of James Eastham. The adopted daughter married, and had issue.

Anthony Thistlethwaite (112), born 2nd June, 1746, at Spicegill, in Dent. He "was remarkable for his abstemiousness and for his great skill in curing the diseases of domestic animals." *

   * Alice Chorley's Record,

When our common ancestor, William Thistlethwaite (1) of Harborgill, died in 1766, his eldest son, Richard, whose wife had died four years previously, probably went to live there with his three sons, all of whom were unmarried at the time. At any rate the second son of Richard Thistlethwaite (2) died there in 1778, and his youngest son, Anthony Thistlethwaite (112) was married from there in 1779. Anthony's seven eldest children were born there between the years 1780 and 1792, and in 1793 his father, Richard Thistlethwaite (2) died there. Anthony then moved with his wife and family to Spicegill, his mother's farm, where his parents began their married life in 1727. And Anthony's eldest brother, William Thistlethwaite (3), who had been living at Hollow Mill, now become owner of Harborgill, whence his elder daughter, Alice Thistlethwaite (4) was married in 1796. He died, however, in 1801, and his only surviving son, Richard Thistlethwaite (13), lived there with his widowed mother, until he went with his family to America in about 1820.

In the meantime Anthony Thistlethwaite (112) had been living at Spicegill since his father's death, and his eighth child was born there in 1794. Two more children were born in 1797 and 1801 respectively, and Anthony died there 30th August, 1815, aged sixty-nine years. His grandson, Thomas Bradley (414), of Bearpark, near Carperby, tells me that according to the family tradition his grandfather, Anthony Thistlethwaite (112), is supposed to have left Spicegill jointly to his sons Thomas and Anthony, and, owing to the latter dying unmarried, the whole fell to Thomas.

In any case, the third son, Thomas Thistlethwaite (279), left Spicegill to his eldest son, Anthony Thistlethwaite (281), long known as " Anthony of Spicegill," for the ancient custom calls the statesmen by their Christian name and their property, rather than by their surname. So, too, was the son known by his father's Christian name if the latter were living, and my grandfather, Jeremiah Thistlethwaite (1218), son of William Thistlethwaite (1217), was colloquially known as " Jerry o' Bill's." To revert to Spicegill, the property has now fallen to the great nephews of the last " Anthony of Spicegill," named Sedgwick.

His grandfather, the Anthony Thistlethwaite (112) of our present paragraph, married 8th January, 1779, Mary Ion, of Street, in Ravenstondale.   They had ten children,

 i. Richard Thistlethwaite (113), whom see.
 ii. William Thistlethwaite (196), whom see.
 iii. Elizabeth Thistlethwaite (200), whom see.
 iv. Thomas Thistlethwaite (279), whom see.
 v. Agnes Thistlethwaite (299), born at Harborgill, 21st June, 1788, died there 19th October, 1791, aged three years.
 vi. Ann Thistlethwaite (300), born at Harborgill, 28th March, 1790, and is said to have gone to America, unmarried, about 1830.
 vii. Agnes Thistlethwaite (301), whom see.
 viii. Alice Thistlethwaite (307), whom see.
 ix. Anthony Thistlethwaite (387), born at Spicegill, 30th October, 1797, and is supposed to have died unmarried.
 x. Mary Thistlethwaite (388), whom see.

Richard Thistlethwaite (113), born at Harborgill, 25th January, 1780 ; lived at Swineley, in Widdale (between Hawes-in-Wensleydale, and Dent Dale) 1808-1813, at which latter date his son, William, was born. The birthplace of his children John and Mary is described as Mid-Widdale, and the youngest child, Betty, was born in 1819, at Studellagarth,* at the head of Dent Dale, where he lived for many years, removing in his old age to Leayat, where he died 14th March, 1851.

He married at Hawes Meeting House, 27th May, 1807, Margaret Hunter, daughter of Simon or Simion Hunter (see Chart III.), and she died at Leayat, in Dent, 9th February, 1857, aged seventy-seven years.   Her father's sister, Agnes Hunter, daughter of John and Jane Hunter, of Carr End, in Wensleydale, married another Richard Thistlethwaite (580), who was first cousin once removed to the Richard Thistlethwaite (113) of this paragraph.

   * Studellagarth fell into ruins shortly after he left it.

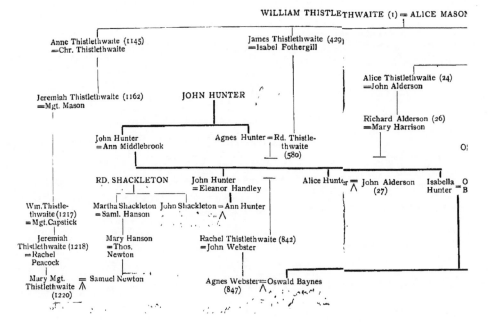

WILLIAM THISTLETHWAITE (1) = ALICE MASON

Anne Thistlethwaite (1145)
=Chr. Thistlethwaite

James Thistlethwaite (429)
=Isabel Fothergill

Alice Thistlethwaite (24)
=John Alderson

Jeremiah Thistlethwaite (1162)
=Mgt. Mason

JOHN HUNTER

Richard Alderson (26)
=Mary Harrison

John Hunter
=Ann Middlebrook

Agnes Hunter = Rd. Thistlethwaite
(580)

O

RD. SHACKLETON

John Hunter
=Eleanor Handley

Alice Hunter = John Alderson
(27)

Isabella O
Hunter = B

Wm.Thistle-
thwaite (1217)
=Mgt.Capstick

Martha Shackleton John Shackleton = Ann Hunter
=Saml. Hanson

Jeremiah
Thistlethwaite (1218)
=Rachel
Peacock

Mary Hanson
=Thos.
Newton

Rachel Thistlethwaite (842)
=John Webster

Mary Mgt. = Samuel Newton
Thistlethwaite
(1220)

Agnes Webster=Oswald Baynes
(847)

    i.   Anthony Thistlethwaite (114), whom see.

    ii.   Alice Thistlethwaite (158), born at Swineley, in Widdale, 6th August, 1809, and lived many years with her father's second cousin, William Thistlethwaite (1217), at Leayat. When her parents came to live at Leayat, she removed to Sedbergh, and died there 24th January, 1881, aged seventy-one years, unmarried.

    iii.   Simon Thistlethwaite (159), whom see.

    iv.   William Thistlethwaite (165), whom see.

    v.   John Thistlethwaite (166), whom see.

    vi.   Mary Thistlethwaite (182), born at Mid-Widdale, 5th November, 1816, and died 13th June, 1836, at Studellagarth, aged nineteen years, unmarried.

    vii.   Betty Thistlethwaite (183), whom see.

Anthony Thistlethwaite (114), born at Swineley, in Widdale, a very outlying farm some distance to the left of the road, going from the head of Dent to Hawes, 14th June, 1808. Married 14th November, 1832, to Elizabeth Altham, of Calf Cop, near Lower Bentham, daughter of John Altham, surgeon, by his wife Elizabeth.

In 1835, he was a flour dealer at Holbeck, near Leeds, and for many years was workhouse-master at Sedbergh. He died 18th October, 1874. His first wife, Elizabeth Altham, was born 12th September, 1807, and died 10th January, 1857. He married a second wife, Mary ——, who survived him without issue.

    i.   Richard Thistlethwaite (115) whom see.

    ii.   Elizabeth Thistlethwaite (134), born at Holbeck, 16th August, 1836, and probably died in infancy.

    iii.   John Altham Thistlethwaite (135) whom see.

    iv.   Mary Margaret Thistlethwaite (150) whom see.

    v.   Jane Thistlethwaite (157) married —— Fletcher, of Bradford, shoemaker, who died there, *s.p.*, after which she went to live with her sister, Mary Margaret Edmundson (150), in

Iowa, U.S.A. Here she married Peter Dyhr, who was born in Denmark, and died at West Branch, Iowa, November, 1907. Jane Dyhr (157) is still living at West Branch, Iowa, *s.p.*

Richard Thistlethwaite (115), born at Holbeck, near Leeds, 3rd February, 1835. For many years in the employment of Messrs. Holdsworth, furniture dealers, of Wakefield. Died 19th December, 1904, at his residence, 4, Warren Terrace, Wakefield. Married at St. Andrew's Church, Wakefield, to Elizabeth Turner, daughter of —— Turner, by his wife Martha Haldane, both of Wakefield. She was born at Wakefield, 30th June, 1835, and died there 20th January, 1899.

    i.   John Altham Thistlethwaite (116), whom see.

    ii.   William Thistlethwaite (122), born at Wakefield, 21st January, 1862; apprenticed as teacher at Ayton Friends' School, and afterwards teacher in many Friends' Schools in England. Now one of the staff of the Friends' Provident Institution, Bradford.

    iii.   Charles Thistlethwaite (123), born 1st June, 1864, at Wakefield, and died there an infant, 1st May, 1865.

    iv.   Elizabeth Thistlethwaite (124), born at Wakefield, 7th September, 1867; lived with her father until his death; married at Iquique, Chili, South America, 17th July, 1908, to Henry Senior, cable operator there, son of a clerk in holy orders.

    v.   Annie Thistlethwaite (125), born 15th June, 1870, at Wakefield, married, 3rd July, 1897, to Joe Roberts, now of Wakefield.

        i.   Harold Roberts (126) born 28th August, 1898, at Wakefield.

    vi.   Anthony Thistlethwaite (127), born 7th March, 1872, at Wakefield; married May, 1904, to Annie E. Buxton. Now of Wakefield.

        i.   Arthur Thistlethwaite (128), born and died at Wakefield, 1905.

    ii. Mary Thistlethwaite (129), born 13th June, 1906, at Wakefield.

vii. Richard Herbert Thistlethwaite (130), born 21st June, 1875, at Wakefield.   Now ironmonger at Wakefield.

viii. Constance Mary Thistlethwaite (131), born 22nd June, 1877, at Wakefield, married 21st May, 1903, to Ernest Judge, an artist, in 1908, of Burniston, near Scarborough ; employed by E. T. W. Dennis and Sons, Ltd., printers, of Scarborough. In 1910 he is a general dealer at Appleton-le-Moors, Yorkshire.

    i. Constance Clare Judge (132), born 23rd June, 1904, at Scarborough.

    ii. Ernesta Judge (133), born 28th February, 1908, at Scarborough.

John Altham Thistlethwaite (116), born at Wakefield, 21st May, 1860, now of Eccleshill, near Bradford, for thirty-two years one of the staff of the Friends' Provident Institution, Bradford. Married, 11th September, 1888, to Mary Smith Baxter, born 25th May, 1865.

    i. Eric Thistlethwaite (117), born at Eccleshill, 5th October, 1891, died there, 18th March, 1903.

    ii. Leslie Thistlethwaite (118), born at Eccleshill, 25th August, 1892.

    iii. Hilda Thistlethwaite (119), born at Eccleshill, 25th March, 1894.

    iv. Wilfred Thistlethwaite (120), born at Eccleshill, 13th July, 1899.

    v. Henry Thistlethwaite (121), born at Eccleshill, 31st March, 1907.

John Altham Thistlethwaite (135), born 31st May, 1840, died at Bradford, 4th September, 1895. Married Matilda Richardson, who was born 23rd January, 1838, and is now living at Bradford.

    i. George Richardson Thistlethwaite (136), born 8th February, 1864, now manager of Wm. North and Sons' Dye Works, Bradford. Married Sarah Newbould, who had one child.

      i.   Annie Thistlethwaite (137), born 14th June, 1889, at
             Bradford, and died there 12th September, 1893.

   ii.   Mary Margaret Thistlethwaite (138), born 25th January, 1869,
      married April, 1897, to Tom Craven, now of Bradford. She
      died 29th January, 1899, at Bradford, three days after the
      birth of her only child, and her husband married again.

      i.   Margaret Craven (139), born 26th January, 1899, at
             Bradford ; now living there with her grandmother,
             Matilda Thistlethwaite.

  iii. Elizabeth Thistlethwaite (140), died in infancy.

  iv. Thomas Thistlethwaite (141), died in infancy.

   v. Anthony Thistlethwaite (142), born 27th July, 1873. In 1908
      of 10, Poplar Terrace, Levenshulme, Manchester, but now
      with Wm. North and Sons, Bradford.   Married, 15th
      January, 1895, to Emma Waite.

      i.   Alice Thistlethwaite (143), born 30th July, 1896, at
             Bradford.

     ii.   Edith Thistlethwaite (144), born 8th February, 1904.

    iii. Annie Thistlethwaite (145), born 23rd September,
             1907, at Levenshulme.

  vi. Ellen Thistlethwaite (146), married 10th December, 1894, to
      Richard Nixon, who died November, 1908, at Bradford.
      She is now living at Bradford.

      i.   Harold Nixon (147), born 31st December, 1895, at
             Bradford.

     ii.   George Fergus Nixon (148), born 16th September,
             1898, at Bradford.

    iii. Charles Thistlethwaite Nixon,(149) born at Bradford,
             and died there in infancy.

Mary Margaret Thistlethwaite (150), married Edward Edmundson of Leeds (born 31st July, 1843), and emigrated to America, where

they settled on a farm at Ida Grove, Iowa, U.S.A. He died 1909, and his widow now lives at Desmoines, Iowa. They had two children.

    i.   Elizabeth Alice Edmundson (151), born 19th May, 1869, at West Branch, Iowa ; married to Gavin Crosbie, who was born 2nd July, 1869, son of Archibald Crosbie. They are now farmers at Ida Grove, and have four children.

        i.   Sophia Florence Crosbie (152), born at Ida Grove.

        ii.   Edward Archibald Crosbie (153), born at Ida Grove.

        iii.   Jessie Elizabeth Crosbie (154), born at Ida Grove.

        iv.   Sydney Altham Crosbie (155), born at Ida Grove.

    ii.   Sophia Jane Edmundson (156), born 28th April, 1871, now of Ida Grove, unmarried.

Simon Thistlethwaite (159), born at Swineley, in Widdale, 11th April, 1811, and died at Hawes, in his old age. He married Elizabeth Helme in 1842, who died at Hawes, 1st January, 1888, aged seventy-seven years. He was a carrier and carter at Hawes.

    i.   Richard Thistlethwaite (160), died in infancy.

    ii.   Richard Thistlethwaite (161), died in infancy.

    iii.   Mary Thistlethwaite (162), of " The Holme," Hawes, who is now carrying on her late brother's business as grocer.

    iv.   James Thistlethwaite (163), grocer, of Hawes, in Wensleydale, Yorkshire. Born 1849 ; married Anna Baker, of Dublin, who was at the Mount School, York, 8 mo. 1869 to 6 mo. 1870, and died at Kingstown, Dublin, 1st August, 1877, aged twenty-five years, leaving one child.

        i.   —— Thistlethwaite (164), who died young (a daughter).

William Thistlethwaite (165), born at Swineley in Widdale, 17th April, 1813 ; went to the school of his second cousin, John Alderson (27), at Leayat, in Dent, then for two years to Ackworth School, which he had to leave in 1827 on account of his age. He returned to Dent, and in 1828 was placed under James Thistlethwaite (581), clogger and leather cutter, of Bainbridge, in Wensleydale.

He appears to have been somewhat precocious, and at the age of seventeen was found discussing with his employer " Doddridge's Rise and Progress of Religion in the Soul," a feat which we may admire rather than envy. That Paley's " Moral Philosophy " was his favourite book, further testifies to his fondness for Metaphysics. One is not surprised to find that he left leather cutting for pedagogy, and conducted the school at Counterside, near Bainbridge, until 1834, when he became of age.

He applied for, and received, the headmastership of Penketh Friends' School at the age of twenty-one years. He left there in 1846, and became Master on Duty at Ackworth School, but shortly afterwards took up a boarding school at Tulketh Hall, near Preston, with his future brother-in-law, Dr. Satterthwaite, whose sister Hannah Satterthwaite he married in 1847. The school was moved to Lindow Grove, near Wilmslow, Cheshire, in 1853.

William Thistlethwaite (165) was recorded a minister of the Society of Friends in 1864, and published several books on Quaker and other matters, *viz.*, " On Education in Prussia " (1850) ; " Thoughts on Religious Education " (1856) ; " An Address delivered in Manchester " (1858) ; " Four Lectures on the Rise, etc., of the Society of Friends " (1865), etc. He died at Wilmslow, 28th January, 1870, aged 56 years.*

His wife survived him, and died at Wilmslow, 5th September, 1893, aged seventy-seven years. She was also a minister in the Society of Friends, and travelled as such in America and elsewhere. *Sine prole*, see Chart V.

John Thistlethwaite (166), born at Mid-Widdale, 22nd March, 1815. In his early days he was with the firm of Harrisons and Crosfield, tea-merchants, of Liverpool and London. At the recommendation of Daniel Harrison, of this firm (who married Anna Botham, sister-in-law of Harrison Alderson (81) who was second cousin to John Thistlethwaite (166), see

* Compare the account in "The Annual Monitor," 1871.

Chart II.), he joined the firm of Wm. Rathbout and Co., of Liverpool. Subsequently he went out to Shanghai, China, and eventually returned to Harrisons and Crosfield, until he retired. He died at Birkenhead, 28th April, 1884.

He married Deborah Barlow, daughter of John Barlow, of Alderley Edge, by his wife Deborah Neild, of which latter family J. J. Green, of Tunbridge Wells, has compiled a genealogy. Deborah Thistlethwaite, *née* Barlow, was born at the Oak, Alderley Edge, Cheshire, 7th October, 1823, and married at Morley Meeting House, Cheshire, May, 1856. She died at Birkenhead, 9th September, 1879, aged fifty-five years.

    i. Margaret Thistlethwaite (167), whom see.
   ii. Richard Henry Thistlethwaite (172), whom see.
  iii. Mary Hannah Thistlethwaite (174), whom see.
  iv. Maria Thistlethwaite (176), whom see.
   v. Helen Thistlethwaite (180), born at Birkenhead, died an infant, and buried at Liscard, F.B.G., Cheshire.
  vi. John Barlow Thistlethwaite (181), born at Kenyon Terrace, Birkenhead, 24th May, 1866, educated at Bootham School, York, 4 mo. 1877 to 6 mo. 1883. Bachelor of Arts, and Solicitor in Manchester. Married, November, 1901, at Grange-over-Sands Church, to Edith Bennett, of that place. *Sine prole.* Resides at Wilmslow.

Margaret Thistlethwaite (167), born 14th February, 1857, at Kenyon Terrace, Birkenhead. Educated at the Mount School, York, 1 mo. 1873 to 6 mo. 1874. Married, 1st September, 1880, at Hemingford Street Meeting House, Birkenhead, to her fourth cousin, William John Cudworth (831), of Darlington, whom see. They lived, in 1909, at Butts Close, Tadcaster Road, York, and had four children.

    i. Margaret Cudworth (168) born 5th October, 1881, at Darlington. Educated at the Mount School, York, 1mo. 1896 to 12 mo. 1899.

ii.   Mary Cudworth (169), born 13th August, 1883, at Darlington ;
       educated at the Mount School, York, 9 mo. 1898, to 7 mo.
       1902.

iii.   William Oswald Cudworth (170), born 25th October, 1885, at
       Darlington, educated at Bootham School, York, 1 mo. 1898
       to 7 mo. 1901, and at Leighton Park, Reading.

iv.   Helen Cudworth (171), born 30th August, 1887, at Darlington
       educated at the Mount School, York, 9 mo. 1901 to 12mo.
       1903.

Richard Henry Thistlethwaite (172), born 29th October, 1858, at
Kenyon Terrace, Birkenhead. Married, at Bismark, Dakota, U.S.A.,
20th June, 1888, in the house of his bride, Mary Castlemaine. I understand that he is, or has been, a judge in Dakota.

i.   Walter Barlow Thistlethwaite (173), born in Dakota, 1889.

Mary Hannah Thistlethwaite (174), born 2nd August 1860, at
Kenyon Terrace, Birkenhead ; educated at the Mount School, York, 8 mo.
1874 to 6 mo. 1876. Married, 20th June, 1882, at Hemingford Street
Meeting House, Birkenhead, to Richard Thompson (808), her fourth
cousin, and a first cousin to her brother-in-law, William John Cudworth
(831). As will be seen on reference to Chart IV., Richard Thompson (808)
and William John Cudworth (831) were fourth cousins to their respective
wives, through the Thistlethwaite blood, but third cousins through the
Hunter relationship. See under Richard Thompson (808).

i.   Geoffrey Thompson (175), born 10th August, 1883 ; educated
       at Bootham School, York, 9 mo. 1896 to 7 mo. 1899.

Maria Thistlethwaite (176), born at Kenyon Terrace, Birkenhead,
9th June, 1862 ; educated at the Mount School, York, 8 mo. 1876 to 12

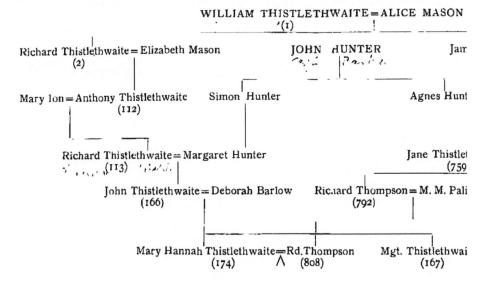

WILLIAM THISTLETHWAITE=ALICE MASON
(1)

Richard Thistlethwaite=Elizabeth Mason   JOHN HUNTER   Jam
(2)

Mary Ion=Anthony Thistlethwaite   Simon Hunter   Agnes Hunt
(112)

Richard Thistlethwaite=Margaret Hunter   Jane Thistlet
(113)   (759

John Thistlethwaite=Deborah Barlow   Richard Thompson=M. M. Pali
(166)   (792)

Mary Hannah Thistlethwaite=Rd.Thompson   Mgt. Thistlethwai
(174)   Λ   (808)   (167)

CHART IV. FURTHER HUNTER CONNECTIONS.
I am much indebted to Wm. Shackleton, of
Pudsey, for permission to use his Hunter
Family Chart. See also Chart III.

mo. 1878. Married February, 1886, at Morley Meeting House, Cheshire, to William Darby, of Birmingham.

    i.   Ruth Darby (177), born 19th September, 1887; educated at the Mount School, York, 9 mo. 1901 to 7 mo. 1905.

    ii.   Henry Basil Darby (178), born 1891,; educated at Leighton Park, Reading, January, 1905 to April, 1909.

    iii.   Roger Darby (179), born 1894; educated at Leighton Park, Reading, April, 1907 to July, 1907.

Betty Thistlethwaite (183), born at Studellagarth, at the head of Dent Dale, 18th February, 1819. Died at Sedbergh, 14th July, 1888. Married 5th November, 1850, to John Guy, who died at Sedbergh, 14th October 1883, aged seventy years. He was a grocer at Sedbergh, but turned this business over to his son and became bank manager at Sedbergh.

    i.   Thomas William Guy (184), whom see.

    ii.   Rachel Margaret Guy (189), born at Sedbergh and died an infant.

    iii.   Richard Thistlethwaite Guy (190), born at Sedbergh and died an infant.

    iv.   Isabella Guy (191), whom see.

Thomas William Guy (184), formerly a grocer of Sedbergh, now a restaurateur in London. Married Annie Winn, whose sister, Elizabeth Winn, married Anthony Bradley (391), of Ambleside, a second cousin of Thomas William Guy (184).

    i.   Agnes Isabella Guy (185), who was married at the Friends' Meeting House, Westminster, 10th May, 1910, to Llewellyn King, third son of Arthur Henry and Ellen King, (both deceased). Her parents then resided at 166, Cambridge Street, London, S.W.

    ii.   John Henry Guy (186), an accountant, now in New York.

    iii.   George Herbert Guy (187).

    iv.   Winifred Mary Guy (188).

Isabella Guy (191), married Thomas Wright, secretary of Ackworth School. They emigrated to New Zealand with their family in about 1902.

    i.   Charles William Wright (192), a twin with Ernest Henry Wright (193).

   ii.   Ernest Henry Wright (193).

  iii.   Harold Wright (194).

   iv.   Percy Guy Wright (195).

William Thistlethwaite (196), born at Harborgill, in Dent, 22nd December, 1781. He is described as husbandman in the parish of Whalley, Lancashire, in the years 1806, 1808, and 1811. He married Betty Hebden, and had at least three children, but I can trace no further descendants. He was apparently disowned by the Society of Friends for marriage with a non-member.

    i.   Mary Thistlethwaite (197), born 9th December, 1806, at Blackowfoot, in the parish of Whalley.

   ii.   Anthony Thistlethwaite (198), born 7th November, 1808, at Little Stone Edge, in the Chapelry of Colne, parish of Whalley.

  iii.   Betty Thistlethwaite (199), born 6th September, 1811, at Little Stone Edge, within Barrowford Booth, Forest of Pendle, parish of Whalley.

Betty or Elizabeth Thistlethwaite (200), born at Harborgill, 24th March, 1784. Married 28th May, 1807, at Dent Meeting House, to her second cousin, Thomas Carter (1132), a cordwainer of Leayat, whom see. She died in 1812, and her husband married again.

    i.   Thomas Carter (201), whom see.

   ii.   Anthony Carter (206), whom see.

  iii.   Alice Carter (261), whom see.

Thomas Carter (201), born 1st June, 1808, at Aldries, near Leayat, in Dent Dale, since pulled down. He was in business at Preston, Lancashire, as a cattle dealer and pork-butcher, and died 29th October, 1884, aged seventy-six years. He was married 16th December, 1840, at Yealand, a village near Carnforth, Lancashire, to Mary Brunton, of Yealand. She was born 4th October, 1812, and died 11th April, 1875.

 i. Elizabeth Carter (202), born 6th November, 1841, at Preston ; died 8th September, 1867, unmarried.

 ii. Thomas Carter (203), born 18th December, 1849, at Preston ; died at Lancaster, 18th March, 1908, unmarried.

 iii. Margaret Alice Carter (204), whom see.

 iv. John Carter (205), born 4th August, 1857, at Preston; died at Lancaster, 21st April, 1875, unmarried.

Margaret Alice Carter (204), born 3rd June, 1852, at Preston, Lancashire. She was married at Yealand, 25th September, 1889, to Joseph Marriage Jesper, practical engineer, of Birmingham. I understand that he was a near relative of the late Sir Richard Tangye, in whose engineering works at Birmingham he is employed. Joseph M. and Margaret A. Jesper were living in 1910 at 42, Crockett's Road, Handsworth, Birmingham..

 i. Constance Jesper (204*a*), born 28th August, 1890, at Handsworth, Birmingham.

 ii. Wilfrid Jesper (204*b*), born 13th January, 1892, at Handsworth, Birmingham.

 iii. Elsie Jesper (204*c*), born 16th October, 1893, at Handsworth, Birmingham.

Anthony Carter (206), born 1st July, 1810, at Aldries in Dent ; died at Dent's Town, 2nd January, 1883. He was trained as a tea-dealer and coffee-roaster, and was also for over forty years Relieving Officer of Sedbergh Union. In these duties he was at one time assisted by his

third cousin, Jeremiah Thistlethwaite, later of Great Ayton.   Anthony
Carter was also Registrar of Births and Deaths, Assessor of Income Tax,
local constable, will-maker for most of the Dent's people, and amateur
doctor.   Besides this, he farmed about four acres of land, and was a very
well-known character in the Dale.

He lost his membership in the Society of Friends on account of his
marriage in the latter part of 1847 to Betty Allen, a non-Quaker.   She
was born 11th January, 1824, at Millhead Brow (now pulled down), on
the road between Dent and Sedbergh.   She died at Dent's Town 26th
June, 1876.

Betty Allen was daughter of Christopher Allen, of Chapel in Dent,
by his wife Agnes Sedgwick, of the Sedbergh or Howgill Sedgwick family.
This family was not nearly connected with the Dent Sedgwick family,
from which sprang Adam Sedgwick, the eminent geologist.   Betty Allen
was second cousin to George Allen, Margaret Allen and Robert Allen, who
respectively married Anthony Carter's first cousins, Margaret Mason
(363), George Mason (366), and Agnes Mason (386).

    i.   Elizabeth Carter (207), whom see.
   ii.   Thomas Carter (225), whom see.
  iii.   Christopher Anthony Carter (227), whom see.
  iv.   Agnes Alice Carter (240), whom see.
   v.   Mary Isabella Carter (251), whom see.
  vi.   John Allen Carter (254), whom see.
 vii.   Emma Carter (258), whom see.

Elizabeth Carter (207), born in Dent's Town, 15th November, 1848.
In 1910 she was living in Dent's Town.   She was married in 1872 or 1873
to Miles Capstick, a cabinet-maker of Dent's Town.

Miles Capstick had been previously married, and had three children
by his first wife.   He was the only son of Thomas Capstick, by his wife
Alice Bainbridge, whose brother George Bainbridge became a clergyman.
Thomas Capstick was the nephew of Margaret Capstick, who married
William Thistlethwaite (1217) of Leayat.   See Chart VI.

Elizabeth Capstick (207), married secondly John Powley, by whom she had no issue. By her first husband she had issue as follows.

    i. Betsy Elizabeth Capstick (208), born at Dent, 12th December, 1873, married William Metcalfe, of Hawes.

        i. Robert Metcalfe (209), born about 1900.

        ii. Carter Metcalfe (210), born 1901.

        iii. Daisy Metcalfe (211), born 1902.

        iv. Lena Metcalfe (212), born 1903.

        v. Emma Metcalfe (213), born 1904.

    ii. Anthony Carter Capstick (214), born 10th April, 1875, at Dent. In 1910 he was a butcher and horse-dealer in Dent, unmarried.

    iii. William Capstick (215), born 15th May, 1876, at Dent. He was innkeeper at the Sun Inn, Dent's Town, and married Mary Chapman. He died in 1905.

        i. Miles Capstick (216), born May, 1903.

        ii. William Capstick (217), born 1905.

    iv. Mary Alice Capstick (218), born 27th July, 1877, at Dent. She was married to Richard Bentham, originally of Dent. In 1910 they were cow-keepers at 5, Clevedon Buildings, South Liverpool.

        i. William Bentham (219), born 12th November, 1898.

        ii. Elizabeth Jane Bentham (220), born 24th December, 1899.

    v. Emma Capstick (221), born 7th February, 1879, at Dent. She was married to Charles A. Midgley, headmaster of Dent Elementary School.

        i. Ella Midgley (222), born at Dent, 1903.

    vi. Bell Capstick (223), born 19th March, 1883, at Dent. She was married to David Raw, carrier, of Dent.

        i. Dora Margaret Raw (224), born at Dent, 1908.

        ii. Elizabeth Raw (224a), born at Dent, 13th April, 1910.

Thomas Carter (225), born in Dent's Town, 2nd March, 1851. He was at one time a sergeant in the Liverpool Police Force, but had retired on his pension before 1910, when he was employed at a skating rink in Liverpool. He married Mary Irving, of Dumfries, Scotland.

    i.   Ella Carter (226), born 1876 or 1877. In 1910 she was living in Manchester, married to John Henry, but without issue.

Christopher Anthony Carter (227), born in Dent's Town, 13th September, 1853. He first went to a dame's school, where he learnt to read and knit, knitting being a common employment of nearly all the Dales-people. In due time he went to the National School, and afterwards to the Grammar School, at Dent, proceeding, in 1864, to King Edward VI. Grammar School at Sedbergh, where he remained eight years, during the last two of which he was head of the school.

In 1872, he entered St. John's College, Cambridge, where he won a Lupton and Hebblethwaite exhibition and an open sizarship. He graduated in the Mathematical Tripos in 1876. St. John's College always had an intimate connection with the Grammar School at Sedbergh, indeed, there were two closed fellowships reserved for Sedbergh scholars, one of which the subject of this sub-section would in all probability have held, had not the foundation been altered by Act of Parliament.

He was married at Somersham, Huntingdonshire, 20th October, 1874, to Lavinia Elizabeth Mordecai, born about 1849, only child of Daniel Mordecai, a printer, of Cambridge, by his wife Lavinia Newman, of Hunsdon, Hertfordshire. The last named died 10th December, 1909, at Cambridge, aged eighty-five, and in 1910 her widower was living with his daughter in Liverpool, aged eighty-six. Mrs. Carter's first cousin, Miss E. L. Newman, of London, is a musical composer of some note.

Immediately on taking his degree, Christopher Anthony Carter (227) became usher in a private school at Budleigh Salterton, South Devonshire, and fifteen months later went to a similar post at Folkestone, where, in September, 1877, he was ordained by Dr. Tait, Archbishop of Canterbury, and licensed to the Sunday Curacy of Hawkinge-with-Swingfield.

In 1878, he accepted a curacy at St. Mary's, Kirkdale, Liverpool, under Canon Major Lester, the well-known philanthropist and friend of children. During the seventeen years of his curacy here, he baptised 14,044 persons, and married 1,798 couples. The total population of the parish was about 27,000.

In 1896, he was appointed Vicar of St. Titus, Liverpool, a poor parish with a population of about 5,000 ; indeed, one street, since rebuilt, had a population of 3,800. Since the recent religious riots the population of this parish has become almost entirely Roman Catholic. St. Titus Vicarage is situated in St. Domingo Grove, Everton, Liverpool.

Christopher Anthony Carter (227) stands six feet two inches in height, and has always taken great interest in athletics. At Sedbergh Grammar School he was captain of the cricket eleven two years before leaving. At Cambridge he pulled in the St. John's first boat for two years. At St. Mary's, Kirkdale, he was captain of the Sunday School cricket and football clubs, and still fills the position of judge in the Liverpool Elementary Schools Athletic Festival each year.

He has had wide experience in school management, and is now an expert and referee in educational matters in the Liverpool district. He is one of the honorary secretaries of the Liverpool and District Association of Church School Managers and Teachers, and, on the formation of the Liverpool Diocesan Church Schools Association, under the Voluntary Schools Act, 1897, he was elected a member of the Governing Body.

He has had twelve children, six of whom died young.

   i.   Percival Anthony Daniel Carter (228), whom see.

   ii.   Thomas Carter (232), whom see.

  iii.   Elizabeth Lavinia Carter (235), born at Liverpool, 7th February, 1879 ; in 1910 living at home unmarried.

  iv.   Charles Christopher Carter (236), whom see.

   v.   Daisy Alice Carter (238), born at Liverpool, 23rd January, 1886 ; in 1910 a teacher in an elementary school in Liverpool ; unmarried.

    vi. William Herbert Carter (239), born at Liverpool, 2nd August, 1889. He was educated at the Liverpool Collegiate Institution, and the Liverpool College, and in 1910 was an undergraduate at St. John's College, Cambridge. He is a Bell University scholar, and holds an £80 open Scholarship at John's, besides holding a Gladstone Exhibition from Liverpool College.

Percival Anthony Daniel Carter (228), born at Cambridge, 5th August, 1875. He was at one time assistant master at a school in the South of England, but in 1910 was Examining Officer in H.M. Customs at Liverpool. He married Jessie Georgette Stenhouse, of Bootle, daughter of George Athanase Doré Stenhouse, a clerk in the Liverpool Municipal Office.

    i. Agnes Elizabeth Lorraine Carter (229), born at Gravesend, 8th November, 1899.

    ii. Ivy Margaret Carter (229a), born 8th October, 1901, at Liverpool; died there 27th December, 1907.

    iii. Elsie Jane Carter (230), born at Liverpool, 20th April, 1903.

    iv. Alice Doreen Carter (231), born at Liverpool, 26th September, 1907.

Thomas Carter (232), born in Devonshire, 14th November, 1876. In 1910 he was accountant to Addenbrooke's Hospital, Cambridge. He married Eleanor Amy Banham, daughter of a robe-maker of Cambridge.

    i. Irene Winifred Carter (233), born at Cambridge, 14th October, 1903.

    ii. Christine Alice Carter (234), born at Cambridge, 9th February, 1906.

Charles Christopher Carter (236), born at Liverpool, 3rd March, 1882. He obtained a scholarship to St. John's College, Cambridge, as tenor in the College Chapel Choir. He took his B.A. degree in a music special, and at the same time went through the Cambridge Day Training College. In 1910 he was a master in an elementary school in Liverpool. He married Emily Wright, daughter of John Wright, a builder and celebrated cornet-player, of Spondon, Derbyshire.

i. Gladys Lilian Carter (237), born 14th July, 1908, at Spondon, Derbyshire.

ii. Christopher Allan Wright Carter (237a), born 31st March, 1910, at Spondon.

1164915

Agnes Alice Carter (240), born 22nd November, 1856, at Dent's Town. She married Edward Hall, farmer, of Countersett, in Raydale, Wensleydale.

i.   Margaret Hall (241), born 10th December, 1885. Married George Terry, of Bainbridge.

  i.   George Stanley Terry (242), born 18th June, 1909.

ii.   Benjamin Hall (243), born 8th September, 1887.

iii. Mary Isabella Hall (244), born 2nd April, 1889.

iv.   Elizabeth Hall (245), born 19th January, 1891.

v.   William Hall (246), born 26th November, 1892.

vi.   Anthony Hall (247), born 30th September, 1894.

vii. Edward Hall (248), born 9th June, 1896.

viii. John Hall (249), born 2nd January, 1898.

ix.   Thomas Hall (250), born 12th December, 1899; died 31st July 1900.

Mary Isabella Carter (251), born at Dent's Town, 9th August, 1859; died 31st October, 1887. Married William Christopher Metcalfe, of Hawes, who was, in 1910, a constable in the Liverpool Police Force.

i. Christopher Anthony Metcalfe (252), born 27th October, 1885; in 1910 employed in the Liverpool Post Office.

ii. Constance Metcalfe (253) born 7th February, 1887 ; now in
     Liverpool ; unmarried.

John Allen Carter (254), born at Dent's Town, 23rd July, 1863.
A police sergeant at Liverpool. Died there 7th December, 1904. He
married Jane Metcalfe, of Hawes, sister of Wm. Chr. Metcalfe, his brother-
in-law.

   i. Anthony Carter (255), born 3rd December, 1888 ; now employed
     in Liverpool Post Office.
  ii. John Allen Carter (256), born 13th January, 1893.
 iii. Charles Carter (257), born 1st September, 1896.

Emma Carter (258), born at Dent's Town, 23rd July, 1867. Now a
widow living at Dent's Town. Married Stanley Hawkings, of Liverpool.
   i. Norman Stanley Hawkings (259), born 5th March, 1895.
  ii. John Harold Hawkings (260), born 14th April, 1897.

Alice Carter (261), born at Aldries, in Dent, 19th December, 1811.
The Memoir in the *Annual Monitor* says she was born at Scotchergill ;
but it was some time later that her father lived at the latter place. She
was deprived by death of her mother when about two weeks old, and
thus became the special care of her grandmother. From the age of
seventeen to twenty-two she was governess to the children of Thomas
Backhouse, of York.

She married, in 1843, Thomas Salthouse, of Fleetwood, Preston, and
Liverpool, painter and drysalter. He survived her, and died at
Southport.

They first lived at Fleetwood, where four sons were born, two of
whom died in infancy. The only daughter was born after removal to
Preston. Alice Salthouse was a well-known local philanthropist, and
died 25th May, 1891, aged seventy-nine years, at Liverpool.

    i.   Thomas Carter Salthouse (262), whom see.

    ii.   William Salthouse (274), born at Fleetwood, about 1850 ; a drysalter, and oil and colourman, at Clapham, South London ; died there about 1902. Married Nanny Twiss, of Dublin, who now carries on his business. He lived at Upper Tooting, Balham.

        i.   George Salthouse (275), born in London.

        ii.   Lilian Salthouse (276), born in London.

        iii.   Thomas Salthouse (277), born in London.

    iii.   Mary Alice Salthouse (278), born at Preston, 17th October, 1853 ; died about 1903. Educated at the Mount School, York, 8 mo. 1869 to 12 mo. 1870. Married, first, Robert Esdaile ; second, William Colbert ; third, John Kay. *Sine prole.*

    Thomas Carter Salthouse (262), born at Fleetwood, 22nd August, 1845 ; died 10th April, 1903, at Liverpool, where he was a coal-agent. He was educated at Bootham School, York, 8 mo. 1859 to 6 mo. 1860. He married Emily Nuttall, daughter of —— Nuttall, of Nutgrove Hall, St. Helens, Lancashire, bottle manufacturer.

    i.   Edith Louisa Salthouse (263), born Liverpool, 2nd April, 1873 ; married John Nightingale, clerk, of Liverpool.

        i.   Elsie Nightingale (264), born 14th June, 1896.

        ii.   Frank Nightingale (265), born 11th February, 1905.

    ii.   Alice Elizabeth Carter Salthouse (266), born Liverpool, 17th September, 1875, married Frederick Steele.

        i.   Francis Frederick Steele (267), born 8th May, 1906.

    iii.   Thomas Francis Salthouse (268), born 12th September, 1877, at Liverpool. Married —— Robinson.

        i.   Nadine Isabel Salthouse (269), born 24th March, 1909.

    iv.   Florence Emily Salthouse (270), born 2nd March, 1880, at Liverpool. Married Arthur Lund.

        i.   Oswe Trelfa Lund (271), a boy, born 14th August, 1 906

  v. Hilda Salthouse (272), born Liverpool, 6th September, 1881 ;
        in 1910 living, unmarried, with her eldest sister.
 vi. Constance Mabel Salthouse (273), born Liverpool, 10th July,
        1883 ; in 1910 living, unmarried, with her eldest sister.

Thomas Thistlethwaite (279), born 15th January, 1786, in Dent
Dale. He married Jane Pickthall, lived and died at Spicegill, and was
buried at Leayat. His father, Anthony Thistlethwaite (112) is said to
have left the Spicegill property jointly to his younger sons, Thomas and
Anthony, but the latter dying without issue, the whole fell to Thomas.

   i. Mary Thistlethwaite (280) born 14th April, 1820, at Spicegill,
        in Dent, and died unmarried.
  ii. Anthony Thistlethwaite (281), born 9th March, 1822, at Spice-
        gill. His father left him the two Spicegill estates, and here
        he lived until his death, 8th February, 1903. He was the
        last Thistlethwaite " statesman " of Dent Dale. He
        married, when middle-aged, a Miss Burton, also middle-
        aged, and had no issue. She was sister to the wife of
        Thomas Parrington (1254) of Leayat. His property he left
        to his only nephew.
 iii. John Thistlethwaite (282), born 8th July, 1826, at Spicegill,
        where he died at the age of thirty-six years, unmarried.
  iv. Elizabeth Thistlethwaite (283), whom see.

Elizabeth Thistlethwaite (283), born 10th January, 1830, at
Spicegill. She married Leonard Sedgwick, and they emigrated to
America, where her three children were born. She is said to have died
at Smithtown in Canada, and her husband returned home with the
children, who were, I believe, brought up at Spicegill.

   i. Agnes Sedgwick (284), whom see.
  ii. Mary Jane Sedgwick (287), whom see.
 iii. Thomas Thistlethwaite Sedgwick (292), whom see.

Agnes Sedgwick (284), was born in Canada, and married Lawrence Bayne of Rayside, in Dent. She died three years after her only child was born. Lawrence Bayne is a marble-polisher by trade, and lived at one time at Bradford. He now lives at Clint in Dent with his daughter and son-in-law.

    i. Alice Bayne (285), married George Allen, and lives at Clint, a house on the side of the Dent Valley opposite to Spicegill. She has three young children, the eldest of whom bears the name,

        i. Lawrence Allen (286).

Mary Jane Sedgwick (287), married James Brown, who has lived at Kettlewell in Wharfedale, and near Hawes Junction. They were both living in 1909, and have issue.

    i. Richard Brown (288), now living unmarried at Kettlewell, Yorkshire.

    ii. Agnes Brown (289), living near Bradford, married, and has one child.

    iii. Mabel Brown (290), in service at Bradford.

    iv. Elizabeth Brown (291), in service at Bradford.

Thomas Thistlethwaite Sedgwick (292), was born at Smithtown in Canada. He owned the Spicegill estates, and was the last Thistlethwaite descendant to be a "statesman" in Dent Dale. Shortly before his uncle's death he contemplated the adoption of "Thistlethwaite" as his surname, but this was not done. But, as is stated elsewhere in this work, the "statesman" is locally known by his Christian name coupled with that of his property; in witness of which, when staying in Dent Dale in 1909, my hostess was well acquainted with "Tom of Spicegill," but an inquiry as to his surname had to be referred to her husband, another "statesman." Thomas Thistlethwaite Sedgwick (292) married a Miss Stenton, of Sedbergh.

On 1st December, 1909, he was taking a "stag" (*i.e.* an unbroken horse) over the moors towards Hawes when he was overcome by the snow, and was found a few days later frozen to death. His land was left to his two sons, who were farming it when last heard of.

    i. Frederick Sedgwick (293), born in Dent Dale. He is unmarried, and emigrated to Canada a year or two ago, but was on his way home when his father died.

   ii. Leonard Sedgwick (294), now of Spicegill, unmarried.

  iii. Elizabeth Sedgwick (295) married John Whinfield, of Long Preston, and has one child.

       i. Ivor Whinfield (296).

   iv. Nancy Sedgwick (297) married Richard Fawcett, who was employed, and killed near Dent, on the Midland Railway. She has four children, and lives at Spicegill.

    v. Agnes Sedgwick (298), now of Spicegill, unmarried.

Agnes Thistlethwaite (301), born 4th March, 1792, at Harborgill in Dent. She married John Baynes, whose nephew of the same name married her niece, Jane Bradley (409), see Chart III. She emigrated to America about 1830, and they had a farm on the " Flats " in Pennsylvania.

    i. William Wallis Baynes (302), was a farmer, and an inspector of schools : a much respected man. I have been unable to trace issue of him and his brothers and sisters.

   ii. John Baynes (303) fought in the American Civil War, and was presented with a farm for his services.

  iii. Timothy Baynes (304) lived at London in Canada. Among other issue his son

       i. John Baynes (305) once visited England.

   iv. Mary Baynes (306), married Edwin Macaulay, a Scotchman, who had a farm at Rochester, New York State.

Alice Thistlethwaite (307), born 20th May, 1794, at Spicegill. She married Thomas Mason, of Dent Dale, and they emigrated to America. As in the case of her youngest sister, here her husband died, and she returned to England with her young family.

She lived at Borren Head, a house on the left side of the Dent Valley as one is going from Dent's Town to Leayat.   In about 1849 eight members of the family are said to have been ill with typhus fever at the same time.   It was found difficult to obtain satisfactory nurses, and several of the family died.   These included Alice Mason (307), mother of the family, her eldest son John Mason (308), and her daughter-in-law, the latter's wife, who was born Harker.

Many of Alice Mason's descendants are still living in the Dent district.   Indeed, with rare exceptions, her father's descendants are the only descendants of William Thistlethwaite (1), of Harborgill, who are still resident in the vicinity of Dent Dale.

  i. John Mason (308), married Simon Harker's sister. Both he and his wife died of typhus fever in or about the year 1849.

      i. David Mason (309), born a few years before his parent's death. He is said to be a provision dealer in Harrogate, Yorkshire.

      ii. Thomas Mason (310), died young.

  ii. Mary Mason (311), whom see.

  iii. Ann Mason (319), whom see.

  iv. Betty Mason (346), whom see.

  v. Anthony Mason (362), born about 1826, married Ellen Allen, but had no issue. He emigrated to America.

  vi. Margaret Mason (363), born 1829. She married George Allen, of Hill, Leayat, whose cousins married her brother and sister respectively.

      i. William Allen (364), born about 1852.

  vii. Isabella Mason (365), born about 1831 ; married James Metcalfe, and died without issue.

viii. George Mason (366), whom see.
  ix. Agnes Mason (386), born about 1837 ; married Robert Allen,
       whose sister Margaret Allen married her brother George
       Mason. They emigrated to America : I do not know
       whether they had offspring.

Mary Mason (311), married Thomas Bushby and had issue.
  i. Thomas Bushby (312), born 18th May, 1843 ; married Mar-
      garet Fothergill and had issue.
        i. Thomas Bushby (313), born 13th January, 1875,
            now milk-dealer in Liverpool. He married Kate
            Ward, of York, and has no issue.
  ii. Betty Bushby (314), married Matthew Metcalfe, of Gaw-
      throp, and had issue.
        i.   John Metcalfe (315), born 1874.
        ii.   Thomas Metcalfe (316), born 1876.
        iii. Elizabeth Metcalfe (317), born 1878.
        iv.   Mason Metcalfe (318), born 1882.

Ann Mason (319), born in 1822, died 1907. She married William
Parrington, farmer and butcher, of Loaning, in Dent Dale, and had
issue.
   i.   Dorothy Parrington (320), whom see.
   ii. Thomas Parrington (326), whom see.
   iii. Alice Parrington (329), whom see.
   iv. Agnes Parrington (338), whom see.
   v.   John Mason Parrington (339), whom see.
   vi. Margaret Parrington (345), whom see.

Dorothy Parrington (320), born 1849, married James Mason, who
lived in 1910, at Dilicar Farm, Dent, and had issue.
    i. William Mason (321), born in 1878, living at home in 1910,
        unmarried.

ii. Annie Mason (322), born in 1880, recently married to John Mackereth, of Craggses Farm, Dent ; no issue.

iii. Elizabeth Mason (323), born in 1881. She was married about four years ago to Richard Mason, who in 1910 was a milk seller at 5, Gilpin Street, The Dingle, Liverpool. She has had two children, who died in infancy.

iv. Agnes Mason (324), born 1886. In 1910 she was living at home unmarried.

v. Margaret Mason (325), born 1888. In 1910 she was living at home unmarried.

Thomas Parrington (326), born 1851, married Jane Baine, and had issue.

i. Annie Parrington (327), died young.

ii. Dorothy Parrington (328), married Joshua Blades, a mason, of Dent's Town, and has one daughter six months old.

Alice Parrington (329), born in 1853. She married Thomas Fawcett, whose mother was an Oversby. He is a shoe-maker in Dent, and has issue.

i. Agnes Fawcett (330), married a Mr. Peaker, a schoolmaster, who resides at Beeston Hill, Leeds, and has two children.

ii. William Fawcett (331), of High Farm, Dent, married Margaret Brown, and has four children.

iii. Richard Fawcett (332), a schoolmaster, married, but without issue in 1910.

iv. Dora Fawcett (333), living at home, unmarried.

v. Mary Alice Fawcett (334), usually known as " May," an assistant teacher at Dent school, unmarried.

vi. Ada Fawcett (335), an assistant teacher at Dent school, unmarried.

vii. Thomas Fawcett (336), a shoe-maker with his father, unmarried.

viii. Annie Fawcett (337), married and living at Appleby, Westmorland.

Agnes Parrington (338), born 1855. She married George Baine,
who was in 1910 a quarryman at Horton-in-Ribblesdale, Yorkshire.

i. George Baine (338*a*), died young.

ii. Jane Ann Baine (338*b*), born 1887, in 1910 living at home
unmarried.

iii. William Baine (338*c*), in 1910 a quarryman at Horton-in-
Ribblesdale, unmarried.

iv. Mason Baine (338*d*), in 1910 a quarryman at Horton-in-
Ribblesdale, unmarried.

John Mason Parrington (339), born in 1857. He married Betsy
Margaret Baynes, and died, leaving issue.

i. Elizabeth Parrington (340), married Alfred King, of Burnley
and was living in 1910 at Carlisle.

    i. Thomas Reginald King (340*a*), born in 1907.

    ii. Catherine King (340*b*), born August, 1909.

ii. William Parrington (341), born December, 1887. In 1910
he was a milk seller, living at 7, Gilpin Street, The Dingle,
Liverpool. He married Annie Mason, and has issue.

    i. Edith Bessie Parrington (341*a*), born 10th January,
1908.

    ii. Agnes Annie Parrington (341*b*), born 25th Novem-
ber, 1909.

iii. Ernest Parrington (342), living unmarried in 1910.

iv. George Parrington (343), living unmarried in 1910.

v. John Parrington (344), living unmarried in 1910.

Margaret Parrington (345), born 1859. She married Thomas Middleton, of Crummuck Farm, near Austwick, son of John Middleton, of Deepdale Head, near Dent.

    i.   John Middleton (345*a*), born about 1892.

    ii.   William Middleton (345*b*), born about 1894.

    iii.   Armer Mason Middleton (345*c*), born about 1896.

Betty Mason (346), born 1824, died 1906 in Dent, married George Morland, of Hawes, and removed to Liverpool.

    i.   Leonard Morland (347), whom see.

    ii.   Thomas Mason Morland (359), born 1856 ; is married, but have no more information to hand.

    iii.   George Scarr Morland (360), born 1858 ; married, but no information.

    iv.   John Morland (361), married, no information.

Leonard Morland (347), born 25th May, 1852. He is a stevedore at Liverpool, and married Ann Jolly, of Poulton-le-Fylde, Lancashire.

    i.   George Morland (348), born 20th November, 1876, died young.

    ii.   Sarah Morland (349), born 26th August, 1878 ; married George Catchpole, an engineer, and has issue,

        i.   Gladys Catchpole (350), born 15th August 1908.

    iii.   Mabel Morland (351), born 23rd October, 1880, died young.

    iv.   Leonard Morland (352), born 5th July, 1883 ; married Elizabeth Green, and has issue,

        i.   Leonard Morland (353), born 28th May, 1905.

        ii.   Frank Morland (354), born 1st June, 1907.

    v.   Bessie Morland (355), born 20th November, 1884, unmarried.

    vi.   Frank Morland (356), born 13th June, 1889, unmarried.

    vii.   Reginald Morland (357), born 10th June, 1892, unmarried.

    viii.   Herbert Morland (358), born 19th July, 1894, unmarried.

George Mason (366), born 1833, died 1894. He married 10th February, 1854, Margaret Allen, born 1829, died 1903, sister of Robert Allen who married George Mason's sister, Agnes Mason (386).

   i.   Thomas Mason (367), born 2nd January, 1855, died 29th April, 1874, unmarried.

   ii.   John Mason (368), born 1st July, 1856 ; was married at Kansas City, U.S.A., to Ann McKinney, and died recently in America, leaving issue,

       i.   George Mason (369), born 1895.

       ii.   Thomas Mason (370), born 1897.

       iii.   John Mason (371), born 1899.

   iii.   Alice Mason (372), whom see.

   iv.   Ann Mason (378), born 29th February, 1860 ; married James Nuttall Bold, clerk in the Corporation Offices, Liverpool.

       i.   Margaret Nuttall Bold (379), born 24th April, 1888.

       ii.   George Mason Bold (380), born 22nd May, 1892.

       iii.   William Bold (381), born 1901.

   v.   Mary Mason (382), born 26th March, 1867. She is a confectioner at West Derby, Liverpool, unmarried.

   vi.   William Mason (383), born 19th April, 1870 ; emigrated to the United States. He married Emily Jones, and has issue,

       i.   George Mason (384), born 25th January, 1895.

       ii.   Mary Mason (385), born 23rd January, 1897.

Alice Mason (372), born 13th June, 1858 ; married Frederick Williams, then of Garsdale, and now a cowkeeper in Liverpool.

   i.   William Arthur Williams (373), born 23rd May, 1883, now in a bank in London. He married Lydia Ainsley, of London, and has issue,

       i.   Irene Williams (374), born April, 1909.

   ii.   George Mason Williams (375), born 23rd April, 1885, unmarried.

   iii.   Frederick Williams (376), born 24th June, 1887, unmarried.

   iv.   Allan Williams (377), born 20th November, 1896.

Mary Thistlethwaite (388), born at Spicegill in Dent Dale, 3rd April, 1801, married at Leayat Meeting House 30th April, 1823, to Timothy Bradley, who was born at Rash in Leniker, Dent Dale, 4th June, 1796, son of John Bradley, miller, and Mary his wife.

Timothy and Mary Bradley emigrated to the United States with their two eldest children about 1827. Timothy Bradley died 6th November, 1837, at Rochester, N.Y., within twenty-four hours of the birth of his youngest child. His widow brought her seven children back to England, and lived in Dent Dale and at Kendal, and latterly with her son Thomas Bradley (414).

-   i. Mary Bradley (389), born at Rash Mill in Dent, 6th June, 1824, died at York aged about sixty years.
-   ii. John Bradley (390), whom see.
-   iii. Anthony Bradley (401), whom see.
-   iv. Jane Bradley (409), whom see.
-   v. Ann Bradley (411), whom see.
-   vi. Thomas Bradley (414), born at Rochester, Monroe County, New York State, U.S.A., 18th December, 1834, for many years a leather merchant in Liverpool. On his retirement he purchased Bearpark, an ancient mansion near Carperby, in Wensleydale, and has since lived there unmarried. Under his direction, the gardens and grounds, skirting the river near Aysgarth falls, have become one of the most beautiful sights in Wensleydale.
-   vii. William Timothy Bradley (415), whom see.

John Bradley (390), born at Rash Mill in Dent, 19th September, 1826, lived at Kendal, died at Arnside, aged 45-50 years. He married Margaret Copplethwaite, of near Kendal, who is now living at Ambleside, near Windermere.

-   i. Anthony Bradley (391), born at Kendal, now of Ambleside, married Elizabeth Winn, whose sister married his second cousin Thos. Wm. Guy (184). *Sine prole.*

ii. Mary Bradley (392), born at Kendal, now of Ambleside,
unmarried.

iii. Jane Bradley (393), born at Kendal, married John Wood-
house, farmer, of Preston Patrick, near Kendal. *Sine
prole.*

iv. Margaret Bradley (394), born at Kendal, now of Ambleside
unmarried.

v. Frederick Bradley (395), born at Kendal, now insurance
agent at Barrow-in-Furness, Lancashire. He married
Elizabeth ——, and has four children.

    i. Lilian Bradley (396), born at Kendal.

    ii. Dorothy Bradley (397), born at Kendal.

    iii. Norah Bradley (398), born at Kendal.

    iv. John Bradley (399), born at Kendal.

vi. Esther Annie Bradley (400), born at Kendal, married 3rd
March, 1908, at St. Mary's Church, Ambleside, to William
H. Hardy, of Rothay House, Ambleside, boat proprietor.

Anthony Bradley (401), born at Rochelle, West Chester County,
New York State, U.S.A., 18th December, 1828 ; a carpenter. He died
in Manchester aged 72 years. His widow Sarah Bradley now lives in
Manchester, and had seven children, all of whom were born in Liverpool.

i. John Bradley (402), now commercial traveller of Liverpool,
married Ellen Beck, and has two children.

ii. Mary Bradley (403), married an engineer, and has issue.

iii. Anthony Bradley (404), sub-manager in carriage works at
Manchester ; married, and has issue.

iv. William Bradley (405), died unmarried, aged about thirty
years.

v. Sarah Bradley (406), married Joseph Bowyer, an engineer
at Montreal, Canada. *Sine prole.*

vi.   Edith Bradley (407), married Alfred ——, and is *sine prole*.

vii. Thomas Bradley (408), now employed in carriage works at Manchester, unmarried.

Jane Bradley (409), born 25th December, 1830, at Rochester, Monroe County, New York State, U.S.A., married at Carperby Meeting House, near Aysgarth, to John Baynes, farmer, of Aysgarth : (for Baynes intermarriages, see Chart III). She died at Bear Park, her brother's residence, near Aysgarth, 27th October, 1885.

i.   Oswald Bradley Baynes (410), Bachelor of Arts, teacher at Bootham School, York, from 1885 to 1907. Married 20th August, 1907, at Saltburn-by-the-Sea Meeting House, to Helen Bayes, B.A., of Polam Hall, Darlington. She, then of Hammersmith, was educated at the Mount School, York, from 8 mo. 1879 to 6 mo. 1882, was a teacher there from 8 mo. 1883 to 6 mo. 1885, and from 1 mo. 1888 to 6 mo. 1893. She is now one of the Principals of Polam Hall Private School for Girls, Darlington.

Ann Bradley (411), born 23rd February, 1833, at Rochester, N.Y., died at Preston, Lancashire, aged about 60 years. She married John Smith, who died at Preston.

i.   William Henry Smith (412), born at Liverpool, sometime missionary in India, now resident at the Isle of Man.

ii.   Mary Ellen Smith (413), born at Liverpool, married — Tickle, and has two children both born at Preston.

William Timothy Bradley (415), born 5th November, 1837, at Rochester, N.Y. He travelled as an infant to England with his mother, but when a young man he returned to America, where he lived three years. He visited his father's grave at Rochester, the family of his aunt Agnes Baynes, *née* Thistlethwaite (301), who lived on the Flats in Pennsylvania, and the family of his second cousin once removed, William Thistlethwaite (1598), of Richmond, Indiana. He returned to England to join his brother Thomas Bradley (414), in the leather business at Liverpool, from which he has since retired, and lives with his wife and youngest daughter at Hallgarth, Carperby, Yorkshire.

He married, 1st March, 1870, at Askrigg Church, Wensleydale, Elizabeth Longmire Willis, who was born at Preston, Lancashire, 26th February, 1839, daughter of Matthew Willis, of Wensleydale. She was adopted by her uncle John Willis, and her father emigrated to America with other members of his family. See Alice Thistlethwaite (1131).

    i.   Mary Alice Bradley (416), born at Liverpool 8th February, 1871, married 14th October, 1896, at Carperby Meeting House, to Simon Hunter Willan, solicitor, of Hawes, Wensleydale, Yorkshire.

        i.   Esther Hunter Willan (417), born 6th September, 1897, at Hawes.

        ii.   Gordon Willan (418), born 18th May, 1899, at Hawes.

        iii.   Thomas Willan (419), born 26th January, 1902, at Hawes.

        iv.   William Willan (420), born 24th June, 1903, at Hawes.

        v.   Mary Willan (421), born 10th April, 1908, at Hawes.

    ii.   Eleanor Jane Bradley (422), born at Liverpool, 4th May, 1872, married 26th June, 1902, at Carperby Meeting House, to Robert William Fraser, engineer, of Liverpool. *Sine prole.* Of Hoylake in 1910.

    iii.   Rose Bradley (423), born at Liverpool, 26th October, 1873, died 18th April, 1884, buried at Crosby Church, near Liverpool.

iv. May Bradley (424), born 11th March, 1875, now in the United States, a journalist, and authoress of three novels, one of which, "Craiktrees," deals with Wensleydale. Educated at the Mount School, York, from 8 mo. 1890 to 6 mo. 1891. Her pen-name is "Watson Dyke."

v. William Timothy Bradley (425), born at Summerdell, West-morland, 9th October, 1876, educated at Bootham School, York, 1 mo. 1888 to 6 mo 1893, B.A. of Liverpool University, employed in the North Eastern Railway Offices, York, and living at Harrogate.

vi. Willis Bradley (426), born at Liverpool 1st April, 1879, now a farmer at Mineral Point, Wis., married 16th October, 1908 Marie Nielson Lykke, of Denmark. He was educated at Bootham School, York, 1 mo. 1892 to 12 mo. 1893.

vii. Elizabeth Bradley (427), born at Liverpool 15th July, 1881, unmarried.

viii. Thomas Bradley (428), born at Blundellsands, near Liverpool, 31st January, 1886, died 30th September, 1906, buried in Aysgarth Churchyard. Educated at Bootham School, York, 5 mo. 1897 to 12 mo. 1901.

PART TWO.

DESCENDANTS OF

JAMES THISTLETHWAITE (429),

SECOND CHILD OF

WILLIAM THISTLETHWAITE (1) OF HARBORGILL.

PART TWO.

James Thistlethwaite (429), born 26th May, 1708, at Harborgill, in Dent Dale, Yorkshire. I have fortunately been able to borrow his original marriage certificate, which is now in the possession of the widow of his great-great-grandson, Alfred Yeardley (586). Mrs. Lucy Yeardley (1451) is herself a Thistlethwaite descendant. The certificate reads as follows :—

" James Thistlethwait of Dent in the parrish of Sedbergh and County of York and Isabell ffothergill of Mossdall in the pish of Aisgarth & county afors[d] haveing Declared their Intentions of takeing Each other in Marriage before severall publick meetings of the people called Quakers within Sedbergh & Richmond Monthly Meetings whose proceedings therein after a Deliberate consideracon thereof were allowd by the s[d] meettings they haveing Consent of parants & Relations concerned.

" Now these are to Cirtifie all whome it may concern that for the full Accomplishment of their said intentions this nineteenth day of the Tenth month in the year According to the English account one thousand seaven Hundred Thirty & Three They the s[d] James Thistlethwait & Isabell ffothergill appeared in a publick Assembly of the afors[d] people met together in their publick Meetting place at Haws in the said County and in a solemn Manner he the s[d] James Thistlethwait takeing the s[d] Isabell ffothergill by the hand did openly Decared as followeth friends in the fear of God & p[r]sence of this assembly doo I take this my ffriend Isabell ffothergill to be my married wife promiseing through Gods assistance to be unto her a loveing & faithfull Husband untill Death separat us or words to like Effect.

" And then and there in the s[d] assembly the s[d] Isabell ffoth[r]gill

Did in like manner Declare as followeth Jn the fear of God & p^{r}sence of this assembly doo I Take this my ffriend James Thistlethwait to be my Husband promiseing through gods assistance to be unto him a loveing & Duityfull wife untill Death seperate us, or words to like Effect.

"And the s^d James Thistlethwait & the s^d Jsabell ffothergill but now Jsabell Thistlethwait as a further confirmacon thereof Did then & there to these p^{r}sents set their hands.

"And we Whose names are hereunto subscribed being p^{r}sent amongst oth^{r}s at the solemnizeing of their said Marriage, and subscription in mann^r afors^d as witnesses thereunto have also to these p^{r}sents subscribed our names the day & year above written.

James Thistlethwaite
Isabel Thistlethwait

W^m. Thistlethw^t ⎱
Rachel Fothergill ⎰ parants

Richard Thistlethw^t [brother to the bridegroom]
John Thistlethwaite   [brother to the bridegroom]
Edmond Fothergill   [brother to the bride]
Richard Burton
John Burton
Isabell Burton
Thomas Mason
Ruth Holme
Joseph Pratt
Hannah Pratt
John Burton
[end of right-hand column]
Richard Burton
Jane Pratt
Margary Moor
Margret Pratt
William Fawcet
Richd Robinson

Amos Robinson

John Binks

Alexander Fothergill   [brother-in-law to the bridegroom]

Joseph Wetherald

W^m. Blakey

Eph Robinson

[end of middle column]

John Harrison

John Lambert

Ruth Metcalfe

Elizabeth Wetherald

Joshua Robinson

Leonard Mason

George Mayson

[end of left-hand column].

Memorand that this Cirtifigate was written upon a five shillings stamp."

From the above certificate and from the Quaker register it appears that James Thistlethwaite (429), was married at Hawes Meeting House 19th October, 1733, to Isabel Fothergill.   The certificate shows her mother to have been Rachel Fothergill, and as her second son was named Richard we may conclude with little hesitation that her father was Richard Fothergill.   Alice Chorley (1020), states that Isabel was daughter of Edmond Fothergill.   However, Edmond Fothergill was almost certainly her brother.   In 1764 he was distrained in Wensleydale for tithe; he then possessed ten cows and eight calves.   I suspect that Edmond and Isabel Fothergill were members of the Ravenstondale family, and not at all nearly related to Alexander Fothergill, who married James Thistlethwaite's sister, Margaret Thistlethwaite (877).

James and Isabel Fothergill lived in Dent Dale until 1745, but in 1748 they had moved to Raysgill in Langstrothdale, a lonely valley eight miles south of Hawes, where rises the river Wharfe.   In 1752 they are described as " of Scarhouse Meeting."

Isabel Thistlethwaite died at Mossdale 13th July, 1770, aged 59 years, and was buried on the 15th at Hawes. James Thistlethwaite (429) died 24th February, 1786, at " Stalyan Busk " or Stalling Busk, a hamlet at the head of Semerwater, near Bainbridge, Wensleydale. He was buried 1st March at Bainbridge, aged 77 years.

    i.   William Thistlethwaite (430), whom see.

    ii. Alice Thistlethwaite (533), whom see.

    iii. Rachel Thistlethwaite (560), whom see.

    iv. Richard Thistlethwaite (580), whom see.

    v. Margaret Thistlethwaite (864), whom see.

    vi. John Thistlethwaite (866), born 6th May, 1748, at Raisgill in Langstrothdale, at the head of Wharfedale, Yorkshire. He died, probably unmarried, at Preston in Lancashire, 27th October, 1783, aged about 34 years, and was buried at Preston on the following day.

    vii. Anthony Thistlethwaite (867), whom see.

William Thistlethwaite (430), born 7th February, 1736, in Dent Dale. Alice Chorley (1020), describes him as " of middle stature and of fresh ruddy complexion."

He was married at Dent 14th June, 1783, to Agnes Banister, of Cowgill, in Dent. Her father was probably named Edmund Banister, whence the name of her second son Edmund Thistlethwaite (434). She had a nephew named Edmund Banister, who was living at Cowgill about 1850. The Banisters had a worsted mill near Cowgill, close beside the river Dee, which was burned down nearly a century ago, and never rebuilt. Only a few courses of stone were remaining in 1909 to indicate its situation. Here worsted was made, and given out to the women and men of Dent Dale, who knitted it into stockings. Southey, in his " Doctor " writes of " the terrible knitters of Dent."

As the Banisters were a " Church " family, William Thistlethwaite (430) was probably married at Church, and disowned therefor by the Society of Friends. His marriage is not in the registers of the Society, .

but they contain the death entries of himself and his wife. The Banister family is said to have been largely responsible for the founding of Cowgill Church in the upper part of Dent Dale. It was a custom in the family that a member of each generation should become a clergyman.

William Thistlethwaite (430) lived at Spicegill in Dent Dale. He was in his forty-eighth year when he married, and was nearly fifty-eight years of age at the time of his death, 3rd December, 1793. His wife died thirteen days later,* on the 16th December, 1793, at Cowgill, aged forty-two years.

He "was killed driving on a dangerous road one dark night," or, according to Alice Chorley's account, "he unfortunately fell down a precipice one snowy night, and, not being found till morning, he was then taken up dead." His wife died "very shortly afterwards of shock and grief."

His only daughter was adopted by his brother Richard Thistlethwaite (580), who lived at Carr End, near Semerwater, Wensleydale. His two elder sons were adopted by other Thistlethwaite relatives, but the youngest child, John Thistlethwaite (475), aged only three years, was taken by the Banisters, and brought up with a Banister, who was long vicar of Pilling, in Lancashire, and whose only son is now vicar of Preston.

 i. James Thistlethwaite (431), born in Dent Dale, 22nd May, 1784. He was a farmer in Dent Dale, and died before June, 1836. His widow, Jane Thistlethwaite, died at Salford, near Manchester, 13th June, 1836, aged thirty-four. She was buried at Mount Street, Manchester, 16th June, a "non-member."

  i. Agnes Thistlethwaite (432), born at Cowgill, 4th April, 1824.

* My copy of the registers shows that William died 3. xii. 1792 and his wife 16. xii. 1793, but I think the years should be the same, as their grand-daughter tells me her grandmother died of grief and shock "very shortly after." I have not checked my extracts.

> ii. William Thistlethwaite (433), born at Stonehouse, in
> Dent Dale, 30th January, 1828. I do not know
> whether he or his sister married or had descendants.

ii. Edmund Thistlethwaite (434), born in Dent, 29th August, 1786,
buried, 31st March, 1863, at Bentham, Yorkshire. He
married Susannah Lister and had children married before
1850. His (only ?) son died aged twenty-one years. I
cannot trace any descendants.

iii. Isabella Thistlethwaite (435), whom see.

iv. John Thistlethwaite (475), whom see.

Isabella Thistlethwaite (435), was born 28th December, 1787,
in Dent, probably at Spicegill. She married, 2nd November, 1812, Thomas
Guy, of Ingleton. They lived on a farm at Chapel-le-dale for many years,
but retired in their old age, and went to live near their only son at Bradford.
Thomas Guy died 29th July, 1867, and is buried in Undercliffe Cemetery,
Bradford. His wife was still living in 1869.

> i. Mary Guy (436), whom see.
> ii. Agnes Guy (458), whom see.
> iii. Margaret Guy (460), whom see.
> iv. William Guy (467), whom see.
> v. Sarah Guy (474), married Joseph Bentham, who died in 1870.
> I do not know whether they had issue.

Mary Guy (436), married Henry Thomas Sedgwick Ellershaw,
grandson of Rev. Henry Ellershaw, who was for thirty-three years Vicar
or Curate-in-charge of Chapel-le-dale, near Ingleton. Mary Ellershaw, *née*
Guy, died when her eldest child was about twelve years old. Her husband
did not marry again, and the children became scattered. He died 15th
June, 1891, aged seventy-three, and was buried 19th June, at Chapel-
le-dale.

> i. Thomas Ellershaw (437), whom see.
> ii. Henry Ellershaw (442), died about 1881, leaving a widow, *sine
> prole.*

iii. William Guy Ellershaw (443), whom see.

iv. Isabella Ellershaw (454), whom see.

v. James Ellershaw (457), lived in Manchester. He died about twenty years ago, leaving a widow and six children, whom I cannot trace.

Thomas Ellershaw (437), born 20th April, 1843, at Chapel House, Chapel-le-dale, Ingleton Fells. He lived at Bradford, and died 5th March, 1905. He was married 25th August, 1875, at All Saints Church, Bradford, to Elizabeth Ann Sordoff Wright, who was born 24th November, 1850, daughter of James Wright by his wife Rachel Sordoff. She now lives at 142, New Cross Street, Bradford.

i. Thomas Ellershaw (438), born 1st June, 1876, married 24th September, 1902, at St. Stephen's Church, West Bowling, Bradford, to Bessie Smith, daughter of John James Smith, by his wife, —— Hartley.

i. Kathleen Muriel Ellershaw (439), born 3rd August, 1905, at Stetchford, near Birmingham.

ii. George Harold Ellershaw (440), born 24th March, 1878, unmarried.

iii. Helen Elizabeth Ellershaw (441), born 21st November, 1886, unmarried.

William Guy Ellershaw (443), born 31st August, 1847, at Broadrake Farm, Ingleton Fells, lived at Manchester, and died there 8th January, 1906; buried in Friends' Burial Ground, Ashton-on-Mersey. He was married, 6th September, 1871, at Manchester, to Sarah Jones, fifth daughter of John and Mary Jones, who was born 5th November, 1847, at Denbigh, North Wales. Their seven children were all born in Manchester.

i. Mary Isabella Ellershaw (444), born 8th September, 1872, living with her mother, unmarried.

ii.   William Guy Ellershaw (445), born 1st September, 1873, died 26th May, 1874, buried Ardwick Cemetery, Manchester.

iii. Jane Agnes Ellershaw (446), born 8th December, 1874, died 25th November, 1881, buried in Ardwick Cemetery, Manchester.

iv.   John Herbert Ellershaw (447), born 6th June, 1876; married at Manchester Meeting House, 14th August, 1902, Nellie Pool, of Manchester. They live there, and have one child.

  i.   Marion Dorothy Ellershaw (448), born 25th April, 1908, at Manchester.

v.   Sarah Emma Ellershaw (449), born 21st January, 1878, married at Manchester Meeting House, 16th August, 1905, to Joseph Edwin Smith, of Manchester. *Sine prole.*

vi.   Letitia Ann Ellershaw (450), born 23rd October, 1881, married at Manchester Meeting House, 2nd June, 1906, to Herbert Lowe, of Whaley Bridge, Derbyshire, now of Manchester.

  i.   Eric Arthur Lowe (451), born 27th February, 1907, at Manchester.

  ii. Ernest Stanley Lowe (452), born 5th June, 1908, at Manchester.

vii. Arthur Guy Ellershaw (453), born 18th January, 1888, now resident with his mother and eldest sister at 108, Gt. Western Street, Moss Side, Manchester.

Isabella Ellershaw (454), born 13th August, 1849, at Chapel-le-dale, Ingleton Fells, Yorkshire. She was married some time in 1876 to Julius Mason, a cashier, and they appear to have lived at Bradford, Yorkshire. He was born 1st April, 1854, and died 10th July, 1885, buried 14th July, at Undercliffe Cemetery. His widow died 19th February, 1891, and was buried 23rd February, at Bowling Cemetery.

  i.   William Mason (455), born 4th June, 1877, at Bradford. In 1910 he was manager for Mason and Booth, Ltd., Store

Chemists, of Hull and Beverley. He was married in Hull, 12th August, 1903, to Mary Sarah Tinkler, who was born 3rd January, 1882, at Hull, only daughter of Thomas Gibson Tinkler. They live at 10, Willow Grove, Beverley, and are without issue.

i. Beatrice Mason (456), born 9th March, 1882, at Bradford. She was married at Hull in 1907 to Alfred Sutton, Wholesale Fruit Merchant, of Hull.

    i. Vera Sutton (456a), born 19th January, 1910.

Agnes Guy (458), born 1819, died 1888, married John Braithwaite, and had one child.

i. Jane Guy Braithwaite (459), born 1842. She died unmarried in 1908, at the residence of her first cousin, John Anthony Guy (469), Eccleshill, near Bradford. When young she was brought up by her grandfather, Thomas Guy, and did not use her name " Braithwaite " until middle aged. She was a junior teacher at Ayton Friends' School, Great Ayton, Yorkshire, and for many years was governess at Penketh Friends' School, near Warrington, Lancashire. After this she was governess in North London to the family of Doyle Penrose, father of Doyle Penrose, the artist, who married the daughter of Alexander, first Lord Peckover of Wisbech, the only Quaker Peer. On leaving the Penrose family she lived in London with her aunt, Margaret Bilton (460). In about 1895 the latter returned to the North of England, and Jane Guy Braithwaite lived for some years at Airton, near Skipton, Yorkshire, with Martha Ecroyd Baynes, widow of Oswald Baynes, whose first wife had been Agnes Webster (847), second cousin once removed to Jane Guy Braithwaite.

Margaret Guy (460), married Edward Bilton, of Bradford, who died there in 1870, aged sixty-one years. She lived a short time in London with her niece Jane Guy Braithwaite (459), but died in Bradford 25th September, 1898, soon after returning to the North, aged seventy-three.

    i.   Edward Vipont Bilton (461), whom see.

    ii.   John Bilton (464), whom see.

Edward Vipont Bilton (461), was a draper at Bradford, where he died a few years ago. He married first, Mary Jane Ward, by whom he had two children. His second wife, Esther Woolman, survived him, without issue, and married again.

    i.   Mary Elizabeth Bilton (462), born 16th August, 1874, died unmarried, 30th May, 1904.

    ii.   Harry Ward Bilton (463), born 14th May, 1878, died 14th February, 1893.

John Bilton (464), died at Bradford, March, 1882, aged twenty-eight years. He became the second husband of Charlotte, born Beanland, who married firstly, Webster, thirdly ——, and fourthly Rev. Holdroyd, all of whom she has survived. She had children by her first three husbands, those by John Bilton being,

    i.   Charlotte Margaret Bilton (465), born about 1880, now of Christchurch, New Zealand, unmarried.

    ii.   John Edward Bilton (466), born about 1881, now in the North of England, unmarried.

William Guy (467), born 1827, wool merchant, of Bradford, where he died in 1890. He married Charlotte Crabtree, who was born at Bradford, married there 1851, and died in 1898.

    i.   Thomas A. Guy (468), born 1854, wool merchant, of Bradford, died unmarried, 1905.

   ii.   John Anthony Guy (469), born 1856, now of Eccleshill, near Bradford, and wool merchant of Nelson Street, Bradford. He married, in 1888, Eleanor Watson, who was born in 1863, and is still living.

       i.   A. Clifford Guy (470), born 1892.

  iii.   Charles Herbert Guy (471), born 1858, now of Holm Leigh, Menston, Yorkshire, and bank-manager of Bradford. He married, 1887, Clara Parkinson.

       i.   Herbert Guy (472), born 1888.

      ii.   William Leslie Guy (473), born 1891.

John Thistlethwaite (475), born in Dent Dale, 1st October, 1790, and at the age of three years was adopted by the Banisters of Dent, his mother's relatives. He entered the woollen business carried on in Darlington by the Quaker family of Pease. At the Monthly Meeting of the Society of Friends held 16th October, 1827, he applied for membership therein, and at the Monthly Meeting held 18th March, 1828, stated his intention of marriage with Isabel Ion, a member of Sedbergh Monthly Meeting. Anthony Thistlethwaite (1164), of Darlington, his second cousin, was appointed to make inquiry as to his clearness from other women, and the report given at the meeting held 15th April, 1828, being satisfactory, he was married at Dent, 30th April, 1828.

His wife, Isabel Thistlethwaite, died 1st May, 1829, at Hollins, in Dent, aged thirty-two years, and was buried on the 6th at Leayat, without issue.

At the Monthly Meeting held 22nd February, 1831, John Thistlethwaite (475), of Darlington, stated his intentions of marriage with Esther Eliza Dickinson, of Maryport, Cumberland, whom he married 25th March, 1831, at Maryport. Their three eldest children were born at Darlington, but in 1836 John Thistlethwaite (475) was sent to manage the Pease woollen business at Bradford. By an extraordinary coincidence, this business had been opened by his second cousin, another John Thistle-thwaite (1319), who was now recalled to Darlington. The latter had married the same year, 1831, Hannah Pease Frank, a grand-daughter of George Pease, of Darlington.

The John Thistlethwaite (475) of this paragraph died at Bradford 18th August, 1863. His wife Esther Eliza Thistlethwaite, died there September 1868. She was born 28th January, 1806, the daughter of John Dickinson, of Maryport (died 1822), by his wife Jane Harris (died 1870), of Cocker-mouth, where her relatives, the present Quaker Harrises of Papcastle, manufacture large quantities of linen thread. Isabella Harris, niece of Jane Harris, married Joseph Jackson Lister, F.R.S., father of Lord Lister, F.R.S., the eminent surgeon, and of Jane Lister, who became second wife of Smith Harrison, youngest brother of Daniel Harrison, who married Anna Botham, sister of Mary Howitt, the authoress. See Chart II.

Esther Eliza Dickinson's son William Thistlethwaite (497), married his first cousin, the daughter of her brother John Dickinson, of Liverpool. John and Esther Eliza Thistlethwaite had children as follows :—

   i.   Jane Agnes Thistlethwaite (476), whom see.

   ii.   John Dickinson Thistlethwaite (478), born at Darlingon 7th December, 1833, died 7th July, 1863, unmarried.

   iii. Mary Ann Thistlethwaite (479), whom see.

   iv. Eliza Thistlethwaite (488), whom see.

   v.   William Thistlethwaite (497), whom see.

   vi. Sarah Hannah Thistlethwaite (513), whom see.

   vii. Isabella Thistlethwaite (518), whom see.

  viii. Harris Thistlethwaite (522), whom see.

   ix. Arthur Thistlethwaite (532), born 10th December, 1853, at Bradford, educated at Bootham School, York, 8 mo. 1868 to 6 mo. 1870 ; married in Australia, and now resident on a fruit-farm in Queensland, with nine children.

Jane Agnes Thistlethwaite (476), born at Darlington 4th January, 1832, died 9th April, 1858, aged twenty-six years. She married, 15th

October, 1856, Edward Tuke, of Bradford, who was born 7th December, 1826. He married secondly Rebecca, daughter of Edwin Turner, of Bradford. By his first wife he had issue :—

    i. Herbert Thistlethwaite Tuke (477), born 1st April, 1858, died 17th March, 1859.

Mary Ann Thistlethwaite (479), born at Darlington, 4th February, 1836, married 17th December, 1862, at Bradford, to Edward Clark, of Doncaster, who was born there 14th August, 1834, educated at Bootham School, York, 8 mo. 1849 to 6 mo 1850, and died at Ripon, 12th December, 1891. Mary Ann Clark (479), now lives with her son at 40, Woodland Terrace, Darlington. Her husband was a wool merchant at Bradford.

    i. Clare Emily Clark (480), born 21st March, 1864, at Bradford, married Arthur Thomson Griffin (born 1857), of 3, Turner Street, Coatham, Redcar, Co. York, and of the Middlesbrough Estate, Ltd.

        i. Arthur Edward Griffin (481), born 24th January, 1895, at Saltburn, Yorkshire.

    ii. Edward Victor Clark (482), born 22nd January, 1866, at Bradford, now of Manchester. Married, 1900, Ethel Watson (born 1875).

        i. Kenneth Watson Clark (483), born 7th October, 1904, at Eccles, Lancashire.

    iii. Katherine Maud Clark (484), born 7th January, 1868, at Bradford, now of London, unmarried.

    iv. Hilda Marian Clark (485), born 29th September, 1874, at Ripon, recently of London. She was married 30th April, 1910, at Darlington, to Charles Edward Louis Simpson, son of Thomas Simpson, surgeon, of Middlesborough (who died young), by his wife, a Swiss lady.

v. Lionel Burrows Clark (486), born 2nd May, 1876, at Ripon, now of Pease's Woollen Mills, Darlington, unmarried.

vi. Lawrence Clark (487), born 24th August, 1878, at Ripon, now of Sheffield, unmarried.

Eliza Thistlethwaite (488), born 12th December, 1837, at Bradford, resident at Brisbane, Queensland, about forty years. Returned to England 1908, with her two daughters, and is now resident at Durban, Natal, South Africa. Married Frederick Ashworth, who was born at Bolton, Lancashire, 17th April, 1833 ; educated at Bootham School, York, 8 mo. 1845 to 10 mo., 1850, and died at Brisbane, 4th August, 1895.

i. Albert Ernest Ashworth (489), born at Bradford, 21st March, 1862, died in Queensland, 11th November, 1894, unmarried.

ii. Frederick William Ashworth (490), born at Bradford 10th June, 1865, died at Brisbane, 20th March, 1866.

iii. Louis Naish Ashworth (491), born at Brisbane, 4th October, ——, died there 23rd May, 1906.

iv. Dora Ashworth (492), born at Brisbane, 17th March, 1873, now of Durban, unmarried.

v. Evelyne Esther Ashworth (493), born 24th November, 1876, at Brisbane, now of Durban, unmarried.

vi. John Arthur Ashworth (494), born at Brisbane, 20th October, 1879, now of Durban ; married Mabel Eveline Girdlestone, of Brisbane.

  i. Frederick Henry John Ashworth (495), born 1906, at Durban.

  ii. —— Ashworth (496), a daughter, born 1908, at Durban.

William Thistlethwaite (497), born 12th September 1843, at Bradford, died 4th June, 1890, at Leeds. Married, 24th April, 1867, at

St. Bride's Church, Liverpool, to Jane Harris Dickinson, who was born at Liverpool, 28th September, 1844, daughter of John Dickinson, eldest son of John Dickinson, of Maryport, by his wife, Jane Harris, of Cockermouth. Consequently William Thistlethwaite and his wife were first cousins. In 1909 she resided at 27, Princes Avenue, Old Trafford, Manchester, but in 1910 was living at 45, Rossett Road, Blundell Sands, near Liverpool. William Thistlethwaite was a wool merchant.

i. John Dickinson Thistlethwaite (498), whom see.

ii. Beatrice Thistlethwaite (505), born at Bradford, 15th December, 1869, now at Blundell Sands, unmarried.

iii. William Thistlethwaite (506), born at Bradford, 7th February, 1871, died there 2nd March, 1871.

iv. Dora Isobel Thistlethwaite (507), born at Bradford, 8th January, 1873, died there 4th October, 1873.

v. Arthur Stanley Thistlethwaite (508), born at Bradford, 22nd January, 1874. In 1910 he was chief engineer of one of the Leyland boats of Liverpool. He was married at St. Kilda's Church, Jarrow-on-Tyne, Co. Durham, 2nd August, 1899, to Charlotte Evelyn Anderson, who was without issue in 1909.

vi. Carl Bertie Thistlethwaite (509), born at Bradford, 25th July, 1875. He is an engineer and in 1910 had charge of a coal mine in South Africa, unmarried.

vii. Guy Wilfrid Thistlethwaite (510), born at Bradford 25th October, 1876. In 1910 he was a cabinet-maker, unmarried.

viii. George Frederick Thistlethwaite, (511), born at Bradford 14th October, 1878. In 1910 he was an electrical engineer, unmarried.

ix. Ruby Thistlethwaite (512), born at Liscard, Cheshire, 10th July, 1883, now at Blundell Sands, unmarried.

John Dickinson Thistlethwaite (498), born at Bradford, 9th March, 1868; in 1910 was manager of the Brisbane Dredging and Engineering Works, Queensland. He was married at St. Paul's Cathedral,

Rockhampton, Queensland, Australia, 29th February, 1895 (?) to Hannah
Norton.

    i.   Lilian Ruby Thistlethwaite (499), born at Maryborough,
        Queensland, 4th May, 1896.

    ii. Doris Eveline Thistlethwaite (500), born at Brisbane, Queens-
        land, 2nd February, 1898.

    iii. Geoffrey Norton Thistlethwaite (501), born at Brisbane, 7th
        November, 1899.

    iv. Leonard Harris Thistlethwaite (502), born at Brisbane, 11th
        March, 1903, died 11th July, 1904.

    v.   John Dickinson Thistlethwaite (503), born at Brisbane, 28th
        September, 1905, a twin, died November, 1906.

    vi. Esther Alice Thistlethwaite (504), born at Brisbane, 28th
        September, 1905, a twin.

Sarah Hannah Thistlethwaite (513), born at Bradford 25th
December, 1846, married Joseph Henry Huthwaite, who was born 12th
September, 1844, at Maryport, Cumberland.   They now live in Queensland.   She was educated at the Mount School, York, 1 mo. 1860 to 12 mo,
1861.

    i.   Esther Ethel Huthwaite (514), born at Gallon, 16th June, 1879,
        unmarried.

    ii. Eva Rachel Huthwaite (515), born at Gallon, 10th August,
        1881, unmarried.

    iii. Annie Catherine Huthwaite (516), born at Brisbane, 15th
        February, 1885, unmarried.

    iv. Lewis Henry Huthwaite (517), born at Brisbane, 26th July,
        1886, unmarried.

Isabella Thistlethwaite (518), born at Bradford, 17th October,
1848, married at Tawantin, Australia, to Alfred Scott, and now lives

in Queensland.   She was educated at the Mount School, York, 8 mo., 1862 to 12 mo. 1863.

    i.   Edith Scott (519), unmarried.

    ii.   Constance Scott (520), unmarried.

    iii.   Boy Scott (521), unmarried.

Harris Thistlethwaite (522), born at Bradford, 1st April, 1850, educated at Bootham School, York, 1 mo. 1865 to 12 mo. 1865, married in Australia, now farmer of Grantham, Queensland. He married Helen Anne Robinson, who was born at Sydney, New South Wales, 13th September, 1853.

    i.   Mabel Thistlethwaite (523), born at Grantham, Queensland, 26th May, 1878, unmarried.

    ii.   Kenneth Thistlethwaite (524), born at Grantham, 30th June, 1879, unmarried.

    iii.   Edgar Thistlethwaite (525), born at Grantham, 1st January, 1881, died there 9th December, 1882.

    iv.   Ruth Thistlethwaite (526), born at Grantham, 26th September, 1882, unmarried.

    v.   Garnet Thistlethwaite (527), born at Grantham, 14th October, 1884, unmarried.

    vi.   Gordon Thistlethwaite (528), born at Grantham, 26th March, 1886, unmarried.

    vii.   Hilda Thistlethwaite, (529), born at Grantham, 24th May, 1888, unmarried.

    viii.   Wallace Thistlethwaite (530), born at Grantham, 10th December, 1890, unmarried.

    ix.   Dorothy Thistlethwaite (531), born at Grantham, 27th April, 1896, unmarried.

Alice Thistlethwaite (533), born 20th November, 1737, in Dent Dale. She was married 6th November, 1765, to Thomas Lund, of

Garsdale, the broader dale parallel with, and immediately north of, Dent
Dale. As their four children were born in Garsdale, they evidently lived
there for some years after their marriage, probably all their remaining
years.

   i.   Elizabeth Lund (534), born 2nd October, 1766, in Garsdale,
       Yorkshire. She was married at some church, about 1795,
       to William Thistlethwaite (1092), her mother's first cousin,
       who was born 1st June, 1747. Their six children and
       descendants are traced under his name in Part Four.

  ii.   Samuel Lund (535), born 9th July, 1768, in Garsdale. No
       Quaker marriage entry appears in the district for this
       Samuel Lund, but I know nothing further.

 iii.   Isabella Lund (536), whom see.

 iv.   James Lund (559), born 8th October, 1772, in Garsdale. His
       great-niece, Isabella Walton (555), writes me as follows :
       " My two brothers, in their young days, before Thomas
       married, visited the Dale belonging to the Lund family,
       and saw the old gentleman, James Lund—he had a daughter
       keeping house for him, who married a man named Tennant,
       who farmed the land and dwelt in the house, as the old man
       was past work. A son of James Lund lived on the other
       farm in the Dale. I cannot tell his name, but when I
       mentioned the name Samuel, my brother said, ' I believe
       that's the name.' No doubt some members of the Lund
       family reside there still."

Isabella Lund (536), born 22nd September, 1770, in Garsdale. A
certain yeoman, who was to become Isabella Lund's grandfather-in-law,
owned some land in the upper part of Wensleydale, Yorkshire. This he
let, preferring to rent for his own use a pleasant house situated near
Askrigg, named Wood Hall. He was named Christopher Metcalfe, and
his daughter had married Richard Walton, a sea-captain, of Sunderland,
Co. Durham. The latter died, or was lost, at sea, and his widow did not

long survive him, leaving three young children. Christopher Metcalfe then rode to Sunderland, and brought his orphan grand-children on horse-back to his home at Wood Hall, the baby being carried in a basket. Here they were brought up : the youngest son, John Walton, died a bachelor, the second, Christopher, has descendants living in Darlington, and the eldest son, William Walton, married Isabella Lund, of Garsdale, the subject of this paragraph.

In 1798, William Walton is described at husbandman, of Burtersett, a hamlet near Hawes, in the parish of Aysgarth, Wensleydale. In his old age he removed to Bishop Auckland, Co. Durham, near his son, and here he died 25th June, 1851, and was buried in the local Friends' Burial Ground, aged over eighty years.

    i.   Christopher Walton (537), whom see.

    ii.   Isabella Walton (557), whom see.

Christopher Walton (537), born 19th November, 1798, at Burtersett, a hamlet about a mile down the dale from Hawes, Yorkshire. He was married at Hawes, probably in May of 1830, to Emma Robinson, and was living, in November, 1831, a farmer at Gayle, half a mile from Hawes. In October, 1833, he was still here, but in March, 1836, he was living at Low Row, in Swaledale.

He left here in 1838 or 1839, and came to be cashier at Black Boy Colliery, near Bishop Auckland, under Jonathan Backhouse. When the Colliery changed hands, he remained in the employment of the new owners until shortly before his death. He died at 3, High Tenters Street, Bishop Auckland, 24th March, 1874. His wife was born 11th July, 1805, and died 3rd September, 1888.

    i.   William Walton (538), born 15th November, 1831, at Gayle, in the parish of Aysgarth, Yorkshire. He died when between two and three years of age, and was buried in the Friends' Burial Ground, Hawes.

    ii.   Thomas Walton (539), whom see.

iii. Isabella Walton (555), born 24th March, 1836, at Low Row, in
the parish of Grinton, Swaledale, Yorkshire. She is now
(1909) living unmarried, with her brother, at 3, High
Tenters Street, Bishop Auckland.

iv. John William Walton (556), born 23rd June, 1839, at Black
Boy Colliery, near Bishop Auckland. He was a grocer in
Durham Chare, Bishop Auckland, but retired from business
9th June, 1905. He is unmarried.

Thomas Walton (539), born 10th October, 1833, at Gayle, a hamlet
half a mile from Hawes, in Wensleydale. He carried on for many years a
celebrated high-class private boarding school at Oliver's Mount, Scarborough. This he gave up a few years before his death, and bought a
mineral water business a few miles from his ancestor's home at Wood
Hall, in Wensleydale. He died 26th May, 1907, at Harrogate.

He was married, 5th July, 1865, to Mary Lean, daughter of William
and Hannah Lean, of Birmingham. In 1910 she was living at Harrogate,
Yorkshire, a widow.

Her sister, Anna Maria Lean, married Frederick Andrews, B.A., who
has been for many years headmaster of Ackworth School, near Pontefract,
Yorkshire. Her brother, William Scarnell Lean, was formerly superintendent of the Flounders Institute, Ackworth ; in later life a clergyman
of the Church of England; and finally a Quaker. One of his daughters
married Herbert Jones, M.A., of Colwall, formerly headmaster of Leighton
Park School, Reading.

i. Herbert Walton (540), whom see.

ii. Sidney Walton (542), whom see.

iii. Hugh Walton (545), whom see.

iv. Ethel Walton (548), born 23rd October, 1870. In 1910 she
was living unmarried, with Mr. and Mrs. Joseph Rowntree,
of York.

v. Hilda Walton (549), born 24th February, 1872. In 1910 she
was a student at Somerville College, Oxford, unmarried.

vi. Mabel Walton (550), born 5th April, 1874. In 1910 she was Warden at Friedensthal, Scalby, a Quaker Guest House founded by her brother-in-law, J. Wilhelm Rowntree, near Scarborough, Yorkshire.

vii. Gertrude Walton (551), whom see.

Herbert Walton (540), born 21st May, 1867. In 1910 he was a schoolmaster at Huddersfield, Yorkshire. He was married 8th August, 1897, to Edith Elizabeth Burnell Mellorie, and has issue one child,

i. Mary Joyce Mellorie Walton (541), born 24th April, 1899.

Sidney Walton (542), born 12th September, 1868. In 1910 he was an architect and surveyor at Buxton, Derbyshire. He was married 11th November, 1899, to May Whittaker, and has issue,

i. Hereward Royden Walton (543), born 2nd September, 1901.

ii. Marjorie Walton (544), born 19th March, 1903.

Hugh Walton (545), born 27th September, 1869. In 1910 he was an engineer in London. He was married 15th January, 1896, to Sarah S. Crasby, and has issue,

i. Richard Geoffrey Walton (546), born 29th October, 1896.

ii. Philip Walton (547), born 2nd May, 1900.

Gertrude Walton (551), born 25th October, 1876. She was married 8th August, 1900, to Joseph Stephenson Rowntree, M.A. Cantab., J.P., in 1910 of Leadhall Grange, Harrogate.

He is a son of Joseph Rowntree, of York, by his wife Antoinette Seebohm, and a director of Messrs. Rowntree and Co., Ltd., the celebrated chocolate manufacturers of York. His brother, the late John Wilhelm Rowntree, of Scalby, near Scarborough, was a celebrated minister in the Society of Friends : another brother, Benjamin Seebohm Rowntree, is author of well-known sociological works.

Thistlethwaite connections exist with the three Quaker cocoa families : Eleanor Taylor of Part VIII., married Joseph Storrs Fry, of Maldon, Essex : and George Cadbury's daughter recently married Bertram Fothergill Crosfield, whose grandmother was Hannah Thistlethwaite of the Wensleydale family.

Gertrude Rowntree has issue,

    i.   Doris Mabel Rowntree (552), born 2nd March, 1902, at Harrogate.

   ii.   Geoffrey Christopher Rowntree (553), born 21st May, 1905, at Harrogate.

  iii.   Thomas Stephenson Rowntree (554), born 25th July, 1909, at Harrogate.

Isabella Walton (557), was probably born about 1800 at Burtersett, a hamlet near Bainbridge in Wensleydale. She married James Burton and was living at Bradford, Yorkshire, in 1847. Her husband died in 1849 at Manningham, near Bradford ; and she, writing from Manningham in 1850, speaks of her wish or intention of going to America with her eight children. I cannot ascertain whether they all went, but in any case, her eldest son, William Burton (558), emigrated to Utah, U.S.A. When the United States took over the Mormon Settlement at Salt Lake City, he removed to the State of Arizona, and correspondence with his English relatives ceased.

    i.   William Burton (558), and seven others.

Rachel Thistlethwaite (560), born 13th January, 1739 (or 1740, by our present method of reckoning). She was born in Dent Dale, some years before her parents removed to Langstrothdale. She was married about 1767, to George Brown, leather cutter, of Preston, Lancashire, son of John and Ann Brown. Her brother, Anthony Thistlethwaite (867), married George Brown's sister Ann. Rachel Brown (560), became a "public friend," or a minister among the Quakers, and had issue. She died 4th January, 1784, at Preston, and was buried there on the 7th. George Brown died 7th June, 1795, aged sixty-four, at Preston, and was buried there on the 10th.

i. Margaret Brown (561), born 30th March, 1768, at Preston, and died there 2nd May, 1771, and buried the following day.

ii. Isabel Brown (562), born 10th May, 1769, at Preston; died there 29th May, 1771, and buried there on the 31st.

iii. William Brown (563), born 29th March, 1771, at Preston. He died 7th November, 1826, at Standish, in Lancashire, aged fifty-five years, and was buried two days later at Langtree. No further particulars appear in the Quaker register, but as he died a "non-member," it is not unlikely that he was married and had issue. He was a clogger.

iv. James Brown (564), born 10th November, 1772, at Preston; died there 23rd January, 1775, and buried there two days later.

v. George Brown (565), born 12th October, 1773, at Preston; died there 10th October, 1774, and buried there two days later.

vi. Alice Brown (566), whom see.

vii. John Brown (572), born 21st November, 1776, at Preston. He appears to have been a land-surveyor in Manchester, where he died 18th August, 1829, aged fifty-four years, and was buried at Manchester five days later. As he is entered as a "non-member," it is not unlikely that he married and had issue.

viii. Rachel Brown (573), whom see.

ix. George Brown (576), born 3rd July, 1779, at Preston; died there 27th December, 1779, and was buried there two days later.

x.   Christopher Brown (577), born 28th July, 1780, at Preston.
No further information.

xi.   Anthony Brown (578), born 15th September, 1781, at Preston,
died there 20th January, 1782, and was buried there three
days later.

xii.   Hannah Brown (579), born 14th November, 1783, at Preston.
She appears to have married a Robinson, of Kendal, where
she was living about 1837. I do not know whether she
had issue.

Alice Brown (566), born 24th October, 1775, at Preston. She was
married 25th August, 1802, at Preston Meeting House, to John Burton,
cotton manufacturer of Preston, son of John (yeoman) and Sarah Burton
of Dent, Yorkshire. In 1814 and 1817, John and Alice Burton were
entered as " non-members." I have not been able to trace farther than
their children.

i.   Rachel Burton (567), born 6th June, 1803, at Preston ; died
there 29th August, 1806, and buried there two days later.

ii.   Mary Burton (568), born 10th September, 1804, at Preston ;
no further information.

iii.   George Brown Burton (569), born 21st April, 1806, at Preston ;
no further information.

iv.   John Burton (570), born 1814, died 21st August, 1814, at Preston,
aged one month, and buried there two days later.

v.   John Burton (571), born 3rd November, 1817, at Preston, his
father being described as " land-surveyor." No further
information to hand.

Rachel Brown (573), born 20th January, 1778, at Preston, Lancashire. She was married at Preston Meeting House, 4th March, 1807,
to Samuel Fielden, grocer, of Lancaster, son of Samuel Fielden, grocer and
draper, of Todmorden, Co. York, and of Hannah his wife. Samuel Fielden,

of Lancaster, was drowned on Lancaster Sands in 1808. His widow died 3rd March, 1865, at Halifax, aged 87 years.

    i. Hannah Fielden (574), whom see.

Hannah Fielden (574), born 5th April, 1808, at Lancaster. She was married at Calder Bridge Meeting House, Yorkshire, 22nd September, 1830, to Joseph Thorp, of Halifax, and died in 1834, leaving one child. Joseph Thorp married a second time, and died in Halifax, Yorkshire, 1873, aged seventy years. A man of intellectual attainments and a minister in the Society of Friends. His widow, Hannah Thorp, died at Halifax in 1879, aged seventy-eight, leaving an only child, who had married Dr. Waite, of Halifax.* By his first wife, Joseph Thorp had issue,

    i. Fielden Thorp (575), whom see.

Fielden Thorp (575), born 1832, at Halifax. He was educated at Bootham School, York, 8 mo. 1844 to 6 mo. 1847, and was a master there from 1850 to 1853. He then took his Bachelor of Arts degree from London University, and returned to Bootham in 1856. Ten years later he became headmaster, from which position he retired in 1875. He has since lived at 18, Blossom Street, York. He married Amy Jane Clark, of Street, in Somerset, whose brother married Helen Bright, daughter of the Rt. Hon. John Bright, M.P., the eminent Quaker orator. Fielden Thorp is *s.p.* He is a well-known Quaker minister, foreign traveller, and linguist.

Richard Thistlethwaite (580), born 13th November, 1742 or 1743, in Dent Dale, Yorkshire. At the date of his marriage, 1776, he was living with his father at Carr End, about three miles from Bainbridge, Wensleydale. He lived at Carr End until after all his children were born. The family then removed to Shawcote, a house about five miles from Carr End by road, on the opposite side of the Wensleydale Valley. They were

* Dr. Waite's daughter, Clare Waite, married Dr. J. F. Gill, of Halifax, who is my second cousin through our mutual descent from David Fox, of Dewsbury.

here in 1816, but removed to Semerdale House, about half-way between Carr End and Bainbridge, before Richard Thistlethwaite (580) died 11th October, 1820.

His daughter, Jane Thompson (759), removed from Hawes to Kendal in 1822, and thither his widow, Agnes or Nancy Thistlethwaite, frequently rode on horseback to visit her daughter and grandchildren. Agnes Thistlethwaite died 21st July, 1834, at Semerdale House, Wensleydale, Yorkshire, aged seventy-seven years. For the gift of their marriage certificate I am much indebted to Mrs. Yeardley, widow of Richard and Agnes Thistlethwaite's great-grandson, Alfred Yeardley (586).

The will of Agnes Thistlethwaite's father, John Hunter, was proved 15th September, 1767. He left four children, all under age ; the two sons being, John Hunter, sometime of Hebblethwaite Hall, and Simon Hunter, sometime of Appersett, near Hawes. For the numerous Hunter Thistlethwaite intermarriages, the inquisitive must refer to Chart II.

" Whereas Richard Thistlethwaite, son of James and Isabel Thistlethwaite, of Car-End, and Agnes Hunter, Daughter of John and Jane Hunter, late of Car-End, Deceased, both in the parish of Aisgarth and County of York, Having declared their Intention of taking each other in Marriage before several Public Meetings of the People called Quakers, according to the good Order used amongst them ; whose proceedings therein, after a Deliberate Consideration thereof, were approved of by the said meetings, they appearing clear of all others in that respect ; And having consent of Parents and Guardians—

"Now these are to Certify all whom it may concern, that for the full Accomplishment of their said Intentions this Eighth Day of the fifth month called May, in the Year of our Lord one Thousand seven Hundred and seventy Six. They, the said Richard Thistlethwaite and Agnes Hunter appeared in a Public Assembly of the aforesaid People and others met together, in their public Meeting House at Counterside, and in a Solemn Manner," etc., etc.

Richard Thistlethwaite.
Agnes Hunter.

Witnesses :

    James Thistlethwaite [(429) father to bridegroom]
    William Thistlethwaite [(430) brother to groom]
    John Thistlethwaite [(866) brother to groom]
    Anthony Thistlethwaite [(867) brother to groom]
    Alice Lund [(533) sister to groom]
    Rachel Brown [(560) sister to groom]
    Margaret Thistlethwaite [(864) sister to groom]
    John Hunter [brother to bride]
    Ann Hunter [*née* Middlebrook, wife of above]
    Simon Hunter [brother to bride]
    Alice Hunter
    Isable Hunter [sister to bride]
    James Middlebrook
    Alex^r Fothergill [married groom's aunt (877)]
    Margaret Fothergill [(877) aunt to groom]
    Ann Freeman [(879) daughter of above]
    William Fothergill [(1021) brother of above]
    Anthony Thistlethwaite [(112) first cousin to groom]
    Edm^d Fothergill [uncle to groom]
    Richard Fothergill [uncle to groom]
    Simon Thwate
    Thomas Lambert
    Jane Robinson
    Hannah Robinson
    John Robinson ⎫
    Eliza Robinson ⎭
    Chris^r Myers [married groom's sister (864)]
    Joseph Wetherald
    Elizabeth Wetherald
    Mary Blakey
    Margaret Sedgwick
    William Middlebrook

Matthew Middlebrook [married groom's first cousin (1245)]
Joseph Baynes
Joseph Wetherald
Daniel Harrison
Oswald Baynes.

I have shown above, so far as I am able, the relationships borne by the witnesses to the bride and bridegroom. Only the simpler relationships are dealt with.

Counterside, or Countersett, is a village close to the lake of Semerwater, and lies mid-way between Semerdale House and Carr End, about three-quarters of a mile from each. The house at Carr End occupied by the Thistlethwaites stood at right angles to that occupied by the Fothergills.

Richard Thistlethwaite (580), had issue :

i.   James Thistlethwaite (581), born 30th March, 1777, at Carr End, Wensleydale, Yorkshire. He was a clogger, near the Meeting House, in Bainbridge, three miles from Carr End. In 1828 his second cousin, Richard Thistlethwaite (113), of Dent, placed his son, William Thistlethwaite (165) with his bachelor relative to learn clogging and leather-cutting. Master, aged fifty-three, and apprentice, aged seventeen, were one day found discussing Doddridge's " Rise and Progress of Religion in the Soul." William became a prince among pedagogues, and James died a clogger and un-married.

ii.   John Thistlethwaite (582), whom see.

iii.   Isabel Thistlethwaite (583), whom see.

iv.   Jane Thistlethwaite (759), whom see.

v.   Anthony Thistlethwaite (841), born 13th July, 1785, at Carr End, co. York. He died 5th October, 1822, at Shawcote, Wensleydale, and was, I think, unmarried. He was interred at Bainbridge.

vi. Rachel Thistlethwaite (842), whom see.
vii. William Thistlethwaite (862), born 23rd October, 1792, at Carr
      End, Co. York. He died 6th July, 1830, at Semerdale
      House, one-and-a-half miles from Carr End, "of an asthma."
      I think he was unmarried; his great-nephew notes that
      he had "no family."
viii. Richard Thistlethwaite (863), whom see.

John Thistlethwaite (582), born 20th February, 1779, at Carr End,
Wensleydale, Co. York. He is said to have married, firstly, Sarah M.
Smith, who died without issue.* After his father's death, in 1820, "he
went with his mother to Semerdale House." At the age of sixty-one, he
married at Counterside, 27th February, 1839, Elizabeth Routh, aged
about fifty-seven. She was the daughter of John Thompson, hosier of
Hawes (1742-1803), by his wife Margaret Routh; and her brother, John
Thompson, junr., had married John Thistlethwaite's sister Jane. Elizabeth
Thistlethwaite, *née* Thompson, married, firstly, Thomas Tennant, and had
issue several children. Her second husband was Thomas Routh, probably
a relative of her mother, and by him she had no children.

John Thistlethwaite (582), is said to have managed the Carr End farm
for his brother-in-law, John Thompson, junr., while the former lived at
Semerdale House, but he and his wife Betsy lived after this at the Grange,
Askrigg. She died at Bainbridge, 5th November, 1856, aged seventy-
four years, and John Thistlethwaite died at Bedale, Yorkshire, 22nd
September, 1858.

An extract from a letter written 4th September, 1898, by his great-
niece, may be of interest : —"We slept at 'The White Hart,' at Hawes ;
it looked more quaint than ever, a sheep-fair bringing in all the country
people in the evening. Mary Thistlethwaite† took us to an original old

---

* My authority for this statement is a chart privately printed by his great-niece,
Mrs. F. I. Reckitt, of Hull, 1898. I have heard of a man who says that his grandfather was John Thistlethwaite, a Quaker, of Wensleydale.

† Second cousin twice removed to John Thistlethwaite (582).

man, who knew some of our ancestors. He had lived near Carr End and told us such histories—I wish you could have been there to hear him.

"Our great-uncle, John Thistlethwaite, was nearly starved to death in prison because he would not enter the army, and he was kept in prison till the war was over. And A. Blakey at the same time was hidden in a cave near Hawes, supplied with food at night by his daughter, and came out at the end of the war so fat and flourishing, such a contrast to poor uncle J.T., who was only skin and bone. Such a fine old man he was, and how he enjoyed telling us these stories, slapping his knees, and roaring with laughter when Sophie reminded him of some of Uncle John's stories of his boyhood's days."

The witnesses to John and Elizabeth Thistlethwaite's marriage were as follows :—

Margaret Tennant.
Richard Thistlethwaite (863).
John Thompson, Jr. (760).
Agnes Webster (847).
John Tennant.
Samuel Tennant (1375).
Alice Tennant (1374).
Jane Routh.
Mary Ann Tennant (1445).
Henry Tennant (1446).
Ann Baynes.
Oswald Baynes, Jr.
John Slinger.
Mary Baynes, Jr.
Mary Blakey.
William Blakey.
Richard Blakey.
William Simpson.

Richard Routh.
John Baynes.
Oswald Lambert.
Joshua Blakey.
William Blakey.
Joseph Smith.
Hannah Lambert.
George Paley.
William Routh.
Thos. Routh.
William Smith.
Emma Metcalfe.
John Metcalfe.
Rebecca Mason.
William Metcalfe.
Robert Hutchinson.
Benjamin Hall.

Isabel Thistlethwaite (583), born 5th March, 1781, at Carr End, in Wensleydale, Yorkshire. As her father's eldest daughter she was, of course, named after her paternal grandmother, Isabel Fothergill. She · was married from Carr End, at Counterside Meeting House, 21st January,* 1803, " to John Wetherald, of Hulme, near Manchester, in the County of Lancaster, son of Joseph Wetherald, of the same place, Butcher, and Mally, his wife."

Joseph Wetherald seems to have been sprung from the Wensleydale family bearing his surname, and to have moved thence to Lancashire. He later went to America.

· John and Isabel Wetherald resided at Little Marsden, in the parish of Whalley, Lancashire, 4th April, 1805 ; and at Burnley, in the same parish, December, 1806, December, 1808, and April, 1811. On these four dates John Wetherald is described as a butcher. In 1812, the family removed to Healaugh (pronounced " Heela "), near Reeth, in Swaledale, Yorkshire. Here their youngest child was born in September, 1824, but before long they removed to Wakefield, Yorkshire, where Isabel Wetherald *née* Thistlethwaite (583), died of consumption, 19th March, 1826.

John Wetherald and his family appear to have lived at Wakefield until their departure from England, as his daughter Agnes was living there when she married in 1831. His daughter Ann was married in England in 1833, but I do not know where. The marriages of his other children took place in America.

On the 8th of February, 1834, John Wetherald, with his son Joseph, and daughter Jane, sailed from Liverpool in " The Virginian," and arrived at New York on the 19th March. His brother, Thomas Wetherald, " had gone over some time before. He was a minister, and very much esteemed by the Hicksites," one of the sections into which the Society of Friends in America had divided.

On the 22nd of March, 1834, John Wetherald and his son and daughter left New York by steamer for Albany, a town 160 miles up the River Hudson, to reach which, they sailed from seven o'clock in the morning

*Their son Thomas gives this date as " 21st 3rd mo. 1803."

until midnight.   On the following day, they travelled by rail fifteen miles
to Schenectady, N.Y., and thence by coach eighty-one miles to Utica,
N.Y., where they arrived on the 24th of March.   They left Utica by " The
Stage," at four o'clock on the following morning, and travelled in twenty-
four hours the eighty miles to Oswego, N.Y., a town on the Southern
shore of Lake Ontario.

Thence they sailed on the 27th in a schooner seventy miles to
Kingston, in Canada, near the exit of the St. Lawrence river from Lake
Ontario, and here they had to remain some days for want of a con-
veyance.   At eleven o'clock in the evening of the seventh of April, they
left Kingston by steamer, and arrived at seven p.m. next day at York—
now the City of Toronto.

At York (Toronto), John Wetherald left his son and daughter, and
took steamer on the 11th for Burlington Bay, at the head of Lake Ontario,
with a friend, John Howitt, from Long Eaton, near Nottingham, England.
They walked to Dundas the same evening, and on the 13th of April,
travelled about thirty miles inland to Guelph.   " Grandfather [John
Wetherald] staid here some days, going about in different directions to
see the country, and eventually purchased one hundred acres of land in the
township of Puslinch, about three miles distant from Guelph, when he
wrote for Jane and Joseph to join him.   Grandfather bought the land of
John Michel, giving him 250 dollars for his right and title, and in addition,
270 dollars to the Government Agent in Toronto, payable in nine annual
instalments, the first due the end of 8th mo.   Total, 520 dollars for 100
acres, one acre only cleared. "

The ship " Hibernia," sailed from Liverpool on the 12th March, 1835,
carrying a third detachment of the Wetherald family, bound for the New
World.   This included four more children of John and Isabel Wetherald
—Mary, William, Thomas, and John, junior—besides Joseph Wetherald,
the grandfather of the latter, and other relatives.   Indeed, I should be
more correct in describing this as a " fourth detachment," for Joseph
Wetherald Sr.'s niece, Elizabeth Thistlethwaite, *née* Wetherald, had
emigrated to Indiana with her husband and family so early at 1818, or

thereabouts.* However, the detachment of which I am now speaking, arrived at New York on the 14th of April, 1835, and at Puslinch on Saturday, the 2nd of May. After staying about seven weeks, all the newly-arrived members of the family, excepting John Wetherald's four children, removed to Toronto.

It will now appear that all the surviving children of John and Isabel Wetherald had crossed to America, excepting Agnes and Ann, who had married before their father left England. Ann's husband, Oswald Foster, went over alone in 1843, and she with her three children followed in 1846. Neither Agnes nor her husband, John Yeardley, were ever in America, but as their only child died without issue, there are no living descendants of John and Isabel Wetherald in England.

John Wetherald gave up the management of his farm to his sons Thomas and John in 1847. He died of apoplexy, at his home in Puslinch, 5th August, 1852, aged seventy-two years and one month. He had issue eleven children.

    i.   Mary Wetherald (584), born 4th April, 1805, at Little Marsden, in the parish of Whalley, Lancashire. She died before her parents left Burnley in 1812.

    ii.   Agnes Wetherald (585), whom see.

    iii.   Jane Wetherald (587), whom see.

    iv.   Ann Wetherald (642), whom see.

    v.   Joseph Wetherald (658), whom see.

    vi.   Rachel Wetherald (689), born at Healaugh, in the parish of Grinton, Swaledale, Co. York, 9th September, 1814. She died unmarried, 20th January, 1834, the same year that her father went to America.

    vii.   Mary Wetherald (690), whom see.

* For the Wetherald descendants in Indiana see Part Eight, under William Thistlethwaite (1598), and for the Wetherald-Haworth-Fothergill connection, see Part Three, under Alexander Fothergill (1062). I intend to give, in my second volume, a much fuller account of the Wetherald ancestry and connections, and of the branch which settled at Wilmington, Delaware.

viii. Richard Wetherald (728), born 12th June, 1818, at Healaugh, in Swaledale. He died unmarried, 11th May, 1831, at Ackworth School.

  ix. William Wetherald (729), whom see.

   x. Thomas Wetherald (744), whom see.

  xi. John Wetherald (758), whom see.

Agnes Wetherald (585), born 29th December, 1806, at Burnley, in the parish of Whalley, Lancashire. She removed with her parents to Swaledale, in 1812, and from there in about 1825 to Wakefield. She was married 27th October, 1831, to John Yeardley, of Ecclesfield, near Sheffield, son of Thomas Yeardley, of the same place, flax spinner, by his wife Elizabeth Hodgson.

Elizabeth Hodgson had a widowed sister named Mary Oddie, who married secondly Robert Graham, of Ackworth near Pontefract, Yorkshire. Their only daughter, Jane Graham, married George Esthill Peacock, whose sisters Rachel and Esther, married respectively, Jeremiah Thistlethwaite (1218) and Charles Webster (1747).

John Yeardley was born 29th February, 1808, at Barnsley. His sister Sarah married his wife's uncle, Richard Thistlethwaite (863), whom see.

Agnes Yeardley (585) died 29th November, 1863, at Rochdale. Her husband was for many years an invalid, and died 9th July, 1883, at Hathersage, and was interred at Bakewell, Derbyshire.

   i. Alfred Yeardley (586), whom see.

Alfred Yeardley (586), born 20th April, 1833, at Ecclesfield, near Sheffield, Yorkshire. He was initiated into business in the counting-house of Edward Briggs, hat manufacturer and silk spinner, Castleton Mills, and in 1851 entered that of James McLaren and Nephew, merchants and shippers, Manchester. He later became a cashier. He died at Clifton, Bristol, aged sixty-five years, 6th June, 1898, without issue.

He was married at Yatton Meeting House, Somerset, 20th April, 1884, to Lucy Taylor (1451), who was born 30th October, 1837, daughter of John Taylor (1450), by his wife Sophia Tew, daughter of William Tew,

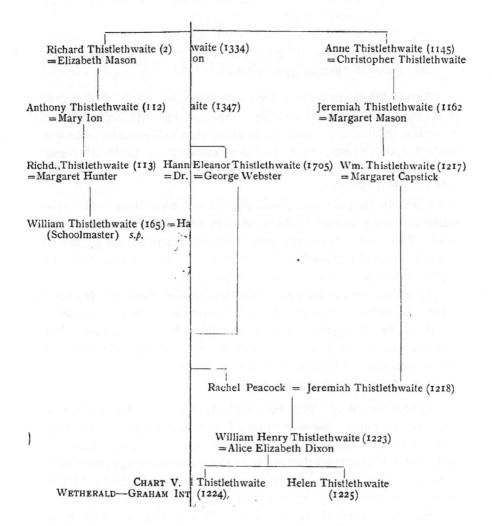

Richard Thistlethwaite (2)   waite (1334)   Anne Thistlethwaite (1145)
  = Elizabeth Mason   on   = Christopher Thistlethwaite

Anthony Thistlethwaite (112)   aite (1347)   Jeremiah Thistlethwaite (1162
  = Mary Ion   = Margaret Mason

Richd.,Thistlethwaite (113) Hann Eleanor Thistlethwaite (1705) Wm. Thistlethwaite (1217)
  = Margaret Hunter   = Dr. = George Webster   = Margaret Capstick

William Thistlethwaite (165) = Ha
  (Schoolmaster) *s.p.*

                    Rachel Peacock = Jeremiah Thistlethwaite (1218)

                    William Henry Thistlethwaite (1223)
                      = Alice Elizabeth Dixon

}

viii. Richard Wetherald (728), born 12th June, 1818, at Healaugh,
in Swaledale. He died unmarried, 11th May, 1831, at
Ackworth School.

ix. William Wetherald (729), whom see.

x. Thomas Wetherald (744), whom see.

xi. John Wetherald (758), whom see.

Agnes Wetherald (585), born 29th December, 1806, at Burnley,
in the parish of Whalley, Lancashire. She removed with her parents to
Swaledale, in 1812, and from there in about 1825 to Wakefield. She was
married 27th October, 1831, to John Yeardley, of Ecclesfield, near
Sheffield, son of Thomas Yeardley, of the same place, flax spinner, by his
wife Elizabeth Hodgson.

Elizabeth Hodgson had a widowed sister named Mary Oddie, who
married secondly Robert Graham, of Ackworth near Pontefract, Yorkshire. Their only daughter, Jane Graham, married George Esthill
Peacock, whose sisters Rachel and Esther, married respectively, Jeremiah
Thistlethwaite (1218) and Charles Webster (1747).

John Yeardley was born 29th February, 1808, at Barnsley. His sister
Sarah married his wife's uncle, Richard Thistlethwaite (863), whom see.

Agnes Yeardley (585) died 29th November, 1863, at Rochdale. Her
husband was for many years an invalid, and died 9th July, 1883, at
Hathersage, and was interred at Bakewell, Derbyshire.

i. Alfred Yeardley (586), whom see.

Alfred Yeardley (586), born 20th April, 1833, at Ecclesfield, near
Sheffield, Yorkshire. He was initiated into business in the counting-
house of Edward Briggs, hat manufacturer and silk spinner, Castleton
Mills, and in 1851 entered that of James McLaren and Nephew, merchants
and shippers, Manchester. He later became a cashier. He died at Clifton,
Bristol, aged sixty-five years, 6th June, 1898, without issue.

He was married at Yatton Meeting House, Somerset, 20th April,
1884, to Lucy Taylor (1451), who was born 30th October, 1837, daughter
of John Taylor (1450), by his wife Sophia Tew, daughter of William Tew,

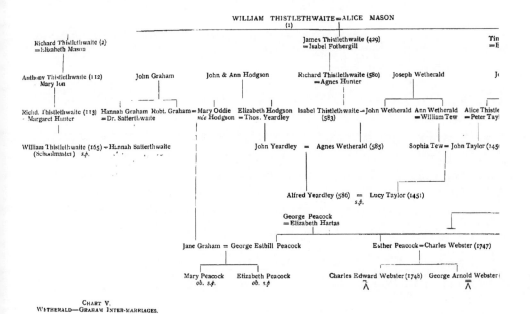

WILLIAM THISTLETHWAITE＝ALICE MASON
(1)

Richard Thistlethwaite (2)
＝Elizabeth Mason

James Thistlethwaite (429)
＝Isabel Fothergill

Tin
＝E

Anthony Thistlethwaite (112)
Mary Ion

John Graham

John & Ann Hodgson

Richard Thistlethwaite (580)
＝Agnes Hunter

Joseph Wetherald

Jo

Richd. Thistlethwaite (113)
Margaret Hunter

Hannah Graham
＝Dr. Satterthwaite

Robt. Graham＝Mary Oddie
née Hodgson

Elizabeth Hodgson
＝Thos. Yeardley

Isabel Thistlethwaite＝John Wetherald
(583)

Ann Wetherald
＝William Tew

Alice Thistle
＝Peter Tayl

William Thistlethwaite (165) ＝ Hannah Satterthwaite
(Schoolmaster) s.p.

John Yeardley ＝ Agnes Wetherald (585)

Sophia Tew＝ John Taylor (145

Alfred Yeardley (586) ＝ Lucy Taylor (1451)
s.p.

George Peacock
＝Elizabeth Hartas

Jane Graham ＝ George Esthill Peacock

Esther Peacock＝Charles Webster (1747)

Mary Peacock
ob. s.p.

Etizabeth Peacock
ob. s.p

Charles Edward Webster (1748)
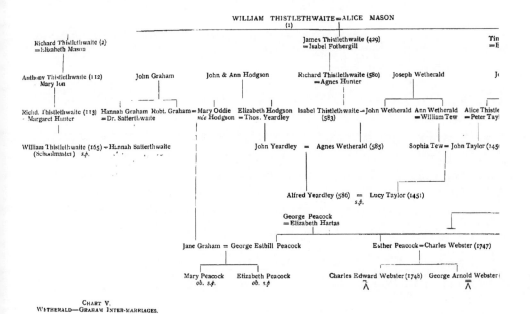

George Arnold Webster

CHART V.
WETHERALD—GRAHAM INTER-MARRIAGES.

of Halifax, by his wife Ann Wetherald. As this Ann Wetherald was sister to Alfred Yeardley's grandfather, Alfred and Lucy Yeardley were second cousins. And I have good reason to believe that John Taylor's maternal grandmother, Elizabeth Wetherald, was sister to Alfred Yeardley's great-grandfather, in which case Alfred and Lucy Yeardley were third cousins. And they were certainly fourth cousins, because of their common descent from William Thistlethwaite (1) of Harborgill.

In 1910, Lucy Yeardley (1451), was living at 9, Wellington Park, Clifton, Bristol, England, a widow.

Jane Wetherald (587), born 27th December, 1808, at Burnley, in the parish of Whalley, Lancashire. In 1834, she crossed from England to America, in the ship "Virginian," with her father and her brother Joseph. Their journey across country and final settlement at Puslinch, near Guelph, Ontario, Canada, is described in the account of Isabel Thistlethwaite (583), her mother.

Jane Wetherald (587), was married 3rd November, 1836, in the township of Pelham, seventy miles from Puslinch, to John Harris, "who has a good farm of 230 acres, twenty or thirty acres cleared," within the township of Eramosa, and near Rockwood and Puslinch. He was forty-seven years of age at the time of his marriage; his wife was nearly twenty-eight.

In 1837, John Harris "gave three acres of land, and timber to build a meeting-house thereupon, at Eramosa; the rest of the ground to be used at a graveyard. They began to meet in this new Meeting House in 3 mo. 1839." In this year John Harris began to speak in Meeting. While attending Pelham Quarterly Meeting in September, 1841, John and Jane Harris "met cousin Mary Thistlethwaite, widow of Anthony, of Dent.* She was one of the Yearly Meeting's Committee appointed to attend the opening of this said Quarterly Meeting."

* Mary, widow of Anthony Thistlethwaite (1164), landed in New York from England 29th August, 1840, accompanied by her two sons. See Part VI.

In September, 1845, " John Harris, still a teacher." In December, 1846, his nephew writes, " Uncle William Wetherald [then aged twenty-six] resides with Uncle and Aunt Harris, and teaches a district school. He has just bought forty-seven acres of land of them, and is engaged to be married to John Harris' niece, Jemima Balls." " Aunt Ann Foster left Toronto, and on 2 mo. 21 [1847], went to live with Uncle and Aunt John and Jane Harris at Eramosa. On 4 mo. 8, Henrietta and Richard went to live with their mother at the same place."

Before 1848, Jane Harris (587), had adopted a little girl named Mary Reed, who was born in the spring of 1839. She later acted as housekeeper to some of her unmarried foster-brothers, and in 1866 married a Mr. Ryckman.

At the end of November, 1848, Ann Foster and her three children left the Harrises, and returned to her husband in Toronto.

In 1853, it appears that a railway was " in course of construction from Toronto to Sarnia, at the foot of Lake Huron, with a station at Rockwood."

Jane Harris (587) was recorded a minister of the Society of Friends in the summer of 1854.

" On 3rd day, 30th of 12 mo. [1856], Uncle John Harris was driving towards Guelph with his son Samuel [then aged twelve years] when a foal belonging to another team kicked his horse, which bolted off the road into the woods. Uncle was thrown out and received fatal injury from his head behind the ear striking a knot on a fallen tree. He died on 2nd day, 5th of 1 mo., 1857. He was interred in the Friends' Burial Ground at Rockwood, in the grave adjoining grandfather's."

Jane Harris (587), " after a time of severe suffering, died about nine o'clock p.m., on 8 mo. 26, 1871."

One of the sons of John Harris writes to me : " I have heard my father say that his forefathers were of an English family, and that one of them of whom we are lineal descendants went over to Ireland as a soldier under William, Prince of Orange, in 1690, and remained there afterwards. When they made the commendable change from soldiers to Quakers I do not know." John Harris was born in March, 1789, son of Thomas Harris, paints, oils and glass merchant, in the city of Cork, Ireland, by his first wife, Mary Chamberlaine. I copy below an original letter recently lent me, written by Thomas Harris to his mother, Sarah Harris, shortly before his first marriage.

"Clonmel, 5 mo. 17, 1784.

"Dear Mother.

"I now adress thee on an Affair of importance towards my future peace & Welfare (which I have had this some before me) for thy advice thereon, it is respecting the Changing my Condition.

"I thought it requisite before I acquainted thee of my intention, to advise some of my friends thereof who were acquainted with the Young Woman, namely Mary Chamberlaine, sister in law to Richard Allen, and first Cousin to Richard Abell (who is married to Cousin Betty Beale), in order that I might be enabled to inform thee of their sentiments thereon. I therefore laid it before Aunt Harris (Uncle being in Leinster), Edward Hatton and John Davis.

"Aunt seemed much prepossessd in the young womans favour and said it was an Affair that required deliberate consideration, but that at the time she saw nothing to object to it, or words to that import. Edward and John each expressed themselves much to the same purpose. Samuel Neale being from home, I have written to him about it, a Copy of which I here enclose. Hoping thou wilt let me have a few lines as soon as convenient, I am, with dear Love to thyself, to Bro^r and sister Langstaff and Children, Cousin Joseph Russell and Family,

"thy truly Affec^te. Son,

"Thos. Harris.

"Please to direct to me at George Corletts, Cork, where I have dieted and lodged these 12 mos. past."

Thomas and Mary Harris had at least two children : Sarah, of whom I write below, and John, born in 1789, less than five years after the date of the above letter. Thomas Harris married a second time, and died when his son, John, was thirteen years of age. After his death the family seems to have been broken up.

A son of John Harris writes : " For ten years my Father followed a seafaring life in English mercantile trade. Coming back from the Mediterranean with a cargo of fruit for an English port, his vessel was captured by a French privateer in the English Channel, and he was taken to France, and held there a prisoner for fourteen months, being released when Napoleon was first conquered and sent to Elba." For ten years he was a member of Yarmouth Monthly Meeting. In the spring of 1818 he was at Scarborough, " when Dr. Wills told him he must give up the sea and keep his feet dry or he would never be well." *

His son writes further : " In 1818, he first took up land at the old homestead adjoining what is now the village of Rockwood, at that time an unbroken forest, and all his supplies for his first start were carried in on his back from the shore of Lake Ontario, a distance of twenty-two miles. A few Friends were attracted to that vicinity by the Government Surveyor's accounts of good land, and they prevailed on my father to be one of the number. I do not think that Sarah Balls came to this country till several years later, probably from 1824 to 1827." However, Sarah Harris had married Samuel Balls, and had two children, Samuel and Mary, born before 3rd March, 1830, the day on which was born, at Rockwood, her third and youngest child, Jemima Harris Balls, who seventeen years later married John Harris's brother-in-law, William Wetherald (729).

John Harris and his wife Jane Wetherald (587) had issue six sons.

   i.   John Richard Harris (588), whom see.
   ii. Thomas Harris (597), whom see.
   iii. Joseph Harris (611), whom see.
   iv. Samuel Harris (625), whom see.
   v.   William Harris (633), born 9th December, 1845, in the township of Eramosa, Ontario ; died 24th August, 1846.
   vi. James Harris (634), whom see.

---

* Thus his nephew, Alfred Yeardley (586), who states that John Harris went to Canada in 1820. His son Thomas Harris (597) thinks " that it would be in 1816 or 17 that my Father came to America."

John Richard Harris (588), born 29th August, 1837, probably in Eramosa township. He founded the Rockwood Woollen Mills, Ontario, which are well-known throughout the Dominion of Canada.

He was married 21st October, 1863, at Norwich, Canada West (now Ontario), to Marianna Trefry. He died 1st April, 1899. His parents had six sons and no daughters, he had five sons and no daughters, and his three married sons have each an only child, a son.

    i.   William Harris (589), whom see.

    ii.   Charles Harris (591), whom see.

    iii.   Edwin Harris (593), whom see.

    iv.   John Harris (595), died in infancy.

    v.   Richard Harris (596), born 24th April, 1879, unmarried in 1910. He is working out for a farmer near Everton, about three miles from Rockwood, Ontario.

William Harris (589), born 15th October, 1864. He now owns and carries on the Rockwood Woollen Mills, which formerly belonged to his father. He was married, 15th May, 1888, to Edith Walker, and has an only child.

    i.   Edgar Harris (590), born 12th March, 1889.

Charles Harris (591), born 26th February, 1867. He has been working in his brother William's Woollen Factory at Rockwood, but recently purchased a fruit-farm in the township of Pelham, Welland County, Ontario. He was married 4th November, 1903, to Emily Pearen, and has an only child.

    i.   Charles Gordon Harris (592), born 20th December, 1904.

Edwin Harris (593), born 21st June, 1869. He " is the owner of a pretty fruit farm, set out in apples, plums, and peaches, near St. Catherines, Ontario, about fifteen miles from Chantler." He was married firstly, 19th August, 1898, to Edith Argue, by whom he had an only child. She died 4th December, 1905, and he married, secondly, 24th September, 1908, Annie Haines Carlfield, who was without issue in 1910.

    i. George Argue Harris (594), born 29th November, 1905.

Thomas Harris (597), born 2nd June, 1839, at Eramosa, Ontario. His first cousin made a note : " 4th month 28th, 1863 : Aunt Jane Harris' sons Thomas and Joseph own a nice good lot of land in the township of Hibbert, in the County of Perth, where they expect to settle this autumn with Mary Reed for housekeeper." And another note, dated 1st month 9th, 1866, states " Cousin Thomas Harris spent last year in Peel, learning the Woollen Manufacture. Joseph will sell the farm at Hibbert, give up possession on 3rd mo. 1, and join his brother." " 9 month 4th, 1866 : They have purchased a mill site at Rockwood and expect to have the Mill at work next spring."

Thomas Harris (597), gave up the woollen business, was at one time a coal company's agent, and eventually bought Moresby Island, situated in the Gulf of Georgia, between Vancouver Island and the mainland of British Columbia. Here he and his family were living in January, 1910. Their life must be charmingly Arcadian in character. He writes, " The coldest day or night here this winter there was only twelve degrees of frost, and just an inch or two of snow that was all gone within forty-eight hours. The grass is green, and the sheep have been out on the island range all winter; we often do not see them for months at a time. There are 1,440 acres in the Island, and about 140 cleared, so you can see what a range they have. There are no wild animals to hunt them; I have only seen mink and mice."

He was married 16th March, 1868, to Mary Ann Zulima Bowerman, of Whitby, Ontario. She was born 16th May, 1846, and was living at Moresby Island in January, 1910.

    1. Agnes Harris (598), whom see.

    ii.   Lucy Harris (602), born 26th December, 1870, and was living unmarried at Moresby Island, in January, 1910.

    iii. Mary Josephine Harris (603), born 11th November, 1872, and died 1st July, 1889.

    iv. Alice Harris (604), born 5th May, 1875, and died 27th July, 1894.

    v. Joseph Arthur Harris (605), born 8th April, 1877, and died 8th August, 1878.

    vi. Howard Bowerman Harris (606), whom see.

    vii. George Stanley Harris (609), born 9th March, 1881, and unmarried in January, 1910.

    viii. Clara Ethelwyn Harris (610), born 23rd September, 1890. In March, 1910, she was attending school at Vancouver, B.C., unmarried.

Agnes Harris (598), born 22nd March, 1869. She was married 21st June, 1899, to Samuel Marshall Busselle, Assistant Manager of the Domestic Department of the Imperial Oil Company, New York. They reside 26, Broadway, New York City. The surname is pronounced with the accent on the second syllable.

    i. Samuel Marshall Busselle (599), born 30th July, 1900, died 13th February, 1901.

    ii. Samuel Marshall Busselle (600), born 10th June, 1903, and was living in New York in January, 1910.

    iii. Margaret Busselle (601), born 9th October, 1904, and died 19th February, 1907.

Howard Bowerman Harris (606), born 28th June, 1879. He was married 16th May, 1906, to Clara Menzies, and has a saw-mill and wood-working machinery at Pender Island, near Moresby Island.

    i. Irene Ethelwyn Harris (607), born 19th May, 1907.

    ii. Dorothy Zulima Harris (608), born 29th December, 1908.

Joseph Harris (611), born 25th September, 1841, at Rockwood, Ontario. In 1863 he and his brother Thomas began farming at Hibbert, Perth County, Ontario. They sold this property in 1866 and purchased a site for a woollen mill at Rockwood, which they expected to have working in the spring of 1867. His cousin, Alfred Yeardley (586), notes, " 1875, Cousin Joseph Harris left Rockwood and built a mill at Mount Forest, forty miles off. He was burnt out in 10 mo., 1875, and lost all, but the townspeople called a meeting and collected sufficient money to start him afresh." However, Joseph eventually gave up the woollen business, and went out to the State of Washington, U.S.A., where he made a fortune in hop-growing. He is said to resemble his brother Thomas in personal appearance and in his characteristics.

He was married 8th May, 1867, to Mary Gainer, born 27th July, 1844, daughter of Jacob and Susan Gainer. She was born in Thorold Township, Ontario, Canada, and was living with her husband at Kapowsin, Washington State, U.S.A., in February, 1910.

    i.   Asenath Harris (612), whom see.

    ii.   Clara Jane Harris (617), whom see.

    iii.   Thomas Fredreck Harris (621), whom see.

    iv.   Rachel Sandom Harris (624), born 28th September, 1878, at Rockwood, Ontario, Canada. She was married, 20th August, 1902, at Auburn, Washington State, U.S.A., to Perry Hand Walbridge, farmer. In February, 1910, they were living at Kapowsin, Washington, without issue.

Asenath Harris (612), born 27th February, 1870, at Rockwood, Ontario, Canada. She was married 30th November, 1892, at Sumner, Washington State, U.S.A., to Oro Oliver, and they now (February, 1910) live at Bismarck, Washington State.

    i.   Richard Harris Oliver (613), born 3rd September, 1893, at South Prairie, Washington State.

    ii.   Charles Fred Oliver (614), born 6th June, 1895, at South Prairie, Washington State.

iii. Orella Josephine Oliver (615), born 6th April, 1897, at Tacoma, Washington, and died there, 2nd November, 1897.

iv. Orno Renell Oliver (616), born 6th June, 1901, in Tacoma, Washington State, U.S.A.

Clara Jane Harris (617), born 8th December, 1872, at Rockwood, Ontario, Canada. She was married 28th January, 1903, at Auburn, Washington State, U.S.A., to Samuel Edward Fix, machinist, and they now (February, 1910) live at Kapowsin, Washington State.

 i. Pauline Mildred Fix (618), born 3rd February, 1905, at Kapowsin, Washington, U.S.A.

ii. Russell Oro Fix (619), born 3rd October, 1906, at Anaheim, California, U.S.A.

iii. Ione Edna Fix (620), born 15th February, 1909, at Kapowsin, Washington, U.S.A.

Thomas Fredreck Harris (621), born 16th January, 1877, at Rockwood, Ontario, Canada. He was married 3rd October, 1904, at Auburn, Washington State, U.S.A., to Lula Mae Tanner, and they were living there in February, 1910, " He has sixty milch cows on a hundred acres of land and sells his milk to an evaporator."

 i. Ethelwyn Josephine Harris (622), born 2nd December, 1905, at Auburn, Washington.

ii. Margaret Gladys Harris (623), born 12th August, 1908.

Samuel Harris (625), born 29th March, 1844, at Rockwood, Wellington County, Ontario. In 1868 he was learning spinning in his eldest brother's mill at Rockwood. In 1870, " Cousins Samuel and James have arranged to settle on their father (John Harris's) farm." In 1910, Samuel Harris had a hundred acres of land in Rockwood.

He was married 27th April, 1874, to Susannah Starr, who was born near Newmarket, in the County of York, Ontario, youngest daughter of Mordecai and Sarah Starr. Her brother, Charles Starr, of Newmarket, married Samuel Harris's first cousin, Hannah Hustler (692).

    i.   Wasley Harris (626), whom see.

    ii.   Charles Henry Harris (627), whom see.

    iii.   Jane Harris (629), born 14th June, 1879, at Rockwood; died 1st September, 1879.

    iv.   Albert Harris (630), born 2nd November, 1880, at Rockwood; died 21st June, 1881.

    v.   Joseph Arthur Harris (631), born 23rd September, 1882, at Rockwood; died 27th May, 1883.

    vi.   Elwood Harris (632), born 1st September, 1885, at Rockwood; died 27th January, 1887.

Wasley Harris (626), born 26th June, 1876, at Rockwood, Ontario. He was married 29th March, 1902, to Annie M. Pasmore, who was born at Conestogo, Waterloo County; daughter of Dr. W. J. Pasmore. He has a farm at Effingham, about ten miles from Chantler, Welland County, and is without issue.

Charles Henry Harris (627), born 7th November, 1877, at Rockwood, Ontario. In 1910, he was working his father's farm, at Rockwood. He was married 7th June, 1905, to Emily W. Kitching, who was born at Corwhin in the County of Halton, daughter of John and Elizabeth Kitching. She died 4th September, 1908, leaving an only child.

    i.   Elwood Kitching Harris (628), born 24th June, 1906.

James Harris (634), born 21st July, 1848, at Rockwood, Wellington County, Ontario. In 1870 he and his brother Samuel arranged to settle on their father's farm near Rockwood. He later lived at Meaford, Grey

County, Ontario, a town on the shores of Georgian Bay, a part of Lake Huron. James Harris died at Meaford, 13th January, 1890.

He was married 14th May, 1874, at Rochester, New York State, U.S.A., to his cousin Elizabeth Ventress Park. She was his second cousin. I do not know the exact steps* of the relationship, but it was through his grandfather, John Wetherald. James Harris's first cousin, Alfred Yeardley (586), writes " 9 mo. 25, 1850, Grandfather [*i.e.*, John Wetherald] visited cousins John and Rachel Park this year." Elizabeth Ventress Harris was living at Meaford, Ontario, in January, 1910. She returned there in December, 1909, after spending more than a year with her sons in the West.

    i.   Rachel Jane Harris (635), born 30th September, 1875 ; died 13th May, 1876.

    ii.   Lewis James Harris (636), born 7th March, 1878. He has 320 acres of land in Alberta, which he is farming ; unmarried.

    iii.   Joseph Allan Harris (637), born 3rd October, 1879. He has 320 acres of land in Alberta, which he is farming ; unmarried.

    iv.   Mary Alice Harris (638), whom see.

    v.   Bessie Harris, (640) born 16th May, 1886, died the same day.

    vi.   Harvy Thomas Harris (641), born 7th October, 1889. He has 160 acres of land in Alberta, which he is farming ; unmarried.

Mary Alice Harris (638), born 2nd May, 1884. She was married at Meaford, 19th June, 1907, to David Grenfield.

    i.   Ventress Lydia Grenfield (639), born 19th June, 1908.

Ann Wetherald (642), born 27th December, 1808, at Burnley, in the parish of Whalley, Lancashire, a twin with her sister Jane, who married John Harris. In 1812, her parents and family removed to Healaugh, near Reeth, in Swaledale, Yorkshire. About 1825, they removed to Wakefield, Yorkshire, where her mother died in the following year. As her father lived at Wakefield until he went to Canada in 1834, she was probably married at the Friends' Meeting House there.

* These are now discovered, and shown in Chart IX.

She was married 20th June, 1833, to Oswald Foster. Her nephew, Alfred Yeardley, writes, " 5 mo., 14, 1843, Oswald Foster sailed from Liverpool in the ' Roscius,' reached Staten Island 6 mo. 20, and New York next day, and, after travelling about in the States, to Niagara, and amongst our other relatives in Canada, settled down for the winter in Toronto, at my Great-uncle James Wetherald's." " 10 mo. 30, 1846, on or about this date Aunt Ann Foster, with [her three children] Henrietta, Richard, and William Henry, sailed [from England], and arrived at New York about 11 mo. 28." Oswald Foster met his wife and children at Rochester, N.Y., at the house of their cousins, J. and R. Park.

Ann Foster (642), arrived at Yorkville (near Toronto) two days short of three weeks after reaching New York. On the 21st February, 1847, she left Toronto, and went to live with her twin sister in Eramosa. On the 8th April she was joined by her children Henrietta and Richard. While living here her son Oswald, junr., was born, 2nd September, 1847. At the beginning of 1848, Oswald Foster left Yorkville and went to live " twelve miles up Yonge Street," (a district running between Toronto and Lake Simcoe). At the end of November, 1848, Ann Foster (642), left Eramosa and returned with her three children to her husband in Toronto.

In the spring of 1870, Oswald and Ann Foster removed to Newton Brook, a farm eight or ten miles above Yorkville. During the last twelve years of her life Ann Foster was an invalid, cared for by her only daughter. She died 24th May, 1875. Her husband married a second time.

i. Henrietta Foster (643), born in England, between 1833 and 1843. Emigrated to Canada with her mother and two brothers in 1846. She tended her mother through her long illness, and died unmarried, aged over sixty years.

ii. Richard Foster (644), born in England between 1833 and 1843. Emigrated to Canada with his mother and sister and brother in 1846. On the 8th April, 1847, he went with his sister to live at Eramosa with his mother and his aunt Jane Harris (587). In 1848 they returned to Toronto. He died of heart disease, 28th April, 1856.

    iii.   William Henry Foster (645), born in England between 1833 and 1843. Emigrated to Canada with his mother and sister and brother in 1846. Shortly after arrival he " was put to school with a person named Cook, a nice woman, living twelve miles from Yorkville, on Yonge Street." He died of epilepsy, about July, 1856.

    iv.   Oswald Fiennes Foster (646), whom see.

Oswald Fiennes Foster (646), was born 2nd September, 1847, near Rockwood, in the township of Eramosa, and County of Wellington, Ontario, Canada. He was married, firstly, at Toronto, Canada, 16th September, 1869, to Mary Symonds Chidley, who was born 2nd January, 1850, probably at Guelph, Ontario, and died 19th February, 1895, at Buffalo, New York State, U.S.A. By her he had seven children.

He was married secondly, at Buffalo, N.Y., 30th June, 1896, to Dena Emma Badger. who was born 1st April, 1862, at East Elma, N.Y. He died, without issue by his second wife, 20th January, 1909, at Buffalo, N.Y.

    i.   Oswald Edward Foster (647), born 11th September, 1870, at Toronto, Canada ; died before 1880.

    ii.   Minnie Etta Foster (648), born 14th December, 1872, at Toronto, Canada ; died before 1880.

    iii.   Fred Foster (649), born at Toronto, Canada ; died before 1880.

    iv.   Robert Charles Foster (650), whom see.

    v.   Annie Ethel Foster (653), whom see.

    vi.   Clara Foster (656), born at Toronto, Canada ; died about 1881.

    vii.   Harold Edwin Foster (657), born 26th July, 1887, at Buffalo, New York State, U.S.A. He died 2nd June, 1901, at Buffalo.

Robert Charles Foster (650), born 25th May, 1877, at Toronto, Canada. He was married 5th June, 1900, at Erie, Pennsylvania, to Emma Priscilla Bauschard, who was born October, 1876, at Erie.

    i. Harold Edwin Foster (651), born 22nd April, 1901, at Erie,
        Pennsylvania.

    ii. Carl William Foster (652), born 8th August, 1906, at Erie,
        Pennsylvania.

Annie Ethel Foster (653), born 18th December, 1879, at Toronto,
Canada. She was married 27th September, 1905, at Buffalo, N.Y.,
to Joan Blanchard Marks, who was born 30th June, 1876, at Albany,
Oregon, U.S.A.

    i. Herbert Ivan Marks (654), born 26th June, 1907, at Buffalo,
        N.Y., died there of scarlet fever 29th November, 1909.

    ii. Wilson Everett Marks (655), born 1st November, 1908, at
        Buffalo, N Y., died there 2nd December, 1909, of scarlet
        fever.

Joseph Wetherald (658), born 10th April, 1811, at Burnley, in
the parish of Whalley, Lancashire. During the next year his parents
removed to Healaugh in the parish of Grinton, Swaledale, Yorkshire.
About 1825, they removed from Swaledale to Wakefield, where in 1826
Joseph Wetherald's mother died.

On the 8th February, 1834, John Wetherald, his son Joseph and
his daughter Jane left England for America. Their journey is described
in the account of Joseph's mother, Isabel Thistlethwaite (583). In
October, 1835, " Uncle Joseph took a farm of 150 acres, 1½ miles from
Guelph, for 7 years, at a rent of 30 Cords of Wood per year=12
dollars. The pine and oak upon it will more than pay the rent by a
great deal."

On the 27th April, 1836, " Uncle Joseph married to Sarah Jarmy
of Dundas, who was only 18 the day after they were married, not a
friend [*i.e.*, Quaker], but in all other respects everything that could be
wished." He was then twenty-five years of age. Sarah Jarmy was

the eldest daughter of Capt. Thomas and Sarah Mason Jarmy. Her sister Catherine Jarmy married Dr. James Cobban, whose son's (Dr. Matthew Cobban's) widow married Joseph Wetherald's eldest son as her second husband.

In February, 1842, Joseph and Sarah Wetherald had been living in Toronto more than a year. In March, 1843, " Uncle Joseph's brother-in-law Dr. Cobban offers him 100 acres of land (40 acres cleared) for 500 dollars and plenty of time to pay for it in." In April, 1847, it is reported that " Uncle Joseph has begun business as a Friction Match Manufacturer at Yorkville in Toronto Home District, Canada West."

· Joseph Wetherald (658), died 29th May, 1886. His widow Sarah Wetherald died 3rd June, 1895 : she was born 28th April, 1818.

    i.   Isabel Wetherald (659), born 4th March, 1837, in Guelph, Wellington County, Ontario, Canada. She died unmarried in Toronto, 27th February, 1867.

   ii.   Joseph John Wetherald (660), whom see.

  iii.   James Cobban Wetherald (670), whom see.

   iv.   Richard Wetherald (673), born 19th October, 1842 ; died 16th August, 1843.

    v.   Henry William Wetherald (674), whom see.

   vi.   Catherine Ann Wetherald (675), whom see.

  vii.   William Wetherald (682), born 17th July, 1849, in Toronto, Ontario. He died there 29th November, 1852.

 viii.   Emily Wetherald (683), whom see.

   ix.   Thomas Jarmy Wetherald (686), whom see.

Joseph John Wetherald (660), born 27th November, 1838, at Guelph, Ontario, Canada. In 1863 he was a carpenter in Elk City, Oregon, U.S.A., but had returned to Canada before 1867. He spent the last twenty-five years of his life as a successful farmer at Blenheim, Ontario, Canada. His first wife, whom he married in March, 1871, was Jane Thompson Cobban, widow of his first cousin Dr. Matthew Cobban. By her he had two sons, as below.

He married secondly, 6th December, 1875, Frances A. Pegg, born at Burlington, 12th December, 1850, only daughter of —— Pegg, of Blenheim. Joseph John Wetherald died at Blenheim, 2nd November, 1896, when his widow kept house for her younger step-son until he married. Since the death of his wife she has again been keeping house for him at Blenheim. She is without issue.

 i. Joseph John Wetherald (661), whom see.
 ii. Charles Thompson Wetherald (667), whom see.

Joseph John Wetherald (661), born 14th December, 1871, at Blenheim, Kent County, Ontario. His father left him a farm there, where he was living in 1910. He married Ida Leng, who was born 15th March, 1871, near Hagersville, Haldimand County, Ontario.

 i. Gladis Ilene Wetherald (662), born 5th September, 1895, at Blenheim.
 ii. Thomas Earl Wetherald (663), born 15th September, 1898, at Blenheim.
 iii. Elva Odessa Wetherald (664), born 27th October, 1900, at Blenheim.
 iv. Lodena May Wetherald (665), born 10th August, 1902, at Blenheim.
 v. Joseph Murry Wetherald (666), born 13th January, 1908, at Blenheim.

Charles Thompson Wetherald (667), born 27th December, 1872, at Blenheim, Ontario. His father left him a farm there, where he was living with his step-mother in 1910. He married Mary Alice Douthwait, who was born 20th August, 1879, in Howard. She died 25th June, 1909, in San Diego, where she had gone for her health.

 i. Edna May Wetherald (668), born 6th March, 1903.
 ii. Joseph Harold Wetherald (669), born 19th June, 1905, at Blenheim.

James Cobban Wetherald (670), born 29th November, 1840.
In the spring of 1863, he was living with his brother Joseph, at Great
Elk City, Salmon River, Oregon, U.S.A., but later in the same year he
was "at Beaver Mines, 300 miles nearer Canada than Elk City." He was
living in 1910 at Georgetown, Halton County, Ontario. "He has
for some years given his time to buying and shipping cattle mostly to
Toronto market. When he first went into that business, he used to ship
horses to Manitoba, but gave it up." He was married in 1874 to Mary
Telford McKay, born 2nd February, 1852, second daughter of Hugh
McKay, of Georgetown.

    · i. Hubert McKay Wetherald (671), whom see.
      ii. Josephine Jarmy Wetherald (672), born 18th July, 1877,
          living at home unmarried in 1910.

Hubert McKay Wetherald (671), born 2nd September, 1875.
He was a teacher in the Georgetown Collegiate, but in 1910 was managing
the business affairs of his uncle S. F. Mackinnon, a millionaire. The
latter has been in poor health for some time: he is brother-in-law to
Hubert McKay Wetherald's mother. Hubert McKay Wetherald (671),
was married to Eleanor McLeod, of Georgetown, Ontario, who was born
in Georgetown 3rd September, 1874, daughter of Wm. Macleod. *Sine
prole.*

Henry William Wetherald (674), born 28th September, 1844.
In 1863, he was a "confectioner near his father." He was married
about 1892 to his first cousin Agnes Ann Hustler (727), who was born
in the latter part of 1862, youngest child of Jeremiah Hustler by his wife
Mary Wetherald (690). When last heard from they had four children,
and were living at Aberdeen, Washington State, U.S.A.

Catherine Ann Wetherald (675), born 8th December, 1846, at
Toronto, Canada. She was married 1st January, 1874, to James Munn,

jeweller and watchmaker, Toronto, Ontario, Canada, who died several
years ago. In 1910, she was living a widow in Toronto with her two
unmarried daughters.

  i.   Elizabeth Agnes Marjory Munn (676), whom see.
  ii. William Wetherald Munn (678), born 26th January, 1877.
       In 1910, he was a prosperous jeweller, at 800, Yonge Street,
       Toronto, unmarried.
  iii. May Hamilton Munn (679), born 23rd November, 1879. In
       1910 she was a teacher in a graded school near her home,
       unmarried.
  iv. Frederick James Munn (680), born 13th January, 1882. In
       1910, he was a practising physician in Toronto. He was
       married October, 1909, to Cecilia Louise Noble.
  v.   Kathleen Jean Munn (681), born 28th August, 1887. In
       1910, she was living unmarried at home.

   Elizabeth Agnes Marjorie Munn (676), born 8th February, 1875.
She was married 8th May, 1908, to William H. Richards, and in 1910
they were living at Killarney, Manitoba, Canada.

  i.   William Wetherald Richards (677), born 20th October, 1909.

   Emily Wetherald (683), born 25th May, 1852, at Toronto. She
was married in 1879 to H. David Johnson. In 1910, he was employed
at an automobile factory. They reside at 795, Roosevelt Avenue,
Detroit, Michigan, U.S.A.

  i.   Irene Johnson (684), born 1885, and died 1897.
  ii. Alma Johnson (685), born September, 1887. In 1910 she
       was a teacher, unmarried.

   Thomas Jarmy Wetherald (686), born 21st August, 1854, at
Toronto. He learned the jewellery and watchmaking business in Canada,

but emigrated to Australia, and for some years has had " a position on a newspaper in Sydney." He was married 4th February, 1895, to Helen Bowie Philp. In 1909, his address was, " Ontario," Kurraba Road, Neutral Bay, Sydney, New South Wales.

    i. ————Wetherald (687), a child which lived only two days.

    ii. Keith Bowie Wetherald (688), born 29th March, 1898.

Mary Wetherald (690), born 14th November, 1816, at Healaugh, in the parish of Grinton, Swaledale, Yorkshire. In 1835, she crossed from England to America, in the ship " Hibernia," with her three younger brothers, and other relatives. Until her marriage she lived with her father at Puslinch, near Guelph, Ontario, Canada. She first appeared in the Quaker ministry in 1842, a contemporary letter remarking that " she has a most beautiful delivery." She died in 1889.

She was married 8th June, 1843, to Jeremiah Hustler, who was then thirty-three years of age, son of Jeremiah Hustler by his wife Hannah Scott. He emigrated with his parents to the United States from Yeadon near Leeds, Yorkshire, and at the time of his marriage was living at Trafalgar, forty miles nearer Toronto than Puslinch. He and his wife settled upon a farm adjoining that of his parents in the township of Trafalgar and county of Halton, Ontario. Here they resided all their lives, Jeremiah Hustler dying in January, 1890 or 1891.

    i. Jeremiah Hustler (691), born 9th March, 1844, in Trafalgar. In January, 1910, he was residing at Hamilton, Ontario. His niece cannot supply further particulars, but I do not think he married.

    ii. Hannah Hustler (692), whom see.

    iii. Isabel Wetherald Hustler (699), born 28th September, 1847, in Trafalgar, and died unmarried in 1888.

    iv. Benjamin Hustler (700), whom see.

    v. Rachel Ann Hustler (713), whom see.

    vi. Sarah Jane Hustler (720), born 28th March, 1855. She lived with her sister and brother-in-law, Hannah and Charles Starr, but a few years ago left their family to reside with her sister and brother-in-law, Rachel and John Anderson, at Vandorf, York County, Ontario. Here she was living unmarried in January, 1910.

vii. Mary Agnes Hustler (721), born 1858, still-born.

viii. John Wetherald Hustler (722), whom see.

ix. Agnes Ann Hustler (727), whom see.

Hannah Hustler (692), born 8th October, 1845, in Trafalgar, Halton County, Ontario. She was married 19th May, 1874, at Rockwood, Ontario, to Charles Starr, farmer, son of Mordecai Starr by his wife Sarah Wesley. The latter were " of Pennsylvania Quaker stock, which emigrated to this province [Ontario] in the early days of the Nineteenth Century."

The eldest daughter of Charles and Hannah Starr writes, " my parents took up their abode on the farm where we now reside [Newmarket, York County, Ontario], engaging in agricultural pursuits ; and here, or upon the farm opposite, which was purchased from my grandfather, they have passed their days." Charles Starr's sister married his wife's first cousin Samuel Harris (625).

i. Sarah Jane Starr (693), born 23rd February, 1875, at Newmarket, Ontario, where she was living unmarried in February, 1910.

ii. Mary Agnes Starr (694), born 23rd March, 1877, at Newmarket, Ontario, where she was living unmarried in February, 1910.

iii. Isabel Esther Starr (695), born 3rd March, 1879, at Newmarket, Ontario. In February, 1910, she was living " in town," unmarried.

iv. Anna Louisa Starr (696), born 20th May, 1881, at Newmarket, Ontario, where she was living unmarried in February, 1910.

v. John Starr (697), born 21st August, 1884, still-born.

vi. Mordecai C. Starr (698), born 17th May, 1886, at Newmarket, Ontario. He died 16th August, 1888.

~~~~~~~~~~~~~~~~~~~~~~~~~~~~~~~~~

Benjamin Hustler (700), born 11th February, 1850, at Trafalgar, Halton County, Ontario. He was married 1st October, 1877, in the Methodist Church, Milton, to Ann Elizabeth Irwin, daughter of James Irwin by his wife Elizabeth Newel, both of whom were Irish. By her he had issue,

i. William James Hustler (701), born 18th January, 1879; died 18th November, 1883, " aged three years and ten months " (?)

ii. Joseph John Hustler (702), born 16th February, 1883. He was married 16th February, 1910, to Ethel May Crewson, and they live on a farm in East Luther.

Benjamin Hustler's first wife, Ann Elizabeth Irwin Hustler, died 10th November, 1883, aged twenty-five years and five months. He was married secondly, 23rd December, 1884, to Louisa McKersie, who was born 5th April, 1857, on her parents' farm in the township of Eramosa, Wellington County, Ontario, Canada. She was the daughter of Gavin McKersie, who was born at Paisley, Scotland, 22nd August, 1818 (still living 1910), by his wife Louisa Reeve, who was born in London, England, 14th March, 1820. Benjamin Hustler and his second wife were living on a farm near Wesley, Dufferin County, Ontario, in February, 1910. They had issue,

iii. Mary Louisa Reeve Hustler (703), whom see.

iv. Florence Olivia Winters Hustler (706), whom see.

v. Irwin Bruce Hustler (708), born 3rd March, 1889, unmarried February, 1910.

vi. Fanny Katie Hunter Hustler (709), born 23rd March, 1891, died 25th March, 1891.

    vii.   Olive Myrtle May Hustler (710), born 9th February, 1894, unmarried February, 1910.

   viii.   Elwood Stanley Hustler (711), born 27th January, 1896.

    ix.   Annie Ettie Pearl Hustler (712), born 29th April, 1899.

Mary Louisa Reeve Hustler (703), born 1st October, 1885. She was married to Albert James McHardy 29th March, 1905, at her parents' home in the township of West Luther, Wellington County, Ontario, by Rev. James Pollick. In 1905 and 1907 they were living on a farm in West Luther.

     i.   Hazel Pearl McHardy (704), born 18th December, 1905, in West Luther.

    ii.   Velma Bernie McHardy (705), born 6th December, 1907, in West Luther.

Florence Olivia Winters Hustler (706), born 1st April, 1887. She was married to Robert Wilson, 20th February, 1906, at her parents' farm home in the township of West Luther, Wellington County, Ontario, by Rev. James Pollick. In 1909 they were living on a farm in West Luther.

     i.   Sarah Edna Wilson (707), born 6th May, 1909, in West Luther.

Rachel Ann Hustler (713), born 28th September, 1852, in the township of Trafalgar, Halton County, Ontario. She was married 1st February, 1877, to John Anderson, who was born in the same township, in 1843. He and his father Henry Anderson were born on the same farm. Henry Anderson's wife was born at Appleby in the county of Westmorland, England; she was the daughter of Michael Hall, of Appleby, by his wife Hannah Alton of the same place.

    John Anderson writes that his mother was connected with the Fothergill and Wetherald families of Yorkshire, but as to the precise relationship " it is so long ago that I heard it talked over that I have forgotten most of it." In February, 1910, John and Rachel Anderson were living on a farm in Vandorf, York County, Ontario.

  i.   Bertie Victoria Anderson (714), died an infant.
  ii. Anson Ernest Anderson (715), born 9th February, 1879, unmarried February, 1910.
  iii. Russell Oliver Anderson (716), born 6th August, 1883, unmarried February, 1910.
  iv. Sarah Millissa Anderson (717), born 10th August, 1885, unmarried February, 1910.
  v.   Marianne Anderson (718), died an infant.
  vi. Herbert Stanley Anderson (719), born 29th August, 1892, unmarried February, 1910.

John Wetherald Hustler (722), born 26th July, 1859, on Lot 14, No. 10 Concession, Trafalgar township, in the county of Halton, Ontario. He was married 7th June, 1898, to Harriet Alice Cowan, who was born on Lot 12, No. 11 Concession, Trafalgar township, 24th October, 1869, youngest daughter of Joseph and Margrate Cowan. Joseph Cowan was born 19th January, 1809 ; his wife was born 6th January, 1826 ; both came from Tipperary, Ireland.

John Wetherald Hustler (722) is a farmer, and owns twenty acres, West Part of Lot 1, No. 6 Concession, Chinguacousy township, Peel County, Ontario. His postal address in March, 1910, was Lisgar, Peel County.

  i.   John Richard Hustler (723), died an infant.
  ii. Joseph Wetherald Hustler (724), born 3rd November, 1902.
  iii. Mary Alice Hustler (725), born 24th September, 1904.
  iv. Florance Margrate Alfretta Hustler (726), born 8th January, 1907.

Agnes Ann Hustler (727), born 1862. She was married about 1892-1894 to her first cousin, Henry William Wetherald (674), born 28th

September, 1844, son of Joseph Wetherald (658), by his wife Sarah Jarmy. When last heard from their address was Aberdeen Post Office, Washington State, U.S.A. They had four children.

William Wetherald (729), born at Healaugh in Swaledale, York-shire, 26th September, 1820. In 1835, he crossed from England to America in the ship "Hibernia" with his two younger brothers, his sister Mary, and other relatives. He went first to live with his father at Puslinch, near Guelph. His nephew notes "29th 12 mo. 1846, Uncle William Wetherald resides with Uncle and Aunt Harris [at Eramosa] and teaches a district school. He has just bought forty-seven acres of land of them and is engaged to be married to [Uncle] John Harris's niece . . . 4th mo. 27th, 1847. Uncle William Wetherald was married on 3rd month 17th [1847] to Jemima Harris Balls, who was seventeen years and two weeks old on that day."

Jemima Harris Balls was born 3rd March, 1830, at Rockwood, Ontario, Canada, youngest of the three children of Samuel Balls by his wife Sarah Harris. Sarah Balls, *née* Harris, was a school-teacher and a woman of unusual refinement and force of character. Her brother, John Harris, married William Wetherald's sister, Jane Wetherald (587), whom see.

William Wetherald (729), took over the school at Eramosa from 1st January, 1848, but in May, 1851, writes from his private boarding school at Rockwood, near Guelph. In December, 1855, he "moved into his new stone house four stories high," and in this year founded Rockwood Academy. In September, 1864, he took the position of Superintendent of Haverford College near Philadelphia, Pennsylvania, U.S.A., which was and still is the highest institution of its kind in the Society of Friends in America. He retired from his position at Haverford, on the 31st January, 1866, sold his Rockwood property, and settled on a fruit-farm in the township of Pelham, Welland County, Ontario.

In case those who read the portions of this book dealing with America should be confused by the American form of rural address, it may be stated here that the province of Ontario is divided into a number of counties, which are each sub-divided into townships. Thus Welland County, in which lie the Falls of Niagara, is formed of seven townships, of which Pelham is one. Until recently the nearest post-office to William Wetherald's farm was at Fenwick, a growing village two miles north-ward; but now the address is Chantler, a new post-office a mile and a quarter to the south-east. William Wetherald's father settled in the township of Puslinch, three miles from the town of Guelph, and in the County of Wellington. William Wetherald and his sister Jane Harris lived near the village of Rockwood, which lies in the township of Eramosa, also in the County of Wellington. William Wetherald's old house was half-a-mile from the village of Rockwood which lies nine miles north-east of Guelph. In the same way, kinsfolk who were formerly addressed Sheridan, Indiana, are now addressed Hortonville, Indiana, although living on exactly the same farms.

William Wetherald (729), made his fruit-farm a home and occupation for his sons, but he himself was never a farmer. He was a minister of the orthodox branch of the Society of Friends, and, after leaving Haver-ford in 1866, made preaching the chief work of his life. When in the vicinity he preached regularly at the meeting held two miles from his home, and he travelled in the ministry with a Minute from Canada Yearly Meeting to very many Yearly and Quarterly Meetings in the United States. His nephew notes that " he left home the beginning of 9th mo. [1863] to attend the opening of Iowa Yearly Meeting, a distance of about 800 miles." His daughter writes, " I doubt if any Friends' minister in this country or the U.S.A. has travelled more, or been more widely known."

His daughter writes further, " One of my father's Rockwood pupils who has since become famous in the business world is J. J. Hill, one of the richest millionaires in the United States. In 1880, when he was President of the St. Paul, Minneapolis and Manitoba Railway, J. J. Hill invited father to visit him, and wished him to be a tutor to his own sons.

9

On Father replying that his life work was preaching, J. J. Hill offered to give positions in his railway office to any of Father's sons." Accordingly in 1881 two of them went to live at St. Paul for that purpose.

William Wetherald (729), died 21st August, 1898, while visiting England, at Wykham Park near Banbury, the home of his first cousin, Mrs. Mewburn. The latter was born Maria Tew, daughter of William Tew, of Halifax, Yorkshire, by his wife Ann Wetherald, daughter of Joseph and Mally Wetherald. Ann Wetherald was sister of John Wetherald, who married Isabel Thistlethwaite (583), and mother of Sophia Tew, who married John Taylor (1450), besides being mother of Maria Tew, who married William Mewburn, a successful stockbroker, sometime of Stokesley and Halifax, Yorkshire.*

Jemima Harris Wetherald lived ten years after her husband's death, chiefly on his fruit-farm near Chantler, with her sons William and Herbert and her daughter Agnes. She visited her sons Samuel John and Frederick, near St. Paul, Minnesota, U.S.A., and was in the habit of going to Rockwood for a visit of two or three weeks each year of the latter years of her life. She died 31st October, 1908, at Chantler, Welland County, Ontario.

    i.   Rachel Wetherald (730), born 11th August, 1848, at Rockwood, Ontario: died 29th January, 1861, of heart disease.

    ii.   Richard Wetherald (731), born February, 1850, at Rockwood, and died the same day.

    iii.   Samuel John Wetherald (732), born 23rd February, 1851, at Rockwood, Ontario. Through the influence of J. J. Hill, in 1881 he was given a position in the St. Paul office of the St. Paul, Minneapolis and Manitoba Railway Company, now called the Great Northern Railway. He rose to be paymaster, which position ill-health obliged him to give up. After a year's absence he accepted a position in the land department, but has lately retired from business altogether. He is an enthusiastic traveller, has been in every State in

* Two of William and Maria Mewburn's daughters married respectively Sir Mark Oldroyd and Sir R. Perks.

the Union, and in 1910 was living unmarried at St. Paul, Minnesota, U.S.A.

iv. James Wetherald (733), born 19th May, 1853, at Rockwood, Ontario. In 1910 he was unmarried, living on a farm near Hamilton, Ontario.

v. William Wetherald (734), born 21st May, 1855, at Rockwood, Ontario. In March, 1910, he was unmarried, and living on his father's fruit farm at Chantler, Welland County, Ontario, with his brother Herbert and his sister Agnes.

vi. Agnes Wetherald (735), born 26th April, 1857, at Rockwood, Ontario. In May 1910, she was unmarried, and living with her brothers William and Herbert at Chantler, Welland County, Ontario. She is well known in Canadian literary circles, and has published four volumes of verse under the name of "Ethelwyn Wetherald." Her latest book, "The Last Robin and Other Poems," produced a complimentary letter from Earl Grey, Governor-General of Canada, with an order for twenty-five copies.

vii. Jane Wetherald (736), born 13th May, 1859, at Rockwood, Ontario. In April, 1910, she was Chief Corresponding Clerk for the Agricultural Department at Edmonton, Alberta, Canada; unmarried.

viii. Charles Wetherald (737), whom see.

ix. Frederick Henry Wetherald (738), whom see.

x. Lewis Wetherald (742), born 2nd August, 1870, on his father's fruit farm, near Fenwick, Ontario. He has not communicated with his relatives for many years.

xi. Herbert Wetherald (743), born 19th April, 1872, near Fenwick, Welland County, Ontario. In March, 1910, he was living unmarried on his father's fruit-farm there, with his brother William, and sister Agnes.

Charles Wetherald (737), born 24th September, 1861, at Rockwood, Ontario, Canada. Through the influence of J. J. Hill, in 1881, he was given a position in the St. Paul office of the St. Paul, Minneapolis and Manitoba Railway, now called the Great Northern Railway. However, the climate of Minnesota proved too rigorous for him and he is now Chief Accountant to the Western Meat Company at Oakland, near San Francisco, California. He and his wife live in a flat in the Roslyn; at Oakland, without issue.

He was married 8th March, 1905, at San Francisco, to Isabella McClelland, as her second husband. She was born 23rd March, 1872, daughter of Robert Henry White, by his wife Isabella Emily Wardman. Isabella Wetherald, her mother Isabella, and her grandmother Isabella, were all born on 23rd March. She was first married 3rd July, 1897, to Thomas Jefferson McClelland, who died 18th February, 1900.

Frederick Henry Wetherald (738), born 21st June, 1865, at Haverford, Pennsylvania, U.S.A. In March, 1910, he had a fruit-farm near St. Paul, Minnesota, U.S.A., and is the only one of his father's eleven children to have issue.

He was married at St. Paul, Minnesota, 11th September, 1894, to Josephine Nadean, a Roman Catholic of French-Canadian extraction. She was born 21st January, 1873, daughter of Sylvain and Isabella Nadean.

    i.   Lillian Wetherald (739), born 11th November, 1895, at St. Paul, Minnesota.

    ii. René Wetherald (740), born 20th March, 1898, at St. Paul, Minnesota.

    iii. Grace Wetherald (741), born 9th February, 1902, at St. Paul, Minnesota.

Thomas Wetherald (744), born 9th July, 1822, at Healaugh, a village near Reeth, in the parish of Grinton, Swaledale, Yorkshire. Reeth is eleven miles by the map from Carr End, in Wensleydale,

the home of Thomas Wetherald's mother, Isabella Thistlethwaite
(583). Swaledale and Wensleydale run due east and west, Swaledale
on the north. Moor-roads cross the six or seven miles of hills
dividing the two valleys : I have myself been lost in a mist while crossing.
In about 1825, Thomas Wetherald's parents and family removed from
Swaledale to Wakefield, and here his mother died in 1826. In 1835, he
crossed from England to America in the ship " Hibernia," with his
brothers William and John, his sister Mary, and other relatives.

His father had settled on a farm about three miles from the town of
Guelph, in the township of Puslinch, Ontario. His two youngest sons
lived here, and apparently helped on his farm until 1847, when he gave up
" the management of the farm to Thomas and John, who are to pay him
a rent and to keep him." Their father died in August, 1852, and John,
his son, was married in October of the same year. Their nephew notes :
" 4 mo. 13th, 1854, Uncles Thomas and John Wetherald, all grandfather's
legacies being paid, dissolved partnership in the best of brotherly love
and affection, and after dividing equally between them all the personal
property, Thomas purchased John's share of the Puslinch freehold."

" Uncle Thomas Wetherald was married on 8 mo. [August] 3rd,
[1854], to Mary Collom, about two years his senior, who emigrated to
Canada about two years ago from near Tavistock, in Devonshire, where
she was convinced of Friends' Principles, and received into membership."
Mary Collom was born 7th November, 1820, daughter of Joseph and
Elizabeth Collom. She was married at Pelham Friends' Meeting House,
Welland County, Ontario.

In 1865, Thomas Wetherald sold the homestead at Puslinch, and
went to live at Rockwood. His wife Mary Wetherald died 4th June,
1867. She had issue three children, as below. Within the next few
years Thomas Wetherald seems to have removed to Maryland, U.S.A.

" On the 21st day of the 4th mo., 1874, Thomas Wetherald and
Elizabeth Haviland, daughter of Daniel P. and Lillias Haviland, of
Bryantown District, Charles County, Maryland, were married in a public
meeting of the Society of Friends, held at the home of the said Lillias

Haviland." Elizabeth Haviland was born 7th August, 1831. Her
niece married Thomas Wetherald's son by his first wife. In April,
1910, Thomas Wetherald (744), aged nearly eighty-eight years, and
his second wife, were living on the same farm (but not in the same house)
as his son Edward at La Plata, Maryland. His second wife is without
issue.

    i. Richard Wetherald (745), born 21st March, 1856, in Puslinch,
        Ontario. He died 12th November, 1885, unmarried.

    ii. John Edward Wetherald (746), whom see.

    iii. Mary Jane Wetherald (757), born 8th May, 1860, in Puslinch,
        Ontario ; died 21st August, 1860, an infant.

John Edward Wetherald (746), born 25th November, 1857, in
Puslinch, Ontario, Canada. In 1910 he owned a grain-mill at La Plata,
Maryland, U.S.A. He and his family live on the same farm, but not in
the same house, as his father.

He was married at a public meeting of the Society of Friends (held
in the home of the bride's parents), 13th October, 1881, to Lillias Gertrude
Haviland, who was born 2nd June, 1861, daughter of Philip H. and
Abigail A. Haviland, of Bryantown District, Charles County, Maryland,
U.S.A.

    i. William Philip Wetherald (747), born 29th December, 1882,
        near Bryantown, Md.

    ii. Mary Collom Wetherald (748), born 7th August, 1886, near
        Bryantown, Md.

    iii. Thomas Edward Wetherald (749), born 14th February, 1889,
        near Bryantown, Md.

    iv. Lewis Haviland Wetherald (750), born 30th June, 1890, near
        Bryantown, Md.

    v. Esther Wetherald (751), born 29th March, 1892, near Bryan-
        town, Md.

    vi. Joseph John Wetherald (752), born 23rd April, 1894, near
        Bryantown, Md.

vii. Alfred Edwin Wetherald (753), born 15th October, 1896, near Bryantown, Md.

viii. Samuel Wetherald (754), born 18th December, 1898, near Bryantown, Md.

ix. Lillias Gertrude Wetherald (755), born 19th June, 1903, near Bryantown, Md.

x. Edna E. Wetherald (756), born 11th February, 1905, near Bryantown, Md.

~~~~~~~~~~~~~~~~~~~~~~~~~~~~~~

John Wetherald (758), born 19th September, 1824, at Healaugh in the parish of Grinton, near Reeth, Swaledale, Yorkshire. While he was an infant his family removed to Wakefield, where his mother died in 1826. In 1835, he crossed from England to America in the ship " Hibernia," with his brothers William and Thomas, his sister Mary, and other relatives, and lived for some years on his father's farm at Puslinch, Ontario. In 1847 the latter gave up the management of the farm to his sons Thomas and John.

John Wetherald (758), was married in the Friends' Meeting House at Rockwood, Ontario, 20th October, 1852, to Sarah Matilda Smith, of Mountmellick, Queen's County, Ireland, who was born in Ireland 18th May, 1834.

In 1854 he sold his share of the Puslinch property to his brother Thomas, and " bought 100 acres of land near Rockwood, thirty cleared, ten chopped, a small log-house, and a good log barn for 1,500 dollars, which was considered reasonable, property having risen 150 per cent. in value in two years." His nephew notes, " 11 mo. 24, 1858, Uncle John Wetherald has let his farm, his lameness preventing his working it. His address now is Spring Grove Cottage, Rockwood." " 9 mo. 8, 1872, Uncle John and Aunt Sarah Matilda Wetherald have sold their farm and bought a ten acre lot about seven miles south of Rockwood, in Nassagawia."

In April, 1910, John and Sarah Matilda Wetherald were living a t Collins, New York State, U.S.A., without issue. The former has been an invalid for some time. He is a member of the Society of Friends, as are most of the descendants of his parents.

Jane Thistlethwaite (759), born 8th March, 1783, at Carr End, near Bainbridge, Wensleydale, co. York. She was married at Counterside Meeting House, 26th February, 1806, to John Thompson, born 15th January, 1781, hosiery manufacturer of Hawes, a small market town four miles higher up Wensleydale than Bainbridge, and about the same distance, by the moor-road, from Carr End. John Thompson was the son of John Thompson, hosier of Hawes (1742-1803), by his wife and first cousin, Margaret Routh, daughter of Richard Routh, of Appersett, by his wife Margaret Wetherald. On the 24th of April, 1822, they left Hawes for Kendal, Westmorland, where their youngest child was born.

John Thompson wrote an interesting diary, some extracts from which I have obtained. He writes on the 7th of 9th month 1812, " Stephen Grellett,* from America (but a native of France), came here on second day, had a public meeting here that evening, one on third day evening at Counterside, fourth-day at the old meeting-house in Swaledale, fifth day in Arkendale, and next day came to Carr End. On First day at 2 o'clock, the 13th of 9th month, a publick meeting in a field at Burton in Bishopdale, at which it was supposed there were 2,000 present. He came to our house that night."

Jane Thompson (759), died 7th November, 1847, at Kendal, and was buried in the Friends' Burial Ground there. John Thompson died 20th December, 1865, at Kendal, and was buried there also. It will be recollected that his sister Betsy married for her third husband, his wife's brother, John Thistlethwaite (582). John and Jane Thompson had issue :—

* One of the most famous Quaker ministers, a member of a " noble " French family.

i. John Thompson (760), whom see.

ii. Agnes Thompson (791), born 22nd January, 1809, at Hawes ; died 30th October, 1835, at Kendal, and buried there 3rd November, unmarried.

iii. Richard Thompson (792), whom see.

iv. William Thompson (814), born 30th July, 1813, at Hawes ; died 4th January, 1824, at Kendal, and was buried there.

v. Margaret Thompson (815), born 21st September, 1815, at Hawes; died 1881, unmarried.

vi. James Thompson (816), whom see.

vii. Sarah Thompson (817), whom see.

viii. Mary Thompson (830), whom see.

ix. Thomas Routh Thompson (840), born 15th January, 1824, at Kendal, and died there 25th February, 1824, an infant.

John Thompson (760), born 28th February, 1807, at Hawes, a small market town near the head of Wensleydale, Yorkshire. In 1822, he removed with his parents to Kendal, a larger old-fashioned town in the county of Westmorland. Here he was in partnership with his father in the hosiery business, but in 1853, he went to Leicester, and entered the fancy hosiery business. In 1865, he removed to Glasgow, and became a partner in the firm of Gray, Dunn & Co., the celebrated biscuit manu-facturers. He was a man of considerable local importance, and much respected. In 1889, he resided at Govan Park, Govan, Co. Lanark, a suburb of Glasgow, and died in the same district, 18th January, 1898, aged nearly ninety-one years. He was married first, 8th November, 1841, to Mary Spencer, of Bransby, Lincolnshire, who had issue an only child, and died 17th July, 1843.

i. John Thompson (761), whom see.

He was married secondly, 30th July, 1846, at Tirrel Meeting House (Co. Westmorland, on the road between Penrith and Pooley Bridge, Ulleswater), to Emma Wilson, born 18th August, 1821, daughter of John Wilson, of Netherfield, Kendal. She was living in July 1908, at Meadside,

Kilbarchan, Renfrewshire, and died there 10th January, 1909. She had issue,

> ii. Mary Emma Thompson (775), born 22nd July, 1847, at Kendal, and died unmarried, at Meadside, Kilbarchan, 17th April, 1906.
>
> iii. Jane Thompson (776), born 3rd November, 1848, at Kendal. In July, 1908, she was living unmarried at Meadside, Kilbarchan.
>
> iv. Sarah Agnes Thompson (777), born 23rd September, 1850, at Kendal. She died unmarried, at Leicester, 3rd March, 1860, and was buried there.
>
> v.   Sophia Thompson (778), born 17th November, 1851, at Kendal. She was living, unmarried, in July, 1908.
>
> vi. Wilson Thompson (779), born 30th April, 1853, at Kendal. In July, 1908, he was a grain merchant in Glasgow, and resided unmarried, with his mother, at Meadside, Kilbarchan.
>
> vii. James Thompson (780), born 1855, at Leicester, where he died in 1857.
>
> viii. Margaret Ann Thompson (781), whom see.
>
> ix. Alice Thompson (786), born 15th June, 1860, at Leicester. In July, 1908, she was living, unmarried.
>
> x.   Lucy Ellen Thompson (787), whom see.
>
> xi. James Alfred Thompson (790), born 11th September, 1864, at Leicester. He died there 25th February, 1865, the year in which his parents removed to Glasgow.

John Thompson (761), born 8th July, 1842, probably at Kendal. He emigrated to New Zealand in 1862, and was married 11th December, 1866, at Hepburn Street, Auckland, N.Z., to Christina Pollock.

> i. Mary Emma Thompson (762), whom see.
>
> ii. Christina Thompson (769), whom see.

iii. John Spencer Thompson (773), born 26th October, 1871 ;
     unmarried 1908.

iv. Frank Tertius Thompson (774), born 17th June, 1874. He
     was married 26th April, 1899, at Parnell, Auckland, New
     Zealand, to Eliza Matilda Ball, who was without issue
     in 1908.

Mary Emma Thompson (762), born 23rd November, 1867.
She was married 4th May, 1887, at St. Luke's Church, Mount Albert,
Auckland, New Zealand, to Henry White.

i. Rita White (763), born 11th September, 1888.

ii. Claude Spencer White (764), born 28th March, 1893.

iii Stanley Ward White (765), born 26th February, 1896.

iv. Mavis Victoria White (766), born 20th February, 1900, a twin.

v. John Valdare White (767), born 20th February, 1900, a twin.

vi. Arnold Carlisle Kessell White (768), born 2nd August, 1906.

Christina Thompson (769), born 2nd September, 1869. She was
married 11th September, 1899, at Knox Church, Parnell, Auckland, New
Zealand, to James Hamilton Buchanan.

i. Alma Hazel Buchanan (770), born 24th January, 1901.

ii. Olive Winnifred Buchanan (771), born 15th April, 1903.

iii. Ruby Joyce Buchanan (772), born 7th August, 1907.

Margaret Ann Thompson (781), born 23rd September, 1856,
at Leicester. She was married 1882, at Glasgow Friends' Meeting House,
to Robert Bird, a lawyer in Glasgow. He is the author of " Jesus of
Nazareth," a charming account of the life and surroundings of the human
Jesus, the miraculous or controversial elements being omitted.

i. Harold Robert Bird (782), born 8th April, 1884, at Glasgow.

ii. Wilfrid John Bird (783), born 8th December, 1887, at Glasgow.

iii. Ethelyn Margaret Bird (784), born 4th February, 1893, at
      Glasgow.

iv.   Elfrida Dorothy Bird (785), born 14th October, 1897, at
      Glasgow.

~~~~~~~~~~~~~~~~~~~~~~~~~~~~~~~~

Lucy Ellen Thompson (787), born 25th October, 1861, at
Leicester. She was married 6th September, 1894, at Gryffe House,
Bridge of Weir, Renfrewshire, to Thomas Smeal, tea-planter, of Assam,
India. He was born in 1842, youngest child of Dr. Smeal, of Glasgow,
and died 18th January, 1910, on landing from India. His eldest sister
married Richard Webster (843), who was first cousin to Lucy Ellen
Thompson's father.

i.   Routh Wigham Smeal (788), born 28th June, 1895, at Glasgow,
      Scotland.

ii.   John Thompson Wigham Smeal (789), born 14th April, 1897,
      at Glasgow.

~~~~~~~~~~~~~~~~~~~~~~~~~~~~~~~~

Richard Thompson (792), born 15th March, 1811, at Hawes, in
Wensleydale, Yorkshire. Shortly before and after his marriage he lived
in Whitehaven, Cumberland, but in about 1838, he removed to Gainsborough, in Lincolnshire. Here he spent the rest of his life, and died
20th May, 1888, a minister in the Society of Friends. He was a grocer
and tea dealer.

He was married, in 1836, to Mary Maw Palian, daughter of Thomas
and Ann Palian. Thomas Palian was convinced of the principles of the
Society of Friends before he married Ann Maw, of Gainsborough.

i.   Agnes Ann Thompson (793), born 28th May, 1837, at White-
      haven ; educated at the Mount School, York, 8 mo. 1853
      to 6 mo. 1854. In 1909, she was living unmarried at 6,
      Morton Terrace, Gainsborough.

ii. Louisa Thompson (794), born 17th August, 1839, at Gains-
     borough. In 1909 she was unmarried, and living at 6,
     Morton Terrace, Gainsborough.

iii. Caroline Thompson (795), whom see.

iv. Richard Thompson (808), whom see.

v.   Charles Thompson (809), whom see.

vi. Mary Jane Thompson (812), whom see.

vii. Sophia Thompson (813), born 22nd February, 1854, at Gains-
     borough ; educated at the Mount School, York, 1 mo. 1869
     to 6 mo, 1871. In 1909 she was living unmarried, at 6,
     Morton Terrace, Gainsborough.

Caroline Thompson (795), born 26th February, 1841, at Gainsborough, Lincolnshire. She was married 29th June, 1865, at Gainsborough
to Joseph John Robson, wholesale and retail grocer and tea-dealer, of
Saffron Walden, Essex.

Alderman Joseph John Robson, J.P., was born in 1828, and married
firstly, Elizabeth Bayes, who died, I believe, without issue. He was a
son of John Stephenson Robson, of Saffron Walden (uncle of Joseph
Joshua Green, the genealogist), by his wife Rachel Green (aunt of Joseph
Joshua Green).   John Stephenson Robson was son of Elizabeth Stephenson, by her husband Thomas Robson, of Liverpool, who was son of
Thomas Robson, of Darlington, by his wife Margaret Pease, daughter of
the first Edward Pease, of Darlington, by his wife Elizabeth Coates. See
Chart VIII.

Joseph John Robson gave up his business nearly two years ago, and
in June, 1910, was living with his wife at Westbourne, Saffron Walden.

i.   Francis John Robson (796), whom see.

ii. Mary Adelaide Robson (799), whom see.

iii. Charles Edward Robson (803), whom see.

iv. Caroline Josephine May Robson (807), born 1st May, 1872, at
     Saffron Walden, and was unmarried in 1910.

Francis John Robson (796), born 30th March, 1866, at Saffron Walden, Essex. He was married 9th April, 1901, at Devonshire House Meeting House, London, to Emily Adelaide Taylor, of Peterhead, and was assistant to Theobald & Son, grocers, of Bath, in 1910, having previously assisted his father.

    i. Eric John Robson (797), born 12th August, 1904, at Saffron Walden.

    ii. Charles Harold Alwyn Robson (798), born 30th August, 1908, at Saffron Walden.

Mary Adelaide Robson (799), born 9th August, 1867, at Saffron Walden, Essex, and educated at the Mount School, York, 1 mo. 1882 to 6 mo. 1885. She was married 17th April, 1895, to Harold John Morland, son of Charles Morland, of Croydon, by his wife Jane Fryer. They reside at Khoja, Harewood Road, Croydon, near London. Harold J. Morland is a Master of Arts, and partner in the firm of Price, Waterhouse & Co., Chartered Accountants, London, and elsewhere. He was an assistant master at Bootham School, York, from 1888 to 1891.

    i. Kenneth Harold Morland (800), born 1st March, 1900, at Croydon.

    ii. Oscar Charles Morland (801), born 23rd March, 1904, at Croydon.

    iii. Joseph Morland (802), born 10th March, 1909, at Croydon.

Charles Edward Robson (803), born 27th December, 1868, at Saffron Walden, Essex. He was married at Kelvedon, 13th April, 1898, to Mary Jesup Barratt, daughter of George and Sarah Barratt, of Kelvedon. They were living at Elsenham, Essex, in 1909, he having previously been in his father's business.

    i Dorothy Mary Robson (804), born 30th January, 1900, at Saffron Walden.

ii. Alice Margaret Robson (805), born 25th April, 1903, at Saffron Walden.

iii. Kathleen May Robson (806), born 1st May, 1909, at Elsenham, Essex.

Richard Thompson (808), born 15th September, 1842, at Gainsborough. He has lived in York since the latter part of 1859, where he is a manufacturer of artificial manure. He has been Sheriff of the City of York. He was married 20th June, 1882, at Birkenhead, to Mary Hannah Thistlethwaite (174), daughter of John and Deborah Thistlethwaite, whom see. By their Hunter ancestry they were third cousins, and by their Thistlethwaite ancestry fourth cousins. See Chart IV.

i. Geoffrey Thompson (175), born 10th August, 1883, educated at Bootham School, York, 9 mo. 1896 to 7 mo. 1899. He was unmarried in 1910.

Charles Thompson (809), born 1st May, 1845, at Gainsborough. He was married 20th April, 1887, to Florence Parker, daughter of Hewson and Maria Parker, of Grimsby. In 1909, he was in business as grocer, in Gainsborough.

i. Hugh Vernon Thompson (810), born 8th February 1888, at Gainsborough.

ii. Edward Leslie Thompson (811), born 11th March, 1896, at Gainsborough.

Mary Jane Thompson (812), born 25th December, 1847, at Gainsborough. She was married in May, 1893, to Frederick Isaac Reckitt, of Hull, as his second wife. He was a son of Isaac and Ann Reckitt, and brother to Sir James Reckitt, Bart., head of the firm of blue manufacturers, Hull. They were living in Hull in 1910 without issue.

James Thompson (816), born 29th May, 1817, at Hawes in Wensleydale, Yorkshire. He resided for many years at Singleton Park, Kendal, Westmorland, where he was a card manufacturer. He died 14th June, 1895, aged seventy-eight years, without issue. He was married in the summer of 1858, at Brighton, to Sarah Bass, only daughter of Isaac and Sarah Bass, of Brighton.

Sarah Thompson, *née* Bass, was born in 1819, " cousin to Daniel Pryor Hack. After leaving school she became associated with her mother in a great variety of philanthropic and charitable agencies ; and to the end of her life she delighted to minister to the wants of the ignorant and destitute, by whom her visits were warmly welcomed. Being deprived of her mother in 1852, and continuing to live with her father during the two or three remaining years of his life, she sought with great filial devoted-ness to contribute to his comfort and happiness, and to soothe his declining years."

She was a minister in the Society of Friends. " In the year 1865 she accompanied Rebecca Collins of New York, in a religious visit to Friends in Germany and the South of France, for which she was somewhat specially qualified ; not only by her ability to sympathise with the exercises of her dear companion and to take part with her in meetings for worship, but also by her knowledge of the German and French languages, and by the lengthened visits she had previously paid to some intimate friends in the South of France and at Minden." She died at Kendal, 29th October, 1869, aged fifty years.

Sarah Thompson (817), born 4th May, 1819, at the " Holme," Hawes, in Wensleydale, Yorkshire. Her parents and family removed to Kendal, Westmorland, in 1822, and here she was married 24th October, 1850, to Samuel Alexander Jefferys.

She was a minister in the Society of Friends, and " resided at Melksham upwards of twenty years, beloved by all who knew her." " Indeed, beyond the home circle she had the power of giving herself out to others in large-hearted sympathy, so that persons of all ages and classes found in her a true helper ; and it was her great desire to lead them from a dependence upon human aid and counsel, to the only sure source of strength and comfort . . . her valuable assistance and counsel in the management of the British School are greatly missed." She died at Melksham, 17th June, 1871, aged fifty-two years, and was buried in the Friends' Burial Ground there.

Samuel Alexander Jefferys was born 17th August, 1804, at Melksham. He resided at Coburg Place, Melksham, until 1875, when he removed to Cirencester, Gloucestershire. Here he died 20th May, 1880, and was buried in the local Friends' Burial Ground. His parents were Thomas Jefferys, of Melksham (born 21st of 2 mo., 1773, died 17th of 12 mo., 1850), and his wife Martha Alexander, of Needham Market (born 1775, died 3rd of 2 mo., 1851 at Melksham). Samuel Alexander Jefferys' daughter writes : " on my father's side we have good charts carrying us back prior to the rise of Friends in the Jefferys, Alexander and Gurney* families."

   i.   Samuel Alexander Jefferys (818), born 2nd October, 1851, at Melksham. In 1909 he was living unmarried, not in business.

   ii.   Edward Jefferys (819), born 20th July, 1853, at Melksham. He died unmarried 28th December, 1885, and was interred at Davos Platz Cemetery, Switzerland.

   iii.   John Henry Jefferys (820), whom see.

   iv.   Jane Mary Jefferys (828), born 29th March, 1857, at Melksham. In 1910 she was residing at Upperthorpe, Darlington, unmarried.

   v.   Martha Louisa Jefferys (829), born 18th May, 1859, at Melksham. In 1910 she was residing at Upperthorpe, Darlington, unmarried.

John Henry Jefferys (820), born 21st April, 1855, at Melksham, Wiltshire. He resided near Kendal, Westmorland, in which town his

* See "The Gurneys of Earlham," 2 vols., by Augustus J. C. Hare. The Gurneys were famous Quaker bankers.

business as card manufacturer was situated. He died 31st July, 1903, and was buried in the Friends' Burial Ground, Kendal.

He was married 20th April, 1887, at Rochdale Meeting House, to Mary Agnes Smithson, who was born 23rd November, 1855, daughter of Thomas and Emma Smithson of Facit, Rochdale, Lancashire. In 1909 she and her family were living at Kendal.

i.　Millicent Jefferys (821), born 24th February, 1888, at Kendal ; unmarried April 1910. Educated at Polam Hall, Darlington, and Somerville College, Oxford.

ii.　Bryan Jefferys (822), born 21st July, 1889, at Kendal. He was educated at Leighton Park School, Reading, 9 mo., 1903, to 4 mo., 1908, and in April, 1910, was employed in his father's business in Kendal.

iii.　Edward Jefferys (823), born 9th November, 1890, at Kendal. He was educated at Leighton Park School, Reading, 9 mo., 1903 to 7 mo., 1909.

iv.　Cecily Jefferys (824), born 3rd January, 1892, at Kendal ; educated at Polam Hall, Darlington.

v.　Barbara Jefferys (825), born 18th July, 1893, at Kendal ; in 1910 at Polam Hall, Darlington.

vi.　Nancy Jefferys (826), born 11th November, 1894, at Kendal ; in 1910 at Polam Hall, Darlington.

vii.　Guy Jefferys (827), born 11th July, 1898, at Kendal.

Mary Thompson (830), born 30th July, 1821, at Hawes in Wensleydale, Yorkshire. She was married at Kendal in 1847 to William Cudworth, an engineer, who for many years lived at Darlington in the employment of the North Eastern Railway. He was a much respected man, and died at Darlington in 1906. His wife, Mary Cudworth (830), died in 1882.

i.　William John Cudworth (831), whom see.

    ii.   Francis Cudworth (832), born at Darlington in 1850, died in 1858.

   iii.   Rachel Mary Cudworth (833), whom see.

   iv.   Jane Cudworth (838), born at Darlington, 10th October, 1854, died in 1873, unmarried.

    v.   Alfred James Cudworth (839), born at Darlington, 13th July, 1857. He married Anna Bethia Smith, of Braintree, who was educated at the Mount School, York, 2 mo., 1871 to 6 mo., 1873. In 1909, he was a member of the firm of Impey, Cudworth & Lakin-Smith, Chartered Accountants, Birmingham. He is without issue.

William John Cudworth (831), born 5th April, 1849, at Darlington. Until within a few months of his death in 1910, he was head engineer for the northern half of the North-Eastern Railway. He resided at Butt's Close, Tadcaster Road, York.

He was married 1st September, 1880, at Birkenhead, to his fourth cousin, Margaret Thistlethwaite (167), whom see.

For particulars of their children see Part One. See also Chart IV. and Chart VIII.

    i.   Margaret Cudworth (168), whom see.

   ii.   Mary Cudworth (169), whom see.

   iii.   William Oswald Cudworth (170), whom see.

   iv.   Helen Cudworth (171), whom see.

Rachel Mary Cudworth (833), born 4th April, 1853, at Darlington. She was married 18th September, 1879, at Darlington, to Brightwen Binyon, an architect by profession, and a pupil of Alfred Waterhouse, R.A. He was born 30th May, 1845, and died 21st September, 1905.

    i.   Janet Binyon (834), born 6th August, 1880, at Ipswich. She was educated at the Mount School, York, 9 mo., 1896, to 7 mo., 1898, while her parents were living at Felixstowe. She then studied at Westfield College, London, and in 1901

became Bachelor of Arts of London University. She was
unmarried in June, 1910.

ii. Mary Sims Binyon (835), born 22nd May, 1882, at Ipswich,
unmarried in June, 1910.

iii. Basil Binyon (836), born 23rd April, 1885, at Ipswich. He
was educated at Bootham School, York, 9 mo., 1897, to
7 mo., 1902, and at Leighton Park School, Reading, September, 1902, to July, 1904. He studied at Trinity College,
Cambridge, and took his B.A. degree in 1907. He is now
an engineer employed at the Marconi Wireless Telegraphy
Station, Slough. In June, 1910, he was living with his
mother at Burlington House, High Street, Slough, unmarried.

iv. Olive Binyon (837), born 4th April, 1888, at Ipswich. She
was educated at the Mount School, York, 9 mo., 1902, to
12 mo., 1904, and was unmarried in June, 1910.

Rachel Thistlethwaite (842), born 28th October, 1789, at
Carr End, in Wensleydale. While her parents were living at Shawcote she
was married at Bainbridge Meeting House, Wensleydale, 19th September,
1816, to John Webster. He was a linen manufacturer, of Sowerby, near
Thirsk, Yorkshire. He was born 21st February, 1780, son of Francis
Webster, husbandman, of Sowerby, by his wife Elinor.

John Webster died at Sowerby, aged forty-one years, 20th November,
1821, a "linen-weaver," and was buried 25th November, at Thirsk. His
widow died in 1834.

i. Ellen Webster (843), born 22nd July, 1817, at Sowerby. She
died 29th December, 1829, "aged about 12½," at Ackworth,
and was buried there 3rd January, 1830.

ii. Richard Webster (844), whom see.

iii. Agnes Webster (847), whom see.

Richard Webster (844), born 1st June, 1819, at Sowerby, near Thirsk, Yorkshire. He lived at Blackburn, in Lancashire, where it is said that he was a tea-merchant, and later a mill-owner. He was married (? in 1862) to Hannah Smeal, eldest daughter of Dr. Smeal, of Glasgow. Her youngest brother (there were at least five in the family), who was born in 1842, married Richard Webster's first cousin once removed, Lucy Ellen Thompson (787).

Richard Webster (844), is said to have died " in his daughter's childhood." His widow, Hannah Webster, died about four years ago, somewhere in Australia, where she had gone to see her children.

     i.   Frank Webster (844a), was a mining engineer, and married Ruby Macintyre, of Melbourne, Australia. He died before 1909. He had issue two girls and one boy.

   ii.   Jane Smeal Webster (845), was married 29th September, 1909, at the Grand Hotel, Glasgow, to James Hodge, of Ardgarten, Pollokshields, Glasgow, tobacco-merchant, son of the late James and Catherine Hodge.

  iii.   Alfred Webster (846), studied medicine at Glasgow University, and was practising somewhere in Western Australia in 1909. He married, and has issue one boy.

***

Agnes Webster (847), born 10th June, 1821, at Sowerby, near Thirsk, Yorkshire. She was married about 1842 to Oswald Baynes, a Quaker horse-dealer. She and her husband and her uncle, Richard Thistlethwaite (863), are said to have lived together " for many years at Carr End, near Semerwater," Wensleydale. Agnes Baynes (847) died 28th June, 1879, at Rimington, near Guisburn, Yorkshire, aged fifty-eight years.

Oswald Baynes was born 28th June, 1818, at Carperby, in Wensleydale. He was married secondly at Birkenhead, 1st January, 1881, to Martha Ecroyd Smith. She was born 6th April, 1833, at Doncaster, Yorkshire, ninth daughter of Henry and Maria Smith. Oswald Baynes, whose residence was then at Airton, Bell Busk, near Skipton, Yorkshire, died 7th February, 1891, and was buried at Sawley. In 1909, his widow was living at Airton, *sine prole*.

Oswald Baynes appears to have been son of Oswald Baynes by his wife Isabella Hunter, daughter of John Hunter, of Hebblethwaite Hall, by his wife Ann Middlebrook. See Chart III. From the Chart it will be seen that Oswald Baynes who married Agnes Webster (847) had an uncle John Baynes, who married Agnes Thistlethwaite (301), and a brother John Baynes, who married Jane Bradley (409).*

Agnes Baynes (847) had ten children, most of whom were born at Craikhall, near Kendal. Four of them died in early childhood, probably at Bramhall, near Stockport. Those who survived were as follows, viz. :—

    i.   John Baynes (848), who, at the age of twenty-one, was a cotton-broker on the Exchange at Calcutta, India. He married Nellie ——, who is said to have been the daughter of an Indian General. He apparently emigrated to America, and was deceased in 1909, but his widow was surviving.

        i.   Ernest Harold Baynes (849), who was in 1909 a journalist, married, and living at Meriden, New Hampshire, U.S.A. He is said to have successfully trained bison as domestic animals.

        ii.   Lilian Baynes (850), who married an artist who lived in New York, but she is said to be without issue.

        iii.   John Reginald Baynes (851), living in America in 1909, married.

    ii.   Oswald Baynes (852), born in 1845. He was married 1st October, 1873, at Downham Market, Norfolk, to Eliza Bunkall, daughter of William Bunkall of the same place. He was a horse-dealer in New York, U.S.A., and died 23rd October, 1895, without issue. His widow married a second time. After removing to America she preferred to be

* I have not proved this Baynes genealogy from the registers.

known as Azile, using the letters of her Christian name
reversed.

iii. Richard Baynes (853), whom see.

iv. Rachel Baynes (858), born 2nd April, 1848, died in Greenbank
Hospital, Darlington, unmarried, 19th July, 1894, buried
at Sawley.

v. Isabel Baynes (859), born in 1850, died unmarried, in 1868.

vi. Joseph Webster Baynes (860), born in 1852. He lived in
Glasgow, and appears to have been a printer. He died
14th July, 1893, and his widow was surviving in 1909.

i. Bernard Baynes (861), born in 1882, died in 1894.

Richard Baynes (853), born in 1846 at Craikhall, near Kendal,
Westmorland. He was married 21st May, 1873, at Carlisle, to Patience
Sutton, who was born 7th June, 1841, at Houghton, near Carlisle, daughter
of Clement Sheldon and Mary Sutton. Richard Baynes (853), died 13th
July, 1899, probably at Penrith, and his widow was living in 1909, at
Ranmere, Upton Park, Chester.

i. Ida Mary Baynes (854), born 1874, at Lysham. Died unmarried, in 1902.

ii. Richard Algernon Baynes (855), born 1878, at Martin Top, near
Clitheroe. He was married at Moosejaw, 31st January,
1910, while resident at Broadview, to Mattie Bird, of
Broadview, Saskatchewan, Canada.

iii. Mabel Agnes Baynes (856), born 1879, at Liscard in Cheshire.
She was married 19th February, 1907, at Carlisle, to Dr.
G. H. Grills.

iv. Herbert Oswald Baynes (857), born 1883, at Liscard in Cheshire,
unmarried in 1910.

Richard Thistlethwaite (863), born 28th October, 1797, at
Carr End in Wensleydale. " Richard Thistlethwaite, of Blackburn, in
the county of Lancaster, tea-dealer, son of Richard Thistlethwaite,

of Carr End, farmer, and Agnes his wife (both deceased), and Sarah
Yeardley, of Rochdale in the county of Lancaster, daughter of Thomas
Yeardley, of Ecclesfield in the county of York, flax spinner, and Elizabeth
[Hodgson] his wife (both deceased) " were married at Rochdale Meeting
House, 13th April, 1859.   The following witnesses signed the marriage
certificate :—

Relations :

John Yeardley

Agnes Yeardley (585)

Ann Yeardley

Rd. Webster (844)

Oswald Baynes

Agnes Baynes (847)

Frances Yeardley

Alfred Yeardley (586)

Joseph Deaville

Frances Deaville

————

Maria White

Martha Midgley

Elizabeth Midgley

Henry King

Mary H. Martindale

Esther Bancroft

Agnes Sharp

Sarah Beresford

Ruth Ashworth

Margt. Elizth Bright

Maria Briggs

Edw. Briggs

Helen P. Bright

Ursula M. Bright

Catharine White

Thomas Blakey

Mgt. E. White

James Mills

John Mills

John A. Bright

John Smithson

Wm L. Bright

Mary H. Bright

John Harman

Lydia Rous

Hannah Benson

Martha West

Sarah Mills.

Richard Thistlethwaite (863) appears to have lived at Carr End
for some time with his niece Agnes Webster (847), and her husband,
Oswald Baynes.   His *wife*, Sarah Yeardley, was sister to John Yeardley,
who married his *niece*, Agnes Wetherald (585).   Richard Thistlethwaite
(863) died at Bough Hey, near Preston, in Lancashire, 2nd July, 1864,
without issue.   His widow, Sarah Thistlethwaite, lived for some years

at Bristol, with Lucy Taylor (1451), who had married Alfred Yeardley (586), the former's own nephew and her husband's great-nephew. She died while visiting Weston-super-Mare, 6th April, 1888, aged seventy-seven years.

Margaret Thistlethwaite (864), born 4th December, 1745 or 1746, in Dent Dale. "Margaret Thistlethwaite, daughter of James Thistlethwaite, husbandman, and Isabel, his wife, deceased, of Carr End," was married at Countersett Meeting House, 7th April, 1779, to Christopher Myers, of Woodend House. Except that they had at least one child, I know nothing further of either Christopher or Margaret Myers.

    i.   Isabel Myers (865), who appears to have lived unmarried at Burtersett, in Wensleydale. She died 5th November, 1868, probably at Burtersett.

Anthony Thistlethwaite (867), born 23rd March, 1752, within the compass of Yorkshire Quarterly Meeting of the Society of Friends. His parents, James and Isabel Thistlethwaite, are described as "of Scarhouse Meeting" at the time of his birth. Anthony Thistlethwaite of Preston, in Lancashire, clogger, son of James and Isabel Thistlethwaite of Wensleydale, was married at Preston Meeting House, 7th June, 1786, to Ann Brown, daughter of John and Ann Brown, of "Skepton," Yorkshire.

Anthony Thistlethwaite (867), appears to have removed from Preston to Manchester in 1791, and to have become a confectioner at the latter place. He died at Manchester, 3rd January, 1823, aged seventy-one years, and was buried there on the 7th January, a "non-member."

His widow, Ann Thistlethwaite, died at Manchester, 12th February, 1829, aged sixty-eight years, and was buried there on the 15th February, a "member." Her brother, George Brown, married her husband's sister, Rachel Thistlethwaite (560). I have been able to trace no living descendants of Anthony and Ann Thistlethwaite. They had issue :—

i. James Thistlethwaite (868), born 26th March, 1787, at Preston, died at Manchester, 15th June, 1811, buried 18th June, at Lancaster, aged twenty-four years.

ii. John Thistlethwaite (869), born 21st December, 1788, at Preston ; no further information.

iii. Richard Thistlethwaite (870), born 11th February, 1791, at Preston. He died there 25th October, 1791, aged eight months, and was buried there two days later.

iv. Isabel Thistlethwaite (871), whom see.

v. William Thistlethwaite (872), whom see.

vi. Ann Thistlethwaite (874), born 15th May, 1796, at Manchester ; died there " a spinster " aged forty years, 18th February, 1837. She was buried at Mount Street, Manchester, 23rd February, a " member."

vii. Rachel Thistlethwaite (875), born 25th October, 1800, at Manchester. She died there 11th June, 1828, unmarried, and was buried there 15th June.

viii. Anthony Thistlethwaite (876), born 15th September, 1803, at Manchester. He died there 8th November, 1804, aged fourteen months, and was buried there on 11th November.

Isabel Thistlethwaite (871), born 8th September, 1792, at Manchester. She appears to have died unmarried in her old age, leaving a will which required a pedigree making, showing her first cousins on both her father's and her mother's sides. A copy of such a pedigree, in which she is described as " Isabel Thistlethwaite, the Testatrix," was lent me by the grandson of her first cousin, Isabella Guy, *née* Thistlethwaite (435). This pedigree bears the date " November, 1869." It shows that her mother had a sister, Sarah Brown, who was married 19th December, 1792, at Kirkham, Lancashire, to John Taylor, and had issue a son, John Taylor, who was born 23rd April, 1794, and baptised at Preston. No mention of any of Isabel Thistlethwaite's brothers or sisters is made in the pedigree.

William Thistlethwaite (872), born 16th June, 1794, at Manchester. He appears to have been a book-keeper at Hollinwood in the township of Oldham, Lancashire, in 1832. He died at Manchester, 24th February, 1834, aged forty years, a book-keeper, and was buried on 27th February, at Mount Street, Manchester, a "non-member." He was probably disowned for his marriage to Martha ————, who appears to have been a non-Quaker. They had at least one child, but no birth entries appear in the Quaker Register.

    i. Henry Thistlethwaite (873), died 11th February, 1832, aged nineteen months, at Hollinwood, and was buried 15th February, at Manchester.

PART THREE.

DESCENDANTS OF

MARGARET THISTLETHWAITE (877),

THIRD CHILD OF

WILLIAM THISTLETHWAITE (1), OF HARBORGILL.

PART THREE.

Margaret Thistlethwaite (877), born 25th April, 1710, at Harborgill, in Dent Dale. She was married 26th December, 1737, to Alexander Fothergill, farmer and lawyer of Carr End, near Bainbridge, Wensleydale, Yorkshire. He was born at Carr End, 22nd November, 1709, and had married in 1732, as his first wife, Jane Blakey, who died at Carr End, 1st March, 1735, having issue two daughters. Of these, Margaret was born 29th February, 1734, and died three days later ; Jane was born 28th February, 1735, and married a Harker. See Chart VII.

Alexander Fothergill was the eldest son of the celebrated Quaker preacher and traveller, John Fothergill* of Carr End (2nd 11 mo., 1675 to 13th 11 mo., 1744), by his first wife Margaret Hough, of Marsh Gate, near Sutton, in Cheshire, whom he married 5th March, 1709.

From the Quaker Tithe-Book now at Carperby, Wensleydale, it appears that on the 13th of April, 1764, Alexander Fothergill possessed one cow and one calf, for which, with costs and arrears, the tithe amounted to eleven shillings and a penny. One ham was distrained, which at $5\frac{3}{4}$d. per lb. for 20-lbs. made 9s. 7d., leaving one shilling and sixpence in arrears.

---

* See the " Memoirs of Samuel and John Fothergill," published 1843 (Liverpool : Marples ; London : Gilpin) compiled by George Crosfield, who married Margaret Chorley, grand-daughter of Samuel Fothergill's brother, Joseph Fothergill. John Fothergill spent many years in America, and his son Samuel travelled in that country with my great-great-great-great-great-great-uncle, Joshua Dixon, of Raby, another Quaker minister. Samuel's and Alexander's brother, John Fothergill, jun., was the eminent doctor and founder of Ackworth School. Only Alexander and Joseph left descendants : the latter's two sons died young, but his daughters had issue. I hope to treat the Fothergill family fully in my second volume.

Alexander Fothergill died at Counterside, 21st January, 1788, and was interred at Bainbridge. The Carr End property passed to his second surviving son, William Fothergill (1021). Margaret Fothergill (877), widow, died 30th April, 1798, at Carr End, and was interred at Bainbridge, on the 3rd of May. She had issue :

i.   Alexander Fothergill (878), born 8th or 9th October, 1738, at Carr End. According to the Quaker register, he died " 21st 10 mo., 1750, aged twelve years and twelve days, a boarder at the school at Skipton, and was buried at Skipton."

ii.   Ann Fothergill (879), born 19th December, 1741, at Carr End (Old Style). She married James Freeman ; I never heard of descendants, but there may have been such.

iii. John Fothergill (880), whom see.

iv.   Alice Fothergill (1020), born 7th September, 1745, at Carr End. She married John Chorley, of London, retired linen-draper, residing at Tottenham. Alice Chorley (1020) died at her house in Tottenham, 11th April, 1828, and was interred at Winchmore Hill, the 18th day of the same, *sine prole.* While living at the " village of Tottenham," 1795, she dictated to her niece, Elizabeth Fothergill, an interesting account of her Thistlethwaite relatives, most of which has been split up, and appears in various parts of this volume.

v.   William Fothergill (1021), whom see.

vi.   Thomas Fothergill (1089), born 19th August, 1751, at Carr End, co. York. He was resident in London in the profession of the law, and died at the house of his sister, Alice Chorley (1020), in Tottenham, 11th October, 1822, unmarried.

John Fothergill (880), born 7th March, 1743, at Carr End. He married, in 1771, Mary Ann Forbes, daughter of Timothy Forbes, of Coleman Street, London. She died 20th January, 1797, aged fifty years, at Poppleton near York, and was buried at York. Her brother, Charles Forbes, had large coffee plantations in Jamaica, and in his grounds her son, Dr. Samuel Fothergill, was buried. She was also sister to James Forbes, an artist, who died at Aix-la-Chapelle, whose daughter married Marc René, Comte de Montalembert, and became mother, in 1810, of Charles Forbes René, Comte de Montalembert, the celebrated French Catholic author and politician. Timothy Forbes was a kinsman of the present nineteenth Baron Forbes, premier baron of Scotland. They both descend from the first Lord Forbes, who married a daughter of the King of Scotland in the thirteenth century.

. John Fothergill (880) is described as ironmonger of Leeds from 1772 to 1777, and after 1778 as " comb-maker " and " ivory-manufacturer " of York. There he died 13th March, 1807, and there he was buried. He was married secondly, in 1803, to Susannah Reynolds, by whom he had no issue. She died 5th August, 1807, aged forty-two years, and was buried on the 13th August, at Croydon, near London.

    i.   Mary Ann Fothergill (881), born 3rd December, 1772, at Leeds, Yorkshire. She died 20th December, 1774, at Leeds, and was buried there.

    ii.   John Fothergill (882), whom see.

    iii.   Alexander Fothergill (912), born 13th June, 1776, at Leeds. He died 4th January, 1797, when his father was living at Poppleton, near York, and was buried at York, unmarried.

    iv.   Elizabeth Fothergill (913), born 23rd August, 1777, at Leeds. In 1795 she was living with her aunt, Alice Chorley (1020), at Tottenham ; she died at York, 25th February, 1856, unmarried.

    v.   Samuel Fothergill (914), born 6th September, 1778, at York ; died there 13th September, 1778, and was buried there.

    vi.   Samuel Fothergill (915), whom see.

    vii.   Charles Fothergill (925), whom see.

    viii.   Margaret Fothergill (1017), whom see.

ix. Mary Ann Fothergill (1019), born 19th April, 1786. She is
      said to have married Daniel Mayer, but left no surviving
      issue.

John Fothergill (882), born 5th February, 1774, at Leeds,
Yorkshire. He was married 9th September, 1801, at St. Peter's, Nottingham, to Rebecca Bott, he being then described as of the parish of St. Trinity,
York. He followed the same occupation as his father, namely that of
manufacturer of ivory combs and the like articles. He died 16th April,
1823, at Acomb, near York. Rebecca Bott was the daughter of George
Bott, a dentist in Nottingham, and London in the season ; there her
portrait was painted by Romney in payment of a debt for dentistry.

i. Rebecca Fothergill (883), born 18th July, 1802, at York ;
      died 26th March, 1837, at Edinburgh, unmarried.

ii. John Alexander Fothergill (884), born 10th November, 1804,
      at York ; died 13th May, 1826, at Acomb, unmarried.

iii. Mary Ann Fothergill (885), whom see.

iv. Elizabeth Fothergill (905), born 28th September, 1808, at
      York. She was married 1830 to Edward Cruickshank,
      and died 24th September, 1838, at Edinburgh, having issue :

  i. Susan Anna Cruickshank (906), died aged eleven
        months.

  ii. Anna Eliza Cruickshank (907), died 1838, aged ten
        months.

v. Anna Fothergill (908), born 2nd June, 1810, at York, died
      there 1832, unmarried.

vi. Margaret Fothergill (909), born 12th December, 1811, at York,
      died there 14th July, 1834, unmarried.

vii. George William Fothergill (910), born 19th August, 1813, at
      York, died there 15th August, 1840, unmarried. An
      artist.

viii. Charlotte Fothergill (911), born 24th October, 1817, at York,
      died there 9th December, 1841, unmarried.

Mary Ann Fothergill (885), born 13th February, 1807, at York. She was married 3rd July, 1838, to Robert Watson, of Mansfield, a lace merchant of that place, exporting to South America and the East Indies. She died 12th August, 1860, at Nottingham, having issue :

   i. Forbes Watson (886), born 7th February, 1840, at Mansfield, Nottinghamshire. He was a doctor of medicine in Nottingham, and died there, unmarried, 28th August, 1869.

  ii. Fothergill Watson (887), whom see.

 iii. Margaret Anna Watson (903), born 26th November, 1844, at Mansfield, living 1909 unmarried.

 iv. Henry Whitfield Watson (904), born 12th April, 1849, at Mansfield. He was a dentist, but has not communicated with his relatives for many years.

Fothergill Watson (887), by deed poll transposed his name to Watson Fothergill, December, 1892. He was born 12th July, 1841, at Mansfield, and was, in 1910, an architect at 15, George Street, Nottingham. He married Anne Hage, and has issue :

   i. Marian Watson (888), born 29th June, 1868, at Nottingham. She was married at St. Andrew's, Nottingham, 18th April, 1895, to William Sydney Reid, ship-broker, of Odessa, Russia.

      i. Christian Fothergill Reid (889), born 23rd February, 1896, at Odessa, died 23rd October, 1900.

     ii. Isabelle Fothergill Reid (890), born 10th October, 1900, at Odessa.

  ii. Annie Forbes Watson (891), born 24th November, 1869, at Nottingham. She was married at St. Andrew's, Nottingham, 26th April, 1893, to Philip Boobbyer, doctor of medicine.

      i. Philip Watson Boobbyer (892), born 9th January, 1896, at Nottingham.

     ii. Annie Isobel Boobbyer (893), born 20th July, 1898, at Nottingham.

   iii. Victor Hirst Boobbyer (894), born 19th February,
     1901, at Nottingham.

   iv. Frances Forbes Boobbyer (895), born 16th July,
     1902, at Nottingham.

  iii. Edith Mary Watson (896), born 6th March, 1871, at Notting-
    ham. She was married at Islington Parish Church, Middle-
    sex, 22nd October, 1907, to Rev. James Lewis, Vicar of
    St. Mark's, Nottingham, *sine prole*.

  iv. Eleanor Fothergill Watson (897), born 25th June, 1872, at
    Nottingham. She was married at All Saints', Nottingham,
    25th July, 1894, to Georg Ellenberger, professor of music.

   i. George Fothergill Ellenberger (898), born 10th July,
     1895, at Nottingham.

   ii. Clarita Lilian Ellenberger (899), born 29th January,
     1897, at Nottingham.

  v. Samuel Fothergill Watson Fothergill (900), born 23rd December,
    1874, at Nottingham, unmarried 1909.

  vi. Harold Hage Watson Fothergill (901), born 28th April, 1876,
    at Nottingham, died 1st September, 1905, unmarried.

  vii. Clarice Watson Fothergill (902), born 21st September, 1877,
    at Nottingham, unmarried 1909.

Samuel Fothergill (915), born 23rd March, 1780, at York. His
widow, at the age of eighty-four, wrote a short account of his life, from
which I gain the following particulars :

He went to a good school at York ; thence he travelled to London
and served his time with eminent practitioners, named Pope and
Lottall, living at Staines. After this he took his degree at Glasgow
University, and returned to London. When living in Leicester
Square he was appointed physician to " the Asylum in the Westminster
Road and many other Institutes of eminence in London." He was also

physician to Queen Victoria's mother, the Duchess of Kent, when she was at Weymouth for her health.

"He then practised most successfully for several years in Leicester Square, when [circa 1815] he broke a bloodvessel on the lungs, and had to resort to Madeira for a few weeks, also to the South of Italy. He came back benefited by the voyage and change," but accepted an invitation from his uncle, Charles Forbes, to visit Jamaica. The island climate suited his health so well that he decided to continue there ; he therefore bought a local practice from a certain Dr. Forbes.

His wife left her elder son with a lady at Hastings ; and, taking with her her son Henry, then about six months old, she joined her husband in Jamaica. The latter died 3rd March, 1822, aged nearly forty-two years, at Prosper House, St. Elizabeth, Jamaica, " and was interred under a Mango Tree in his Uncle Charles Forbes' ground nearly opposite to the dwelling-house, and his dear uncle, with little Henry, attended the funeral, —the former most impressively read the Burial Service over his grave."

Samuel Fothergill (915), married, May 1809, Anna Maria Russell, who survived him and after his decease returned to England with her younger son. She lived to be over eighty-five years old, and had issue three children, viz :—

i. Samuel Fothergill (916), born 1811. His birth note reads : " On the 22nd of May, 1811, born in Leicester Square, in the parish of St. Anne, Westminster, in the City of Westminster, unto Samuel Fothergill, physician, and Anna Maria his wife, a son who was named Samuel." He is said to have married a Curtis, and died 1840, without issue.

ii. Maria Fothergill (917), born 1813. Her birth note reads : " 29th August, 1813, born in Craven Street, in the parish of St. Martin's-in-the-Fields (so called), in the county of Middlesex, unto Samuel Fothergill, Doctor in Medicine and Anna Maria his wife, a daughter who was named Maria." She died 15th May, and was interred in the Friends' Burial Ground, Bunhill Fields. I do not know the year of her decease, but believe she was an infant.

iii.   Henry Fothergill (918), whom see.

Henry Fothergill (918), born 19th August, 1815.   His birth note reads : " born in Craven Street in the parish of St. Martin's-in-the-Fields (so called), in the county of Middlesex, unto Samuel Fothergill, M.D., and Anna Maria his wife, a son who was named Henry.   [signed] John Hooper, surgeon.   Sarah Gibson."

His mother writes : " My   .   .   .   [illegible] together with Henry to a Person who took Friends' children at Wandsworth, but afterwards, Samuel and Henry, placed them to the Rev. John Stedman, of Wandsworth—considered a good school."   Henry Fothergill (918), was for many years country manager in Barnett's Bank, Lombard Street, now amalgamated with Lloyd's Bank.   In 1873, 1875, and 1878, he was living at Brixton, London, S.W.

He was married 1847 to Maria Covington, who died before 1870, without issue.   In the latter year he was married secondly to Eliza Cormick Hughes, who was born 1845, daughter of Professor William Hughes, F.R.G.S., a famous geographer, who produced many maps and atlases. She died in 1895, and her husband died at Brixton.   They had issue,

i.   Maud Anna Fothergill (919), whom see.
ii.   Henry Chorley Fothergill (922), whom see.
iii.   Beatrice Mary Fothergill (924), born 1878, at Brixton, London, S.W.   She was unmarried in 1910.

Maud Anna Fothergill (919), born 1873, at Brixton, London S.W. She was married to Frank Austin Leach, civil servant, of Kingston-on-Thames, in 1910.   They have issue :

i.   Beatrice Maud Leach (920), born 1903, in South Street, Manchester Square, London.
ii.   Cyril Austin Leach (921), born August, 1905, in Battersea, London.

Henry Chorley Fothergill (922), born 1875, at Brixton, London, S.W. His second name was taken from the surname of his third cousin once removed, Henry Fothergill Chorley, grandson of a daughter of Joseph Fothergill, whose brother Alexander married Margaret Thistlethwaite (877). H. F. Chorley was born 15th December, 1808, at Blackley Hurst, near Billinge, Lancashire. He was for many years critic to the *Athenaeum,* and was a personal friend of Charles Dickens, the Emperor Napoleon III.; Mendelssohn, and a legion of other great ones.*

The subject of this paragraph is in Lloyd's Bank, Barnett's Branch, Lombard Street, London. He was resident at 21, Grove Lane, Kingston-on-Thames, in 1910. On 3rd September, 1906, he was married at Kingston Parish Church, to Charlotte Louisa Palmer, daughter of the late Rev. George William Palmer, M.A., vicar of Claydon, Oxfordshire. He has issue :

    i. Philip Henry Fothergill (923), born 14th July, 1907, at Kingston-on-Thames.

Charles Fothergill (925), born 23rd May, 1782, at York. He was married firstly, somewhere in England, during the year 1811, to Charlotte Nevins. They were living at Lachfield, near Leeds, in 1813, and in 1814 at Rockmont, Peel, in the Isle of Man. They emigrated to Canada, and she died in Toronto, about 1820, being buried just north of St. James' Cathedral, Toronto. By her he had issue :

    i. Charles Forbes Fothergill (926), born 22nd February, 1813, at Lachfield, near Leeds. He was drowned in Lake Ontario, in 1841 or 1842, not long after the death of his father. He never married.

    ii. George Alexander Fothergill (927), whom see.

* I hope to describe him more fully in my second volume. See his biography by Henry G. Hewlett in two volumes, published 1873 by Richard Bentley & Son, London. It is a fascinating book.

iii.   William Henry Fothergill (945), birth date unknown. If he ever existed he died an infant.

Charles Fothergill (925), married secondly, Eliza Richardson, the eldest daughter of Joshua and Catherine Richardson. She was born at Mount Monerabe, five miles from Mount Rath, Queen's County, in Ireland, on the 15th February, 1801 ; and was married to Charles Fothergill at the Parish Church, in Port Hope, Newcastle District, Upper Canada, by the Rev. William Thompson, Rector of Cavan, on Sunday, 20th March, 1825. She died at Whitby, Ontario, on the 26th December, 1892, and was buried at the Friends' Burial Ground, Pickering, Ontario.

Charles Fothergill (925), was a literary man, and established a newspaper in Canada. He was also a celebrated naturalist, and had a very large museum. He died in May, 1841, aged fifty-nine years, and was buried in the Friends' Burial Ground at Pickering, Ontario. By his second wife he had issue :

iv.   Caroline Amelia Fothergill (946), whom see.

v.   Mary Ann Adelaide Fothergill (1000), whom see.

vi.   Theodore Augustus Fothergill (1012), born 17th February, 1830, at Ontario Cottage, near Port Hope, Upper Canada. He died unmarried, and was buried in the Friends' Burying Ground, Pickering, Canada.

vii.   John Joshua St. George Fothergill (1013), whom see.

George Alexander Fothergill (927), born 1814, at Rockmont, Peel, Isle of Man. He was married 11th June, 1845, at Toronto, to Margaret Blanchard, who predeceased him. He was drowned in Lake Huron, about 8th September, 1868.

i.   George William Fothergill (928), born 14th September, 1847. He died, unmarried, 4th November, 1866, and was buried at Owen Sound, Ontario, Canada.

ii.   Louisa Fothergill (929), whom see.

   iii. Augustus Theodore Fothergill (940), born 28th September, 1852. He died unmarried, 5th September, 1880, at Ottawa, and was buried at Bowmanville, Ontario.

   iv. Charles Fothergill (941), whom see.

Louisa Fothergill (929), born 19th April, 1849. She was married 5th September, 1872, at Whitby, Ontario, to William James McMurtry, merchant. She is now (1910) living at 403, Huron Street, Toronto, and has issue :

   i. Dora Louisa McMurtry (930), born 2nd January, 1876, at Bowmanville, Ontario. She married George Douglas Atkinson, bachelor of music, and resides at 272, Major Street, Toronto.

       i. Philip McMurtry Atkinson (931), born 8th September, 1909, at Toronto.

   ii. Earnest McMurtry (932), born 2nd July, 1878, at Bowmanville, Ontario. He was married 1st June, 1908, at Toronto, to Henrietta Louise Hostrawer. He is a wholesale grocer, and resides at 42, Bernard Avenue, Toronto, *sine prole.*

   iii. Gertrude Fothergill McMurtry (933) born 5th September, 1879, at Oshawa, Ontario, a twin. She is unmarried, and lives with her parents at Toronto, 1910.

   iv. Constance Nevins McMurtry (934), born 5th September, 1879, at Oshawa, Ontario, a twin. She married the Rev. Edwin T. Lewis, of Brooklyn, New York, U.S.A. They now reside at Grantwood, New Jersey, U.S.A.

       i. Edwin McMurtry Lewis (935), born 30th December, 1906.

       ii. William Tuttle Lewis (936), born 1st August, 1908.

   v. Grace Muriel McMurtry (937), born 18th November, 1881, at Oshawa, Ontario ; now living with her parents in Toronto.

   vi. Roy Fothergill McMurtry (938), born 11th June, 1885, at Port Perry, Ontario. He is unmarried, and a clerk in the Bank of Montreal, at King, Ontario.

vii.   Hope Fothergill McMurtry (939), born 17th February, 1889,
at Toronto, where she resides with her parents, unmarried.

Charles Fothergill (941), born 10th February, 1856.   He was
married 18th September, 1878, at Owen Sound, to Mary Eliza Malone,
and died 5th January, 1904.   He is buried in All Saints' Churchyard,
Cannington Manor, Saskatchewan.   His widow and three children now
(1910) reside at 349, Eighth Avenue East, Vancouver, British Columbia,
Canada.

    i.   Charles Joseph Fothergill (942), born 3rd September, 1879.
He was married 29th May, 1908, at Vancouver, B.C., to
Martha Edna Wright.

    ii.   Mildred Donaldson Fothergill (943), born 13th October, 1884,

    iii.   George Gwynne Fothergill (944), born 7th June, 1887.

Caroline Amelia Fothergill (946), born 20th April, 1828, at
Ontario Cottage, near Port Hope, Upper Canada.   She died 26th September, 1909, at Whitby, Ontario, and was buried at the Union Cemetery
there.   She was the last surviving child of Charles Fothergill (925), the
emigrant.   She was married at Pickering, Ontario, on 17th March, 1846,
by the Rev. J. Lambie, to George McGillivray, farmer, who was born at
Bar-Hill, St. Fergus, Scotland, on 5th October, 1813, and who died at
Whitby, Ontario, on 29th January, 1894, and was buried at the Union
Cemetery, Whitby.

    i.   Elizabeth Fothergill McGillivray (947), whom see.

    ii.   Mary Eliza McGillivray (956), born 21st May, 1848.   She is
unmarried, and lives at Whitby, Ontario.

    iii.   Catherine Amelia McGillivray (957), whom see.

    iv.   John Alexander McGillivray (972), whom see.

    v.   Adelaide Fothergill McGillivray (974), whom see.

    vi.   George McGillivray (980), born 27th April, 1856, at Burnside
Farm, Pickering, Ontario, (lot No, 1, Concession 4).   He

was first married, to Isabella Brown, who died without issue, and he married secondly, Margaret Hutton, who is still living, *s.p.* He is a veterinary surgeon, residing at Spring Valley, Minnesota, U.S.A.

vii. Charles Fothergill McGillivray (981), whom see.

viii. Caroline Jane McGillivray (983), whom see.

ix. Theodore Augustus McGillivray (987), whom see.

x. Florence Helena McGillivray (991), born 1st March, 1864, at Clovendale Farm, lot No. 32, Concession 3, Whitby Township, Ontario. She is unmarried and lives at Whitby, Ontario.

xi. William McGillivray (992), whom see.

xii. Donald McGillivray (996), born 18th May, 1867, at Clovendale Farm, Whitby Township, Ontario. He was married in June, 1906, to Helen Nelson, who is without issue. He is a physician, and lives at No. 60, College Street, Toronto.

xiii. Norman Harold McGillivray (997), whom see.

Elizabeth Fothergill McGillivray (947), born 28th February, 1847, at Burnside Farm, Pickering, Ontario. She was married at Whitby, Ontario, 15th June, 1870, to Michael Hillary, physician. She died 6th October, 1877, at Kingston, Jamaica, where she was buried. Michael Hillary died in 1884, at Detroit, Michigan State, U.S.A.

i. Eileen Augusta Hillary (948), whom see.

ii. George Michael Hillary (954), born 20th March, 1873. He is a mining engineer, and lives in the City of Chihuahua, Mexico. He is unmarried.

iii. Kathleen Ethel Hillary (955), born 13th September, 1875. She is unmarried, and lives at Whitby, Ontario.

Eileen Augusta Hillary (948), born 16th August, 1871, three months before her mother's youngest brother. She was married 22nd August, 1895, to Rev. Thomas G. McGonigle, and they live at "the Rectory," Islington, Ontario.

    i. Rowland Hillary McGonigle (949), born 27th May, 1896.
    ii. Eileen Mary McGonigle (950), born 20th August, 1897.
    iii. William Harold Burton McGonigle (951), born 14th September, 1898.
    iv. George Michael Gerald McGonigle (952), born 14th October, 1900.
    v. Arthur Cormac Robert McGonigle (953), born 2nd June, 1908.

Catherine Amelia McGillivray (957), born 3rd December, 1850, at Burnside Farm, Pickering, Ontario. She was married 19th August, 1875, to David MacLaren, a timber merchant. They reside at Frank Street, Ottawa.

    i. James Gordon MacLaren (958), born 18th May, 1876. He married Menota Isbester, 30th September, 1903, at Ottawa, where they reside.

        i. Katherine Lois MacLaren (959), born 12th August 1904.
        ii. David Gordon MacLaren (960), born 2nd December, 1905.
        iii. James Isbester MacLaren (961), born 24th August, 1908.

    ii. George McGillivray MacLaren (962), born 10th July, 1877. He was married 1st January, 1905, at Montreal, to Florence Evelyn Willett, and they now reside at Ottawa.

        i. Brock Willett MacLaren (963), born 9th March, 1906.

    iii. Charles Henry MacLaren (964), born 22nd November, 1878. He is a barrister, and lives at Ottawa, Canada, unmarried.

    iv. John Alexander MacLaren (965), born 15th October, 1880, and died 4th February, 1905.

    v. Kenneth MacLaren (966), born 2nd July, 1882. He married Bessie L. Dowsley, 16th November, 1908, at Ottawa, where they now reside.

    i. Ian David MacLaren (967), born 2nd November, 1909.

vi. Caroline Anna MacLaren (968), born 18th September, 1885. She was married in February, 1907, to Robert Legrand Johnstone, and they reside at Glen Ridge, New Jersey, U.S.A.

    i. Helen Irene Johnstone (969), born 1st January, 1908.

    ii. Robert MacLaren Johnstone (970), born 9th July, 1909.

vii. Katherine Amelia MacLaren (971), born 26th November, 1890. She is unmarried, and lives with her parents at Frank Street, Ottawa.

John Alexander McGillivray (972), born 19th July, 1852, at Burnside Farm, Pickering, Ontario. He was married 22nd December, 1880, to Zella Augusta Button. He is a barrister, and resides at Uxbridge, Ontario.

    i. Gordon Button McGillivray (973), born at Uxbridge, 31st July, 1885, now of Toronto.

Adelaide Fothergill McGillivray (974), born 21st July, 1854, at Burnside Farm, Pickering, Ontario. She was married 28th January, 1886, to Rev. Robert Gamble, and they reside at Wakefield, Quebec. The five daughters are all unmarried, and living at home.

    i. Laura Adelaide Gamble (975), born 4th September, 1887.

    ii. Kathleen Mary Gamble (976), born 1st February, 1889.

    iii. Florence Caroline Gamble (977), born 22nd August, 1890.

    iv. Clara Louise Gamble (978), born 10th May, 1892.

    v. Eileen Elizabeth Gamble (979), born 17th September, 1894.

Charles Fothergill McGillivray (981), born 26th December, 1857, at Burnside Farm, Pickering, Ontario. He was married 3rd December, 1891, to Caroline Argo. He is a physician, and resides at Whitby, Ontario.

  i. George Argo McGillivray (982), born 9th September, 1900, at Whitby, Ontario.

Caroline Jane McGillivray (983), born 9th February, 1860, at Clovendale Farm, Whitby Township, Ontario. She was married 30th December, 1891, to John Taylor Fotheringham, a physician, now resident at 20, Wellesley Street, Toronto.

  i. Caroline Helen Fotheringham (984), born 1st August, 1894.
  ii Ruth McGillivray Fotheringham, (985), born 9th November, 1895.
  iii. Donald Taylor Fotheringham (986), born 29th April, 1898.

Theodore Augustus McGillivray (987), born 12th July, 1862, at Clovendale Farm, Whitby Township, Ontario. He was married 11th June, 1895, to Helen MacLaren. He is a barrister, and lives at Whitby, Ontario.

  i. Donald John McGillivray (988), born 30th October, 1896.
  ii. Charles Allister McGillivray (989), born 29th July, 1899.
  iii. Helen Marjory McGillivray (990), born 2nd August, 1901.

William McGillivray (992), born 24th July, 1865, at Clovendale Farm, Whitby Township, Ontario. He was married 29th June, 1898, to Luella Taylor. He was a physician, and died 28th November, 1904, at Pipestone, Minnesota, U.S.A., where his three children and widow now reside.

  i. George Theodore McGillivray (993), born 28th March, 1900.
  ii. Florence Jenny McGillivray (994), born 11th July, 1902.
  iii. William Taylor McGillivray (995), born 28th August, 1904.

Norman Harold McGillivray (997), born 29th November, 1871, at Inverlynn Farm, Whitby, Ontario. He was married in June, 1901, to Mary R. Mitchell, and is a clergyman at Cornwall, Ontario.

    i. Margaret Louise McGillivray (998), born 11th July, 1902.

    ii. Jean Caroline McGillivray (999), born 3rd August, 1903.

Mary Ann Adelaide Fothergill (1000), born at Ontario Cottage, near Port Hope, Upper Canada, 17th July, 1832. She was married 2nd January, 1865, at Pickering, to William Henry Clendenan, and died 11th October, 1903, at Whitby, Ontario. She was buried at the Friends' Burial Ground, Pickering, Ontario. William Henry Clendenan was a farmer, and died at Whitby, Ontario, 4th October, 1906. He was also buried at the Friends' Burial Ground, Pickering.

    i. Eliza Clendenan (1001), born 16th October, 1865. She was married 27th June, 1900, to John Reid, merchant. They reside at Wakefield, Quebec.

        i. Mary Fothergill Reid (1002), born 16th December, 1901, at Wakefield.

    ii. Mary Clendenan (1003), born 12th February, 1867. She is unmarried, and lives with her eldest sister, Mrs. Reid, at Wakefield, Quebec.

    iii. Caroline Victoria Clendenan (1004), born 24th May, 1868. She was married 6th December, 1900, to Rev. Alexander Shepherd, and they live at Markdale, Ontario.

        i. William Alexander Shepherd (1005), born 28th December, 1902.

        ii. George Fothergill Shepherd (1006), born 27th July, 1904.

    iv. Kathleen Amelia Clendenan (1007), born 8th March, 1870. She was married 4th September, 1907, to George Shepherd, pattern-maker. They live at Lindsay, Ontario, and are without issue.

v. Georgina Clendenan (1008), born 23rd April, 1873. She was
married 2nd January, 1900, to James Cornell, agent, and
they live at Lindsay, Ontario.

    i. Henry Edward Clendenan Cornell (1009), born 4th
February, 1901.

    ii. William James Clendenan Cornell (1010), born 4th
June, 1903.

    iii. Marianne Fothergill Cornell (1011), born 28th
August, 1906.

John Joshua St. George Fothergill (1013), born at Pickering,
Ontario, on St. George's Day, 23rd April, 1836. He was married at Whitby
18th October, 1883, to Catherine Amelia Jones. He died 29th June, 1908,
at Whitby, Ontario, and was buried at the Friends' Burial Ground,
Pickering, Ontario. His widow and three children reside at Whitby,
Ontario.

    i. Elizabeth Augusta Fothergill (1014), born 16th March, 1885,
now, (January, 1910) unmarried.

    ii. George Jones Fothergill (1015), born 12th February, 1887,
now unmarried.

    iii. Charles Theodore Fothergill (1016), born 7th November, 1888,
now unmarried. His first cousin, Elizabeth Fothergill
McGillivray (947), was born in 1847, forty-one years
previous to his birth. And her grandson, Rowland Hillary
McGonigle (949), was born in 1896, only eight years after
his grandmother's first cousin, the subject of this paragraph.

Margaret Fothergill (1017), born 6th January, 1785, at York.
She was married at York Meeting House, 3rd September, 1812, to Thomas
Blakey, of the City of London, son of Joshua and Mary Blakey, of
York. She died in London, in 1822. She had issue an only child:

    i.   Alfred Blakey (1018), born 1812, and died 25th November, 1854, unmarried. I do not know the occupation of either Thomas or Alfred Blakey, nor whether they were descended from the Wensleydale Quaker family of the same name.

William Fothergill (1021), born 24th October, 1748, at Carr End, Wensleydale, Yorkshire. William Fothergill, yeoman, of Carr End, was married 14th August, 1782, at Counterside Meeting House, to Hannah Robinson, daughter of Amos and Jane Robinson, of Semerdale, the small valley in which Counterside and Carr End lie. William Fothergill, although the second surviving son, succeeded to the family farm and house at Carr End, where he died in February, 1837, aged eighty-eight years. His wife Hannah Fothergill, died at Carr End, 22nd June, 1836, and was buried at Bainbridge.

    i.   John Fothergill (1022), whom see.

   ii.   Thomas Fothergill (1061), born 13th September, 1786, at Carr End, Wensleydale, Co. York, where he died 3rd December, 1789, and was buried at Bainbridge.

  iii.   Alexander Fothergill (1062), whom see.

  iv.   Margaret Fothergill (1087), born 13th November, 1789, at Carr End. She lived to be about ninety years of age, and was buried at Skinnergate, Darlington, unmarried.

   v.   Jane Fothergill (1088), born 14th January, 1793. She was married 31st May, 1828, at Marside, to Thomas Whaley, of Wensleydale. She lived to be about ninety years of age, and was buried at Skinnergate, Darlington, without issue.

John Fothergill (1022), born 13th May, 1785, at Carr End, Wensleydale, Yorkshire. He was a Member of the Royal College of Surgeons, London, and practised medicine in Askrigg, Co. York, and in Darlington, Co. Durham. He was married 25th May, 1815, to Ann Rimington, daughter of Edward Rimington, cabinet-maker, of Liverpool.

   i.   William Fothergill (1023), whom see.

  ii.   Edward Fothergill (1032), born 23rd August, 1817, at Askrigg, in Wensleydale, Co. York. He died young, and unmarried, at Darlington.

 iii.   Samuel Fothergill (1033), whom see.

  iv.   Mary Ann Fothergill (1057), born 10th January, 1821, at Darlington, where she died, aged seventy to eighty years, unmarried.

   v.   Alexander Fothergill (1058), born 28th March, 1823, at Darlington. He was a dentist, and practised in Darlington, where he died at Elton Cottage, in his sixty-ninth year, unmarried.

  vi.   John Rimington Fothergill (1059), born 25th March, 1825, at Darlington. He is now (February, 1910) living at Chorley Cottage, Darlington, and is a Doctor of Medicine, and Justice of the Peace. He married Emily Young, of South Shields, but is without issue.

 vii.   Agnes Fothergill (1060), born 1st March, 1830, at Darlington, where she died unmarried, at Elton Cottage.

William Fothergill (1023), born 29th February, 1816, at Askrigg, Wensleydale, Co. York. He was a dentist at Darlington, and married Jane Mary Ann Sanders, daughter of Joseph Sanders, of Newcastle-on-Tyne (son of Joseph Sanders, of Whitby, Co. York), by his wife Diana Willis, of Whitby.

   i.   John Alexander Fothergill (1024), was a dentist in Darlington, and died at Middleton-in-Teesdale. He married Christian Stuart Armour, who survived him a few years, and died in Norway, 1909.

          i.   John Stuart Fothergill (1025), living at Hammersmith, London, in 1909.

        ii.   Mabyn Fothergill (1026), only daughter.

      iii.   Alan Fothergill (1027).

   iv. Edward Rimington Fothergill (1028).

 ii. William Sanders Fothergill (1029), is now (1910) resident at Nelson Terrace, Redcar, Co. York. He is cashier in Barclay & Co. Ltd.'s Bank, Stockton-on-Tees, Co. Durham. He married Isabella Crichton, who is a well-known lecturer on educational subjects.

   i. William Crichton Fothergill (1030), born September 1900, at Redcar.

 iii. Edward Fothergill (1031), now (1909) resident at Newcastle-on-Tyne. He married Ann Silburn, widow of a solicitor, but is without issue.

Samuel Fothergill (1033), born 13th July, 1819, at Askrigg, Wensleydale, Co. York. After leaving Ackworth School he became a private family tutor, and later conducted private schools at Darlington, Scarborough, and Southampton. "In most of the social and religious controversies of his time he took an active interest, enforcing his views alike by voice and pen. Some articles on "The Principles of Political Economy applied to the Wages Question," which he published in the *Contemporary Review* and afterwards in pamphlet form in the early seventies, created a great stir among the working classes. Although ever in sympathy with the struggling masses, he hesitated not to condemn the policy of Trades' Unions, from which he strongly differed. He also flinched not from crossing swords with men like John Stuart Mill and Professor Fawcett, as is evidenced by his pamphlets on "Liberty, Licence and Prohibition," addressed to the former, and "A Reply to Professor Fawcett on Pauperism, Poor Law, and the Drink Traffic."

 "As we have hinted, he was strongly opposed to the Ritualistic Movement, and wrote many letters and pamphlets in condemnation thereof. His spiritualised ideal religion was entirely out of sympathy with ecclesiastical ceremonials in any form whatever." John Fothergill (1022), as a medical practitioner, advocated total abstinence from intoxi-

cants at a time when probably not a dozen of his professional brethren in
the whole kingdom could be found to support his views. And his son,
Samuel, was a keen Temperance worker, lecturing on behalf of the United
Kingdom Alliance. He also persistently denounced tobacco-smoking.
He was an intimate friend of John Bright, the Quaker orator, and himself
remained a Quaker all his life.

Samuel Fothergill (1033), married, firstly, 27th April, 1848, Priscilla
Deane, of Reigate, Surrey, who was born 20th October, 1827, at Dover,
daughter of James Deane by his wife Sarah Dann. Priscilla Fothergill
died 12th March, 1855. By her he had issue:

  i.   Emma Fothergill (1034), whom see.

  ii. Ann Fothergill (1039), born 14th April, 1850. She was married,
       September, 1900, at the Friends' Meeting House, Darlington,
       to Alfred E. Eccles, of White Coppice, near Chorley, Lan-
       cashire. He was educated at Tulketh Hall, where he
       imbibed his Quaker principles, and has since become a
       Friend. He and his wife are both interested in certain
       branches of social reform. *Sine prole.*

  iii. Sarah Fothergill (1040), born 14th October, 1851. She died
       24th November, 1868, at Southampton, unmarried.

  iv. Samuel Deane Fothergill (1041), born 24th March, 1853,
       at Darlington, and died there 12th November, 1886,
       unmarried.

  v.   Henry Fothergill (1042), whom see.

Samuel Fothergill (1033), married secondly, 18th July, 1864, Emma
Deane, his deceased wife's sister, who was born 25th June, 1829, at Dover,
Kent. She is now (1910) resident at Ashcroft Road, Darlington. He
lived at one time at Keswick, near Derwentwater, Co. Cumberland, but
died at Darlington, 22nd April, 1902. By his second wife he had issue:

  i.   William Edward Fothergill (1056), whom see.

Emma Fothergill (1034), born 18th March, 1849, at Darlington. She was married 22nd December, 1874, to Elbert Sills Clarke, who was born 16th March, 1850, at St. Mary Cray, Co. Kent, about seven miles from Woolwich. He and his wife are missionaries, living (1910) at Hope Vale, Comrie, N.C.R., *via* Maritzburg, Natal, South Africa.

    i.   Evelyn Fothergill Clarke (1035), born 17th September, 1875. In 1900 she became a teacher in the Inanda Zulu Girls' Seminary, and since January, 1909, has been Lady Principal of the Girls' Part of the Amanzimtote Training Institute for those desiring to obtain Government Certificates as qualified Zulu teachers for their own people. Her address is Adam's Mission Station, Amanzimtote, *via* Durban, Natal. She is unmarried.

    ii.   Minnie Clarke (1036), born 19th February, 1877. In 1910 she is head of the Girls' Seminary, Mount Silinda Mission Station, Melsetter, Rhodesia. Both this and the Institute at Adam's Station are in connection with the American Board of Missions. She is unmarried.

    iii.   Bertha Clarke (1037), born 19th November, 1879. Now unmarried; missionary helper to her parents at Hope Vale, Natal.

    iv.   John Fothergill Clarke (1038), born 3rd October, 1880. Unmarried. On February 4th, 1910, he arrived at Ogada, in Central Africa, sixteen miles north of Lake Victoria Nyanza. Here he is carrying on missionary work "in the Luwo Tribe, in the Kavirhondo Country, where the people are of Nilotic extraction." He is "not very far from" the neighbourhood where Willis Hodgkiss and American Friends are labouring.

Henry Fothergill (1042), born 12th September, 1854, at Darlington, Co. Durham. He was married 22nd July, 1879, at Belper, near Derby, to Mary Elizabeth Hughes, of Crich, Derbyshire, who was born there 14th September, 1858, daughter of William and Mary Hughes. Henry Fothergill (1042), is a minister of the United Methodist Free Church, in 1909, of Clarence House, Loughborough, Leicestershire, and in 1910, of Stafford Road, Weston-super-mare.

    i.   Elbert Percy Fothergill (1043), born 19th July, 1880, at Mansfield, Nottinghamshire. He is unmarried, and secretary of a firm in Paris.

    ii.   Ethel May Fothergill (1044), whom see.

    iii.   Gladys Fothergill (1050), born 29th July, 1883, at Swansea, Glamorganshire, Wales. She died 7th March, 1884.

    iv.   Clarice Lilian Fothergill (1051), born 13th October, 1885, at Irlams o' th' Height, Lancashire. Unmarried.

    v.   Agnes Jessie Fothergill (1052), born 24th August, 1887, at New Mills. Unmarried.

    vi.   Harold Fothergill (1053), born 31st March, 1892, at Tamworth.

    vii.   William Hughes Fothergill (1054), born 12th May, 1895, at Birkenshaw, near Leeds, Yorkshire.

    viii.   Samuel John Rimington Fothergill (1055), born 10th March, 1898, at Market Rasen, Lincolnshire.

Ethel May Fothergill (1044), born 25th September, 1881, at Codnor, Derbyshire. She was married to George Arthur Pickering, of Market Rasen, Lincolnshire, born 3rd December, 1879, now farmer, of Thorpe-le-Fallows, near Lincoln.

    i.   William Stuart Leslie Fothergill Pickering (1045), born February, 1900.

    ii.   Arthur Douglas Pickering (1046), born 22nd August, 1902.

    iii.   Jessie Fothergill Pickering (1047), born January, 1904, died 31st January, 1908.

iv.   Ethel Janet Pickering (1048), born April, 1907.

v.   Dorothy Pickering (1049), born May, 1909.

William Edward Fothergill (1056), born 4th October, 1865, at Southampton, Hampshire. He is M.A., B.Sc., M.D., C.M., of Edinburgh University. He obtained the Gold Medal for his M.D. Thesis, and the Milner-Fothergill Gold Medal for a professional investigation, and was awarded the Essay Prize of the Edinburgh University Club of London, for an essay on " The Relation of Literature, Science, and Philosophy in University Education." He is Lecturer in Obstetrics and Gynaecology in the Victoria University of Manchester, and Assistant Gynaecologist to the St. Mary's Hospitals and the Royal Infirmary, Manchester. He published in June, 1896, a very successful " Manual of Midwifery," now in its fourth edition, and has contributed six articles to the " Encyclopædia Medica," 1899, *et seq.*, besides publishing four other separate works and a multitude of papers in the Scientific Journals.

He was married, in 1895, to Edith A. Woon, of Swan Walk, Chelsea, London. She was the daughter of Joseph Dillon Woon, of Grampound, Co. Cornwall, by his wife Mary Ribey, of Withamwick, Co. York, and was living in 1909. They are without issue, and reside at 337, Oxford Road, Manchester.

Alexander Fothergill (1062), born 18th May, 1788, at Carr End, near Bainbridge, Wensleydale, Yorkshire. While a farmer at Carr End, he was married 25th May, 1815, at Rochdale Meeting House, Lancashire, to Elizabeth Haworth, daughter of Jonathan Haworth, grocer, of Rochdale, by his wife Sally. By her he had six children, all of whom were born at the family farm, Carr End.

i.   Hannah Fothergill (1063), born 27th January, 1816. She accompanied her father and step-mother to the United States of America in 1842, but eventually returned to

England, and died unmarried, at Sunderland, 2nd November, 1884.

ii. Thomas Fothergill (1064), whom see.

iii. Sarah Fothergill (1073), whom see.

iv. Susannah Fothergill, (1074), born 20th December, 1821. She went to America in 1842, and died 7th January, 1851, in Philadelphia, unmarried.

v. Eliza Fothergill (1075), born 11th December, 1824. She went to America, in 1842, died unmarried, at the Episcopal Church Home, Baltimore, Maryland, 7th January, 1895, aged seventy years ; and was buried in Wilmington and Brandywine Cemetery, Wilmington, Delaware.

vi. Alice Haworth Fothergill (1076), born 14th November, 1826. She was married 6th October, 1876, to Joseph Tatum, of Woodbury, New Jersey, who died about five years later. She lived about fifteen years in the Sanitorium at Clifton Springs, New York, and died there in 1898. She was buried in Wilmington and Brandywine Cemetery, Wilmington, Delaware, *sine prole.*

Alexander Fothergill's first wife died 12th December, 1826, at Carr End, not long after the birth of their youngest child, and he became a land-agent at Rochdale, Lancashire. While living here he was married, 13th September, 1828, at the Meeting House at Little Marsden, in the parish of Whalley, Lancashire, to Jane Robinson, of Rochdale. Her father, then deceased, was Richard Robinson, a grocer, of Longfield, near Todmorden, Yorkshire, son of John and Alice Robinson, of Park House, Colne, Lancashire. There seems to have been no relationship between this family, and the Robinson family of Semerdale, to which Alexander Fothergill's mother belonged. Richard Robinson, of Longfield, had married Sarah Greenwood, and she appears to have been living in 1828, a widow, at Horsforth, near Leeds, Yorkshire.

They lived at Sunny Bank, and at Roach Place, Rochdale, but in 1832 or 1833 they removed to Waithland, within the same Parish. In

December, 1835, Alexander Fothergill is still described as a land-agent, but he shortly afterwards became a cotton-spinner, and failed in the panic of 1837. In this year William Fothergill (1021), of Carr End, died, leaving, it is said, his farm to his sons John and Alexander. Owing to the misfortune of the latter, it was sold, and I am told that John made no claim for his share. It now belongs to a Mr. Jackson, of Sunderland.

J. Henry Lancashire, of Rochdale, in September, 1909, recollects a visit paid to his uncle Alexander Fothergill, at Carr End, before 1842. The latter " was a keen sportsman : he had recently shot a wild swan on Semerwater, and being also very kind he took me with him expeditions, chiefly fishing, near at hand."

Alexander Fothergill (1062), left England for America with his wife and nine of his children on the 8th of August, 1842. They landed at Philadelphia, Pa., 18th September, 1842, and spent the winter in Wilmington, Delaware. In the spring a farm was rented near Chester, Pennsylvania, but on the 2nd of October, 1843, Alexander Fothergill (1062) died, aged fifty-five years, at the home of his first wife's sister, Mary Wetherald, Wilmington, Delaware, where he had gone with his wife to spend a few days. He was buried in the Friends' Burial Ground, Fourth and West Streets, Wilmington.

His widow, Jane Fothergill, died 9th January, 1874, aged seventy-five years, at the home of her son William, Chester, Pennsylvania ; and she was buried in Wilmington and Brandywine Cemetery, Wilmington.

Alexander Fothergill's first wife's sister, Mary Wetherald, was the wife of Joseph Wetherald, of Wilmington, whose brother, John Wetherald, of Puslinch, Ontario, married Isabella Thistlethwaite (583) second cousin to Alexander Fothergill. See Part II.

By his second wife Alexander Fothergill had issue.

vii. Ann Fothergill (1077), born 1st May, 1830, at Rochdale, probably at " Sunny Bank." She went to America in 1842 with her parents, and was living, January, 1910, at 319½ Arctic Avenue, Atlantic City, New Jersey, with her sister Margaret, both being unmarried.

viii.   Mary Fothergill (1078), born 21st October, 1831, at Rochdale, Lancashire, probably at " Roach Place." She went to America in 1842, and died, unmarried, at Wilmington, Delaware, 16th December, 1854, aged twenty-three years. She was buried in the Friends' Burying Ground, Fourth and West Streets, Wilmington.

ix.   Margaret Fothergill (1079), born 3rd June, 1833, at Waithland, Rochdale, Lancaster. She went to America in 1842, and was living, January, 1910, at 319½ Arctic Avenue, Atlantic City, New Jersey, U.S.A., with her sister Ann, both being unmarried.

x.   William Fothergill (1080), whom see.

xi.   Henry Fothergill (1081), whom see.

Thomas Fothergill (1064), born 30th July, 1817, at Carr End, Wensleydale, Yorkshire. He was senior partner in the firm of Fothergill and Harvey, yarn and cloth agents, of Manchester. He was married in June, 1850, to Anne Coultate, daughter of William and Judith Coultate, of Burnley, Lancashire. He died 5th August, 1866, at Bowdon, Cheshire, and his widow died 16th August, 1888, at Withington, Manchester.

i.   Jessie Fothergill (1065), whom see.

ii.   Alexander William Fothergill (1066), born 17th January, 1853, at Cheetham Hill, Manchester. He died 3rd November, 1870, at Littleborough, Lancashire, and was buried at Calderbrook, Littleborough.

iii.   Constance Fothergill (1067), born 30th July, 1854, at Bowdon, Cheshire. She died 12th September, 1858.

iv.   Sophia Fothergill (1068), born 2nd July, 1856, at Bowdon, Cheshire. In September, 1909, she was living at Richmond Hill, Bowdon, Cheshire, unmarried.

v.   Caroline Janet Fothergill (1069), born 1st April, 1858, at Bowdon, Cheshire. In September, 1909, she was living, and unmarried. I believe that she resides in London, and is an authoress of some repute.

vi. Charles Fothergill (1070), born 30th January, 1860, at Bowdon, Cheshire. He died an infant.

vii. Reginald Harry Fothergill (1071), born 6th May, 1861, at Bowdon, Cheshire. He was at one time in India, but died in London, 5th November, 1900, unmarried.

viii. Elizabeth Cecilia Fothergill (1072), born 29th June, 1863, at Bowdon, Cheshire. In September, 1909, she was living at Richmond Hill, Bowdon, Cheshire, unmarried.

Jessie Fothergill (1065), born 7th June, 1851, at Cheetham Hill, Manchester. She died at Bern, Switzerland, 28th July, 1891, aged forty years, unmarried. She was a celebrated novelist. Among her numerous publications is " The First Violin," which originally appeared in the *Temple Bar* Magazine, and was published in three volumes, 11th October, 1878 ; it has been many times reprinted, and is an entrancing story of musical life in Germany. She also wrote " Borderland," " Aldyth," " Probation," etc.

But the most important to my history is her " Kith and Kin," the first edition of which appeared in 1881. This novel describes in a brilliant way the upper part of Wensleydale, the district in which resided so many of her ancestors and the ancestors of others mentioned in my history. I strongly recommend a perusal of this fascinating book to all those Thistlethwaite descendants interested in the surroundings of their ancestors.

" Yoresett-in-Danesdale " refers to Askrigg in Wensleydale, which is accurately described in the chapter so headed, " Yoresett House " being the old Manor House in Askrigg market place. " Shennamere," on the opposite side of the valley is Semerwater, and " Scar Foot," the charming old house overlooking this little lake, is Carr End. " Bainbeck " is, of course, Bainbridge, and " Stanniforth," with its falls and enormous parish, disguises Aysgarth, some of the most beautiful parts of which are contained in the grounds of Bearpark, at present the property of a Thistlethwaite descendant.

~~~~~~~~~~~~~~~~~~~~~~~~~~~~~~~

Sarah Fothergill (1073), born 29th September, 1819, at Carr End, Wensleydale, Yorkshire. She and her brother Thomas were the only members of Alexander Fothergill's family of eleven who did not go to America. She was married at Darlington Meeting House, 23rd May, 1850, to Arthur Thistlethwaite, grocer, of Sunderland, son of William Thistlethwaite, of Pontefract, Yorkshire. This family of Thistlethwaites were Quakers from the seventeenth century, but do not appear in this volume, as they sprang from the Wensleydale Thistlethwaite stock to which belonged my great-great-great-grandfather, Christopher Thistlethwaite, of Aysgarth in Wensleydale, who married in 1751, Anne Thistlethwaite (1145), daughter of our common ancestor, William of Harborgill. I intend to trace this family in full in my second volume.

Arthur and Sarah Thistlethwaite lived in their latter years at Hurworth-on-Tees, near Darlington. He was buried 12th February, 1885, at the Friends' Burial Ground, Darlington. His widow died at Hurworth 5th July, 1885, and was buried at Darlington Friends' Burial Ground, on the 8th. Arthur Thistlethwaite was born 26th September, 1818, at Pindar Green, Methley, Yorkshire. His mother was born Hannah Hardwick of Pontefract, daughter of John and Mary Hardwick, and was baptised 4th January, 1778. Arthur and Sarah Thistlethwaite had no issue.

~~~~~~~~~~~~~~~~~~~~~~~~~~~~~~~

William Fothergill (1080), born 22nd December, 1835, at Waithland in the parish of Rochdale and the county of Lancaster. He went to America in 1842, his father dying the following year. He and his brother Henry learned pattern-making in the same shop in Wilmington, Delaware, and always followed that occupation. " William has mostly worked and lived in Chester, Pennsylvania." He was married 15th March, 1866, to Jane Yarrow Eldredge, of Wilmington, daughter of John and Margaret

Eldredge. She died without issue 12th November, 1884, aged forty-eight years, and was buried in Wilmington and Brandywine Cemetery. William Fothergill (1080), was living on the 1st of October, 1909, in Chester, Pennsylvania.

Henry Fothergill (1081), born 6th December, 1837, at Church Stile, Rochdale, Lancashire. He went to America in 1842, his father dying in 1843, when Henry was only six years of age. He learned pattern-making with his brother William at Wilmington. In 1876, he went to Steelton, Pennsylvania, to take charge of the pattern-shop at the Pennsylvania Steel Works. He died at Steelton, 28th March, 1885, aged forty-seven years, and was buried in the Wilmington and Brandywine Cemetery, Wilmington, Delaware. He was married 25th June, 1867, to Rachel Maria Poinsett, daughter of Asa and Ann Poinsett of Wilmington.

He, and his brother Thomas, were the only members of Alexander Fothergill's eleven children to have issue, and as none of Thomas' children are likely to have issue, Henry, the youngest of the eleven, is the only one by whom this branch of the family will be perpetuated. He had issue,

    i.   Alexander Poinsett Fothergill (1082), whom see.
    ii. Henry Robinson Fothergill (1083), whom see.
    iii. William Greenwood Fothergill (1086), whom see.

Alexander Poinsett Fothergill (1082), born 22nd November, 1869, at Wilmington, Delaware, U.S.A. At the age of sixteen, he entered the office of the Diamond State Iron Company in Wilmington, and remained there about seven years. Since then, he has filled different positions with other firms, sometimes as manager, secretary, or salesman. He was, in October, 1909, Vice-President of the Cleveland Steel Tool Company, Cleveland, Ohio, where he was living. He was married 12th June, 1904, to Anna Maria Kinch, of Reading, Pennsylvania. He had no children in October, 1909.

Henry Robinson Fothergill (1083), born 10th January, 1873, at Wilmington, Delaware. He learned mechanical draughting with the Diamond State Iron Company, in Wilmington, but it proved too quiet and sedentary for him. In about 1906, he removed to Greenville, South Carolina, to take charge of a short line of electric road. The climate did not suit his tendency to asthma, and after a year's residence, he was obliged to leave the locality. He obtained a temporary position at Youngstown, Ohio, and in October, 1909, he was superintending the building of some water-works at Girard, a little town about five miles from Youngstown.

He was married 27th October, 1897, to Eliza Groves Quigley, daughter of Winfield Scott Quigley, of Wilmington, Delaware, by his wife Lola Gould. They have issue,

    i.   Elizabeth Fothergill (1084), born 24th February, 1899.

    ii.   Henry Robinson Fothergill (1085), born 24th August, 1903.

William Greenwood Fothergill (1086), born 19th February, 1877, at Steelton, Pennsylvania. ' At the age of sixteen he went into an electric light plant at Wilmington, Delaware, to learn the business, and remained there three years." While working in New York he met with two serious accidents to one of his hands, which for ever disabled him from doing any kind of hard practical work. Having no inclination for anything except manual work of some sort, he has been for several years at the Concrete Works in Baltimore, Maryland, making the wooden cases in which the concrete is moulded. He was married 6th September, 1905, to Katie May Crawford of Annapolis, Maryland. She was a widow with two children by her first husband, but is without issue by William Greenwood Fothergill.

PART FOUR.

DESCENDANTS OF

JOHN THISTLETHWAITE (1090),

FOURTH CHILD OF

WILLIAM THISTLETHWAITE (1), OF HARBORGILL.

PART FOUR.

John Thistlethwaite (1090), born 27th April, 1712, probably at Harborgill, in Dent Dale, Co. York. His niece, Alice Chorley, writes : " John was accidentally lamed, which occasioned him to be taught the business of clogg-making." In the account of the avalanche of 1752 (which see), it was to his house, at Leayat in Dent, that his relatives at Harborgill fled for safety ; and as he died there in 1800 we may conclude that Leayat was his residence. According to the custom of the Society of Friends, Sedbergh Monthly Meeting drew up a " testimony concerning John Thistlethwaite," as a minister in that body. This is unusually brief, and worthy of quotation :——

" He was the son of our friends William and Alice Thistlethwaite, of Dent, who gave him a guarded and religious Education, which he often expressed had made lasting impressions on his mind. He was careful in the education of his own children and desirous that others would be careful in this important duty. By yielding to the dictates of unerring Wisdom he became measurably qualified to instruct others in the way of Peace and Salvation, and was called to bear a Testimony thereunto in meetings about the fortieth year of his age. His gift in the ministry, though not large, was sound and edifying, and he had at seasons openings into the deep mysteries of man's redemption and with the authority of Truth he had to declare it in Meetings. He was also a good example in Meetings for Discipline, sound and clear in supporting the Testimony of Truth, and liberal in contributing to the services of the Society. And we have this Testimony to give concerning him that as he grew in years he grew in Grace, and laid down his head in Peace. He died the 11th day of 10th month, 1800, and was buried at Leayat, in Dent, the 14th of the same, aged eighty-eight years. A minister about forty-eight years. Signed in, by order and on behalf of Sedbergh Monthly Meeting, held at Brigflatts the 24th day of 2nd mo. 1801."

William Jackson	John Laycock
Simon Alderson	Edward Smith
Jeremiah Thistlethwaite (1162)	James Collinson
Matthew Middlebrook	Joshua Smithson
Richard Alderson (26)	Robert Jackson
John Ion	Richard Wilkinson
John Thistlethwaite (1347)	Charles Holmes
Simon Harker	Thomas Carter
	John Holmes.

He married 31st March, 1744, Margaret Close, of Street, in Ravenstondale, who died 9th May, 1768, having issue.

    i.   Alice Thistlethwaite (1091), born 5th or 15th January, 1745, and died an infant, 27th April, 1745.

   ii.   William Thistlethwaite (1092), whom see.

  iii.   Thomas Thistlethwaite (1130), born 21st March, 1750 ; died at Dent's Head, 22nd September, 1777, " aged about twenty seven," unmarried.

  iv.   Alice Thistlethwaite (1131), whom see.

   v.   Ann Thistlethwaite (1134), whom see.

  vi.   Margaret Thistlethwaite (1139), born 30th August, 1758, and married firstly, 31st March, 1784, John Bezzon, of Woodhall, which was at one time the residence of Christopher Metcalfe (near Askrigg, see under Isabella Lund (536)). Her second husband was John Kershaw, of Standish near Wigan, Lancashire, who died 19th November, 1830, aged eighty-eight years. She died 19th February, 1851, aged ninety-two years ; without issue.

 vii.   Isabel Thistlethwaite (1140), born 8th January, 1764, and died, unmarried, 12th January, 1780, aged sixteen years.

William Thistlethwaite (1092), born 1st June, 1747, in Dent Dale. He appears to have married at some church, about 1795, his first cousin once removed, Elizabeth Lund (534), who was born in Garsdale, Yorkshire, 2nd October, 1766, daughter of Thomas Lund, by his wife Alice Thistlethwaite (533), daughter of William Thistlethwaite's uncle, James Thistlethwaite (429).   The Quaker rules forbade cousin marriage,* therefore William and Elizabeth Thistlethwaite were disowned, and the births of their children entered in the Quaker register as " non-members."

According to the register, his first five children were born at Manchester, 1796 to 1804, but his grand-daughter writes me that before going to Manchester he " had a Mill (presumably a cotton-mill) at Marsden," Lancashire. " It was while he had the mill at Marsden that the people rose against the new machinery. Hearing that the mob were on the way with destructive intent, W. Thistlethwaite went out to meet them, carrying only his staff. When he came up to them he reasoned with them so calmly and convincingly that they retired without doing any injury."

He was about forty-eight years old when he married, and was engaged in some business in Manchester with a Quaker named Taylor. Between 1804 and 1808 he removed to Penketh,† where he became schoolmaster, and taught in a room near the Meeting House. He died 31st December, 1808, " at Sankey, being seized with apoplexy (as we are told) on his way into town with his son Thomas." He was buried at Penketh, Lancashire, 5th January, 1809, aged sixty-two.

His widow, then aged forty-two, appears to have remained at Penketh. " The old lady was a great reader and almost invariably read aloud in an evening, for the benefit of the rest. I well remember her going through

* Karl Pearson, D.Sc., F.R.S., the eminent scientist and biometrician writes : " My great-great-grandfather married his second cousin, Mary Unthank, and both were ejected from the body by the second cousin decree of the York Quarterly Meeting."   Our greatest scientists have shown that cousin-marriage is not detrimental to the offspring, thus contradicting one of our most persistent popular fallacies.   See my second volume for a full account of this subject and the Quaker rules verbatim.

† So says his grand-daughter, Anne West (1125), but the birth-place of his youngest child suggests Sankey, about two miles from Penketh.

Homer's 'Odyssey' and 'Iliad,' as well as the ' Spectator,' ' Tatler,' etc., by
Addison, and also the ' Life of George Fox.'   My connection with the
family was like entering a new world " (*ex* " Autobiography of Robert
Garnett").   She died 10th November, 1848, in Academy Place, Warrington,
at the residence of her son-in-law, Edward West, with whom she had lived
for some years, and she was buried at Penketh.

    i.   John Thistlethwaite (1093), born 29th February, 1796, at
           Manchester, and died there 2nd March, 1797.

    ii.   Thomas Thistlethwaite (1094), whom see.

    iii.   Margaret Thistlethwaite (1107), whom see.

    iv.   Alicia Thistlethwaite (1113), whom see.

    v.   Ann Thistlethwaite (1114) whom see.

    vi.   William Thistlethwaite (1127), whom see.

Thomas Thistlethwaite (1094), born 6th December, 1797, at
Manchester.   He was apprenticed to Sanders, grocers and bankers, of
Whitby, but spent most of his life in Manchester, where he held a respon-
sible position in the bank of Messrs. Lloyd, Entwhistle & Co.   Shortly
after this was taken over by the Manchester and Liverpool Bank he
retired with his wife and daughters to Whitby, where he died 20th
July, 1881, and was interred in the cemetery there.   He was married 12th
July, 1826, at Knaresborough, Yorkshire, to Ann Ripley, who was born
30th October, 1795, and died 22nd April, 1877.   He married a non-
Quaker, and severed his connection with the Society of Friends.

    i.   William Thistlethwaite (1095), whom see.

    ii.   Mary Thistlethwaite (1105), born 9th September, 1829, and
           baptised at the Parish Church, Manchester ; died un-
           married, 21st February, 1895, at Whitby.

    iii.   Ann Elizabeth Thistlethwaite (1106), born 5th September, 1831,
           and baptised at the Parish Church, Manchester ; died,
           unmarried, 7th October, 1897, at Whitby.

William Thistlethwaite (1095), born 2nd December, 1827, and
baptised in the Parish Church, Manchester.   He was manager of the

Manchester and Liverpool District Bank, at Nantwich, Cheshire, and died there, 2nd October, 1896. He was married 15th January, 1861, at the Parish Church, Whitby, to Laura Stephenson, daughter of Appleton and Ann Stephenson, the former a solicitor of Whitby. She was born 22nd April, 1841, and died at Nantwich, 16th August, 1903.

    i.   Clifton William Thistlethwaite (1096), born 29th June, 1866, at Whitby; Master of Arts of Exeter College, Oxford, and Clerk in Holy Orders. In 1909 curate at Wilmslow, Cheshire, but in the spring of 1910, he was licensed to the curacy of Hampton Bishop, Hereford; unmarried. "Clifton" is a family name of the Stephensons.

    ii.   Thomas Vere Close Thistlethwaite (1097), whom see.

    iii.   Arthur Henry Thistlethwaite (1102), born 8th June, 1871, at Whitby, and is farming in New Zealand. He married 1st March, 1904, near or in Tauranga, N.Z., Edith Eleanor Kensington, *s.p.*

    iv.   Annie Laura Thistlethwaite (1103), born 19th August, 1874, at Whitby, now of Nantwich, unmarried.

    v.   Bertie Fleming Thistlethwaite (1104), born 15th March, 1880, at Nantwich, where he is now a bank clerk, unmarried. He derives his middle name from a certain Dr. Fleming, for whom his father was executor.

Thomas Vere Close Thistlethwaite (1097), born 28th September, 1869, at Whitby, Yorkshire. Now wine and spirit merchant, of Nantwich. He married, 14th June, 1898, Frances Laura Elliott, who has issue,

    i.   Vera Laura Thistlethwaite (1098). born 22nd May, 1899, at Nantwich.

    ii.   Mabel Phyllis Thistlethwaite (1099), born 10th December, 1901, at Nantwich.

    iii.   Dorothy Frances Thistlethwaite (1100), born 18th July, 1904, at Nantwich.

iv. William Thistlethwaite (1101), born 24th December, 1908, at
Nantwich.

Margaret Thistlethwaite (1107), born 22nd November, 1799,
at Manchester. While resident at Penketh, she married, 2nd June,
1825, at Penketh Meeting House, Samuel West, woollen draper, of
Warrington, son of William and Elizabeth West, of Shaftesbury, Dorset-
shire. His brother, Edward, married her younger sister Ann. Samuel
West died about 1830, and his widow and daughter lived with Edward
West, at Warrington (on his becoming a widower in 1839), until 1851,
when they removed to Doncaster. Thence they went to Nottingham,
and finally Margaret West lived with her daughter and son-in-law, at
Wymondham, Norfolk, where she died, 26th September, 1884.

    i. Mary West (1108), whom see.
    ii. William West (1112), born 26th January, 1830, at Warrington,
        and died an infant.

Mary West (1108), born 21st March, 1827, at Warrington,
Lancashire. She married 16th July, 1856, at Doncaster Meeting House,
her second cousin, Arthur West, son of William West, chemist, of Leeds.
Arthur West was apprenticed to Kitson, Hewitson and Co., engineers of
Leeds, after which he had a business as lithographic printer at
Nottingham. Partly on account of health he went to Montserrat (West
Indies), to superintend the erection of sugar-cane crushing machinery
for the Sturges. This he accomplished satisfactorily, notwithstanding
a severe accident, by which he lost three fingers of his right hand.
He and his wife and little boy were in Antigua for a short time before
returning to England. He afterwards settled at Wymondham, Norfolk,
as ironmonger, the business eventually passing to his son.

Arthur and Mary West, after the birth of their grand-children,
removed to South Africa on account of their son's health, and the former
died 3rd May, 1908, aged seventy-eight years. Mary West (1108), now
lives near her son, at Sea Point, near Cape Town, South Africa.

    i. Samuel Arthur West (1109), whom see.

Samuel Arthur West (1109), born 18th May, 1857, at Nottingham, and apprenticed to an ironmonger at Whitby. He took over his father's business at Wymondham, Norfolk, which he eventually gave up and went to South Africa on account of his health. There he was at first manager of a hardware store, and is now a small farmer, while his wife carries on a large boarding establishment at Worcester House, Worcester Road, Sea Point, Cape Colony. He married Alice Mary Smith, daughter of a miller living at Carlton Rode, near Attleborough, Norfolk.

    i.   Bernard Tuffen West (1110), born 7th April, 1890, at Wymondham, Norfolk, now in the South African Bank, at Cape Town.

    ii. Margaret Hilda West (1111), born 31st August, 1892, at Wymondham, Norfolk ; now of Cape Town.

Alicia Thistlethwaite (1113), born 28th January, 1802, at Manchester. She married December, 1851, at Warrington, Benjamin Wilson, of Blyth, near Worksop, Nottinghamshire. They lived for some years at Blyth, when Benjamin Wilson gave up his business, that of a general country shop, and they settled at Holly Mount, Nottingham, near to his sister Miriam Armitage. He died there 5th December, 1870, aged seventy-nine years. Alicia Wilson (1113) remained at Nottingham, and died there 1st May, 1875, *sine prole*.

Ann Thistlethwaite (1114), born 11th June, 1804, at Manchester. While resident at Warrington she married 24th March, 1831, at Warrington Meeting house, Edward West, woollen draper of Warrington, son of William West, farmer and later schoolmaster of Shaftesbury, who died at Edward West's, at Warrington. His brother Samuel West married her sister Margaret Thistlethwaite (1107), whom see. Ann West died 17th July, 1839, at Warrington, and her sister Margaret came to live with Edward West until 1851.

Edward West married secondly, in 1852, Hannah Rutter, of Bath, and had by her one child, Edward West, Jr., now of the Steam Laundry, Swinton, Manchester.* Edward West, Sr. died 28th April, 1883, aged eighty-six, while living with his daughter Elizabeth Brown, at Banbury. By his first wife he had issue,

    i.   Samuel West (1115), born 29th August, 1833, at Warrington ; died in infancy.

    ii. Elizabeth West (1116), whom see.

    iii. Anne West (1125), born 3rd April, 1837, at Warrington ; now residing, unmarried, with her sister, Elizabeth Brown, at Banbury. A minister in the Society of Friends.

    iv. Edward West (1126), born 15th June, 1839, at Warrington ; died an infant.

Elizabeth West (1116), born 17th April, 1835, at Warrington, Lancashire. She was married 5th March, 1861, at the Baptist Chapel, Warrington, to Wilks Brown, woollen-draper and commercial traveller ; and they lived some years after their marriage at Kendal, during which period Wilks Brown became a Quaker. His wife was the first member of Hardshaw East Monthly Meeting, who was not disowned for " marrying out." In 1868, they were living at Nantwich, and now reside at 62, Broughton Road, Banbury. Wilks Brown is of Scotch descent, his father, Edward Brown, being " a Congregational minister, educated under the auspices of Matthew Wilks." Edward Brown was a fellow-student and intimate friend of Moffat and Williams, the famous missionaries, and at one time contemplated going to the South Seas, but was chosen instead for mission work in Ireland.

    i.   Elizabeth Bartlett Brown (1117), born 30th December, 1861, at Kendal ; now living unmarried, at 12, Parsons Street, Banbury, being, jointly with her sister, proprietor of the " Original Cake Shop."

* Edward West, jun., married Louisa Gundry, daughter of Joseph Gundry, of Congresbury. Their three children are (i) Mary Louisa West, married Wilfred Irwin, of Manchester ; (ii) Amy Estelle West, married Fred Williams ; (iii) Edward Gundry West, unmarried.

  ii. Ann West Brown (1118), born 23rd February, 1863, at Kendal ; died at Ackworth School, 1st February, 1877.

  iii. Charlotte Brown (1119), born 20th December, 1864, at Kendal ; now in business with her sister as above.

  iv. Edward Wilks Brown (1120), born 3rd September, 1866, at Kendal ; died 10th May, 1867.

  v. Samuel Edward Brown (1121), whom see.

  Samuel Edward Brown (1121), born 20th August, 1868, at Nantwich ; M.A. Cantab., sometime science master at Uppingham School, and now headmaster of the Collegiate Institution, Liverpool. He married 6th January, 1904, at Swanage Church, Margaret Robinson, daughter of Gerald Robinson, mezzotint engraver to the King, and grand-daughter of Sir Charles Robinson, C.B.

  i. Christopher Ernest Gordon Brown (1122), born 31st January, 1905, at Uppingham.

  ii. Marian Elizabeth Brown (1123), born 6th February, 1907, at Uppingham.

  iii. David Gerald West Brown (1124), born 19th March, 1909, at Liverpool.

  William Thistlethwaite (1127), born 26th January, 1808, in the township of Sankey and parish of Prescott, Lancashire. He had a chemist's business at Warrington, and married Sophia Morris, who was apparently a Quaker, as her children were born " members." After his daughter, and shortly before his son, went to Ackworth School, he left England for New Orleans, U.S.A., and appears to have died of yellow fever shortly after arrival.

  i. Elizabeth Thistlethwaite (1128), born 1st January, 1833, at Warrington ; became a teacher at Ayton Friends' School, where she died, unmarried, 7th May, 1851, and is buried in the Friends' Burial Ground, Great Ayton, Yorkshire.

ii.   Theodosius Thistlethwaite (1129), born 20th April, 1834, at
Warrington. He was apprenticed to Joseph Jesper,
clothier, of Preston, after which he spent about a year in a
large store in New York. On returning he was employed
by his uncle, Edward West, at Warrington, and is said
to have married Jane Jones, of Warrington, by whom he
left children. I have been unable to trace living descendants.

Alice Thistlethwaite (1131), born 4th March, 1753, in Dent Dale ;
married 29th September, 1779, to Thomas Carter, of Carperby, near
Aysgarth, Wensleydale, who later lived at Leayat in Dent Dale.

Thomas Carter was born 30th December, 1749. He was a
" cordwainer," an archaic expression for " shoe-maker," derived from
the custom of using " Cordovan " leather, that is, leather from Cordova,
in Spain. Thomas Carter's great-grandson (Rev. C. A. Carter, of Liverpool) writes me as follows :—" When the Professor [Adam Sedgwick,
F.R.S.] visited my father in the ' sixties ' he used to tell a story of how
my father's grandfather [Thomas Carter, of Carperby] visited the Grammar
School at Dent to get the Headmaster to sign a petition against slavery,
and seeing young Adam Sedgwick, he said, ' Let this boy sign, he looks an
intelligent lad.' "

Thomas Carter of Carperby had a sister Ellen (or Jane ?) who married
John Willis and had about nine sons, one of whom, Matthew Willis, was
the father of Bessie Longmire Willis, who married William Timothy
Bradley (415). John Willis had a son Thomas Willis, who was converted
to Quakerism by Stephen Grellet, while the latter was preaching in
Wensleydale. Thomas Willis's grand-daughter, Ethel Marguerite Willis,
married Alfred Rowntree, of Kirkby Overblow, whose father, John
Rowntree, married Ann Webster (1725), See under Jane Thistlethwaite
(759), in Part II.

Thomas and Alice Carter of Carperby had issue two children,

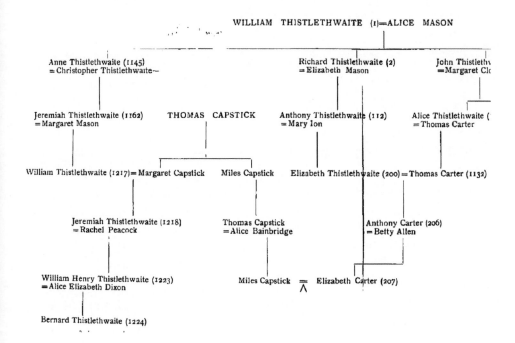

WILLIAM   THISTLETHWAITE   (1)=ALICE   MASON

Anne Thistlethwaite (1145)
= Christopher Thistlethwaite–

Richard Thistlethwaite (2)
= Elizabeth Mason

John Thistlethv
=Margaret Clc

Jeremiah Thistlethwaite (1162)
= Margaret Mason

THOMAS   CAPSTICK

Anthony Thistlethwaite (112)
= Mary Ion

Alice Thistlethwaite (
= Thomas Carter

William Thistlethwaite (1217)= Margaret Capstick

Miles Capstick

Elizabeth Thistlethwaite (200) = Thomas Carter (1132)

Jeremiah Thistlethwaite (1218)
= Rachel Peacock

Thomas Capstick
= Alice Bainbridge

Anthony Carter (206)
= Betty Allen

William Henry Thistlethwaite (1223)
= Alice Elizabeth Dixon

Miles Capstick   =   Elizabeth Carter (207)

Bernard Thistlethwaite (1224)

i. Thomas Carter (1132), born 8th August, 1781 ; died 17th April, 1845. He married, when of Leayat, his second cousin, Betty Thistlethwaite (200), 28th May, 1807, and their descendants are traced under her name in Part I. They lived in Dent Dale, and she died in 1812. He married secondly, 26th March, 1817, Ann Akrigg, who was without issue. He was then living at High Thistlethwaite, a cottage near Harborgill.

ii. John Carter (1133), born 16th January, 1784, at Richmond, Yorkshire. He died unmarried, 20th November, 1856, having been a cattle dealer for many years at Preston.

Ann Thistlethwaite (1134), born 20th December, 1755, in Dent Dale; married 19th October, 1785, at Warrington Meeting House, to John Taylor, corn factor, of Manchester, son of John Taylor, yeoman, of Styal, in Cheshire, by his wife Catherine. Probably he was the Quaker Taylor of Manchester, with whom Ann Thistlethwaite's brother William was in partnership.

i. Ann Taylor (1135), born 26th September, 1787, at Manchester. I do not know what became of her.

ii. Mary Taylor (1136), born 24th September, 1789, at Manchester, married John Lowe and had issue,

    i. John Lowe (1137), an architect, who married, but is said to have had no children.

    ii. Mary Anne Lowe (1138), who married a widower named Fawcett, living somewhere in the North of England, and had no children of her own. I should much like to discover some living descendants of the above Ann Thistlethwaite (1134).

PART FIVE.

DESCENDANTS OF

ISABEL THISTLETHWAITE (1142),

SIXTH CHILD OF

WILLIAM THISTLETHWAITE (1), OF HARBORGILL.

PART FIVE.

Isabel Thistlethwaite (1142), was born 6th July, 1717, in Dent Dale, probably at Harborgill. Her niece, Alice Chorley (1020), writes of her, "Isabel was middle-sized, of literary knowledge, which, added to genteel manners, rendered her an agreeable companion." She was married 26th February, 1749, at Leayat Meeting House, Dent Dale, to Henry Morland, a farmer in Wensleydale.

From the "Tithe Book" of Richmond Monthly Meeting of the Society of Friends, now at Carperby Meeting House, it appears that "Friends Tithe, etc., was adjudge before John Hutton, Esq. and Edward Place, clerk, two Justices of the peace, at the Half-penny house, the 13th 4th mo. 1764, as followeth, viz., [among many others] Henry Morland, four shillings costs," making, with the tithe on 60 sheep, 17 lambs, 5 cows, and 5 calves, a total of £1 1s. 7½d. He is previously 6s. in arrears, and with 2s. for "distress" the sum wanted becomes £1 13s. 7½d. On account of this there was "distrained

	s.	d.
Dozen stockins	10	8
Cheese	6	1
* Beef, 35 at 3½d. and 1d. over	10	3½
In all	£1 7	0½

being 6s. 7d. short, but he is overcharged half a calf which is to be righted next year."

* Note the price of beef per pound 150 years ago.

From Alice Chorley's Record, it appears that her aunt Isabel had at least two children, and very possibly more, for Alice Chorley, in her Record, frequently omits important members of the family.   But I have had search made by Norman Penney, F.S.A., in the Quaker Registers at Devonshire House, neither births, nor marriages, of children being found.   Most unfortunately the registers for Wensleydale during a large part of the eighteenth century have been lost, and the only records apparently remaining are the minute books now kept in an unlocked cupboard in Carperby Meeting House.   From these I have found much of interest in reference to the Wensleydale Thistlethwaites,"* but no light has yet been thrown on Morland descendants.

   i.   Isabel Morland (1143), who had issue, according to Alice Chorley.

  ii.   Alice Morland (1144), who had issue, according to Alice Chorley.

---

* Relatives of my great-great-great-grandfather, Christopher Thistlethwaite, who married, 1751, Anne Thistlethwaite (1145), of Dent.   No local parish registers exist before 1711, and the Aysgarth registers after that date contain only one Thistlethwaite entry.

PART SIX.

DESCENDANTS OF

ANNE THISTLETHWAITE (1145),

SEVENTH CHILD OF

WILLIAM THISTLETHWAITE (1), OF HARBORGILL.

PART SIX.

Anne Thistlethwaite (1145), was born 30th October, 1720, in Dent Dale, probably at Harborgill. Her niece, Alice Chorley (1020), describes her as "much pitted with the smallpox," and "of a religious amiable character." She died in Dent Dale, 30th April, 1772, aged fifty-one years.

She was married 4th July, 1751, to Christopher Thistlethwaite, hosier, of Aysgarth, Wensleydale, Yorkshire. That he was a kinsman of the Dent family I do not doubt, but the relationship was probably distant.

Christopher Thistlethwaite was a son of Jeremiah Thistlethwaite, who was married, 21st September, 1711, to Margaret Burn, of Aysgarth, at the Friends' Meeting House there. Jeremiah's father, Arthur Thistlethwaite, of Carperby, Wensleydale, suffered as a Quaker six years and twenty-nine weeks imprisonment at York. I hope to print a full account of the Wensleydale Thistlethwaites, and their descendants, in a second volume.*

As the name of only Christopher Thistlethwaite's youngest child, born 1763, appears in the Dent Quaker Registers, I conclude that his

---

* It may be mentioned here that the Dent family usually spelled their surname "Thistlethwayte." This spelling is used at the present day by the Thistlethwaytes of Hampshire, whose ancestors probably separated from the Dent Dale stock in the fifteenth century. However, in the marriage certificate of Christopher's parents it is uniformly spelled "Thistlethwait," and the Wensleydale contemporary Quaker minute books suggest that this variant was most commonly used by the Wensleydale family.

Glen Thistlethwaite (1686), of Earlham College, Indiana, writes that among many of the American kinsmen "Thistlewaite" is becoming the permanent *pronunciation*, but not *spelling*, although he personally asks for the full pronunciation. I have noticed that the old Dent farmers invariably say "Thistlethut," which perhaps explains why so awkward a name has persistently retained its full number of consonants.

elder children were born at Aysgarth in Wensleydale, and that he removed into Dent shortly before the above named year.   He died 31st October, 1794, aged seventy-four years, at Hobsons-in-Dent, a house close to Leayat Meeting House, on the other side of the road.

His great-grandson (my grandfather) tells of a tradition according to which Christopher Thistlethwaite, some time before his actual death, recovered from, I suppose, a cataleptic seizure only just in time to prevent his burial.

    i.   Margaret Thistlethwaite (1146), whom see.

    ii. Alice Thistlethwaite (1161), probably born at Aysgarth about 1755, and is mentioned by Alice Chorley as "remaining single."   She died at Hobsons, 11th July, 1825, aged 70 years.

    iii. Jeremiah Thistlethwaite (1162), whom see.

    iv. Ann Thistlethwaite (1245), whom see.

    v. William Thistlethwaite (1257), whom see.

Margaret Thistlethwaite (1146), born probably at Aysgarth, between 1751 and 1763, the Quaker register which should contain the date being lost.   She married at Leayat Meeting House, 26th June, 1777*, James Anderson of Kelso, in the county of Roxburgh, grocer and weaver, son of Michael Anderson of Edinburgh, tanner, and of Kelso, linen manufacturer, by his wife Christian Gray of the City of Old Aberdeen†. Margaret and James Anderson both appear to have been living in 1791, but James died before 1797, and Margaret before 1831.

    i.   Michael Anderson (1147), born at Kelso, Scotland, 27th May 1778, and died aged nineteen years at Edinburgh, 23rd August, 1797, buried the following day in Edinburgh.

    ii. Ann Anderson (1148), whom see.

* The marriage certificate contains the signatures as witnesses of the following Thistlethwaites:—four Williams; two Johns, Alices, and Margarets; and Mary, Isabel, Thomas, Jeremiah, Christopher, Arthur, Agnes, Anthony, and Richard.

† Michael was the son of Patrick Anderson, of Kelso, Scotland, weaver; and Christian, whom he married 9th November, 1728, was daughter of James Gray, of the City of Old Aberdeen, merchant.

   iii. Christian Anderson (1157), whom see.

   iv. Christopher Anderson (1159), born at Kelso, 26th August 1784, died at Kelso 12th June, 1785, and buried there the following day.

   v. Margaret Anderson (1160), born at Kelso, 15th August, 1787, died at Kelso, 3rd September, 1791, aged four years, and and buried there on the fifth.

Ann Anderson (1148), born 9th November, 1779, at Kelso, co. Roxburgh, N.B. She married, about 1803, Thomas Thwaite farmer of Low Blean, in Wensleydale, who died many years before her decease. She first appeared as a Quaker minister about 1815. She lived at Bainbridge, in about 1840, and afterwards at Westhouse in Dent and near Dent's Town, but died at Bainbridge in Wensleydale. At one time she also lived in the cottage at Hobsons in Dent.

   i. John Thwaite (1149), born 8th August, 1804, at Low Blean, in the parish of Aysgarth, probably died young, *s.p.*

   ii. Margaret Thwaite (1150), born 12th of May 1806, at Low Blean, died an infant.

   iii. James Thwaite (1151), born 7th April 1808, at Low Blean, probably died young, *s.p.*

   iv. William Thwaite (1152), born 12th May, 1810, at Low Blean, probably died young, *s.p.*

   v. Elizabeth Thwaite (1153), born 20th March, 1812, at Low Blean, married Matthew King, of Bentham, draper, when she was middle-aged, and had one child which died an infant.

   vi. Margaret Thwaite (1154), born 15th April, 1814, of unsound mind, died unmarried.

   vii. Mary Ann Thwaite (1155), born 14th May, 1818, died unmarried about 1838.

   viii. Thomas Thwaite (1156), born 11th August, 1821, at one time assistant with Bainbridges, drapers, of Newcastle-on-Tyne, died unmarried about 1851.

Christian Anderson (1157), born 11th August, 1781, at Kelso in the county of Roxburgh, Scotland. At the age of nearly fifty she was living at Kendal, and on 13th April, 1831, was married at Preston Patrick Meeting House, in the county of Westmorland, to Joseph Binns of Craw-shaw Booth, in the county of Lancashire, leather-cutter, son of David Binns, of the same place, leather-cutter, and of Ann, his wife, both then deceased. Joseph Binns died at Crawshaw Booth, about 1842-3, and his wife Christian soon afterwards went to live near her son at Castleton, Yorkshire. A little while before he left Castleton, she removed into one of Thomas Richardson's cottages at Great Ayton, in Cleveland, Co. York. Here she died 31st December, 1870, aged eighty-nine years, and was interred in the Friends' Graveyard, where a headstone incorrectly names her as " Christiana Binns." When a girl she was a maid in the London household of the father of Josiah Forster, who was later to become an eminent Quaker, and at the age of about twenty she had a natural child.

   i. William Anderson (1158), born about 1801, and educated at Ackworth School. He was for many years employed by Thomas Baker, grocer and draper, at the " High Shop," Castleton, and when the latter retired on account of ill-health, William Anderson (1158) took over the shop himself, the " Low Shop " at Castleton also becoming his property. Jeremiah Thistlethwaite (1218), of Great Ayton, who had also been assistant to Thomas Baker, and who was after-wards to marry the latter's first cousin, became assistant to William Anderson. In spite of a paying business, the last years of William Anderson's life were unfortunate ; and after giving up the shop at Castleton about 1860 he spent his time walking about the country, making what little money he required by reading in his excellent manner at taverns. He never married, and is said to have died in Skipton Workhouse.

Jeremiah Thistlethwaite (1162), born in 1757, probably at Aysgarth. He married 31st March, 1779, Margaret Mason, who was born 23rd March, 1757, daughter of Anthony Mason,* "public friend," by his wife Elizabeth Adamthait, whom he married 3rd March, 1738.

He lived at Hobsons-in-Dent, opposite Leayat, and here his three children were born. He later lived at Rasett (or Rayside), a house near Leayat, which, my grandfather told me, was his own property. He was apparently obliged to sell this, and removed to Darlington in 1825 at the age of sixty-eight years, where his second son, Anthony Thistlethwaite (1164) had been settled since 1809. He was employed by the Peases as wool-comber.

The minute of Darlington Monthly Meeting held 20th September, 1825, runs : " A certificate has been received from Sedbergh Monthly Meeting, dated 30th of Eighth Month 1825, on behalf of Jeremiah and Margaret Thistlethwaite settled at Darlington, the latter in the station of Minister, which is accepted, and Jonathan Backhouse and Henry Frederick Smith are appointed to urite with women friends and visit them." The following minute was made at the Monthly Meeting held 17th July, 1827 : " One of the overseers of Darlington meeting informs us that Jeremiah and Margaret Thistlethwaite who were recommended from Sedbergh Monthly Meeting are now, in account of the increased age and inability of the former to follow his business as heretofore, requiring the assistance of friends, and have accordingly been relieved. The clerk is requested to send a copy of this minute to Sedbergh Monthly Meeting."

Margaret Thistlethwaite, who had been acknowledged a minister in the Society of Friends by Briggflatts Monthly Meeting in 1797, died at Darlington 15th November, 1832, and was interred in the Friends' Burial Ground on the 18th November, aged seventy-five years. The following minute was made 4th December, 1832 :—" We appoint Edward Pease†

* Anthony Mason was son of Christopher Mason by his wife Agnes Burton, whom he married 3rd March, 1704. For Mason family see my second volume.

† " Edward Pease " founded the first railway in England, and his son " Joseph Pease, Junior " was the first Quaker member of Parliament, and father of Sir Joseph Whitwell Pease, Baronet. Sophia, daughter of Edward Pease's son " John Pease," married Sir Theodore Fry, Baronet.

William Robson, John Thistlethwate, John Pease, and Joseph Pease, jun., to prepare a few lines by way o'minute concerning our dear deceased friend Margaret Thistlethwaite, lat: of Darlington, minister."

Before July, 1833, Jeremiah Tistlethwaite (1162) returned to Dent, and spent the rest of his life with hison, William Thistlethwaite (1217) at Leayat, in the cottage next to the Meting House.   Here he died in 1838, aged eighty-one years, and was bued in the Friends' Burial Ground at Leayat.   My grandfather remembed him as a small thin man of amiable disposition.

    i.   Christopher Thistlethwae (1163), born 12th June, 1780, at Hobsons, died aged nieteen years, unmarried, 4th January, 1800.

    ii. Anthony Thistlethwaite1164), whom see.

    iii. William Thistlethwaite.217), whom see.

Anthony Thistlethwaite (11), born 15th June,1782, in Dent Dale. He was settled at Darlington, May809, and went through the Pease's woollen business with John Pease (l:r of Cleveland Lodge, Great Ayton). " Anthony Thistlethwaite, warehseman, of Darlington," died there 28th December, 1831, aged forty-1e years, and was buried there 1st January, 1832.

He married at Yarm Meetinghouse 23rd December, 1814, Mary Hedley,* of Darlington, daughter ames and Sarah Hedley.   She was born 29th August, 1790, at Low Cocliffe, in the parish of High Coniscliffe, near Darlington, her father tg a flax-dresser.   Her mother was Sarah Hartas, daughter of Williaand Mary Hartas of Danby Dale, Co. York, and sister to George 'tas whose granddaughter, Rachel Peacock, married Anthony Thistlwaite's nephew, Jeremiah Thistlethwaite (1218).   See Chart VII.

On 25th July, 1840, eight ye after her husband's death, Mary Thistlethwaite left England with two sons and landed in New York 29th August, 1840, the day she ' fifty years of age.   She died at

* See " Unhistoric Acts " (Headleothers), by George Baker, of York.

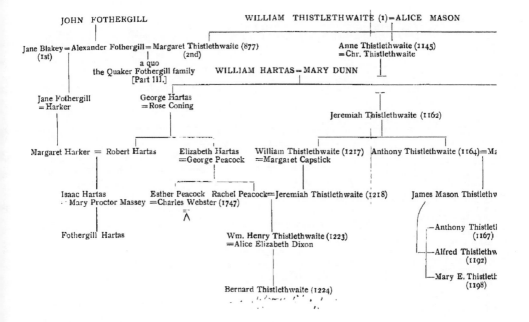

JOHN FOTHERGILL   WILLIAM   THISTLETHWAITE (1)＝ALICE   MASON

Jane Blakey ＝Alexander Fothergill ＝ Margaret Thistlethwaite (877)   Anne Thistlethwaite (1145)
    (1st)   (2nd)   ＝Chr. Thistlethwaite
                              a quo
                    the Quaker Fothergill family   WILLIAM HARTAS＝MARY DUNN
                           [Part III.]

Jane Fothergill   George Hartas
＝Harker   ＝Rose Coning   Jeremiah Thistlethwaite (1162)

Margaret Harker ＝ Robert Hartas   Elizabeth Hartas   William Thistlethwaite (1217) Anthony Thistlethwaite (1164)＝M
                                    ＝George Peacock   ＝Margaret Capstick

Isaac Hartas   Esther Peacock Rachel Peacock＝Jeremiah Thistlethwaite (1218)   James Mason Thistlethw
  Mary Proctor Massey   ＝Charles Webster (1747)

Fothergill Hartas   Wm. Henry Thistlethwaite (1223)   —Anthony Thistletl
                                                    ＝Alice Elizabeth Dixon   (1167)

                                                                                             —Alfred Thistlethw
                                                                                                 (1192)

                                                    Bernard Thistlethwaite (1224)   —Mary E. Thistleth
                                                                                                 (1198)

Macedon, Wayne County, New York State, at the residence of her son Jeremiah, 27th July, 1884, aged nearly ninety-four years.

  i. Margaret Hannah Thistlethwaite (1165), born 18th April, 1816, at Darlington in the County of Durham, where she died 1st March, 1834, aged eighteen years, and was buried 6th March, unmarried.

  ii. James Mason Thistlethwaite (1166), whom see.

  iii. Jeremiah Thistlethwaite (1205), whom see.

  iv. Sarah Thistlethwaite (1216), born 9th December, 1830, at Darlington, where she died 28th October, 1832, aged two years, and was buried 1st November.

James Mason Thistlethwaite (1166), born 6th August, 1820, at Darlington. He is said to have been in Pease's Bank there until he emigrated to America in 1840 with his mother and younger brother. He was thrice married, the first time 21st December, 1842, at Shelby, Orleans County, New York State, to Mary Hawley Haines, daughter of Reuben and Anne Haines, who was born 11th March, 1825. She died 19th June, 1850, aged twenty-five years, leaving three children.

  i. Anthony Mason Thistlethwaite (1167), whom see.

  ii. Sarah Haines Thistlethwaite (1178), whom see.

  iii. Alfred Thistlethwaite (1192), born 5th April, 1850, at Milville, Orleans County, N.Y., now farmer near Tonganoxie, Kansas. He married 8th August, 1882, at Tonganoxie, Emily Baker, who was born 16th April, 1851, near Shotley Bridge, Co. Durham, England. She was his second cousin, and her sister married his brother Anthony Mason Thistlethwaite (1167), whom see. They are *sine prole*, but have an adopted girl named Elsie.

On the death of his young wife, James Mason Thistlethwaite (1166) was fortunately able to entrust his three young children to his mother. On the 23rd January, 1852, she wrote from Milville a letter, from which the following is an extract, to her first cousin, Elizabeth Peacock, *née* Hartas, whose daughter, Rachel Peacock, married four years later the late Jeremiah Thistlethwaite (1218), of Great Ayton, Yorkshire, nephew by marriage to the writer of the letter :—" Thee and I can sympathise in the loss of daughters, and each of us have lost a daughter-in-law ; the loss of mine has left me with the care of three children, the oldest little more than six years old, the care of which, in addition to the care of housekeeping, I find occupyes my time pretty fully ; my health is not very good, but I have a hired girl that has been with me ever since my daughter-in-law died, and we can get help to wash, etc., when we need it. A cottage house belonging to the Farm is occupied by an Englishman, and his wife is willing to go out to wash, a thing rather uncommon in country situations in this part of America ; her husband works for my son James in the summer."

However, James Mason Thistlethwaite (1166), was married for the second time in Shelby, Orleans County, N.Y., 22nd November, 1854, to Ann Eliza Weaver, a widow. She was born 24th January, 1828, daughter of Jonathan and Elizabeth Taber, and married firstly John W. Weaver, by whom she had one child, John Wells Weaver, born 16th March, 1849. She died at Milville, N.Y., 9th July, 1861, aged thirty-three years, leaving by her second husband one child.

    iv.   Edward Joshua Thistlethwaite (1193), born 9th October, 1855, at East Shelby, N.Y., now living in Kansas City, Missouri, unmarried.

James Mason Thistlethwaite (1166), was married for the third time in Orleans County, N.Y., 15th October, 1862, to Sarah Emily Ransome. She was born 22nd March, 1834, in Dutchess County, N.Y., daughter of Joseph and Elizabeth (_née_ Wheeler) Ransome, and died at Tonganoxie, Kansas, 24th January, 1892, aged 58 years. At the age of 84 years, James Mason Thistlethwaite (1166) wrote a letter to my aunt from his residence at Linwood, Kansas. In this he says, " I have twenty-nine children, grand and great-grand, without reckoning their husbands or wives—about equal in number in New York, Missouri, and Kansas— four families here on adjoining farms in Kansas." He died 19th

March, 1906, at Tonganoxie, Kansas, aged eighty-six years. By his third wife, Sarah Emily Ransome,* he had three children.

  v. Ann Eliza Thistlethwaite (1194), whom see.

  vi. Mary Emily Thistlethwaite (1198), whom see.

  vii. Arthur Wensley Thistlethwaite (1202), whom see.

  Anthony Mason Thistlethwaite (1167), born 10th September, 1845, at Milville, Orleans County, N.Y., and is now resident in Kansas City, Missouri. He was married at Tonganoxie, Kansas, 15th November, 1871, to his second cousin, Ann Maria Baker, who was born at Shotley Bridge, Durham, England, 18th April, 1848. His brother and his half-sister married her sister and her brother respectively. See Chart VII.

   i. Lilian Theodora Thistlethwaite (1168), born 3rd December, 1873, at Medina, New York State.

   ii. Sarah Eleanor Baker Thistlethwaite (1169), whom see.

   iii. David Haines Thistlethwaite (1176), whom see.

   iv. Alfred Henry Thistlethwaite (1177), born 12th June, 1883, at Tonganoxie, Kansas, now jeweler (*sic*) at Trenton, Missouri.

  Sarah Eleanor Baker Thistlethwaite (1169), born 29th November, 1877, at Medina, N.Y., married 31st December, 1896, at Tonganoxie, Kansas, to Charles Fox Parham, a preacher, born 4th June, 1873, at Muscatine, Iowa, son of William and Anna Maria Parham.

   i. Claude Wallace Parham (1170), born 22nd September, 1897, at Baldwin, Kansas.

   ii. Esther Mary Parham (1171), born 29th November, 1898, at Topeka, Kansas.

   iii. Charles Theodore Parham, (1172), born 1st March, 1900, at Topeka, and died there 16th March, 1901.

* Sarah Emily Ransome was a descendant of Robert Ransome, of Aldborough, Suffolk, England, who died in 1588, and was son of Thomas Ransome, who lived in the fifteenth and sixteenth centuries. An intermediate ancestor was Richard Ransome, known as the "Quaker miller," who was born 1649, and died 8th November, 1716, in Bristol. He was a miller at North Walsham, Norfolk, became a Quaker in 1676, and was imprisoned fifteen years for his faith.

iv. Philip Arlington Parham (1173), born 2nd June 1902, at Kansas City, Missouri.

v. Wilfred Charles Parham (1174), born 16th March, 1904, at Galena, Kansas.

vi. Robert Parham (1175), born 1st June, 1906, at Keelville, Kansas.

David Haines Thistlethwaite (1176), born 17th August, 1880, at Tonganoxie, Kansas, near which place he is now a farmer. He was married 26th February, 1908, at Kansas City, to Merton Wade, born 1st December, 1886, at Oak, Nebraska, daughter of John R. and Loretta May Wade.

Sarah Haines Thistlethwaite (1178), born 27th May, 1847, at Millville, Orleans County, N.Y. She was married firstly 26th March, 1872, at Shelby, Orleans County, to Oscar Dillingham, who was born 21st June, 1842, at Elba, Genesee County, N.Y., son of Stephen and Anna Dillingham. Oscar Dillingham died 8th February, 1895, and his widow married 15th February, 1898, Warren Gardner, born 24th May, 1832, son of Joel and Gulielma Gardner. She now lives at Palmyra, Wayne County, N.Y., about nine miles from Macedon. By her first husband she had the following children :

i. James Irving Dillingham (1179), whom see.

ii. Alfred Stephen Dillingham (1184), whom see.

iii. Mary Helen Dillingham (1187), whom see.

iv. Ethel Anna Dillingham (1191), born 12th March, 1885, at Elba, Genesee County, N.Y., unmarried.

James Irving Dillingham (1179), born 3rd February, 1873, at Elba, Genesee County ; was married 28th June, 1900, at Glens Falls, N.Y., to Sara Rawson Keates, born 16th February, 1875, in Ireland, daughter of Harry Rowland and Elizabeth Robinson Keates, who were engaged in religious work there at the time.

    i. Elizabeth Keates Dillingham (1180), born 19th October, 1902, at Elba, N.Y.

    ii. Howard Irving Dillingham (1181), born 11th October, 1904, at Elba, N.Y.

    iii. Catherine Sara Dillingham (1182), born 1st September, 1906, at Elba, N.Y.

    iv. Maurice Stanley Dillingham (1183), born 30th March, 1908, at Elba, N.Y.

Alfred Stephen Dillingham (1184), born 25th December, 1874, at Elba, N.Y., and was married 27th September, 1899, at Elba, to Edythe Maritta Blood, born 27th April, 1879, in Cattarangus County, N.Y., daughter of Albert E. and Mary L. Blood of Elba, N.Y.

    i. Eula Belle Dillingham (1185), born 22nd July, 1900, at Elba, N.Y.

    ii. Paul Alfred Dillingham (1186), born 3rd April, 1904, at Auburn, Cayuga County, N.Y.

Mary Helen Dillingham (1187), born 28th January, 1878, at Elba, N.Y., and was married 8th June, 1899, at Elba, to Frederick Allan De Voll, born 3rd April, 1871, son of Allan Potter and Sarah Francis De Voll.

    i. Harold Allan De Voll (1188), born 24th September, 1900, at Newburgh-on-the-Hudson, N.Y.

    ii. Laurence Oscar De Voll (1189), born 3rd September, 1902, at Brighton (now East Rochester), N.Y.

    iii. Raymond Dillingham De Voll (1190), born 8th July, 1905, at Rochester, N.Y.

Ann Eliza Thistlethwaite (1194), born 7th January, 1865, at East Shelby, N.Y., and was married 18th February, 1891, at Tonganoxie, Kansas, to John Caffery Hopkins, born 16th June 1860, near Lawrence, Kansas, son of Thomas and Sarah Agnes Hopkins, and now a farmer near Tonganoxie, Kansas.

    i.   Raymond Curtis Hopkins (1195), born 19th November, 1891, at Linwood, Kansas.

    ii.   Arthur Edward Hopkins (1196), born 3rd December, 1893, at Linwood.

    iii.   Sarah Ethel Hopkins (1197), born 19th April, 1899, at Linwood.

Mary Emily Thistlethwaite (1198), born 8th February, 1867, at East Shelby, Orleans County, N.Y.; married 14th August, 1889, at Tonganoxie, Kansas, to her second cousin, Thomas Hedley Baker, born 24th April, 1854, near Shotley Bridge, Durham, England, son of David and Anna Maria (*née* Thompson) Baker, and now farmer near Tonganoxie. See Chart VII.

    i.   James Thistlethwaite Baker (1199), born 10th June, 1892, at Tonganoxie.

    ii.   Margaret Lucy Baker (1200), born 16th May, 1898, at Tonganoxie.

    iii.   Ruth Baker (1201), born 7th March, 1901, at Tonganoxie.

Arthur Wensley Thistlethwaite (1202), born 28th May, 1871, at East Shelby, N.Y., now jeweler (*sic*) and optician at Tonganoxie. He was married 28th December, 1893, at Lawrence, Kansas, to Linnie Hortans Kemmerling, born 4th August, 1871, at Altoona, Pennsylvania, daughter of Samuel Angus and Blanche Kemmerling.

    i.   Mae Nellie Thistlethwaite (1203), born 12th March, 1898, at Tonganoxie, Kansas.

    ii.   Helen Blanche Thistlethwaite (1204), born 8th August, 1906, at Tonganoxie.

Jeremiah Thistlethwaite (1205), born 12th September, 1824, at Darlington, England, and emigrated to America, aged sixteen years, with his mother and elder brother, in 1840. Writing to England in January, 1852, his mother says, " My son Jeremiah is in the Timber business so that he is but little at home with us, he is lately gone west through Canada, Michagon, and part of Ohio and Wisconson through the South part of Ilinois to a place called Greenbay on the Michigon Lake to buy Timber ; I don't like his taking such long journeys, railway and stage traveling is attended with some risk, especally in this country where railroads are only in most cases put up rather slight, and only a single line, but he seems to like it and hitherto he has been preserved from harm. If he does the business that he anticipates I don't look for him home before next midsummer. . . James' and my love to Wm. Anderson and Jeremiah* if at Castleton, I should like much to hear of Cousin Ann Thwaite, or any of our other relations in Dent. If Wm. A. would like to write to either James or me it would be acceptable."

Jeremiah Thistlethwaite (1205), married 3rd January, 1855, at Macedon, N.Y., Abigail Packard, born 19th November, 1829, at Macedon. She was daughter of Philander Packard (son of Bartimeus and Abigail, *née* Packard, Packard) by his wife Minerva, daughter of Isa and Mary (*née* Beal) Lapham.

The following account is extracted from the *Macedon News-Gatherer*, October 19th, 1901. " Jeremiah Thistlethwaite died at his home in this village, Wednesday evening at nine o'clock, October 16th, 1901, aged seventy-seven years, one month and four days. Deceased was born the twelfth day of September, 1824, at Darlington, England, to Anthony and Mary Thistlethwaite, who were members of the Society of Friends. When a child six years of age his father died—in 1830. He received his education at Wigton School in Cumberland County. In 1840, with his mother and brother James who is still living, he came to this country and settled at Millville, Orleans County.

* *i.e.*, my grandfather Jeremiah Thistlethwaite (1218), of Great Ayton, first cousin to Jeremiah Thistlethwaite (1205), of Macedon.

"Mr. Thistlethwaite first came to Macedon in 1843, when he began his business career as clerk in the store of Alexander Purdy. At that time he remained here nearly two years. He then became interested in the lumber business, and conducted different camps and saw mills in Pennsylvania and Canada and finally located as a wholesale merchant in that commodity at Buffalo in 1850. He remained in Buffalo until 1864, when, retiring from business, he settled in Macedon, where he resided until his death.

"Possessed of unusual good judgment and a habit of thoroughly investigating the smallest details of his business, his success was greater than is common. . . In politics Mr. Thistlethwaite was a Republican and represented Macedon on the Board of Supervisors in 1876, and the year following he was elected to the Assembly from the second district of Wayne County. He was a man from whom advice was frequently sought, and he conscientiously gave it. To be courteous to everyone was one of his aims, and no matter the provocation or the anger he may have felt, no one saw him different than a gentleman in the full meaning of the word. He could say no to those asking favours which he could not grant and leave them pleased to have asked even if disappointed. Age only tended to ripen his intellect, never to impair it, and up to the time of his last sickness he showed none of the failings old men usually manifest."

  i. Mary Thistlethwaite (1206), born 13th September, 1855, at Buffalo, N.Y., now living with her mother at Macedon, unmarried.

  ii. William Packard Thistlethwaite (1207), whom see.

  iii. Charles Jeremiah Thistlethwaite (1213), whom see.

  iv. Joseph Leayat Thistlethwaite (1214), whom see.

William Packard Thistlethwaite (1207), born 6th February, 1860, at Buffalo, N.Y., married 24th January, 1884 at Bridgeport, Connecticut, Annie Belle Gilbert, born 7th June, 1862, at Weston, Conn., daughter of George Hall Gilbert (son of Joseph and Matilda, *née* Bradley,

Gilbert) by his wife Maria E. daughter of Charles B. and Julia, *née* Kelsey, Flint. In 1900 he entered into partnership with his two brothers in a Grain Drill Factory at Despatch (or East Rochester, N.Y) and he lives at Macedon, 13 miles away.

    i. Leayat A. Thistlethwaite (1208), born 11th August, 1887, at Macedon, married 4th July, 1906, at Macedon, Allan T. Littell, farmer of Macedon, son of Henry M. and Cornelia (*née* Longstaff), Littell.

    ii. Agnes H. Thistlethwaite (1209), born 15th April, 1890, at Macedon.

    iii. Nina Minerva Thistlethwaite (1210), born 23rd March, 1896, at Macedon.

    iv. Abigail Thistlethwaite (1211), born 24th June, 1898, at Macedon.

    v. William Gilbert Thistlethwaite (1212), born 1st September, 1908, at Macedon.

Charles Jeremiah Thistlethwaite (1213), born 19th July, 1867, at Macedon, N.Y., now resident at Fairport, N.Y., and partner in the Drill Factory at Despatch. He married 12th September, 1901, at Minneapolis, Minnesota, Elizabeth Wright Hance, who was born 31st July, 1865, at Aurora, Illinois, daughter of Dr. Samuel Francis Hance (son of Thomas Clare Hance by his wife Esther Aldrich Lapham), by his wife Sarah Elizabeth, daughter of Warren and Betsy (*née* Sill) Wright. *Sine prole.*

Joseph Leayat Thistlethwaite (1214), born 30th April, 1871, at Macedon, N.Y., and practised law for about eight years in Rochester, N.Y., but now lives at Penfield, N.Y., about a mile from the Drill Factory at Despatch in which he is a partner. He was married 9th October, 1901, at Meriden, Connecticut, to Edna Maude Miller who was born 29th

15

November, 1871, at Meriden, Conn., daughter of Edward Gardner Miller
(son of Harrison Plum and Lucy Rand, *née* Johnson, Miller) by his wife
Harriet Prudence, daughter of Aaron Horsford and Eunice Peckham (*née*
Clark) Miller.

    i.   Harriet Miller Thistlethwaite (1215), born 4th March, 1906,
        at Penfield.

    ii. Jeremiah Thistlethwaite (1215a), born 18th June, 1910.

William Thistlethwaite (1217), born 31st January, 1786,
at Hobsons in Dent.   He married Margaret Capstick, daughter of Thomas
and Mary Capstick, of Slack, near Dent's Town ; they were probably
married at Dent Church in the year 1825.   William was a member of the
Society of Friends, and Margaret attended Friends' Meetings and wore a
Quaker bonnet,* but as she was not an actual member William was
disowned for his marriage, and he never asked for readmission as was
often the custom.   Hence his children were not born Quakers, but their
birth dates appear in the Quaker Register as " non-members," a thing
frequently done in the cases of children of those disowned by the marriage
rule.

William and Margaret Thistlethwaite first lived at Ewegallas (now
called Eugales).   I was fortunate enough to see the old and almost falling
house, nearly half a mile below Leayat, on the south bank of the Dee,
when in Dent about ten years ago, but on calling there this year found
that it had been entirely rebuilt in 1908 on the same site.   It is now
(1909) inhabited by Edward Capstick and his wife, formerly Agnes
Banister, a great niece of Agnes Banister who married the William
Thistlethwaite (430), who was killed driving in the snow.

---

   * All those interested in the first Dent Quakers should read the account in
" First Publishers of Truth " edited by Norman Penney, F.S.A. (Headley, 1907).
Many of the Mason family are mentioned, and among others are James and George
Capstack.   "At and about Gawthorp in Dent, in the grounds of one James Capstack,
were two meetings, where Gervas Benson ministered at one, and Thos. Taylor at the
other " (page 330).

William Thistlethwaite (1217), the subject of this paragraph, removed in about 1833 to the house next the Meeting House at Leayat, living a few months between at Basil Busk in Dent. He had to leave Leayat a few years before his death in order to make way for Richard Thistlethwaite (113), formerly of Studellagarth.* He died 10th June, 1850, at Cowgill, aged sixty-four years, and was buried at Leayat Friend's Burial Ground.

His widow eventually lived at Askrigg with her daughter, Mary Ann Gill (1238), and on the latter's death in 1860 remained with Thomas Gill until he married again, when she removed to her surviving daughter's at 'Bentham, Yorkshire. Here she died in April, 1870, aged seventy-seven years, and was buried at Leayat.

 i. Jeremiah Thistlethwaite (1218), whom see.

 ii. Thomas Thistlethwaite (1229), born 18th April, 1828, at Eugalas in Dent, and was for some time a mechanic at Rotherham. He died 20th April, 1854, at Askrigg, while living with his mother, who had been keeping a school there with her daughters, and he was buried at Leayat.

 iii. Margaret Thistlethwaite (1230), whom see.

 iv. Mary Ann Thistlethwaite (1238), whom see.

Jeremiah Thistlethwaite (1218), born 29th June, 1826, at Eugalas. His third cousin, Simon Thistlethwaite (159), a carrier at Hawes, took him to Rawdon School on horseback. He was apprenticed with Robert Clemesha, a grocer, of Blackburn, and also spent some time as assistant to Anthony Carter (206), of Dent's Town, relieving officer and a tea-dealer. He was later assistant to John Horniman, the far-famed tea merchant, in the Isle of Wight.

From here he went to Castleton in Cleveland, Yorkshire, and was assistant, as was William Anderson, to Thomas Baker at the High Shop. When Thomas Baker retired, Jeremiah Thistlethwaite (1218), remained

---

* This house, which stood at the extreme head of the dale, has for many years been in ruins. The ordnance map writes Studley Garth, but my spelling has the authority of the Quaker registers and local pronunciation, the first syllable accented.

as assistant to Wm. Anderson (1158), who took over the shop. He lived
with William Anderson (1158), to whose housekeeper, Rachel Peacock,
he became engaged. His third cousin, Charles Webster (1747), who had
been with David Baker, grocer, of Guisborough, eight miles away, married
Rachel Peacock's sister Esther at Guisborough Friends' Meeting House,
11th September, 1856, and Rachel went to stay with her at Halifax.

Jeremiah Thistlethwaite (1218), went there a little later, and was
married 2nd October 1856, at Halifax Registry Office, to Rachel Peacock,
born 24th August, 1824, at Woodale Farm, about eight miles from
Castleton, daughter of George Peacock (son of Benjamin Peacock by his
wife Martha Esthill, of Stainton-dale), by his wife Elizabeth Hartas,
daughter of George Hartas of Danby Dale, near Castleton, by his wife
Rose Coning.

They returned to Castleton for a few months, and removed in May,
1857, to the village of Great Ayton in Cleveland, eight miles from the
young town of Middlesbrough. Here he began a grocery and drapery
business, which, on his decease, passed to his only son, who had been
virtually manager for a number of years. In the year 1891, he and George
Dixon, of White House, Great Ayton, entered into partnership for the
purpose of opening and working certain Whinstone Mines under royalties
from Sir Joseph Whitwell Pease, Bart., and Jonathan Backhouse Hodgkin.
About six years ago the partnership was dissolved, and the mines became
the sole property of Jeremiah Thistlethwaite (1218), the management
from that date resting in the hands of his son. George Dixon is Jeremiah
Thistlethwaite's daughter's brother-in-law, and his daughter-in-law's
uncle.

Jeremiah Thistlethwaite (1218), died 17th April, 1910, in the house
in which he had lived since 1857, and was buried on the 20th April, in the
Friends' Burial Ground, Great Ayton. His wife, Rachel Thistlethwaite,
died 6th October, 1902, at Great Ayton, and was buried in the Friends'
Burial Ground there, aged seventy-eight years.

    i.   Elizabeth Ann Thistlethwaite (1219), whom see.

    ii.   Mary Margaret Thistlethwaite (1220), whom see.

    iii.   Lucy Maria Thistlethwaite (1222), born 30th December, 1861, at Great Ayton; educated at the Mount School, York, 8 mo. 1877 to 12 mo. 1878. She is unmarried, and lived with her father until his decease.

    iv.   William Henry Thistlethwaite (1223), whom see.

    v.   Rose Hannah Thistlethwaite (1226), whom see.

Elizabeth Ann Thistlethwaite (1219), born 11th July, 1857, at Great Ayton; educated at the Mount School, York, 8 mo. 1872 to 6 mo. 1874. She was married at Great Ayton Friends' Meeting House, 26th December, 1878, to John Naughton. He was born 21st June, 1846, at Maase North, Westport, in the County of Mayo, Ireland, son of Denis Naughton, by his wife Bridgid Dolan, and great-nephew of the Most Reverend John McHale, D.D., etc., Roman Catholic Archbishop of Tuam, Co. Galway, an eminent man of letters, who is said to have had an excellent prospect of becoming pope, would he have accepted the cardinal's hat.

John Naughton was assistant master at schools in Waterford, Jersey and the Midlands, and finally at the Friends' School at Great Ayton. He then began a private school at Carlton House, Halifax, whence he moved a few years after marriage, and has since been principal of Ellesmere School, Harrogate. *Sine prole.*

Mary Margaret Thistlethwaite (1220), born 28th January, 1860, at Great Ayton, educated at the Mount School, York, 8 mo., 1875 to 12 mo., 1876. She married, 21st January, 1892, at Great Ayton, Samuel Newton, born 11th January, 1849, at Bank Foot, Todmorden, son of Thomas Newton, land agent, of Blackburn (son of Samuel Newton (1775-1861), by his wife, Anne Ogden of Blackburn), by his wife Mary Hanson, daughter of Samuel Hanson, of Todmorden, by his wife Martha Shackleton (See Chart III).

Samuel Newton was articled at the Borough Surveyor's Office, Blackburn, and afterwards lived with his widowed mother at Todmorden, Yorkshire, until her death. He then entered the office of William Phillips Thompson, patent agent, of Liverpool, and about 1885 he came to Great Ayton to live with his brother-in-law George Dixon, spending the next three years in surveying the local estate of Sir Joseph Whitwell Pease, Baronet. A few months before his marriage he became Secretary to the Mildmay Mission to the Jews, Newington Green, London. He died 7th September, 1896, at Plimsoll Road, Finsbury Park, London.

> i. Mary Hanson Thistlethwaite Newton (1221), born 5th April, 1895, at Finsbury Park, now living with her mother at Great Ayton.

William Henry Thistlethwaite (1223), born 24th December, 1863, at Great Ayton, educated at Ackworth, and by his brother-in-law, John Naughton, at Halifax. He entered the office of William Phillips Thompson, patent agent, of Liverpool, for a few months, and then spent about a year in the shop of Amos Hinton, grocer, of Middlesbrough, before entering his father's business. He is now owner of this, and manager of his father's whinstone quarries. He married 29th July, 1886, at Great Ayton, Alice Elizabeth Dixon, born 10th December, 1861, at Great Ayton, second daughter of Ralph Dixon, superintendent of Ayton Friends' School (son of George Dixon, Sen., by his first wife Alice Swinburn) by his wife Elizabeth Fox, daughter of David Fox,* of Dewsbury, by his second wife, Rebecca Payne, of Southwark, London.

> i. Bernard Thistlethwaite (1224), born 18th September, 1888, at Great Ayton, Yorkshire, educated at Leighton Park School, Reading, September 1904 to December 1905, compiler of this family history.

* David Fox was first cousin to the mother of Sir Mark Oldroyd of Hyrstlands, Dewsbury, who married Maria Tew Mewburn, niece of John Taylor (1450). David Fox's daughters and Sir Mark Oldroyd's sisters attended the school at Dewsbury kept by Maria Thistlethwaite (1790), half-aunt to John Taylor (1450). See also under Isabel Thistlethwaite (583), and Chart V.

ii. Helen Thistlethwaite (1225), born 20th March, 1890, at Great Ayton, educated at Polam Hall,* Darlington, now living at home unmarried.

Rose Hannah Thistlethwaite (1226), born 2nd January, 1866, at Great Ayton, educated at the Mount School, York, 8 mo., 1882 to 12 mo., 1883, married at St. Hilda's Parish Church, Middlesbrough, 7th January, 1903, to Charles Frank Dodsworth, grocer and confectioner, of Great Ayton, born 2nd October, 1880, at Great Ayton, grandson of Foster Dodsworth by his wife Margaret Hansell.

i. Lucy Joyce Hartas Dodsworth (1227), born 5th February, 1904, at Great Ayton.

ii. Christine Margaret Dodsworth (1228), born 9th February, 1906, at Great Ayton.

Margaret Thistlethwaite (1230), born 13th April, 1830, at Eugalas, in Dent. She kept a school at Cowgill in Dent and later at Askrigg; at the latter place she became governess with the Winn family. In March, 1854, she was married at Bentham Church to William Cleminson, plumber, of Bentham, Yorkshire, who was born February, 1830, at Lancaster, son of William and Jane Cleminson. He died at Wakefield in 1873.

In 1872, Margaret Cleminson and her family removed from Bentham to Great Ayton, Yorkshire, where they lived for some time at Leayat House, built by her brother Jeremiah. They later carried on a confectionery business, on retiring from which in 1899 they removed to Redcar, Yorkshire, where they still live.

i. Jane Cleminson (1231), born 26th July, 1855, at Bentham, now of Redcar, unmarried.

* Helen Bayes, one of the principals of Polam Hall, married Oswald Bradley Baynes (410), whom see; he is fourth cousin once removed to Helen Thistlethwaite (1225). A number of Thistlethwaite descendants have been educated there.

ii.   Margaret Thistlethwaite Cleminson (1232), born 6th September, 1856, at Bentham, married 1st December, 1883, at Great Ayton Church to Frederick Miles, Inland Revenue Officer of Great Ayton. They removed about 1894 to Kirby Moorside, Yorkshire, where they lived until his death, which occurred while visiting Redcar 20th June, 1907, at the age of sixty-one years. He was buried in the Friends' Burial Ground, Great Ayton, and his widow now lives at that village, *sine prole*.

iii. Mary Ann Cleminson (1233), born 23rd May, 1859, at Bentham, now of Redcar, unmarried.

iv.   William Cleminson (1234), born 23rd January, 1862, at Bentham, now of Redcar, unmarried.

v.   Christiana Barbara Cleminson (1235), born at Bentham and died at Leayat House, Great Ayton, aged nine years.

vi.   Thomas Thistlethwaite Cleminson (1236), born at Bentham, and died there aged one week.

vii. Lucy Maria Cleminson (1237), born at Bentham, and died at Leayat House, Great Ayton, aged about three years.

Mary Ann Thistlethwaite (1238), born 20th October, 1832, at Eugalas in Dent, and was married to Thomas Gill, worsted manufacturer, of Askrigg, in Wensleydale, Yorkshire. She died 21st August, 1860, at Askrigg, leaving two children. Her mother lived with Thomas Gill until he married, secondly, Hannah Morland, by whom he had three children. He later became a farmer, and died at Askrigg in 1908. Thomas and Mary Ann Gill had offspring.

i.   William Gill (1239), whom see.

ii.   Mary Ann Gill (1243), whom see.

William Gill [(1239), born 7th December, 1858, at Askrigg, now farmer and postmaster at Low Row, near Reeth, Swaledale, Yorkshire.

He married 16th June, 1884, at St. Oswald's Church, Askrigg, Ann Isabella Metcalfe, daughter of John Metcalfe.

    i.   Margaret Gill (1240), born 18th December, 1886, at Low Row in the parish of Melbecks, Swaledale, unmarried.

    ii.   James Gill (1241), born 7th December, 1888, at Low Row, unmarried.

    iii.   Thomas Gill (1242), born 25th September, 1892, at Low Row, unmarried.

Mary Ann Gill (1243), born 9th May, 1860, at Askrigg, and married Benjamin Cartwright, a farmer at Carperby, who had formerly been signalman at Askrigg station. They removed to Ripon, and he eventually married again. Mary Ann Cartwright died 19th July, 1902, leaving one child.

    i.   Hannah Mary Cartwright (1244), born June, 1902, at Ripon, and died there the same year.

Ann Thistlethwaite (1245), was born about 1760, probably at Aygsarth. Before 1763, her parents had removed to Dent Dale, and from Hobsons in Dent she was married 26th November, 1783, to Matthew Middlebrook. As all their children were born at Hobsons, they appear to have lived there until 1802, perhaps with her father until he died there in 1794. Matthew Middlebrook died 7th April, 1836, at Leayat in Dent, aged 81, and his widow, Ann Middlebrook, died there 23rd October, 1842, aged eighty-two.

He appears to have been a son of James Middlebrook, of Low Blean, a farm on the banks of Semerwater, near Countersett, Bainbridge, Wensleydale, at which Ann Thwaite (1148) spent her married life. James Middlebrook's daughter, Ann Middlebrook, married John Hunter, of Hebblethwaite Hall, near Sedbergh, who was born at Carr End on the opposite side of Semerwater, and whose sister and niece married respectively Richard Thistlethwaite (580), and Richard Thistlethwaite (113). See Charts III. and IV.

    i.   Christopher Middlebrook (1246), whom see.

    ii.   Matthew Middlebrook (1250), born 7th October, 1788, and probably died young.

    iii.   Margaret Middlebrook (1251), born 5th September, 1790, and probably died young.

    iv.   William Middlebrook (1252), born 11th November, 1792. He lived with his unmarried brother and sister, John and Ann, and jointly with his brother farmed " Liletown," in Dent, and a field called " Ufthra," which latter belonged to his nephew Matthew Middlebrook (1249). They lived at Leayat, in the next house but one to the Friends' Meeting House, and here William died unmarried 23rd January, 1876, aged eighty-three.

    v.   John Middlebrook (1253), whom see.

    vi.   Ann Middlebrook (1255), born 4th February, 1797, lived with her brothers as above, and died unmarried at Leayat 30th May, 1872, aged seventy-five.

    vii.   Alice Middlebrook (1256), born 2nd September, 1802, and probably died young.

Christopher Middlebrook (1246), born 9th June, 1786, at Hobsons in Dent, a hosier, who married, about 1814, Margaret ——. In 1816 he was living at Horton in Ribblesdale, and in 1819 and 1822 in Dent. Both he and his wife died before the memory of his first cousin once removed, Jeremiah Thistlethwaite (1218), of Great Ayton, who was born 1826 in Dent.

    i.   Matthew Middlebrook (1247), born 31st March, 1816, at South House, Horton in Ribblesdale, and died before 28th March, 1822.

ii. Margaret Middlebrook (1248), born 1st January, 1819, at
Dent, married to John Watson, soap-manufacturer, of
Gateshead-on-Tyne, where, it is said, she died.

iii. Matthew Middlebrook (1249), born 28th March, 1822, at Dent,
and married the sister of John Watson of Gateshead, his
brother-in-law. Shortly after marriage they emigrated
to New Zealand, where they have, perhaps, numerous
descendants. His property at Ufthra, and an intake above
Leayat of about thirty acres, were eventually sold on his
behalf.

John Middlebrook (1253), born 14th January, 1795, at Hobsons
in Dent, and lived for many years at Leayat with his brother and sister,
William and Ann, where he died 29th February, 1860, aged sixty-five.
He was unmarried, but had a natural son,

i. Thomas Parrington (1254), who lived many years at Leayat,
in the house next the Meeting-house. He married
—Burton, sister of the wife of Anthony Thistlethwaite (281)
of Spicegill. He was one of the last Quakers in Dent Dale,
and died without issue at Leayat, 22nd January, 1907,
aged eighty-two.

William Thistlethwaite (1257), was born in Dent Dale 19th
September, 1763. He married 2nd October, 1811, Isabel Wynn, of Garsdale, the next parallel valley to the north of Dent Dale. He was a wool-
comber, and died at Stonehouse in Dent, 5th November, 1830, aged
sixty-seven. His widow died at Clough in Garsdale 4th August, 1857,
aged eighty-three years. I have been unable to discover any living
descendants, and think he may have had other children besides the two
shown.

i. William Thistlethwaite (1258), who died 18th February, 1832,
    at Great Bolton, in Lancashire, grocer, aged nineteen years,
    and was buried at Little Bolton on the 22nd February.

ii. Christopher Thistlethwaite (1259), born 1st June, 1814, at
    Hobsons in Dent. I have no further particulars.

PART SEVEN.

DESCENDANTS OF

THOMAS THISTLETHWAITE (1260),

EIGHTH CHILD OF

WILLIAM THISTLETHWAITE (1) OF HARBORGILL.

PART SEVEN.

Thomas Thistlethwaite (1260), born 25th March, 1723, probably at Harborgill in Dent Dale. At the age of nearly forty-two, he married 6th February, 1765, Agnes Mason, aged nearly twenty. Fourteen years later, her youngest sister Margaret married her husband's nephew, Jeremiah Thistlethwaite (1162). They were daughters of Anthony Mason, of Rayside, in Dent, who married Elizabeth Adamthait, 3rd March, 1738. Agnes was born 27th March 1745, and Margaret 23rd March, 1757. Agnes Thistlethwaite died 6th December, 1785, aged forty years, and her husband 11th September, 1786, at Rayside, aged sixty-three years.

Thomas Thistlethwaite (1260), " was extraordinary for his natural turn to mechanics, which afforded him much amusement in constructing various useful articles, especially some curious wooden clocks, entirely the work of his own application and ingenuity."*

Although I am aware that several branches of the Thistlethwaite family possess accounts of a wonderful avalanche which took place in Dent Dale in 1752, yet I think it worth while to record one of the descriptions here, for the benefit of the many kinsmen who have not already seen it, and in order that it may live the relative immortality of printed matter. A few notes may suitably preface the ancient document.

Let us picture for a moment the surroundings of some imaginary ancestor as he walks from Sedbergh up Dent Dale—for many real ones must have followed the route which was recently traced by the present writer. A steep path leads from Sedbergh over the ridge, and falls

* Alice Chorley's Record.

through woods into the Dent high road near Gate, an old-fashioned mansion.   Following the road towards Dent, one may now see on the left
hand side a monument to Miss Elam who made the present new and
higher road, to be used in place of that called " The Floods," which runs
close by the river Dee, and is frequently covered with water.   The comparatively wide part of the dale where the town is situated branches to
the right, and through Deepdale runs the road past Yordas Cave to
Ingleton.   On the left, the Dale of Dent narrows, and runs semi-circularly
first more to the left, and finally to the right.

Shortly after crossing the bridge near Dent's Town our ancestor
would pass on his left the Hall Bank Charity Estate of about eighty acres,
partly purchased with the capital of the perpetual Thistlethwaite Charity
of £5 4s. per annum.*   About two miles further, again on the left, stands
" Gib's Hall," where once lived William and Mary Howitt, the author
and authoress.   The valley grows yet narrower and steeper, and all the
fields slope at a sharp angle to the edge of the curious river, parts of whose
rocky bed remain quite dry except at flood times.   In about a mile, a field
road on the left leads round a projecting hillock to Spicegill, the only
family farm still owned by Thistlethwaite descendants.   Soon the little
valley of Cowgill opens on the left, just past which winds the fearsome
road to Dent Station, 1160 feet above sea level, the highest in England.
At the foot of the road stands Leayat—four cottages and the Friends'
Meeting House and graveyard.   Shortly before reaching here, again on
the left and just behind a more recent cottage close to the road, stands
Hudshouse, perhaps the most ancient-looking house in Dent.

After Leayat the semi-circle of the dale turns to the right, with the
dale-head and the railway viaduct showing in the distance.   Opposite
Leayat is " Hobson's," and the next farm on the left is Harborgill, the
home of our common ancestor, William Thistlethwaite (1).   As the road
here runs at the right, or south, of the Dee, the latter must be crossed by
a narrow bridge, and a comparatively flat field traversed before the house

* Settled by deed of Thomas Thistlethwaite in 1637, for a full explanation of
which, see my second volume.

is reached. It is coloured white, and over the porch stands clearly forth in black " W.T., 1700." High up on the hill behind, there is a stone building still called High Thistlethwaite, formerly a cottage, but now used as a stable and barn. At some elevation from the road, on the side opposite to Harborgill, stands the Hollow Mill. The great avalanche from the other side swept through the river and demolished the wall of the Hollow Mill paddock.*

The fleeing inhabitants of Harborgill had but 400 yards to traverse in a direct line to John Thistlethwaite's at Leayat, yet spent more than two hours upon the journey. High on the hill above Harborgill runs the main line of the Midland Railway, 1200 ft. above sea level, guarded by three ranks of snow-sheds, but much higher still on the side of Widdale Fell lie Monkeybeck Grains, and here, a century before the railway was thought of, wandered these refugees seeking for a way to Leayat. The dale is singularly narrow, rising on the north-east to Widdale Fell (2,203 feet), and on the south to Whernside (2414 feet). Sudden floods are frequent, and the bed of the river is curiously worn and hollowed, the water shooting through narrow channels into deep seething pits, such as Hell's Cauldron.

Those who fled from Harborgill at the time of the avalanche were as follows :—† William Thistlethwaite (1) our common ancestor, his son Thomas Thistlethwaite (1260), who writes the account, aged twenty-eight, his youngest son Timothy Thistlethwaite (1334) aged twenty-six, his grandson Richard Thistlethwaite (580) aged nine, and his housekeeper Elizabeth Atkinson, aged twenty-seven, who married Timothy Thistlethwaite (1334), two years later. His son John Thistlethwaite (1090), with whom they sought refuge at Leayat, was at this time thirty-nine years old, and had married seven years previously. James Thistlethwaite (429), the father of the boy Richard Thistlethwaite (580), seems to have been living in Langstrothdale, ten miles to the south-east.

* The local pronunciation, and even spelling, of the word " paddock " is invariably " parrack "—nothing more or less than the original Anglo-Saxon " pearroc," of which our " paddock " is a corruption.

† See the first key chart.

16

I will now give the account of the avalanche, just as I copied it from the original in the possession of John Anthony Thistlethwaite (1322), of Middlesbrough, a great-grandson of Thomas Thistlethwaite (1260), the writer. I have supplemented a punctuation which is almost absent in the original.

"When any thing Remarkable or Extraordinary falls out in the course of Nature or providence, I think it has been the practice of severall ages to make their observations and Remarks upon them, not thinking such things unworthy or below their Notice as may have a tendancy in them to make us Reflect on the wonderfull protection of providence, Even in the most seeming greatest daingers. Of which I think the 28 day of the 1th month, 1752, Is a very Notable and Worthy Instance, and may very Justly be ranked amongst the greatest Wonders that has hapned of Late years Within some Considerable distance of Us.

"Therefore I thought it might not be improper to make some observations on it, Seeing it so Emmediatly affected me, and being an eye and ear witness of . . . its severall circumstances . . . with the . . . certainly attest the truth of them. And I hope it may be of some satisfaction to me or others When many days may be gone over my head, or Even Children that may be yet unborn may Remember how singularly their fathers and mothers Escaped those dangers without the Least harm, for which Cause I ought in perticular still when I remember it to be thankfull to that power that so wonderfully protected us.

"Therefore to give my friend, Reader, or Kinsman (or in what Relation soever he may stand to me in perticular, it matters not), a true Idea of these things owerly as they hapned woud be too hard a task for me, therefore shall observe that for severall days, or near a week together, successively day after Day it snew excedingly, attended in a very Remarkable manner with Extraordinary great winds, that 'tis hard to determine whether this or the consequence was more singular. For all the the (*sic*) water courses both in the mountains and Elsewhere was almost Quit Leavell by the prdiggous quantity of snow that was blown into them, so that in many places where the gills, so called, was well stored with wood, it weight broke of [*i.e.*, its* weight broke off] the arms of the trees in a surprising manner, and in many places the snow might be 15 or 20 yards thick by computation. Things remaining thus for some time, severall persons curosity was Excited thereby to view these prodgies in Nature with some atention, because they were actualy of a surprising Nature, and seemed to foretell or threaten something Extraordinary both to man and Beast, and in the consequence proved true, for they in the event proved fatal to severall of Both.

" For on the 27th day the atmosphere seemed exceeding Black, and heavin as if Laden and . . . disberth . . . of it weight, so in the morning it began to haill & rain Extreamly and Continued all night without intermission, and about 11 a clock the day following the dismal Scene began ; oh ! shocking to relate without trembling at the very thought of it. For the prodigious quantity of snow had Imbibed almost all the rain that had fall^n for the space of 15 hours in so plentifull a manner, that the snow in the mountains, valleys, & wather courses, could no Longer sustain it self, but Broke and tumbled, or rather Run, down the mountains into the water courses with Incredible fury and velocity, tearing up large Quantities of Earth, Rocks, Stones and trees, and whatever else was in its way, of which I was an Eye witness.

" For when I was at Harbourgill in Dent, in my fathers house, sitting by the fire with the rest of the family, at that time we heard a wonderfull rumbling noise, at which we were surprized and severall of us run out of doors, suposing what what (*sic*) might be the cause, and indeed it was truee, for we directed our course towards the Barn to look at the gill, but we were scarce there before We were glad to run for our Lives. For at the very first sight it was Coming down the pasture, about the middle, with surprising swiftness, tearing up the trees by the roots and Braking others to piecs ; driving all Before it so that we ran for our Lives, shouting, that if posible my father might Escape it fury, he being not got as yet out of doors. Neither did he till every thing in its way was become an heap of the most surprising Rubish that ever my eyse beheld.

* The word "its" being comparatively modern, "it" or "his" were used instead.

" For almost in a moment, in the twinkling of the eye, the peathouse
and stable, and all about, was carried away as the dust before the wind,
not being able to discover the place where it stood by any thing but the
Knowledge of it before.   For all the Earth around was covered with an
Incredible Quantity of snow, wood, Earth, and stone Rocks for two or
three yard thick, so that it looked most dismal to behold ; and we very
narrowly Escaped, for it threw the Slate and timber and the like within a
few yards of us, and my poor father narrowly Escaped out of the dweling
house, for the presently the floods came down betwixt the Barn and
dwelling house, nay, even run round it, Broke down the Garden wall,
and almost filld it with sand and water.   For the flood was turned out
of it course by the vast quantity of Rubish that it Left in the place where
formerly it used to pass, so that it run thro the garden till next day.
It was Very remarkable how the Barn stood the shock of it fury, for it run
the height of the house top, and left sand and Earth upon the roof, and
it remained there many months, plainly to be seen by Every spectator.
And at the end of the Barn it Left Rubish, as Earth, stones, and snow,
the thickness of 3 or 4 yards, it being severall months before the snow
disolved.   It likewise broke open all the doors in the Barn, cramed in
all full of snow and stones, which by it own Natural Coldnes Congeald
to that degrie that it was with dificulty got to pieces with Instruments
so as to be removed out of doors.

" Things being thus remarkibly in confusion, in a moment we were
obliged to Betake our selves to the open fields, that if possible we might
Eskape the Dainger of More of the Like Nature which hapned for severall
hours after that, so we were glad to run from hill to hill to avoid their
Danger, scarcely having got out of one Danger before we were likely to
run foul upon another.   Some of which came within a few yards of us,
whilest others perhaps at some distance, tho in sight, and rored Like
Claps of thunder, drove down the walls & fences for 100 yards to gether,
Carrying the stones along with them ; of which our pasture wall wass
an Instance, and the sheepfould Was driven by its fury quite down and
some of its force was felt on the other side of the River.   For it drove

quite thro it, tho a prodigious flood, and took away the wall of the hollow Mill parrack, so called, and Tossed it to the oposite side. Some of these breaks got 2 horsss of our Neighbour Chapmans, whilest others got 20 or 30 sheep of another Neighbours, Tumbling them Head Long, sometimes in sight and sometimes out of sight, of which I was an eye witness.

" Being in this Disconsolate Condition, & everything apearing with such a dismal aspect as if Nature had being gone to Confusion & the Elements at varience with Each other, We resolved at Last to make an attempt to get to Brother Johns, Beside the Leyeat, not dareing to stay Lest we should perish ; So Set forwards on our intended Journey, being wet to the Naked Skin and almost Starved with Cold, and having eaten Little or Nothing, since fear and danger takes away the apitite after food. And our greates desire was that we might think ourselves pretty free from danger that night, so proceeded on our Journey more Chearfully, and got out at the pasture head & at Length got over harbour-gill and proceeded towards munkey beck, wading thro water & snow almost to the knee. And when we came near it we found it impassible, not being able to get over it, and the Bridge was broke down at Leyet pretty soon that day so that it obliged us to pas further up towards the mountains.

" At Length we got over besides Monkey beck grains, tho with great hazard of our Lives, and almost spent and benumbed with Cold ; yet it gave us good incouragement and we all got safe to Brother Johns Just as it grew dark, having been above 2 hours in going that fateaguing Journey, where we were thankfull to see the faces of one another in a place of safty. My poor father the greatest part of the time had but one shoe on one foot and was upwards of 70 years of age, yet by good providence I do not think that any of us came to any harm thro the Cold or fateague of that dismal day, tho we were 5 in number, viz., My Father, Bro Timothy, Nephew Richard Thistlethwaite & our housekeeper, Elizth Atkinson.

" Next morning before we got out of Bed we heard the melancholy and affecting news that Thomas Stockdalls whole family to the number

of 8 persons was all Buried in Ruins by the Like misfortune.   Even in
a moment they were surprisd by Death, & was no more.   This gave us
fresh cause to be thankfull to heaven for his wonderfull protection in so
manifest dangers.

" In the morning as soon as well Could we came to View Our old but
now forsaken Habitation, which indeed was amazing to behold.   For it
had brought such Quantities of Stones & Large Rocks almost past belief,
nay, quite so to such as did not Come to see them, tho severall hundreds
of persons from severall parts came thro Curiosity to observe them.
Severall of the Largest of these Rocks went quite thro the body of the
peat housse & stable above 40 yards down into the hoame, one of which
I took the pains to find it weight and found it to be above $2\frac{1}{2}$ Tun
weight, & asisted in blowing it in pieces with gunpowder in order to
remove it severall months after.   Getting some of our neighbours to assist
us, we got the snow, stones, & earth, & the like, out of the Barn, tho it
took severall days for that purpose it was so monstrously Congealed
together.   And it spoild the hay very much, tho by good hap we had no
Cows in the barn at that time, Else they must of consiquence have
perished.   Yet we had 2 horses in the high stable, wreaked up as high
as their backs, but being in a Corner was not Crushed, so got them out
next day not much worse.   But the good old horse in the Low Stable
was Crushed to pieces in a moment, & it was several days ere we coud
remove him out of the rubish.

" In this hurly burly we Lost all our peats, Fleese, woll, husbandry
Gear, to a great value, tho we after some time diged for the peats & wool
as in a Coal mine, and got most of the wooll and as many peats as served
us very well the remaining part of that winter.

" The Best reason that I Can assign why the Barn was not thrown
down, was the depth of the gill Just above the End of the Barn ; for the
rocks that Came full upon a Line for the End thereof, was Lodged in
the gill and Left there, so that their force fell short of it, Else it must
certainly have been thrown in pieces, then our dwelling house had   .   .   .
stood a poor chance of better fate.   Some months after, we found one of

the Crocks in the Barn quite broke in two, very probably by the violent shock tho not discovered till after.

"There Likewise was a row of Ash Trees grew by the gill side, some of which it took away & the rest was miserably Shawn of all the Bark, with wood 2 Inches thick knocked of for 1 or 2 yards above ground, so that if they grew and got forwards perhaps the Carpenters (?) an 100 years thence may be at a loss to know the cause of their misfortune when the ax or saw searches the coverd grounds."

· Thomas Thistlethwaite (1260), the author of this account, had the following children :—

    i.   Alice Thistlethwaite (1261), whom see.

    ii.   William Thistlethwaite (1263), whom see.

    iii.   Anthony Thistlethwaite (1279), whom see.

Alice Thistlethwaite (1261) was born 4th November, 1765, in Dent Dale. She married at Leayat Meeting-house, 27th April, 1785, Daniel Harrison, woolcomber, of Hobsons-in-Dent, son of Reuben and Hannah Harrison, of Countersett, near Bainbridge in Wensleydale, where he was born 19th July, 1760. For Harrison intermarriages, see Chart II. In 1786 he is described as hosier, of Cowgill in Dent. I can find record of only one child.

    i.   Alice Harrison (1262), born at Cowgill, 26th August, 1786.

        I have failed to discover whether she married or left issue.

William Thistlethwaite (1263), born 8th August, 1767, in Dent Dale. He was married at Edgeworth in Lancashire, 1st May, 1795, being then yeoman, of Cowgill in Dent, to Peggy Thomasson, daughter of Thomas Thomasson, yeoman, deceased, and his wife Margaret, of Edgeworth in Lancashire. Their first child was born at Cowgill in March, 1796, but on the birth of their second in November, 1797, he is described as cotton spinner, of Edgeworth in the parish of Bolton, and is so described

until 1809. In 1811 he is called "labourer," and in 1814 and 1816
"husbandman." He died 15th January, 1838, at Little Bolton, aged
seventy-two, and his wife, Peggy, at Bolton, 31st January, 1853, aged
seventy-seven. I have been unable to discover any living descendants,
although many such probably exist,

  i. Thomas Thistlethwaite (1264), born at Cowgill in Dent, 16th
    March, 1796. Died aged eighteen years, at Edgeworth,
    15th February, 1814, buried there on the 17th.

  ii. Agnes Thistlethwaite (1265), born at Edgeworth in Lancashire,
    14th November, 1797.

  iii. Margaret Thistlethwaite (1266), born at Edgeworth, 10th
    May, 1799.

  iv. Christopher Thistlethwaite (1267), born at Edgeworth, 28th
    November, 1801.

  v. Alice Thistlethwaite (1268), born at Edgeworth, 18th January,
    1804.

  vi. John Thistlethwaite (1269), born at Edgeworth, 25th August,
    1805, a blacksmith. He died aged thirty-one at Edgerton
    in the township of Turton, parish of Bolton-le-Moors,
    6th May, 1836, and was buried at Little Bolton, 10th May.
    Married Alice —— and had issue,

    i. Margaret Thistlethwaite (1270), born 17th March,
      1827, at Edgeworth.

    ii. William Thistlethwaite (1271), born 3rd February,
      1829, at Cocksgreen in Turton.

  vii. William Thistlethwaite (1272), born at Edgeworth 2nd August,
    1807, a basket maker, of Great Bolton, Lancashire. Married
    Elizabeth —— and had issue.

    i. Thomas Thistlethwaite (1273), born 23rd June,
      1833, at Great Bolton, parish of Bolton-le-Moors.

    ii. Mary Thistlethwaite (1274), born 13th June, 1835,
      at Great Bolton. Died aged seven weeks at Little
      Bolton, 5th August, 1835.

viii. Joseph Thistlethwaite (1275), born at Edgeworth, 3rd July, 1809.

ix. Anthony Thistlethwaite (1276), born at Edgeworth, 19th November, 1811.

x. Isabel Thistlethwaite (1277), born at Edgeworth, 28th February, 1814.

xi. Mary Thistlethwaite (1278), born at Edgeworth, 16th October, 1816.

Anthony Thistlethwaite (1279), born 17th November, 1769, in Dent Dale, probably at Rasett, or Rayside, a house on the north side of the road a little lower down the dale than Leayat. He married, 5th May, 1791, Mary Atkinson, daughter of John and Margaret Atkinson, of Corn Close in Dent. They were married at Briggflatts Meeting House, a well-known and well-preserved old building about two miles from Sedbergh. All their children were born at Stonehouse, the place, about a mile above Leayat, where for so many years the Dent marble was dressed.

They appear to have moved, after 1804, to within the compass of Settle Monthly Meeting, and thence to Darlington in 1818. The following Minute was made by Darlington Monthly Meeting held 17th February, 1818. " A certificate has been received from Settle Monthly Meeting on behalf of Anthony and Mary Thistlethwaite and their two children, Elizabeth and John (all members of Sedbergh M.M., as to maintenance), settled at Darlington, which is accepted. We appoint Edward Pease and William Backhouse to unite with women friends and visit them thereon." I understand that they latterly lived on the Friends' Meeting House premises at Darlington.

Anthony Thistlethwaite (1279), woolcomber, died at Darlington, 24th April, 1820, aged fifty-two years, and was buried there on the 28th April. His wife spent the last years of her life with her son Thomas, and died at Ackworth, near Pontefract, 5th January, 1833, aged sixty-eight years, and was buried there on the 10th January.

i.   Agnes Thistlethwaite (1280), born 15th April, 1792, at Stone-
     house. She spent the last twenty years (or thereabouts) of
     her life with her brother Thomas, at Ackworth. Previous
     to this she had been many years cook at Ackworth School.
     She died at Ackworth, 16th June, 1857.

ii. Margaret Thistlethwaite (1281), whom see.

iii. Alice Thistlethwaite (1284), born 22nd April, 1799, at Stone-
     house. The following minute was made by Darlington
     Monthly Meeting, held 15th August, 1820, " A certificate
     has been received from Hardshaw West M.M. (a part of
     Lancashire), on behalf of Alice Thistlethwaite, which is
     accepted." She had therefore removed from Lancashire
     to Darlington soon after her father's death. She died at
     Darlington, 27th April, 1822, aged twenty-three years, and
     was buried there 1st May.

iv. Thomas Thistlethwaite (1285), whom see.

v.   Elizabeth Thistlethwaite (1318), whom see.

vi. John Thistlethwaite (1319), whom see.

Margaret Thistlethwaite (1281), born 24th February, 1797, at
Stonehouse. She removed before 20th March, 1818, from Brighouse
Monthly Meeting (Leeds and District), to Darlington. At Darlington
Monthly Meeting, held 19th June, 1827, " women friends are requested to
prepare a certificate for Margaret Thistlethwaite, removed to York
Monthly Meeting." At Darlington M.M., held 17th July, 1827, " the
certificate for Margaret Thistlethwaite is deferred, her residence not being
at present known." Nothing further appears until 30th November, 1830,
when " it is reported that Margaret Thistlethwaite left her brother's
house at Selby, vi. mo. 1827, remained about a year in England, and then
went to America, without her parents' knowledge or consent."

She married Frederick Smurthwaite, a schoolmaster, who had been
previously married, and went to America shortly afterwards, when for

nearly thirty years she was lost sight of. She died at Coatesville, Chester County, Pennsylvania.

     i.   Hubert Frederick Smurthwaite (1282), was living, when last heard of, at West Chester, Pa., married and with children.

     ii.   William Smurthwaite (1283), to whom the same description applies.

     Thomas Thistlethwaite (1285), born 31st January, 1801, at Stonehouse, in Dent. At Darlington Monthly Meeting, held 25th December, 1822, a certificate from Pontefract M.M., on behalf of Thomas Thistlethwaite settled at Darlington, was accepted, and Edward Pease and James Backhouse were appointed to visit him thereon. In January, 1829, Thomas Thistlethwaite, " now in Brighouse Monthly Meeting," was censured for intemperate conduct, and in November, 1830, was reported " married contrary to our rules."* A testimony of disownment was drawn up, 19th April, 1831, against him for " marriage by a priest."

He came to Darlington to learn the wool business with the Peases, and then went to Bradford, where he married, at the Parish Church, Mary Wilkinson, born 30th March, 1805, daughter of Samuel and Sarah Wilkinson. He unsuccessfully applied for readmission into the Society of Friends in July, 1836, when he had " resided at Ackworth three-and-a-half years and attended meeting." He was a shop-keeper at Ackworth, and, in his earlier years there, a brewer also. He died at Wragby, near Ackworth, 17th December, 1878, and was buried in Ackworth Friends' Burial Ground. His wife died at Ackworth, Yorkshire, 4th April, 1867, and was buried in the same place.

     i.   —— Thistlethwaite (1286), an unnamed child, who was born at Ackworth, 25th June, 1832, lived only one hour, and was buried there 29th June.

     ii.   Anthony Thistlethwaite (1287), whom see.

* Let not Quaker strictness mislead. Thomas Thistlethwaite (1285), was a genial and honourable man : so tells me one who knew him well.

   iii.   Alice Thistlethwaite (1291), whom see.
   iv.   Samuel Thistlethwaite (1293), born in 1838, and died in infancy.
   v.   William Thistlethwaite (1294), whom see.
   vi.   Sarah Thistlethwaite (1295), whom see.
   vii.   Mary Thistlethwaite (1302), whom see.
   viii.   Maria Thistlethwaite (1309). whom see.

Anthony Thistlethwaite (1287), born 1st June, 1833, at Ackworth, and married in 1866, at Almondbury Church, Huddersfield, to Sarah Jane Lamprey, who is now living at Council Bluffs, Iowa, U.S.A. Anthony Thistlethwaite (1287), died 8th August, 1871, at Hockworthy, Co. Somerset, while visiting his wife's friends, and was buried in the Friends' Burial Ground, Wellington, Somerset.

   i.   Alice Mary Thistlethwaite (1288), born 1866, at Ackworth, and died, unmarried, at Council Bluffs, in 1896.
   ii.   Agnes Jane Thistlethwaite (1289), born 1867, at Ackworth, and died there, 1869.
   iii.   Thomas William Thistlethwaite (1290), born 1869, at Ackworth. Married to Maud Teft, of Gainsborough, England, at Council Bluffs, 1896, where he lives, and has two or three daughters. Address, 3021 Avenue H., Council Bluffs.

Alice Thistlethwaite (1291), born 25th March, 1836, at Ackworth, and married, March, 1862, at the Parish Church, Pontefract, to Thomas Ellis, jeweller. Alice Ellis (1291) died 19th February, 1891, at Bishop Auckland, Co. Durham.

   i.   Mary Ann Agnes Ellis (1292), born 18th March, 1863, and now living unmarried at Bishop Auckland.

William Thistlethwaite (1294), born 1st August, 1840, at Ackworth, and since 1871 has been headmaster of the Friends' School at

Newton-in-Bowland, near Clitheroe, Yorkshire. He was married 26th July, 1876, at Monyash Meeting House, near Bakewell, Derbyshire, to Edith Bowman, born at Cales Farm, Monyash, 5th September, 1854, daughter of Ebenezer and Hannah Bowman. *Sine prole.*

Sarah Thistlethwaite (1295), born 25th January, 1843, at Ackworth, near Pontefract, Yorkshire. She was married, 23rd March, 1876, at the Independent Chapel, Newton-in-Bowland, to Joseph Booth, Congregational Minister, in 1910 of Zion Manse, Gawthorpe, near Osset, Yorkshire, son of the Rev. Bulcock Booth (1805 to 1874).

i.   Ernest Atkinson Booth (1296), born 26th February, 1877, at the Manse, Pocklington, Yorkshire. In 1910 he was headmaster of the County Council School at Highworth, Wiltshire. He was married 25th December, 1905, at Zion Congregational Church, Gawthorpe, to Helen Park Foster, daughter of Nathanael Foster, of Ayr, Scotland.

    i.   Roland Gordon Booth (1297), born 17th June, 1909, at " The Laurels," Highworth, Wiltshire.

ii.   Joseph Alexander Booth (1298), born 12th September, 1878, at Pocklington, now Congregational Minister in Leeds, unmarried.

iii. Rowland Thistlethwaite Booth (1299), born 11th September, 1880, at Pocklington , now a clerk in London, unmarried.

iv.   Agnes Mary Booth (1300), born 1st March, 1882, at the Parsonage, Luddenden Foot, near Halifax, Yorkshire. She died there 2nd December, 1882, and was buried at Luddenden Cemetery.

v.   Esther Hallworth Booth (1301), born 30th January, 1887, at the Parsonage, Luddenden Foot. She died there 28th March, 1888, and was buried at Luddenden Cemetery.

Mary Thistlethwaite (1302), born 9th December, 1845, at Ackworth. She was married 1st December, 1869, at New York, U.S.A., to George Richardson, who was born in 1845, son of Thomas Richardson,* by his wife Elizabeth Jones, of Selby, Yorkshire. She removed with her husband to Omaha, Nebraska, U.S.A., and died 5th June, 1904, at Henley-in-Arden, Warwickshire, while on a visit to England.

    i.   Thomas Bertram Richardson (1303), born 1870, at Omaha, Nebraska. He was married to Ora Maud Kearney, who died at Sandholm Ranch, Nebraska, leaving an only child.

        i. Noel Richardson (1304), born at Sandholm Ranch, Nebraska.

    ii. Alice Maria Richardson (1305), born 1872, at Omaha, Nebraska, and died in childhood.

    iii. Mabel Elizabeth Richardson (1306), born at Omaha, Nebraska, and was married to George Clarke Green. In 1909 she was living at Council Bluffs, Iowa, and had four children, two boys and two girls.

    iv. Mary Catherine Richardson (1307), who was living at Council Bluffs, Iowa, in 1909, unmarried.

    v. Agnes Hope Richardson (1308), who was living at Council Bluffs, Iowa, in 1909, unmarried.

Maria Thistlethwaite (1309), born 20th May, 1847, at Ackworth, Yorkshire. She was married in 1871, at Wragby Parish Church, to Thomas William Fryer, joiner and builder. They lived at Wragby near Ackworth until 1879, when they went to Council Bluffs, Iowa, where they still reside.

    i.   George Bertram Fryer (1310), born at Wragby, Yorkshire, and is now a printer and book-binder, at 35, Main Street, Council Bluffs, Iowa, U.S.A. He was married firstly to

---

* Thomas Richardson was son of Aaron Richardson (1775-1832), by his wife, Deborah Proctor, of Selby. See "The Richardsons of Cleveland," by Anne Ogden Boyce, first cousin to the above Thomas Richardson.

Ida Smith, of Omaha, Nebraska, who died at Council Bluffs. He married secondly Anna May Priestley, of Council Bluffs. By his first wife he has two sons, and by his second wife one son.

ii. William Thistlethwaite Fryer (1311), who is a printer, &c., at Council Bluffs, Iowa. He is married and has three children.

iii. Ernest Fryer (1312), a printer, &c., at Council Bluffs, unmarried.

iv. Agnes May Fryer (1313), born and died at Wragby, near Ackworth, Yorkshire, and buried in the Friends' Burial Ground at Ackworth.

v. Alice Margaret Fryer (1314), living at Council Bluffs, unmarried in 1909.

vi. Arthur Fryer (1315), born and died at Council Bluffs.

vii. Thomas Fryer (1316), born and died at Council Bluffs.

viii. Roy Fryer (1317), born at Council Bluffs, where he was living with his parents in 1909.

Elizabeth Thistlethwaite (1318), born 7th November, 1802, at Stonehouse in Dent Dale. Her Quaker membership was transferred to Darlington, from Settle Monthly Meeting, by minute dated 17, ii. 1818, jointly with that of her parents and her brother John. At the end of the following year she seems to have gone to Newcastle, but returned to Darlington before the end of 1820, the year in which her father died. Quakerism had become at this time excessively "narrow"—so much so that while marriage with a non-Quaker meant immediate disownment, even affecting the company or the "worldly" habits of outsiders was likely to produce a similar result. As this family history has become rather a study in sociology than an orthodox pedigree, it may be permissible to copy some of the minutes in the case of Elizabeth Thistle-thwaite and the Darlington Quakers.*

" 18. ix. 1821. Women friends inform us that Elizabeth Thistle-thwaite, of Darlington, has for some time given her company to a person not a member of our society, and that, much labour having been bestowed without producing the desired effect, they request our assistance ; we therefore appoint John Atkinson, of Stockton, Isaac Stephenson and John Backhouse to unite with them in paying her a visit."

" 9. x. 1821. Report is given that some of the friends appointed to visit Elizabeth Thistlethwaite have attended thereto—she expressed a willingness to accept any situation friends might advise, but gave them little reason to hope that the connection would be broken off—the case is constituted under their care to report to our next or a future meeting."

" 8. i. 1822. Isaac Stephenson reports that he in company with the other friends appointed and a part of the committee appointed by women friends have had several interviews with Elizabeth Thistlethwaite in which she has admitted that she still keeps company with the person before noticed without giving them any expectation of discontinuing to do so. The case has been solidly considered at this time, and is left under the care of the said friends to report to our next."

" 5. ii. 1822. The friends appointed to visit Elizabeth Thistlethwaite hand in the following report :—We, your committee appointed in ninth month last, have to report that we had several opportunities with Elizabeth Thistlethwaite in which much pains was taken to convince her of the impropriety of her conduct, apparently to little or no effect, but in an interview which one of the committee had with her yesterday she ex-pressed herself more inclined to follow the advice of friends, and said it was her intention to give up the connection : signed on behalf of the committee, Isaac Stephenson, John Atkinson, John Backhouse. Upon considering which it is agreed to continue the case under their care."

* I owe many thanks to Albert Wood, of Bishop Auckland, for persuading Darlington Monthly Meeting to grant me permission to examine the Minute Books. I have not yet dared to assail the sanctity of the Women's Minute Books.

"19. iii. 1822. The committee in Elizabeth Thistlethwaite's case have brought in the following report :—We your committee . . . . have had another opportunity with her in which she acknowledges that the connection was again renewed, and we fear there is little reason to hope that she will be induced to relinquish it : Isaac Stephenson, Hannah Stephenson, John Atkinson, Margaret Atkinson, John Backhouse. Upon seriously considering which the said committee is discharged, and George Hall, William Ord, and J. Sams are appointed to draw up a testimony of disownment and bring it to our next that the Society may be cleared of the reproach which her conduct has brought upon it." However the issuing of this was deferred and monthly minutes of continuation occur until

"8. x. 1822. The following acknowledgment has been received from Elizabeth Thistlethwaite :—I wish friends to be informed that the connection which gave them so much uneasiness has for some time been broken off. I regret the trouble and concern I have caused them and hope my future conduct will prove the sincerity of my acknowledgement. Elizabeth Thistlethwaite. On considering which it is agreed that the minute in her case be discharged, and Edward Pease and Isaac Stephenson to unite with women friends and visit her."

But in spite of her somewhat pliable spirit (and may we not attribute part of her wavering to the cooling in ardour of the " person not a member of our Society " ?) she was evidently born with some of the independent qualities which Galton ascribed to the Damaran fore-ox. And at the age of twenty-four she appears to have been disowned for " dissatisfactory conduct."[*] Her nephews tell me that " she died young, unmarried "; to which we, who now know more of her history, may add " Requiescat in Pace."

---

[*] Let it be clearly understood that her " crime " consisted solely in " walking out with," or " courting," a young man *who was not a Quaker.* Evidence of anything improper or immoral would have entailed immediate disownment, with quite a different series of minutes.

John Thistlethwaite (1319), born 26th June, 1804, at Stonehouse in Dent Dale. His Quaker membership was transferred to Darlington from Settle Monthly Meeting by minute dated 17. ii. 1818, jointly with that of his parents and his sister Elizabeth. A minute of Darlington meeting dated 19. ix. 1826, reads, " A certificate being wanted for John Thistlethwaite removed to York Monthly Meeting, we appoint Joseph Pease, Junior, and Joseph Hartas to prepare one for approbation of our next." He learnt the wool trade with the Peases in Darlington and was sent by them to open a branch of the business at Bradford, but before leaving Darlington he had become engaged to Hannah Pease Frank.

He went over to Darlington for a few days, and was married to her at St. Cuthbert's Church, 7th June, 1831. His eldest son was born at Bradford in the following year, and his daughter in December, 1834. Shortly after this he was recalled to Darlington, and his place was taken by his second cousin, another John Thistlethwaite (475), who appears to have been transferred from Darlington to Bradford towards the end of 1834.

The John Thistlethwaite (1319) of this sub-section died at Darlington, 6th April, 1841, from pneumonia brought on through remaining in wet clothes during an angling excursion, angling being his favourite sport. He was buried in the Friends' Burial Ground at Darlington, aged thirty-six years. His widow lived for many years in Darlington, and died 13th May, 1871, while living with her son-in-law, John Storrow, at Middlesbrough. She was buried in the Friends' Burial Ground, Darlington.

Hannah Pease Thistlethwaite was born 17th November, 1798, at Darlington, daughter of John Frank, currier, of Darlington, by his wife Ann Pease, daughter of George Pease (of Barnsley and Darlington) who fought at Culloden. Hannah Pease Thistlethwaite's sister Mary married Jeremiah Dixon, whose niece married George Blundell Longstaff, M.A., M.D., F.S.A., the genealogist. See Chart VIII. George Pease's niece married Jonathan Backhouse, banker, of Darlington, and to their children Hannah Pease Frank was for some time governess. She not infrequently visited the family of her second cousin Edmund Backhouse, M.P., whose

CHART VIII. SHEWING COATES AND PEASE INTER-MARRIAGES.

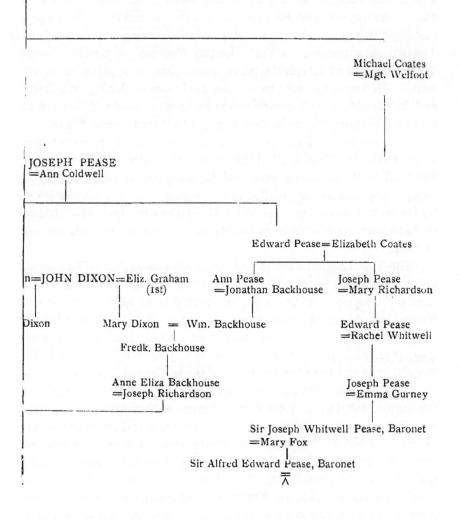

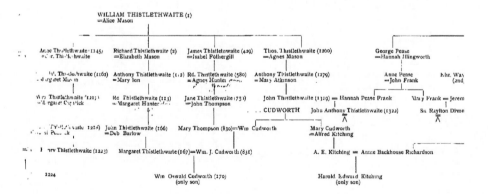

GEORGE COATES 1643-1723
=Elizabeth Shawe

WILLIAM THISTLETHWAITE (1)
=Alice Mason

Anne Thistlethwaite (1145)
=Wr. Thistlethwaite

Richard Thistlethwaite (2)
=Elizabeth Mason

James Thistlethwaite (429)
=Isabel Fothergill

Thos. Thistlethwaite (1200)
=Agnes Mason

George Pease
=Hannah Illingworth

Wr. Thistlethwaite (1162)
=Margaret Mason

Anthony Thistlethwaite (1, 2)
=Mary Ion

Rd. Thistlethwaite (580)
=Agnes Hunter

Anthony Thistlethwaite (1279)
=Mary Atkinson

Anne Pease
=John Frank

Eliz. Way
(2nd

Wm Thistlethwaite (1217)
=Margaret Chadwick

Rd. Thistlethwaite (113)
=Margaret Hunter

Jane Thistlethwaite (753)
=John Thompson

John Thistlethwaite (1319) = Hannah Pease Frank

Mary Frank = Jerem

CUDWORTH

John Anthony Thistlethwaite (1322)

Su Raylton Dixon

Thistlethwaite (1218)
=Peacock

John Thistlethwaite (166)
=Deb Barlow

Mary Thompson (830)=Wm Cudworth

Mary Cudworth
=Alfred Kitching

= Mary Thistlethwaite (1223)

Margaret Thistlethwaite (167)=Wm. J. Cudworth (831)

A. E. Kitching = Annie Backhouse Richardson

1224

Wm Oswald Cudworth (170)
(only son)

Harold Edward Kitching
(only son)

son Sir Jonathan Edmund Backhouse, Bart., M.P., is director of Barclay & Co., Ltd., the well-known bankers.

    i.   William Pease Thistlethwaite (1320), born 29th August, 1832, at Bradford, Yorkshire. He died 11th March, 1848, at Darlington, aged fifteen years, and was buried in the Friends' Burial Ground there.

   ii.   Mary Ann Thistlethwaite (1321), born 9th December, 1834, at Bradford. She was married 6th March, 1869, at Holy Trinity Church, Darlington, to John Storrow, of Middlesbrough, as his second wife. He had previously married Elizabeth Jowsey, who was said to be the first girl born in Middlesbrough, daughter of Richard and Mary Jowsey. Elizabeth Jowsey was sister to Dorothy Jowsey, who married John Storrow's brother-in-law, John Anthony Thistlethwaite (1322). Mary Ann Storrow (1321), died 19th February, 1870, at Middlesbrough, *sine prole*, and is buried in the cemetery there. John Storrow married a third time.

  iii.   John Anthony Thistlethwaite (1322), whom see.

  iv.   Henry Thistlethwaite (1333), born 29th November, 1840, at Darlington, and died there in childhood.

     John Anthony Thistlethwaite (1322), born 14th April, 1837, at Darlington. His birth date is entered in the Quaker Register, but he is described as a " non-member." His grandmother, Anne Pease, lost her membership by marrying John Frank, who was not a member. Therefore her children were not birth-members, although brought up in a Quakerly way. When John Thistlethwaite (1319), a member of the Society of Friends, married her daughter, Hannah Pease Frank, who was technically a " non-member," he was disowned for it, by the Quaker marriage rule, since discontinued. Therefore *his* children were not birth members. Similarly Jeremiah Dixon, a good Quaker, lost his membership through his marriage with Hannah Pease Frank's sister, Mary Frank.

John Anthony Thistlethwaite (1322) became clerk to David Dale, the future baronet, who was, at this time, Secretary to the Middlesbrough and Guisborough Railway. On this becoming part of the old Stockton and Darlington Railway, David Dale took an important position at Shildon Works, and John Anthony Thistlethwaite (1322) went with him.

John Anthony Thistlethwaite (1322) took a keen interest in the volunteer movement of " the fifties." Although he was never a member of the Society of Friends, and not at this time even an attender of their meetings, this interest produced a " warning," by means of David Dale, from the Peases, who held the control of the railway. He therefore left their employment, and obtained an appointment with Hopkins & Co., of Middlesbrough. This firm, which later became Hopkins, Gilkes & Company, was ruined by the disaster to the Tay Bridge, which they built.

John Anthony Thistlethwaite (1322) then became a partner in an iron foundry at Haverton Hill, Co. Durham, and he was afterwards secretary to the North Yorkshire Iron Company. He is now a shipping agent, and resides at 17, St. John's Terrace, Middlesbrough.

He was married 18th December, 1866, at St. Hilda's Church, Middlesbrough, to Dorothy Jowsey, daughter of Richard and Mary Jowsey, the former being a Contractor and Staithe-master to the Stockton and Darlington Railway Company at Middlesbrough. She was living in 1910.

    i.   Mary Jane Thistlethwaite (1323), born 18th July, 1867, at Middlesbrough. She was married 2nd April, 1902, at St. John's Church, Middlesbrough, to Reuben Tomlinson Millott, now a schoolmaster at Mansfield, Nottinghamshire.

        i.   John O'Neale Millott (1324), born 10th November, 1902, at Mansfield.

   ii.   Alice Agnes Thistlethwaite (1325), born 19th March, 1869, at Middlesbrough ; married 22nd August, 1893, at St. John's Church, Middlesbrough, to Edwin Greenwood, lately of Middlesbrough and Leeds, and now advertising contractor of Sydenham, London.

    i. Dorothy Greenwood (1326), born 24th February, 1897, at Batley, Yorkshire.

iii. Frank Arthur Thistlethwaite (1327), born 1st December, 1870, at Middlesbrough ; died there 22nd October, 1874.

iv. Florence Kate Thistlethwaite (1328), born 20th August, 1872, at Middlesbrough, now living at home unmarried.

v. Amy Marion Thistlethwaite (1329), born 18th July, 1875, at Middlesbrough ; married 25th June, 1902, at St. John's Church, Middlesbrough, to James William Taylor, schoolmaster, of Middlesbrough.

    i. Dorothy Taylor (1330), born 29th July, 1906, at Middlesbrough.

vi. Frank Henry Thistlethwaite (1331), born 1st September, 1878, at Middlesbrough, lately with Messrs Dunkerly & Co., iron merchants, of Manchester. In 1910 he was a clerk in London. He was married 1st August, 1910, at Mount Tabor Church, Stockport, Cheshire, to Edith Gertrude Shore, fifth daughter of the late Mr. Charles Shore, and of Mrs. Shore, Rose Villa, Lowfield Road, Stockport.

vii. Richard Jowsey Thistlethwaite (1332), born 28th January, 1881, at Middlesbrough, died there 17th January, 1885.

PART EIGHT.

TIMOTHY THISTLETHWAITE (1334),

NINTH CHILD OF

WILLIAM THISTLETHWAITE (1), OF HARBORGILL.

PART EIGHT.

Timothy Thistlethwaite (1334), born 8th October, 1725, in Dent
Dale ; probably at Harborgill. He married 2nd January, 1754, at
Leàyat Meeting House, Elizabeth Atkinson. She had been his father's
housekeeper at the time of the avalanche in 1752, for further particulars
of which see under his brother Thomas Thistlethwaite (1260). According
to his niece Alice Chorley (1020), " Timothy was tall and thin, social and
kind, inheriting a large portion of his mother's charitable disposition ;
he died of a decline in middle life." In the marriage certificate of his son
John he is described as " late of Harbour Gill." He died 10th July, 1766,
in Dent Dale. His widow died 3rd March, 1801, at Leayat in Dent,
aged seventy-seven years.

    i.   William Thistlethwaite (1335), born 17th January, 1755, in
           Dent Dale, died 29th June, 1767.

   ii.   Alice Thistlethwaite (1336), whom see.

  iii.   John Thistlethwaite (1347), whom see.

  iv.   Mary Thistlethwaite (1791), born 29th September, 1761, in Dent
           Dale, married before 12th November, 1788, to John Bradley,
           and had issue whom I have not succeeded in tracing.

    Alice Thistlethwaite (1336), born 8th January, 1757, in Dent
Dale ; married 27th March, 1782, Thomas Cutforth, then of Burton
in Bishopdale, a village near Aysgarth in Wensleydale, Yorkshire.
Between January 1787 and December 1788, they removed to the small
town of Hawes, about ten miles further up Wensleydale, and here Thomas
Cutforth is described as grocer. They had issue, but I have been unable

to trace living descendants, and can only give a few detached facts,
gleaned from the Quaker registers, except in the case of their daughter
Elizabeth.

    i.   Sarah Cutforth (1337), born 25th May, 1783, at Burton, in
          Bishopdale ; no further information to hand.

   ii.   Elizabeth Cutforth (1338), whom see.

  iii.   Timothy Cutforth (1339), whom see.

  iv.   William Cutforth (1344), born 29th December, 1788, at Hawes.
          He " married a niece of Susan Appleby and died at London
          1827 " ; no further particulars to hand.

   v.   Thomas Cutforth (1345), born 26th July, 1791, at Hawes ;
          no further particulars to hand.

  vi.   Jonathan Cutforth (1346), born 15th June, 1794, at Hawes ;
          no further particulars to hand.

Elizabeth Cutforth (1338), born 13th February, 1785, at Burton,
in Bishopdale. She was known as " Aunt Betty " to the grandchildren
of her first cousin Alice (Mrs. Peter) Taylor (1448), who much appreciated
their visits to her farm near Sedbergh. She died unmarried, at Liverpool,
in 1852. She was at one time engaged to be married to one of the Fosters
of Hebblethwaite Hall, near Sedbergh, but a misunderstanding parted
them. Her *fiancé* was, I believe, Myles Birket Foster, born 4th January,
1785, at Hebblethwaite Hall, who was married 11th April, 1811, at Newcastle-on-Tyne, to Ann King, and became father of the eminent water-
colour artist, Birket Foster, R.W.S. It will be recollected that Elizabeth
Cutforth's brother was a ship-owner at Newcastle, and that her mother's
first cousin Richard Thistlethwaite (580), married Agnes Hunter, sister
of John Hunter, sometime of Hebblethwaite Hall. Myles Birket Foster,
born 1785, was the son of Robert Foster, an extraordinary man respecting
whom Southey wrote to Richard Duffa, on the 23rd February, 1806 :—

   " Oh, Wordsworth sent me a man the other day, who was worth
seeing ; he looked like a first assassin in Macbeth as to his costume, but
he was a rare man ; had been a lieutenant in the navy ; was a scholar

enough to quote Virgil aptly ; had turned Quaker or semi-Quaker, and was now a dealer in wool somewhere about twenty miles off. He had seen much and thought much ; his head was well stored, and his heart was in the right place."* Robert Foster left Hebblethwaite Hall for Newcastle in 1812, and I imagine it was after this date that John Hunter, who died in 1840, resided at the former place.

Elizabeth Cutforth (1338), during the latter part of her life, used a wooden leg. " When she found her knee was very bad, *alone* she took the coach to a distant town . . . had the limb amputated, and returned home to her duties. I call her a noble character."

Timothy Cutforth (1339), born 5th January, 1787, at Burton, in Bishopdale, Yorkshire, shortly before his parents removed to Hawes. He was married 3rd January, 1814, at Colthouse Meeting House, to Margaret Cockbain. He was then described as " Hosier, of Newcastle-on-Tyne," but in 1816 and 1819 he is described as ship-owner of the same place. In the entry of his death he is described as " bank agent." He died, aged 42½ years, on 17th August, 1829, in the township of Westgate, Northumberland, and was buried on the 23rd at Newcastle-on-Tyne. His widow died 1st January, 1834, aged forty-five years, at Newcastle, and was buried there on the 5th. I possess no information regarding possible descendants of his son Thomas or his daughter Alice.

    i.   Thomas Cutforth (1340), born 17th October, 1814, at Newcastle-on-Tyne ; educated at Bootham School, York, January to December, 1829.

    ii.   Mary Cutforth (1341), born 16th September, 1815, at New-castle ; died 28th August, 1825, in the township of Westgate, Northumberland, aged nearly 10 years, and buried at Newcastle on the 31st.

* See " Birket Foster " by H. M. Cundall (Black, 1906).

  iii. John Hadwen Cutforth (1342), born 9th November, 1816, at
        Newcastle ; educated at Bootham School, York, January
        to December, 1829 ; died 29th January, 1833, at Newcastle,
        where he was buried 3rd February.
  iv.   Alice Cutforth (1343), born 9th February, 1819, at Newcastle.

  John Thistlethwaite (1347), was born 3rd November, 1758, in Dent
Dale. He is perhaps the most important person in this pedigree ; the
innumerable descendants of his nineteen children in America and in
England have included many men and women of high capabilities and
attainments—a vice-chairman of the North-Eastern Railway, a president
of Swarthmore College, U.S.A., the inventor of the screw for steamships,
the founder of the Thistlethwaite Bank of Indiana, etc.

  John Thistlethwaite, of Newcloses in Dent (close to Leayat),
yeoman, was married 10th April, 1782, at Bainbridge Meeting House to
Elizabeth Wetherald. She was a daughter of Joseph Wetherald, of
Brough Hill in the parish of Aysgarth, Wensleydale, Yorkshire, by his
wife, Elizabeth Whitehouse, a "public" friend, and cousin to Dr. Whitehouse, of Liverpool. Her sister Jane's grand-daughter married James
Harris (634), her brother George's daughter married William Thistlethwaite (1598), while her brother Joseph's son married Isabel Thistlethwaite (583), and his grand-daughter married John Taylor (1450).*
See Chart IX. She had three daughters, and died at Newcloses in Dent
19th April, 1787,† aged twenty-three years.

  John Thistlethwaite (1347), appears to have given up his farm at
Newcloses in Dent, and removed to Bainbridge in Wensleydale, about
fourteen miles away, where he became a wool-comber. While here he
married, 12th November, 1788, at Bainbridge Meeting House, Eleanor
Atkinson, daughter of John Atkinson, of Frostra, in the parish of Sedbergh,

  * I have not succeeded in tracing the relationship between these Wetheralds
and the grandmother of John Thompson who married Jane Thistlethwaite (759).

  † My transcription reads " 1784 " but it is obviously inaccurate. I think the
above date correct.

husbandman, and Ann his wife. She may have been his cousin* of some degree, as his mother was Elizabeth Atkinson, but I have been unable to fix the relationship.

The witnesses to the marriage of John Thistlethwaite (1347), and Eleanor Atkinson, were as follows.

John Atkinson	George Wetherald
Ann Atkinson	Wm. Sowerby
Mary Blanior [?]	William Middlebrook
Thomas Cutforth	Peggy Sedgwick
Alice Cutforth	Thomas Lambert
John Bradley	Christ' Myers, Jr.
Mary Bradley	John Beezon Baynes
Jane Wetherald	Simon Hunter
Joseph Wetherald	Ann Scarr
Joseph Wetherald	Ann Wilson
Molly Wetherald	Eliz. Lambert
John Wetherald	Rich' Blakey
Richard Thistlethwaite	Mary Hodgson
Agnes Thistlethwaite	Joshua Blakey
Christ' Myers	Ann Thompson
Marg' Myers	Alex' Hunter
William Fothergill	Richard trotter
Bai Hudson	Jane Scarr
John Thompson	Betty Scarr
Margaret Thompson	Penelope Binks
John Routh	Hannah Bayes
George Raw	
Jannet Wilkinson.	

In 1789, 1791, 1792, and 1794 he is described as " of Aysgarth," but in 1796 he was a husbandman at Counterside or Countersett, a hamlet two miles from Bainbridge and close to Semer-water, a small lake nearly

---

* She was probably not *first* cousin, as they were married at a Friends' Meeting House.

a mile in length.   He was here in March of 1798, but in June of 1800 he
is described as wool-spinner, of Milthrop, near Sedbergh.   In April, 1802,
he was back at Newcloses in Dent, and was here also in May, 1804, but in
June, 1806, he was living at Upper (sometimes " High " or " Over ")
Bentham, Yorkshire.   He was here in 1807, and it was here also 22nd
June, 1810, that his second wife died aged forty-one years ; she was buried
on the 24th at Lower Bentham.

In November, 1812, John Thistlethwaite is described as " warehouse-
man of Bentham."   While living here he was married 8th February, 1813,
at Leeds, to Hannah Winn, daughter of John Winn, oil miller of Leeds,
and his wife Miriam.   He soon removed to Holbeck near Leeds, and here
his son Henry was born in January, 1814.

Neither Quaker publications in general nor the Annual Monitors in
particular are especially Meredithean in their development of the Jocular
Spirit, and one regrets that the author of the following account of John
Thistlethwaite should remain anonymous.

" John Thistlethwaite died at Holbeck near Leeds, aged seventy-
seven, on the 22nd of fourth month, 1836.   When young he was much
inclined to jocularity ; but often felt reproved and condemned for the
indulgence of this disposition.   When disposed to enter into a married
state, a little money appeared to him a proper addition to a wife.   Finding
however, that he could not feel satisfaction and peace in looking out for a
companion with this view, he relinquished it ; and to adopt his own
remarks ; ' sought one who he believed to have religion and virtue, and
married one in whom he found both.   But it pleased Him who gave her
to take her to Himself, about five years after they were married.   When
he thought of marrying again, he was again tempted to think of looking
for some brass ; (a common dialectick phrase for property) ; saying to
himself : surely this time I may have liberty.   But feeling a like check
from the Lord, he had peace in giving up that desire.   And though he
had been married three times, he had never sought anything but religion
and virtue in either of his wives ; and in that great blessing he had not
been mistaken.   .   .'   The closing portion of life was attended with

much bodily affliction ; but his end was peaceful. A minister about twenty-five years."

John Thistlethwaite (1347) was, I understand, a grocer at Holbeck. His third wife survived him a number of years, and sometime during "the forties " kept a school at Dewsbury, Yorkshire, assisted by her daughter, Maria Thistlethwaite (1790), who later married Francis Wallis, of Scarborough. She died at Leeds, 2nd October, 1858, aged eighty-three.

John Thistlethwaite (1347) had nineteen children, only eighteen of whom I have discovered. By his first wife, Elizabeth Wetherald, he had issue :

- i. Elizabeth Thistlethwaite (1348), whom see.
- ii. Alice Thistlethwaite (1448), whom see.
- iii. Ann Thistlethwaite (1544), born in Dent Dale, 27th February, 1786 ; died before 14th July, 1796.

By his second wife, Eleanor Atkinson, he had issue :

- iv. Timothy Thistlethwaite (1545), whom see.
- v. John Thistlethwaite (1555), whom see.
- vi. William Thistlethwaite (1598), whom see.
- vii. Mary Thistlethwaite (1703), born 4th May, 1794, at Aysgarth in Wensleydale. While living at Halifax, Yorkshire, she was married at the Meeting House there 23rd April, 1835, to Samuel Bleckly, grocer, of Colchester in the county of Essex, son of William Bleckly, late of the City of York, linen draper, deceased, and Dorothy his wife now surviving. Samuel Bleckly, of Darlington, died 3rd June, 1867, aged sixty-seven years ; buried at Halifax. His widow, of Elton Villas, Darlington, died 10th February, 1868. *Sine prole.*
- viii. Ann Thistlethwaite (1704), born 14th July, 1796, at Counterside in Wensleydale. She died unmarried 10th September, 1820, at Leeds, and was buried on the 13th at Camp Lane Court, Leeds.

ix. Eleanor Thistlethwaite (1705), whom see.

x. Margaret Thistlethwaite (1782), born 2nd June, 1800, at Milthrop, near Sedbergh, Yorkshire. While confectioner at Newcastle-on-Tyne, she was married at the Meeting House there, 11th January, 1827, to George Abbatt, of Newcastle-on-Tyne, druggist, son of William Abbatt, of Kendal, upholsterer, and the late Deborah Abbatt, his wife. *Sine prole.* She died 14th April, 1880, buried Friends' Burial Ground, Liverpool.

xi. Thomas Thistlethwaite (1783), born 9th April, 1802, at New-closes in Dent. He and his brothers, William, James, and Isaac, emigrated to America. William went about 1818, with his wife, and two children, and perhaps his brothers also, although Thomas would then be sixteen, James fourteen, and Isaac eleven years old. It seems more likely that they went out later. Thomas Thistlethwaite (1783) mysteriously disappeared in America about 1830, and had not been heard of in 1843. It is unknown whether he married.

xii. James Thistlethwaite (1784), born 11th May, 1804, at Newcloses in Dent. As stated above, he emigrated to America, and had married and died before 20th March, 1843. His niece writes : " When we last heard of Uncle James' widow she had gone to spend a few months with one of her sisters who lives at Madison on the Ohio river in this State " (*i.e.* Indiana, the State of Kentucky being immediately across the river). I do not know whether he had children. His great nephew Edward Thistlethwaite (1637) writes me that he settled in Virginia.

xiii. Jane Thistlethwaite (1785), born 6th June, 1806, at High Bentham ; died there 19th October, 1807, and buried on the 21st at Low Bentham.

xiv. Isaac Thistlethwaite (1786), whom see.

xv. Rachel Thistlethwaite (1787), born 5th June, 1810, at Upper
Bentham ; died there 13th July, 1810, and buried on the
15th at Low Bentham.

By his third wife, Hannah Winn, he had issue :—

xvi. Henry Thistlethwaite (1788), born 17th January 1814, at Holbeck, near Leeds, emigrated to Australia unmarried, and
was never again heard of by his relatives.

xvii. Joseph Thistlethwaite (1789), born 8th December, 1814,
at Holbeck; died there 10th December, 1814, and buried
on the 11th at Camp Lane Court, Leeds.

xviii. Maria Thistlethwaite (1790), born 25th June, 1817, at Holbeck.
Before her marriage she and her mother kept a school at
Dewsbury.* She became the second wife of Francis Wallis
of Scarborough (son of Abraham Wallis). His first wife's
son, Edward Wallis, married Maria Wallis's half-great-niece,
Annie, daughter of Francis Johnson, by his first wife,
Eleanor Thistlethwaite (1556). *Sine prole.*

Elizabeth Thistlethwaite (1348), born 23rd January, 1783,
in Kirthwaite (*i.e.*, the upper-part of the Dent Valley), probably at Newcloses. She married 26th May, 1802, John Tennant of Counterside, son
of Christopher and Isabella Tennant. She died 29th September, 1861,
at Kendal. He was born 19th October, 1775, and died 27th April, 1847,
at Kendal. He was formerly husbandman, of Counterside in Wensleydale.

His brother Thomas Tennant, saddler, of Ulverston, born 13th June,
1779, married 1804, Elizabeth Thompson, daughter of John Thompson,
of Hawes by his wife, Margaret Routh. Elizabeth Tennant *née* Thompson
married secondly Thomas Routh, and thirdly John Thistlethwaite (582),
whose sister, Jane Thistlethwaite (759) had married her brother, John
Thompson, Jun., of Hawes. John and Jane Thistlethwaite were second
cousins to Elizabeth Thistlethwaite (1348), who married John Tennant.
Elizabeth and John Tennant had issue,

* See footnote under William Henry Thistlethwaite (1223).

i. Isabella Tennant (1349), born 26th April, 1803, at Counterside; died 7th June, 1831, at Counterside, unmarried.

ii. Christopher Tennant (1350), born 12th July, 1804, at Counterside, a tea-dealer in Liverpool, died there 13th April, 1858, *sine prole*. He married Elizabeth Atkinson of Cheshire, who died 10th January, 1864, buried at Nantwich.

iii. John Tennant (1351), born 13th April, 1806, at Counterside; died 19th April, 1837, at Davenham, Cheshire, unmarried.

iv. William Tennant (1352), whom see.

v. Elizabeth Tennant (1372), born 4th August, 1809, at Counterside, died 5th January, 1887, unmarried.

vi. Thomas Tennant (1373), born 1st May, 1811, at Counterside, died March, 1847. His niece " thinks she remembers a daughter of Uncle Thomas coming over from America on a visit, but she fancies her father was killed over there, but knows no particulars."

vii. Alice Tennant (1374), born 1st February, 1813, at Counterside; died 23rd April, 1855, at Kendal, unmarried.

viii. Samuel Tennant (1375), whom see.

ix. James Tennant (1425), whom see.

x. Eleanor Tennant (1444), born 2nd September, 1818; died 18th January, 1837, at Davenham, Cheshire, unmarried.

xi. Mary Anne Tennant (1445), born 21st April, 1821; died 29th June, 1886. She married Thomas Wilson Jesper, as his second wife, 22nd February, 1867, and died without issue 29th June, 1886. Her husband had three children by his first wife, who was her half-first-cousin, Ann Thistlethwaite (1588). Her niece, Maria Tennant (1366), married her stepson, Alfred Jesper (1590), they being half-second cousins to each other.

xii. Henry Tennant (1446), whom see.

xiii. Margaret Tennant (1447), born 4th February, 1829, and was therefore twenty-six years younger than her mother's eldest daughter. She died 25th April, 1848, at Liverpool, unmarried.

William Tennant (1352), born 1st January, 1808, and married Maria Sampson, who died 28th October, 1892. He died 2nd March, 1877, at Liverpool.

 i. William Sampson Tennant (1353), whom see.

 ii. Maria Tennant (1366), whom see.

 iii. Fanny Tennant (1367), whom see.

 William Sampson Tennant (1353), born 18th September, 1846, at Liverpool. He is now manager of the Stores Department of the American, Dominion, and Leyland Lines of steamers at Liverpool, and resides at 40, Belgrave Street, Liscard, Cheshire. He married 6th December, 1868, at St. Michael's, Liverpool, Sarah Jane Francis, who was born 20th May, 1851, at Liverpool.

 i. William Alfred Tennant (1354), born 10th September, 1869, at Liverpool, died 20th September, 1870.

 ii. Amy Gertrude Tennant (1355), born 18th March, 1871, at Liverpool, unmarried.

 iii. Henry Charles Tennant (1356), born 1st February, 1873, lost at sea, 11th November, 1893.

 iv. Eleanor Francis Tennant (1357), born 1st February, 1876, at Liscard, married 22nd October, 1894, Ernest William Witter, stockbroker's clerk.

  i. Harry Ernest Witter (1358), born 18th August, 1895, at Liscard.

  ii. Doris Witter (1359,) born 22nd March, 1900, at Liscard.

 v. Maud Tennant (1360), born 1st July, 1878, at Liscard, unmarried.

 vi. Samuel Tennant (1361), born 15th September, 1880, at Liscard, now with Messrs. Henry Tate and Sons, sugar refiners, unmarried.

vii.   Edith Tennant (1362), born 18th August, 1886, at Liscard, unmarried.

viii. Emma Mary Tennant (1363), born 9th June, 1888, at Liscard, married 7th February, 1909, to George Yeo, clerk in the Board of Trade Offices, Liverpool.

ix.   Jessie Tennant (1364), born 22nd August, 1890, at Liscard, died 11th February, 1891.

x.   Wilfrid Tennant (1365), born 16th December, 1891, at Liscard, clerk with the Liverpool, London and Globe Insurance Company.

Maria Tennant (1366), born 12th September, 1850, at Liverpool. She was married there 16th May, 1877, to Alfred Jesper (1590), her half-second-cousin. She died 24th March, 1906, at York, leaving one child. Further particulars appear under her husband, Alfred Jesper (1590).

Fanny Tennant (1367), born 29th September, 1853, at Liverpool; she was married 28th September, 1881, at St. Michael's-in-the-Hamlet, Aigburth, Liverpool, to Henry Hatton, who was born 21st April, 1854, at Herculaneum, Liverpool. He and his two sons are clerks in Liverpool. Fanny Hatton died 18th July, 1890, at Liverpool, leaving three children.

i.   Fred Hatton (1368), born 25th January, 1883, at Liverpool; married 24th February, 1905, at West Derby Registry Office, Liverpool, to Elizabeth Maude Ellis, daughter of Hugh and Martha Ellis.

    i.   George Albert Hatton (1369), born 12th July, 1906, at Liscard, Cheshire; baptised at Wallasey Parish Church.

ii.   William Hatton (1370), born 3rd May, 1884, at Liverpool, now living unmarried with his father at 14, Adelaide Road, Kensington, Liverpool.

iii. Elsie Hatton (1371), born 27th January, 1888, at Liverpool, now living unmarried with her father.

———————————

Samuel Tennant (1375), born 18th November, 1814, at Counterside, Wensleydale. He married April, 1843, at Newcastle-on-Tyne, Agnes Nicholson. He died 21st September, 1897, at Darlington, having issue,

    i. Isabella Tennant (1376), born 9th November, 1845, unmarried.

    ii. Joseph John Tennant (1377), born 25th February, 1847; died 27th December, 1906, unmarried.

    iii. Agnes Tennant (1378), whom see.

    iv. Margaret Tennant (1394), whom see.

    v. Samuel Henry Tennant (1402), whom see.

    vi. Annie Tennant (1407), born 13th September, 1854, died June, 1855.

    vii. Christopher Tennant (1408), whom see.

    viii. Eleanor Tennant (1411), whom see.

    ix. James Thistlethwaite Tennant (1420), born 23rd January, 1860; married 26th June, 1886, at Barnard Castle Parish Church to Mary Eleanor Bowness, *sine prole.* In 1910 of North Street, Abergavenny, Monmouth.

    x. Jane Alice Tennant (1421), whom see.

Agnes Tennant (1378), born 1st October, 1848. She was married 30th September, 1869, at Darlington Meeting House, to George Mason Goundry,* aged thirty-four, grocer of Chesterfield, son of George Goundry.

    i. Henry Tennant Goundry (1379), born 1870, married 1896 to Harriet Marsden.

        i. Walter Henry Goundry (1380).

        ii. Norman Goundry (1381).

        iii. Nellie Goundry (1382).

    ii. George Frederick Goundry (1383), born 1872, died 1893, unmarried.

* He was the youngest brother of the wife of Henry Tennant (1446), uncle to Agnes Tennant (1378).

    iii. Agnes Rachel Goundry (1384), born 1873, married 1894, at
         Chesterfield Meeting House, to Herbert Taylor, in 1910
         of Holly House, Sibford Ferris, Oxon.

        i. Herbert Taylor (1385).
        ii. Samuel Edward Taylor (1386).
        iii. Agnes Harriet Taylor (1387).
        iv. Alice Eleanor Taylor (1388).
        v. Winifred Taylor (1389).

    iv. Samuel Edwin Goundry (1390), born 1874, unmarried.
    v. Eleanor Goundry (1391), born 1878, unmarried.
    vi. Elsie Goundry (1392), born 1880, unmarried.
    vii. Mary Goundry (1393), born 1882, died 1892.

Margaret Tennant (1394), born 30th June, 1851. She married
John Robson, at Darlington. In 1910 she was resident at 252, Enfield
Terrace, Gateshead-on-Tyne.

    i. Thomas Robson (1395), born 12th February, 1878, unmarried.
    ii. Samuel Raymond Robson (1396), born 6th August, 1879;
        married Adeline Tate at Darlington.

        i. Raymond Robson (1397).

    iii. Richard Robson (1398), born 6th August, 1881; married
        Gertrude Mary Dobbing.

        i. Gwendoline Margaret Robson (1399).
        ii. Kathleen Robson (1400).
        iii. Gertrude Mary Robson (1401).

Samuel Henry Tennant (1402), born 12th March, 1853. He
married Frances Maria Ryan at Darlington.

    i. Agnes Tennant (1403), married at Weston-super-Mare to
        James Dudley of Rawdon.

ii. Julia Tennant (1404), lives at York, with her great uncle Henry Tennant (1446), of the North-Eastern Railway Company, unmarried.

iii. Philip Tennant (1406), unmarried, lately care of Mr. Wright, Box 154, Cherry Creek Farm, Boisserain, Canada.

Christopher Tennant (1408), born 15th October, 1855. He was married at Chesterfield to Mary Eliza Short. He resided in 1910 at Fairfield House, Fairfield Road, Chesterfield.

i. Charles Short Tennant (1409).

ii. Emma Short Tennant (1410).

Eleanor Tennant (1411), born 3rd September, 1857. She was married at Staindrop Meeting House to Charles Brown, son of Charles and Emily Brown of North Shields (see " The Richardsons of Cleveland," by Anne Ogden Boyce : pedigrees at end.) Charles Brown was for many years a grocer at Stockton-on-Tees, and is now secretary to his brother, Dr. Vipont Brown, of Manchester, a well-known Quaker doctor, and man of letters.

i. Ethel Spence Brown (1412), born 8th February, 1881 ; married 3rd October, 1907, at Mount Street Meeting House, Manchester, to Ernest Watson, of the Friends' Mission, Sehore, Central India. He is son of Richard Watson, of Norton Mill, near Stockton (great grandson of William Dixon*, of Old Raby by his wife Sarah Coates of Smelt. House, Co. Durham), by his wife Sarah Jane Peacock.

  i. Nora Jean Watson (1412a), born February, 1910, in Rasulia, Hoshangabad, India.

ii. Charles Richardson Brown (1414), born 28th May, 1882, physician in Manchester, unmarried.

* See Chart viii. for Thistlethwaite-Dixon-Coates intermarriages.

iii. Gwendoline Brown (1415), born 31st July, 1883, lived six days.

iv. Ellen Winifred Brown (1416), unmarried.

v. Hugh Vipont Brown (1417), born about 1888, unmarried.

vi. Henry Tennant Brown (1418).

vii. Emily Kathleen Brown (1419).

Jane Alice Tennant (1421), born 22nd June, 1862. She married 21st December, 1889, at Chesterfield, Richard George, of Llanidloes.

i. Richard George (1422), born 6th October, 1890, and lived six days.

ii. Eva Constance George (1423), born 2nd December, 1891; unmarried.

iii. Helena Gwendolen George (1424), born 28th November, 1894.

James Tennant (1425), born 20th September, 1816, died 2nd February, 1875, at York. He was a colliery agent, and appears to have lived at Penrith in Cumberland, Liverpool and Fleetwood in Lancashire, and finally at York. By his first wife Jane Bell he had issue.

i. John Bell Tennant (1426), born probably in Penrith, for many years secretary to the Friends' Provident Institution of Bradford. He died unmarried at Rawdon near Leeds.

ii. Mary Elizabeth Tennant (1427), whom see.

By his second wife, Katherine Hope, daughter of Philip and Catherine Hope, of Liverpool, he had issue seven children, as follows,

iii. Eleanor Tennant (1436), eldest child, died in infancy.

iv. Henry Hope Tennant (1437), born 10th August, 1849, in Liverpool. In February, 1910, he was employed in an office in Bradford, unmarried.

    v.   Philip Hope Tennant (1438), born 25th April, 1851, in Liverpool, died 17th July, 1882. He was employed in a branch of the woollen trade in Sydney, New South Wales, and died of consumption.

    vi.   Emma Hope Tennant (1439), born 27th December, 1852, in Liverpool. In February, 1910, she was living unmarried at Green Bank, Rawdon, near Leeds.

    vii.   Alfred James Tennant (1440), born 10th November, 1854, in Liverpool; died of consumption without issue 13th November, 1881. He married Dorothy Robinson, of York, who was living in London, a widow, in February 1910. He was employed in a branch of the woollen trade in Sydney, New South Wales.

    viii.   Samuel Tennant (1441), born in Fleetwood, or York, 7th April, 1857. He was employed in a branch of the woollen trade in Bradford, Yorkshire, and died of consumption at sea 3rd December, 1879, while on the way to join his two brothers in Sydney, N.S.W.

    ix.   Charles Edward Tennant (1442), youngest of his mother's children, died an infant.

James Tennant's third wife was a widow, Sarah Rotherford *née* Wood. Her son by her first husband married James Tennant's eldest daughter. By James Tennant she had issue one child,

    x.   Katherine Tennant (1443), who was born and died young at York.

Mary Elizabeth Tennant (1427), was born probably at Liverpool. She was married to John Rotherford, colliery agent of York, son of her father's third wife by the latter's first husband. In January, 1910, she was living at Ingledene, Fulford Road, Scarborough, a widow.

    i.   Eleanor Rotherford (1428), born 15th September, 1866, at York. She was married August 1899, to Robert Ayton Dunn, M.D., and was living at Hertford in January, 1910, without issue.

 ii. Mary Grace Rotherford (1429), whom see.

 iii. Winifred Alice Rotherford (1434), born 24th March, 1880, at York, unmarried January, 1910.

 iv. Margaret Tennant Rotherford (1435), born 20th June, 1882, at York, unmarried January, 1910.

Mary Grace Rotherford (1429), born 9th December, 1868, at York. She was married in August, 1893, to George Alfred Bellerby, Painter and House Decorator, of York.

 i. Margaret Hope Bellerby (1430) born 24th October, 1894.

 ii. John Rotherford Bellerby (1431), born 25th May, 1896.

 iii. Francis George Bellerby (1432), born 4th July, 1900.

 iv. Joyce Mary Bellerby (1433), born 3rd March, 1905.

***

Henry Tennant (1446), born 23rd October, 1823, at Countersett, near Bainbridge, Wensleydale, Yorkshire. He was educated at Ackworth Friends' School, near Pontefract, Yorkshire. He was married 17th February, 1847, to Mary Jane Goundry at the Friends' Meeting House, Pilgrim Street, Newcastle-on-Tyne. She died 19th May, 1900, without issue.

When sixteen years of age he became associated as book-keeper with the firm of Messrs. Charles Bragg & Co., of Newcastle. Two years later he was appointed chief clerk to Mr. James Potts, the secretary of the Brandling Junction line, and this may be said to have been the commencement of his lifelong railway career.

In 1846, he became accountant for the Leeds and Thirsk Railway Company, of which Samuel Smiles, the well-known author of "Self Help," was assistant secretary from 1845 to 1854. Henry Tennant became general manager of this line in 1848, at the age of twenty-five years. In 1854 the North-Eastern Railway was formed by the amalgamation of the York, Newcastle & Berwick Co., the York and North Midland Co., and the Leeds Northern Co. Henry Tennant represented the last-named company in the negotiations, and became accountant of the newly-formed amalgamation.

In 1870, at the age of forty-seven, he became General Manager of the North-Eastern Railway Company. In 1891, when aged sixty-eight, he retired from this position. He was thereupon elected a director of the company, and granted the sum of £10,000, " in recognition of the very valuable services he has rendered." On the 19th November, 1891, at a meeting in the Railway Institute, York, the officers and servants of the Company presented him with an illuminated address, a service of plate, a landau and harness, and several works of art. He became Vice-chairman of the North-Eastern Railway Company in 1905, and was later joined in that office by Lord Knaresborough.

To Henry Tennant "was especially due the important financial arrangement which converted various old stocks of the North-Eastern Railway into ' consols.' Other companies followed suit, and thus Mr. Tennant was the originator of a most important departure in the consolidation of railway stock." A certain type of express engine was named after him.

He was appointed arbitrator by the Irish Secretary, the Board of Trade, and other bodies, and his contested decision respecting the Edinburgh tramways was upheld by the House of Lords.

He was an active director of the Forth Bridge Company, and of the Central London Railway. He was also Chairman of Directors of the York City and County Banking Company until its absorption by the London Joint Stock Bank, Ltd., in January, 1909, when he joined the London board of directors.

For a number of years he was vice-chairman of the York School Board, and "was a great educationist and temperance reformer."

In 1907, he was offered Knighthood, but declined the honour, " having regard to advancing years and somewhat declining health." He lived unostentatiously at Holgate Hill House, York, with his great niece, Julia Tennant (1404), and here he died 25th May, 1910, aged eighty-six years.

He was a valued member of the Society of Friends, and constant in attendance at its meetings for worship and for business. He was buried at the Friends' Burial Ground at Heslington Road, York, 28th May, 1910. His half-first-cousin once removed, Arthur Rowntree, read the ninetieth Psalm. The funeral was a large one, including J. Lloyd Wharton, Esq., Chairman of the N.E.R. ; and Lord Airedale, Sir Hugh Bell, Bart., Sir George Gibb and Arthur Francis Pease, Esq., directors of the Company.

The *Northern Echo* heads a column, " With the death of Mr. Henry Tennant . . . a great railway pioneer has passed away. Indeed the career of that gentleman is practically the history of the North-Eastern Railway Company, for he it was who took the most prominent part in the consolidation of the many smaller enterprises from which the present extensive system has evolved. . . Much of the success of the company may be ascribed to his exceptional powers of organisation and foresight."

Alice Thistlethwaite (1448) born 10th April, 1784, at Newcloses in Dent Dale. She married 3rd December, 1806, at Manchester Meeting House, Peter Taylor, "turner" of Manchester. He was born 8th February, 1784, fourth child of Joseph Taylor, inventor and machine-maker, of Manchester, by his wife, Dorothy Waring. Joseph Taylor was born 31st January, 1750, O.S. (11th February 1750, N.S.) son of David Taylor, sometime Moravian pastor to Lady Huntingdon, and a missionary in Jamaica, who died 1783.

Peter Taylor* lived near Sedbergh, Yorkshire, where he had a rope mill which was burnt down. He inherited an inventive genius which descended to his only son ; they are said to have invented the screw for steamships. He died at his son's house, Deptford, London, 23rd April, 1863, and was interred at Nunhead Cemetery. His wife Alice Taylor (1448), died 27th November, 1842, at Hollinwood, Lancashire.

* Peter Taylor the member of the Society of Friends was not identical with Peter Taylor the member of the Society of Friends of Italy, and the intimate friend of Mazzini, although a contemporary.

i. Ellen Taylor (1449), died aged about one year.
ii. John Taylor (1450), whom see.
iii. Alice Taylor (1466), whom see.
iv. Elizabeth Taylor (1468), whom see.
v. Mary Taylor (1482), whom see.
vi. Sarah Taylor (1504), whom see.
vii. Eleanor Taylor (1539), whom see.

John Taylor (1450), born 28th November, 1807, in Manchester. He was married 29th December, 1836, at Halifax Meeting House, to Sophia Tew, whose father, William Tew, was then a corn and flour dealer of Halifax. John Taylor (1450) died 1st March, 1901, in Bristol, in his ninety-fourth year.

John Taylor (1450), lived in Manchester, in Deptford, London, in India, and finally in Bristol. He was a flax-spinner, a rope and twine manufacturer, and a slate merchant, in England. In 1869 he went to India for the purpose of growing cotton, and of introducing shallow-bottomed boats of his own invention for the navigation of the rivers of India. He returned to England in 1881. He was " of an inventive mechanical genius, and too clever to be much benefit to himself." Before he went to India he did important work in the invention and development of twin-screw propellers for steamships.

In his youth he was an intimate friend and companion of John Bright, the future statesman. Good fortune has enabled me to borrow an interesting pamphlet printed in 1888 by John Taylor (1450), in which he describes his and John Bright's first visit to London together. The young men broached the project to John Bright's father, Jacob Bright, a Quaker mill-owner. The latter replied : " I've partly consented to let him go. Our John has been teasing me about it ; I think thou won't lead him into mischief . . .

" My liberated young friend and I lost no time in securing our places by that renowned 'Red Rover' patent safety coach, which nightly drew wondering crowds of sight-seers round the Albion Hotel, in Piccadilly, opposite the Manchester Infirmary, in response to the musical trumpet-blast flourish, so skilfully played by the gorgeously apparalled guard, who, like his companion, the Coachman who ' Tooled the Ribbons,' wore a beautiful Bouquet of fresh-cut fragrant flowers on his breast, culled expressly, or purchased, for each day's display.

" The ' Red Rover ' was the property of Weatherald and Webster,* friends and relatives of the Taylors, of Hollinwood and Manchester, ' Th' Quakers o' th' Bower.' The nominal owners of that favourite coach used to say jocosely (there's many a true word spoken in jest) that the Coachman and Guards took the tips and proceeds attached to three of the wheels of their coach, and that the responsible Proprietors between them only pocketed the proceeds or returns from *one* of the wheelers, and from *one* of the wheels of the coach.

" There can be no mistake about the date of our departure for the ' Modern Babylon.' It was the very day after the Reform Bill of 1832 had received the Royal Assent, and on our way up to London we encountered not a few somewhat furiously driven ' Four-in-Hands,' with their almost wild with excitement Insiders & Outsiders scattering broadcast printed announcements of the tumultuously and generally joyously welcomed fact of the passing of that historically memorable Bill of 1832.

" Arrived at the ' White Bear,' in Basinghall Street, we ordered a ' knife and fork ' tea, and then went to our bedrooms to ' Wash and Brush up,' and after somewhat hastily despatching our meal, forthwith we rushed off for the House of Commons. . . Side by side with his friend John Taylor, the now world-renowned John Bright took his seat for the first time in the gallery of the British House of Commons, and took his first survey of that great Legislative Assembly, which had only the day before enacted the Reform Bill of 1832.

" And in which, on the very evening afterwards, in our hearing and presence, was being discussed the merits of Mr. Whitmore's important motion for the Repeal of the Corn Laws.

---

* John Webster, brother of George Webster, who married Eleanor Thistlethwaite (1705), John Taylor's half-aunt. John Webster at one time lived at Poynton Towers, the dower-house on Lord Vernon's Cheshire estates.

" Ireland was to the front upon that occasion, and we both listened with intense interest to the debate, which included two short and sharp sentences, in which, with uplifted arms, that great Orator and law-abiding Irish agitator—Daniel O'Connell—denounced the Starvation Corn Laws."

John Taylor (1450) married Sophia Tew. She was born 2nd October, 1815, at Rochdale, in Lancashire, daughter of William Tew, by his wife Ann Wetherald, who was a daughter of Joseph and Mally Wetherald.* William Tew later removed to Halifax. Sophia Taylor *née* Tew died 1st January, 1908, at Bristol, in her ninety-third year.

  i. Lucy Taylor (1451), born 30th October, 1837, at Hollinwood, near Manchester. She was married 20th April, 1884, at Yatton Meeting House, Somerset, to Alfred Yeardley (586), whom see. He was her second, third and fourth cousin. She was living, a widow, at 9, Wellington Park, Clifton, Bristol, in June, 1910. *s.p.*

  ii. Emily Anne Taylor (1452), born 31st January, 1840, at Hollinwood ; died 2nd June, 1855.

  iii. Sophia Taylor (1453), born 14th June, 1841, at Hollinwood. In June 1910 she was living, unmarried, with her eldest sister at 9, Wellington Park, Clifton, Bristol.

  iv. John William Taylor (1454), born 19th March, 1844, at Hollinwood ; died 9th November, 1846.

  v. Eliza Gulielma Taylor (1455), born 16th October, 1846, at Hollinwood. She died 7th January, 1859, at Ackworth School.

  vi. Fenton Kay Taylor (1456), whom see.

  vii. George Stephenson Taylor (1463), whom see.

Fenton Kay Taylor (1456), born 22nd January, 1849, at Hollinwood, near Manchester. He was book-keeper, etc., to a firm of varnish manufacturers in London. He was married 8th March, 1872, to Charlotte Amelia Stevenson, widow of Joseph Stevenson. He died 23rd July, 1884,

---

* See Charts V. and IX., and under Isabel Thistlethwaite (583), Alexander Fothergill (1062), John Thistlethwaite (1347), and William Thistlethwaite (1598).

    i.   Sophia Taylor (1457), born 16th January, 1873. She was married, 22nd December, 1898, to Alan Hadfield (1491), her second cousin, whom see.

        i.   Samuel Alan Hadfield (1458) born 6th April, 1900.

        ii.   Bernard Hadfield (1459), born 17th September, 1901.

    ii.   John Taylor (1460), born 16th November, 1874, unmarried.

    iii.   Lucy Taylor (1461), born 28th April, 1877, unmarried.

    iv.   May Taylor (1462), born 4th December, 1879, a nurse, unmarried.*

George Stephenson Taylor (1463), born 7th February, 1853, near Cheadle, Cheshire. He was married 10th October, 1877, to Cicely Porter Turnbull, of West Hartlepool, Co. Durham, who died 20th May, 1885, near Bristol. He married secondly Elizabeth Anne Low, 12th December, 1887, who is without issue. He lives at Chew Stoke, near Bristol, and is manager of the Winford Iron Ore and Redding Company.

    i.   Maud Taylor (1464), born 28th April, 1879, died 28th September, 1879, at Bristol.

    ii.   Maurice Cecil Taylor (1465), born 1st May, 1885, unmarried.*

Alice Taylor (1466), born at Manchester 6th August, 1812. She married (firstly) David Wright, of Kettering, by whom she had one child· She married secondly in 1861, Samuel Alexander of Leominster, son of Alexander, the bill-broker, of Lombard Street, London. Her third cousin, Sarah Thompson (817), married Samuel Alexander Jefferys, son of Thomas Jefferys by his wife, Martha Alexander, of Needham Market (1775-1851), who was probably aunt of Samuel Alexander. He died 26th May, 1884, in his seventy-fifth year, and his widow Alice Alexander (1466), died 9th March, 1898, at Cheltenham. Samuel Alexander's first wife was Sarah Gundry, of Calne, by whom he had several children.

* At St. John's Church, Clifton, 1st September, 1910, Maurice Cecil Taylor (1465), was married to his first cousin, Mary Taylor (1462).

One of them is Joseph Gundry Alexander, a well-known Quaker traveller and philanthropist, who is interested in the abolition of the opium traffic.

    i.   Phœbe Wright (1467), an only child, died aged about one year.

Elizabeth Taylor (1468), born 30th August, 1816. She married 12th August, 1840, at Prestwich, Manchester, George Hadfield, who was not a Quaker. He and John Hadfield were children of George Hadfield, of Failsworth, near Oldham, Lancashire, by his wife Jane Barlow, whose nephew was Thomas Oldham Barlow, the famous engraver. Possibly they were related to Deborah Barlow, who married John Thistlethwaite (166), of Birkenhead, third cousin to Elizabeth Taylor (1468). George Hadfield was a varnish manufacturer, and was carrying on this business in Paris in 1868. Elizabeth Hadfield (1468) died 23rd March, 1861, at Wetheral, near Carlisle, and her husband died 6th December, 1881. She published at least one volume of poems.

    i.   George Hadfield (1469), whom see.
    ii.   Alice Taylor Hadfield (1480), born 29th June, 1842 ; married 14th January, 1868, at Manchester Cathedral to her first cousin german, Samuel Frederick Hadfield (1503). They lived for several years at Haltwhistle, Northumberland, where he was a varnish-manufacturer, and they retired about two years ago to Lochmaben, Dumfries, Scotland. *Sine prole.*
    iii.   Thomas Hadfield (1481), born 17th February, 1845, married 19th July, 1877, at Carlisle to Eliza Bell. He died without issue 10th May, 1882, at Weston-super-Mare.

George Hadfield (1469), born 16th June, 1841. He was a varnish manufacturer. He formerly lived at Haltwhistle and Carlisle, but in the late seventies he removed to London, where he started the varnish business now carried on by his four sons. He was married, firstly, 28th October, 1874, to S. J. Healey, who died 20th January, 1878. By her he had issue,

    i.   Elsie Hadfield (1470), born 27th August, 1875 ; died 23rd September, 1882.

   ii.   Henry Healey Hadfield (1471), born 10th January, 1878 ; died 19th January, 1878, an infant.

George Hadfield was married, secondly, 3rd September, 1879, to Emily Rogers. She was born 2nd February, 1846, at Stoke Newington, daughter of Ishmael and Jennet Maria Rogers, the former of whom was a provision merchant. Emily Hadfield, *née* Rogers, was living at Wimbledon, in 1910. George Hadfield (1469) lived from 1880 to 1886 at Old Southgate, North London, from 1887 to 1895 at Sutton, in Surrey, and after that at Merton Park. He died 24th February, 1900. By his second wife he had issue.

  iii.   George Hugh Hadfield (1472), born 17th July, 1880, at Old Southgate. He was married at Carlisle, 30th October, 1909, to Jean Duncan Scott. In 1910 he was a partner with his three brothers in the London varnish factory.

  iv.   Samuel Rogers Hadfield (1473), born 23rd November, 1881, at Old Southgate. In 1910 he resided at 105, Broxholm Road, West Norwood, and was a partner with his three brothers in the London varnish factory. He was married 3rd December, 1908, at S. Mary's Parish Church, Wimbledon, to Bertha Mildred Taplin, of Wimbledon. She was born at Brighton, 19th May, 1882, daughter of Robert and Mary Elizabeth Taplin, the former of whom is a builder at Wimbledon.

       i.   Robert Samuel Hadfield (1473a), born 8th September 1909, at West Norwood.

    v.   Mary Blanch Hadfield (1474), born 21st February, 1883, at Old Southgate. She was unmarried in 1910.

   vi.   Cicely Milicent Hadfield (1475), born 9th November, 1884, at Old Southgate. She was unmarried in 1910.

    vii. Alice Winifred Hadfield (1476), born 20th February, 1886, at Old Southgate. She was unmarried in 1910.

  viii. Constance Emily Hadfield (1477), born 7th June, 1887, at Sutton, Surrey. She was unmarried in 1910.

    ix. Harold Roy Hadfield (1478), born 3rd November, 1888, at Sutton, Surrey. In 1910 he was a partner with his three brothers in the London varnish factory; unmarried.

    x. Norman McLaran Hadfield (1479), born 3rd October, 1890, at Sutton, Surrey. In 1910 he was a partner with his three brothers in the London varnish factory; unmarried.

Mary Taylor (1482), born 13th December, 1819. She was married 17th October, 1844, to John Hadfield, varnish manufacturer. He was born 19th October, 1819, son of George and Jane Hadfield, of Failsworth. His brother, George Hadfield, jun., married Mary Taylor's sister, Elizabeth Taylor (1468). Mary Hadfield (1482) died in 1906 or 1907 at the home of her niece and daughter-in-law, Alice Taylor Hadfield (1480), at Haltwhistle.

    i. John Henry Hadfield (1483), whom see.

    ii. Samuel Frederick Hadfield (1503), born 29th September, 1847. He was married 14th January, 1868, at Manchester Cathedral to his double first cousin, Alice Taylor Hadfield (1480). He was a varnish manufacturer at Haltwhistle in Northumberland, but retired in about 1908, and now resides at Lochmaben, Dumfries, Scotland. *Sine prole.*

John Henry Hadfield (1483), born 13th January, 1846. He was a varnish manufacturer, but eventually gave up the business and removed to New Zealand. He is now an agent to " some large house," and lives in Auckland, N.Z. He was married 31st July, 1868, to Mary Clowes. She was born 4th October, 1846, and now resides at 67, Wightman Road, Harringay, London.

    i. Ernest Clowes Hadfield (1484), born 15th August, 1869. He has lived in Australia, but returned to New Zealand a short time ago, where he is now a fruit-grower at Auckland. He married Ida Bostock.

        i. Bernard Hadfield (1485).

        ii. Harold Hadfield (1486).

        iii. Irene Mary Hadfield (1487).

        iv. Vera Faith Hadfield (1488).

        v. Gwendoline Hope Hadfield (1489).

    ii. Lily Mary Hadfield (1490), born 7th January, 1871. In 1910 she was a teacher in London, unmarried.

    iii. Alan Hadfield (1491), born 27th July, 1872. He and his brother Donald have been in business together, for about ten years, as builders and decorators, at Finsbury Park, London. He married his second cousin, Sophia Taylor (1457), 22nd December, 1898.

        i. Samuel Alan Hadfield (1458), born 6th April, 1900.

        ii. Bernard Taylor Hadfield (1459), born 17th September, 1901.

    iv. Francis Leslie Hadfield (1492), born 15th October, 1873. He is a missionary at Bulawayo, Rhodesia, South Africa. He married Lily Marson.

        i. Douglas Leslie Hadfield (1493).

        ii. Gladys Hadfield (1494).

        iii. —— Hadfield (1495), born in 1908, in Matabeleland.

    v. Donald Hadfield (1496), born 7th November, 1874. He and his brother Alan have been in business together for about ten years as builders and decorators at Finsbury Park, London. He married Amy Eleanor Maskins, who was without issue in 1908.

    vi. Bernard Hadfield (1497), born 10th February, 1876; died 26th August, 1876, an infant.

vii. Douglas Hadfield (1498), born 6th July, 1877; died 27th August, 1896.

viii. Mabel Helen Hadfield (1499), born 24th January, 1879, un-married, in 1910 in the Civil Service, London.

ix. Cecil Angus Hadfield (1500), born 15th May, 1880; unmarried, in 1910 land and estate agent at Calgary, Alberta, Canada.

x. Kenneth Hadfield (1501), born 25th August, 1881, unmarried. He is articled to Messrs. Keen, Chartered Accountants, London.

xi. Alice Muriel Hadfield (1502), born 15th October, 1883, un-married, in 1910 in the Civil Service, London.

Sarah Taylor (1504), born 27th May 1823, at Birks, near Sedbergh, Yorkshire. She was married 24th September, 1851, at Egremont Friends' Meeting House to Samuel Moss. His parents came from Frodsham, and lived many years at Kilternan Lodge, Golden Ball, Co. Dublin, where they died. Samuel Moss was born 23rd March, 1812, and lived at Youghal, Ireland, until about 1855, when he removed with his family to Co. Dublin. He was a trunk and box manufacturer, and died at Dundrum, Dublin, 22nd March, 1871, aged fifty-nine years. His widow lives with her daughter, Mrs. Loveridge, at Llandaff, near Cardiff, South Wales.

i. Alice Mary Moss (1505), whom see.

ii. Phœbe Lawton Moss (1521), whom see.

iii. Samuel Moss (1530), born 2nd May, 1856, in Co. Dublin, and died at Dublin aged a little over two years.

iv. Sarah Emily Moss (1531), whom see.

v. Sophia Moss (1534), born 26th March, 1861, in Co. Dublin, now headmistress of the Friends' Schoool, Mountmellick, Queen's County, Ireland, unmarried.

vi. Lydia Moss Moss (1535), born 17th March, 1862, in Co. Dublin, now unmarried at Dublin.

    vii. Anna Elizabeth Moss (1536), born 11th October, 1863, in Co.
           Dublin, died aged six years at Clonskeagh, Co. Dublin.
   viii. Eleanor Moss (1537), born 18th December, 1864, in Co. Dublin ;
           Bachelor of Arts, headmistress at Edgbaston College,
           Birmingham. Unmarried.
     ix. Edith Moss (1538), born 8th August, 1868, in Co. Dublin,
           died aged seventeen days at Clonskeagh, Co. Dublin.

Alice Mary Moss (1505), born 27th December, 1852, at Youghal,
Ireland. She was married 13th August, 1874, to Thomas Loveridge, of
Leominster. He is now ironmonger and ship-chandler, of Cardiff, and
resides at Llandaff, Wales. About half their children were born at
Leominster, and half at Penarth, near Cardiff.

      i. Maria Louisa Loveridge (1506), born 19th January, 1876.
           She was a missionary in China, and married Dr. Stanley
           Jenkins, now of Sianfu, Shensi, North China.   .
           i. Margaret Winifred Jenkins (1507).
     ii. Samuel Moss Loveridge (1508), born 14th June, 1877. He is
           a Baptist Minister, now a missionary living at Culebra,
           Panama, Central America. He married 7th November,
           1905, Ethel Rebecca Pratt, daughter of a minister in
           Kingston, Jamaica.
           i. Guy Loveridge (1509), born 8th September, 1907.
    iii. Thomas Lawton Loveridge (1510), born 25th November,
           1878. He married 10th June, 1905, Florence Emily Neale,
           daughter of a cold-storage proprietor of Penarth. He lives
           at Llandaff, and is a director in his father's business.
           i. Ferrar Lawton Loveridge (1511), born 15th Septem-
              ber, 1906.
           ii. Dorothy Loveridge (1512).
     iv. Alexander Loveridge (1513), born 21st January, 1881, un-
           married.

v. Sarah Winifred Loveridge (1514), born 16th January, 1883, died unmarried 17th July, 1906.

vi. Ernest Ebenezer Loveridge (1515), born 24th May, 1884, unmarried.

vii. Alice Mary Moss Loveridge (1516), born 16th August, 1885, died 17th May, 1899.

viii. Mary Anna Newman Loveridge (1517), born 16th April, 1887, died 1910, unmarried.

ix. Guy Loveridge (1518), born 30th November, 1888, died 25th November, 1890.

x. Arthur Loveridge (1519), born 28th May, 1891.

xi. Sophia Joy Loveridge (1520), born 7th January, 1894.

Phœbe Lawton Moss (1521), born 25th November, 1854, at Youghal, Ireland. She was married 9th June, 1880, in Dublin, to Hugh Wallace, in 1909, of Lowville, Merrion, Co. Dublin, now of Dublin city. His father, Robert Wallace, was a well-known Methodist minister ; another of the latter's sons, Robert Wallace, junior, was member of parliament for Perth until his resignation on becoming Chairman of the London County Sessions. Hugh Wallace is managing director of Wallace Brothers Ltd., Coal and General Merchants. Three of his children were born at Dublin, one at Birkenhead, and two at Gt. Meols, Cheshire.

i. Hugh Ellerslie Wallace (1522), born 9th July, 1881 ; married 15th December, 1905, Maud Reid, and is now in Wallace Brothers' business.

 i. Kathleen Maud Wallace (1523), born 14th March, 1907.

 ii. Hugh Ellerslie Wallace (1524).

ii. Norman Hay Wallace (1525), born 10th December, 1882, unmarried.

iii. Sarah Mayken Wallace (1526), born 8th May, 1884, unmarried.

iv.   Kathleen Dorothea Wallace (1527), born 1st November, 1886, unmarried.

v.   Kenneth Moss Wallace (1528), born 30th December, 1889, unmarried.

vi.   William Eric Wallace (1529), born 3rd February, 1902.

Sarah Emily Moss (1531), born 4th September, 1858, in Co. Dublin. She was married 7th July, 1890, at Birkenhead, to Thomas Robert Sparks, now an agent in Dublin.   He is the son of Richard William and Rose Sparks, and is said to be descended from Archbishop Ussher, who fixed the dates which appear in the Authorised Version of the Bible.

i.   Thomas Robert Sparks (1532), born 15th September, 1893, at Dublin.

ii.   Richard William Sparks (1533), born 19th August 1895, at Dublin.

Eleanor Taylor (1539), born about 1829, married Joseph Storrs Fry, of Chelmsford, at Egremont Meeting House, Cheshire, 24th September, 1851 ; the same day that her sister Sarah married Samuel Moss. She died 27th December, 1876, at Purleigh, Essex, aged forty-nine years. Her husband was a farmer at Maldon, and died 16th January, 1898, aged eighty-five years.

He was son of Thomas Fry, and grandson of Cornelius Fry, who died in Bristol, 1818, aged eighty-one.   Cornelius Fry was the fifth son of John Fry (1701-1775), of Sutton Benger, Wiltshire, by his wife Mary, daughter of Joseph and Katherine Storrs.   Cornelius Fry's eldest brother, Dr. Joseph Fry, of Bristol, is the direct ancestor of Joseph Storrs Fry, head of the chocolate firm, of Sir Edward Fry, an eminent judge, and of Sir Theodore Fry, Bart., lately of Darlington, whose first wife was Sophia Pease, grand-daughter of Edward Pease, " father of railways " (See Chart VIII).

Joseph Storrs and Eleanor Fry, of Maldon, had four children, three of whom died of consumption.

    i.   John Fry (1540) went to New York, where he married and died. He had no children known to his relatives.

   ii.   Henry Fry (1541), born about 1856, "went out farming to Maryland, got his arm caught in a machine at a saw-mill, and had it amputated; returned to England, and died at Barnsbury, London, unmarried, 3rd October, 1883, aged twenty-seven." He was buried in the Friends' Graveyard, Stoke Newington.

  iii.   Eleanor Fry (1542), "was engaged to be married to Cornelius Barritt, of Croydon, who went out to the States to provide a home," but was robbed and murdered there. She died 8th March, 1888, at Purleigh, or Mundon, Essex, aged twenty-nine.

  iv.   Joseph Taylor Fry (1543), born about 1868, killed by his father's hay-cart 1876, aged eight years, at Purleigh, near Maldon, Essex.

Timothy Thistlethwaite (1545), born 16th September, 1789, at Aysgarth, Yorkshire, being the eldest son of the nineteen children, and the eldest child of John Thistlethwaite (1347), by his second wife, Eleanor Atkinson. He was a clogger at Lower Bentham, Yorkshire, in 1812 and 1813. His father was also living here, but on his third marriage (a year after Timothy's marriage), he removed to Holbeck, near Leeds, whither his son Timothy removed about the same time. The latter was a shop-keeper here from 1814 to 1824, but in 1827 and 1829 he was living at Hunslet, another suburb of Leeds. He died at Pontefract 18th March, 1839, aged forty-nine years.

He married Betty Davison, who was born 28th May, 1787, at Mewith near Bentham, daughter of Leonard Davison, stay-maker, by his wife Alice Harrison. For Thistlethwaite-Harrison intermarriages, see Chart

II.   They were married 18th November, 1812, at Lower Bentham
Meeting House, and some of their children went to Australia, with their
mother.   As Harris and Arthur Thistlethwaite of Part II. are the only
Quakers of the name in Australia at present, I presume that Timothy's
descendants are no longer Quakers.   I should much like to correspond
with some representative of the family ; I believe that there are no
descendants in England.*

  i.   John Thistlethwaite (1546), born 27th September, 1813, at
       Lower Bentham.   I know nothing more about him.
 ii.   Leonard Thistlethwaite (1547), born 14th December, 1814, at
       Holbeck, near Leeds.   He died 25th August, 1837, at
       Ackworth, three miles from Pontefract.   His death
       occurred from consumption while visiting Thomas Thistle-
       thwaite (1283) of Ackworth, his father's second cousin, and
       he was buried in the Friends' Burial Ground, Ackworth,
       unmarried.
iii.   William Thistlethwaite (1548), born 2nd March, 1817, at
       Holbeck.   He is said to have emigrated to Australia with
       his mother, and brothers Edward and Timothy Atkinson ;
       and is reported by his first cousin Charles Webster (1747)
       to have been mayor of the town of Geelong, Australia.   Of
       possible offspring I know nothing.
 iv.   Thomas Thistlethwaite (1549), born 16th September, 1819,
       at Holbeck.   I know nothing more about him.
  v.   Alice Thistlethwaite (1550), born 20th November, 1821,
       probably at Holbeck.   She died 21st January, 1838, at
       Pontefract, aged sixteen.
 vi.   Eleanor Thistlethwaite (1551), born 12th January, 1824, at
       Holbeck.   I know nothing more about her.

    * From the Australian directories it appears that a certain Leonard
Thistlethwaite, boot and shoe manufacturer, is living at Naucluse St. Claremont,
Western Australia ; and a certain Maurice Thistlethwaite at Koroit, Victoria.   The
former must almost certainly be a descendant.

vii. Edward Thistlethwaite (1552), born 25th September, 1825,
probably at Holbeck. He is said to have emigrated to
Australia with his mother and two brothers. Of possible
offspring I know nothing.

viii. Timothy Atkinson Thistlethwaite (1553), born 27th November,
1827, at Hunslet, near Leeds. He without doubt emigrated
to Australia before October, 1858, unmarried. In a
Monthly Meeting Minute Book at the Friends' Meeting
House, Scarborough,* I found a minute dated 15th January,
1862, transferring his membership into Melbourne Monthly
Meeting. But the certificate of transfer was returned
together with a copy of disownment issued by Melbourne
Monthly Meeting 20th October, 1858, against Timothy
Atkinson Thistlethwaite, who had married a non-Quaker.
I know nothing more about him.

ix. Eliza Thistlethwaite (1554), born 20th November, 1829, at
Hunslet, where she died 12th September, 1831, and was
buried on the 15th at Camp Lane Court, Leeds.

John Thistlethwaite (1555), born 3rd March, 1791, at Aysgarth,
Yorkshire. He was a shopkeeper at Holbeck, near Leeds, and married,
20th May 1819, at Ackworth, Margaret Walton, daughter of James and
Julia Walton, of York. There seems to have been no near relationship
between her and the late Thomas Walton (539), of Scarborough. He was
at Holbeck in 1820, at Beeston near Leeds in 1821 and 1823, but again
at Holbeck in 1825 and 1826, and here he died 19th October, 1828, and
was buried on the 23rd at Camp Lane Court, Leeds. His widow died
12th April, 1860, at Preston, Lancashire, aged seventy-three years.

* I am indebted to my friend Stephen Robert Steventon, Clerk of Pickering
and Hull Monthly Meeting, for obtaining permission to examine the Quaker books
at Scarborough. His second wife is a daughter of the second wife of Francis
Johnson, whose first wife was Eleanor Thistlethwaite (1556).

  i. Eleanor Thistlethwaite (1556), whom see.
 ii. David Thistlethwaite (1576), whom see.
iii. Edward Thistlethwaite (1587), born 1st February, 1823, at
        Beeston, died 27th February, 1824, at Holbeck, and buried
        on the 29th at Camp Lane Court, Leeds.
 iv. Ann Thistlethwaite (1588), whom see.
  v. John Thistlethwaite (1596), born 12th November, 1826, at
        Holbeck, died 9th December, 1826, at Holbeck.
 vi. Mary Thistlethwaite (1597), born 12th November, 1826,
        a twin with John, died 13th June, 1826, at Holbeck.

Eleanor Thistlethwaite (1556), born 11th February, 1820, at
Holbeck, near Leeds.   She was married at Macclesfield, 15th May, 1851,
to Francis Johnson, who was born 3rd December, 1821, at Richhill, Co.
Armagh, Ireland. He was a tea-dealer in Southwark, London, where
his business is still carried on by his eldest son, Robert Johnson. He
married secondly Susanna Maria Brown, of Earith, Huntingdon, by whom
he had six children. She is now resident at Ashford, Kent. His first
wife died 1867 in London.

  i. Annie Johnson (1557), whom see.
 ii. Robert Johnson (1564), whom see.
iii. Francis Johnson (1569), born at Manchester 13th December,
        1856, was apprenticed to John Rowntree, grocer of Scar-
        borough, whose first wife was born Ann Webster (1725),
        first cousin once removed to Francis Johnson, Junior. The
        last-named is now a country postman living about thirty
        miles from Brisbane, Queensland, Australia. Unmarried.
 iv. Samuel Johnson (1570), whom see.
  v. William Johnson (1572), whom see.
 vi. Henry Johnson (1575), born 29th November, 1862. He was
        married in 1889, to Mary Alice Peters, but was without
        issue in 1910. At this date he was employed in America
        as a civil engineer by the firm of Babcock & Wilcox, Ltd.,

and resided at 491, Union Avenue, Patterson, New Jersey U.S.A.

Annie Johnson (1557), born 10th April, 1852. She was married 10th January, 1877, at Holloway Meeting House, London, to Edward Wallis, grocer of Scarborough, Yorkshire, son of Francis Wallis, grocer and miller of Scarborough by his first wife, Sarah Ann Jeffrey. In 1910 Edward and Annie Wallis were resident at Springfield, West Parade Road, Scarborough.

Francis Wallis married secondly Maria Thistlethwaite (1790), who thus became stepmother-in-law to her half-great-niece, Annie Wallis *née* Johnson (1557). Priscilla Gray Wallis, sister to Edward Wallis, married George Rowntree (1730), grocer of Scarborough, second cousin to Edward Wallis' wife. And two of Edward Wallis's uncles married descendants of the Wensleydale Thistlethwaites, whom I intend to describe in my second volume.

Edward and Annie Wallis had issue :

  i. Eleanor Gray Wallis (1558), born 14th March, 1878, at Scarborough. In 1909 she was demonstrator to George Hamilton Archibald, the well-known lecturer on Children's Sunday Schools. Unmarried.

 ii. Edward Arnold Wallis (1559), born 22nd April, 1880, at Scarborough ; now employed in his father's grocery business at Scarborough, unmarried. He was educated at Bootham School, York, 9 mo. 1896, to 12 mo. 1897.

iii. Arthur Thistlethwaite Wallis (1560), whom see.

 iv. Dorothea Wallis (1561), whom see.

  v. Annie Mabel Wallis (1563), born 21st May, 1885, at Scarborough. She was educated at Polam Hall, Darlington, and in 1909 was living with her parents unmarried.

Arthur Thistlethwaite Wallis (1560), born 25th July, 1881, at Scarborough. He was educated at Bootham School, York, 9 mo., 1897, to 7 mo., 1898, and in 1909 was organiser of religious and social work for the Society of Friends in the Birmingham district.

He was married 21st April, 1909, at Purley Meeting House, Surrey, to Mary Dorothy Knight, daughter of Howard Forester and Harriet Knight, of Uphill, Purley, Surrey. Howard Knight's nephew, Wilfred Marriage Brown, of Weston-super-Mare, married Emily Dixon, sister of Alice Elizabeth Dixon, who married Wm. Hy. Thistlethwaite (1223).

    i.   Mary Joyce Wallis (1560a) born 30th March, 1910, at Birmingham.

Dorothea Wallis (1561), born 13th April, 1883, at Scarborough. She was married 11th June, 1907, at Scarborough Meeting House, to Herbert George Wood, M.A. Cantab., Fellow of Jesus College, Cambridge, and University Lecturer.

    i.   Audrey Wood (1562), born 19th August, 1908.

Robert Johnson (1564), born 24th July, 1854. He entered his father's business, and has been for many years a partner in the firm of Johnson, Johnson & Co., tea dealers, 50, Southwark Bridge Road, London. He was married 19th April, 1883, at Edinburgh, to Sophia Louise Hart, and has issue.

    i.   Francis Montague Johnson (1565), unmarried in 1909.
    ii.   Hugh Lorrimer Johnson (1566), unmarried in 1909.
    iii.   Christian Eleanor Johnson (1567), unmarried in 1909.
    iv.   Annie Louise Johnson (1568), unmarried in 1909.

Samuel Johnson (1570), born 4th November, 1858. He emigrated to California, and married there a Californian girl named Ida Riske, who was then aged about seventeen. After this he went to Australia, and joined his brother William Johnson (1572) in the wholesale merchanting business at Brisbane, Queensland. In 1909 he was trading independently, but in a smaller way of business than his brother.

    i. Eleanor May Johnson (1571), unmarried in 1909.

William Johnson (1572), was apprenticed in Liverpool to Thompson & Capper, the Quaker chemists. At the age of twenty-one he emigrated to Australia, where he managed a business for a chemist. He has been very successful in laying artesian wells near Perth and Freemantle, Western Australia, but is now settled in Brisbane as a large wholesale merchant. He is a Justice of the Peace, and resides at Castle Rawe, Toowong, Brisbane, Queensland. He married Harriet Pollock, a widow who has three children by her first husband.

    i. Eleanor Johnson (1573).

    ii. Winifred Johnson (1574), about fifteen years of age, 1909.

David Thistlethwaite (1576), born 23rd July, 1821, at Beeston, near Leeds. He was a scholar at Ackworth School, near Pontefract, from 1830 to 1835, and was apprenticed there from the latter date until 1838, but gave up the teaching profession and entered into business under Messrs. Binyons, Robinson & Co., tea-dealers, of Manchester. He then went gold-digging to Ballarat, Australia, but returned to England and became manager of Messrs. Fryer, Benson & Forster's Preserve Works at Manchester. When these were given up, he became partner in an unsuccessful laundry. He died 3rd February, 1893, at Hulme, Manchester, aged seventy-one years. He married Ellen Clayton, and had issue.

    i. Margaret Thistlethwaite (1577), married Edwin Harrison, of Rosslair, Monton, Eccles, near Manchester, son of George Harrison, of Manchester.

        i. Frank Harrison (1578).

        ii. Eleanor Harrison (1579).

        iii. Lucy Harrison (1580).

    ii.   Annie Thistlethwaite (1581), married Frank Ponsford Edwards, and is without issue.

   iii.   Eleanor Thistlethwaite (1582), married Herbert Axford, now of 801, Electric Street, Scranton, Pa., U.S.A.

       i.   Gladys Axford (1583).

      ii.   Marjory Axford (1584).

    iii.   Herbert Axford (1585).

    iv.   Eleanor Axford (1586).

Ann Thistlethwaite (1588), born 5th January, 1825, at Holbeck, near Leeds. She was married 21st November, 1850, to Thomas Wilson Jesper, of Macclesfield, Hanley and York, who was born 3rd February, 1827, at Macclesfield. She died 23rd August, 1865, leaving three children, and her husband married secondly her half-first-cousin, Mary Anne Tennant (1445), on the 22nd of February, 1867. She died 29th June, 1886, and Thomas Wilson Jesper married thirdly Alice Esther Ward, 22nd November, 1887, who is still living. He died 2nd May, 1901, at York, being without issue by his second and third wives.

Thomas Wilson Jesper was son of Samuel Jesper, who was eldest son of Samuel Jesper, Sen., of Purleigh, Essex. The fourth son of Samuel Jesper, Sen., named Thomas Jesper, was father of Joseph Marriage Jesper* who married Margaret Alice Carter (204). She was doubly third cousin once removed to Thomas Wilson Jesper's first and second wives. By his first wife he had issue as follows :

     i.   Eleanor Jesper (1589), born 5th September, 1851, at Macclesfield, and was unmarried in 1910.

    ii.   Alfred Jesper (1590), whom see.

   iii.   Charles Jesper (1592), whom see.

Alfred Jesper (1590), born 19th January, 1853, at Hanley. He was married at Liverpool 16th May, 1877, to Maria Tennant (1366), his

---

* Joseph Marriage Jesper was born at Birmingham, 20th May, 1848, son of Thomas and Martha Emma Jesper.

half-second-cousin, and niece to his father's second wife. She died 24th March, 1906, at York, having issue one son ; and her husband married secondly, 28th August, 1907, at York, Lilly Jane Wright, by whom he has no children. He is a coal merchant at 19, Micklegate, York.

    i.   William Alfred Jesper (1591), born 30th March, 1878, at York, and was married 6th June, 1906, at York, to Eleanor Tuff, *s.p.*

Charles Jesper (1592), born 3rd December, 1854, at Hanley. He was married at York, 30th April, 1895, to Agnes Sinclair McKay, and died in London 18th November, 1900. He was goods manager of the North Eastern Railway Company.

    i.   Norman Jesper (1593), born 21st June, 1896, at York, a twin.

    ii.   Leslie Charles Jesper (1594), born 21st June, 1896, at York, a twin.

    iii.   Sydney Watson Jesper (1595), born 6th June, 1900, at York.

William Thistlethwaite (1598), born 3rd April, 1792, at Aysgarth, in Wensleydale, Yorkshire. He married, in England, Elizabeth Wetherald who was niece of his father's first wife, another Elizabeth Wetherald. See Chart IX. They were married about 1814, and lived at Boynton Field House, in the parish of Boynton, and the county of York, where they were probably farmers. Here their first two children were born, but a few months after the birth of the younger, 14th May, 1817, they emigrated to the United States of America.

His brothers Thomas, James and Isaac Thistlethwaite had all emigrated to America before 20th March, 1843, but it seems probable that they crossed some years later than William and his family. One of William's sons, the late George Thistlethwaite (1673), spoke of his father and uncle coming from England to America in 1816 ; but the date is obviously incorrect, and this statement is no sure proof that all four brothers crossed the Atlantic together.

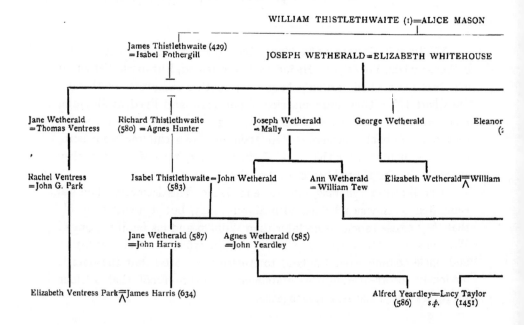

WILLIAM THISTLETHWAITE (1)=ALICE MASON

James Thistlethwaite (429)
=Isabel Fothergill

JOSEPH WETHERALD = ELIZABETH WHITEHOUSE

Jane Wetherald
=Thomas Ventress

Richard Thistlethwaite
(580) = Agnes Hunter

Joseph Wetherald
= Mally ————

George Wetherald

Eleanor
(

Rachel Ventress
=John G. Park

Isabel Thistlethwaite = John Wetherald
(583)

Ann Wetherald
=William Tew

Elizabeth Wetherald = William

Jane Wetherald (587)
=John Harris

Agnes Wetherald (585)
=John Yeardley

Elizabeth Ventress Park = James Harris (634)

Alfred Yeardley = Lncy Taylor
(586)   s.p.   (1451)

half-second-cousin, and niece to his father's second wife. She died 24th March, 1906, at York, having issue one son ; and her husband married secondly, 28th August, 1907, at York, Lilly Jane Wright, by whom he has no children. He is a coal merchant at 19, Micklegate, York.

> i. William Alfred Jesper (1591), born 30th March, 1878, at York, and was married 6th June, 1906, at York, to Eleanor Tuff, *s.p.*

Charles Jesper (1592), born 3rd December, 1854, at Hanley. He was married at York, 30th April, 1895, to Agnes Sinclair McKay, and died in London 18th November, 1900. He was goods manager of the North Eastern Railway Company.

> i. Norman Jesper (1593), born 21st June, 1896, at York, a twin.
> ii. Leslie Charles Jesper (1594), born 21st June, 1896, at York, a twin.
> iii. Sydney Watson Jesper (1595), born 6th June, 1900, at York.

William Thistlethwaite (1598), born 3rd April, 1792, at Aysgarth, in Wensleydale, Yorkshire. He married, in England, Elizabeth Wetherald who was niece of his father's first wife, another Elizabeth Wetherald. See Chart IX. They were married about 1814, and lived at Boynton Field House, in the parish of Boynton, and the county of York, where they were probably farmers. Here their first two children were born, but a few months after the birth of the younger, 14th May, 1817, they emigrated to the United States of America.

His brothers Thomas, James and Isaac Thistlethwaite had all emigrated to America before 20th March, 1843, but it seems probable that they crossed some years later than William and his family. One of William's sons, the late George Thistlethwaite (1673), spoke of his father and uncle coming from England to America in 1816 ; but the date is obviously incorrect, and this statement is no sure proof that all four brothers crossed the Atlantic together.

William Thistlethwaite (1598) settled first near Philadelphia, whence he removed to Richmond, Indiana, a state which is still largely populated by Quakers. He appears to have been a large and successful farmer. At the age of about sixty-four he visited England for a few months, and was the only Thistlethwaite to sign the marriage certificate of his nephew Charles Webster (1747), who was married 11th September, 1856, at Guisborough, Yorkshire. He stayed part of the time in Manchester with his niece Eleanor Johnson, *née* Thistlethwaite, and the wonderful and numerous presents which he took back to America caused considerable interest when opened at the customs-houses. A further account of himself and his family will be found under the account of his daughter, Eleanor Thistlethwaite (1599).

   i.   Eleanor Thistlethwaite (1599), whom see.

   ii.   John Thistlethwaite (1600), whom see.

   iii.   George Thistlethwaite (1673), was born in America. Before 20th March, 1843, he had commenced business as a blacksmith at Cambridge, sixteen miles west of Richmond, Indiana, and was unmarried. He married Leah Shortel, and had one child, but they were all deceased in 1908. I imagine that his only child left no offspring.

   iv.   Thomas Thistlethwaite (1674), was born in America. On 20th March, 1843, his elder sister writes, " Thomas is in Cincinnati learning the saddling and harness trade ; he went there the latter part of last spring.' He married later than this, and his two daughters now live somewhere in Kansas, but I have not yet succeeded in tracing them more definitely, and do not know whether they are married.

   v.   Timothy Thistlethwaite (1675), was born in America. On 20th March, 1843, his elder sister writes that he was unmarried and living at home near Richmond, Indiana. He subsequently married Sarah ———— who has survived him and was living at Richmond, Ind., 9th April, 1908. He had three children.

      i.   William Thistlethwaite (1676), who is married.

      ii.   Mary Thistlethwaite (1677), who is married.

      iii.   Edward Thistlethwaite (1678), who is married.

  vi. Mary Thistlethwaite (1679), whom see.

  vii. William Thistlethwaite (1681) was born in America. On 20th March, 1843, his elder sister writes that he was unmarried and living at home, near Richmond, Indiana. He subsequently married Margaret—— and had three children. His widow was living in California in 1908. One of his children is now deceased ; the two others are,

      i.   Margaret Thistlethwaite (1682), born in America. I do not know whether any of her parents' children married.

      ii.   Alice Thistlethwaite (1683).

  viii. Henry Thistlethwaite (1684), whom see.

Eleanor Thistlethwaite (1599), was born 1st September, 1815, at Boynton Field House, in the parish of Boynton and the country of York. She was the elder of the only two children of William Thistlethwaite (1598), the emigrant, who were born in England. I am glad to know personally her third cousin, William Timothy Bradley (415), who spent some years of his early manhood in America, and was well acquainted with the subject of this paragraph, and such of her relatives as then lived in the vicinity.* She, of course, travelled to America as an infant, and spent most of her life at Richmond, Indiana.

In 1843, when she was but twenty-seven years old, she wrote in reply to her aunt, Eleanor Webster (1705), " Thy supposition that I was settled, afforded my sister a subject for merriment ; she says I am undoubtedly settled for life, in the state of single blessedness." And in fact she never married. For many of her later years she lived a very

---

* I did not discover this until I had conducted considerable correspondence with several of the Indiana Thistlethwaites, whose address I obtained by accident from my second cousin once removed Mary Thistlethwaite (1206) of Macedon, New York State.

retired life as an invalid.   Her letter of 1843 to her aunt, Eleanor Webster
(1705), of Halifax, England, seems to me something of a masterpiece for one
whose education must have been conducted, I imagine, almost entirely
by her parents, and whose social intercourse must have been limited to
a few surrounding farms.   Part of it I will quote.*

After discussing the pecuniary predicament of her uncle Isaac
Thistlethwaite (1786), she says : " Father says it is out of his power to
raise any considerable amount of money.   In consequence of the pressure
of the times a person's inability to pay his debts has ceased to be considered
discreditable to him, and the few that are able are frequently too little
inclined to do so, knowing that the relief laws made by the State render
it almost impossible to collect debts by law.   On this account he is barely
able to obtain sufficient money to get along with.

" The sick and poor are alike affected by the times.   Those who possess
a large amount of property and are considerably in debt are in a most
unenviable situation ; several such in our immediate neighbourhood have
been ruined by the depreciation of property.   Those who own a farm and
are entirely clear of debt, enabled thus to procure food, have reason to
be thankful, and where in addition to this they can manufacture their
own clothing, they may well consider themselves independent even if
they are obliged (which is here generally the case) to make use of barley or
something of the kind as a substitute for coffee and tea ; with such other
trifles, though perhaps an Englishwoman would need Americanising before
she would think it a trifle to do without her tea.   The price of provisions
is extremely low, but this avails nothing to those who are unable to obtain
the means of paying. . .

" Father is always glad to hear from his relations ; but if you knew
what a task it is to him to write, you would not wonder that you hear
from him so seldom.   I have frequently heard him say that, old as he is, he
would rather thrash a week than write a letter.   His sight, too, has failed

---

* The letter mentioned is now in the possession of Eleanor Webster's grandson,
George Arnold Webster (1752), my first cousin once removed, from whom I
borrowed it.

of late, and as he is not in the habit of using spectacles, it has become painful to his eyes. His children are perhaps too backward in undertaking to address those with whom they are personally unacquainted.

"We still live near Richmond. Father concluded he had not met with a neighbourhood that he liked as well ; he therefore again bought a farm here, on which he has lived since 1836. As there is not the least probability of his changing his residence you need not hereafter be at any loss to know where to find him. Our parents have eight children, five of whom are at home, viz. : Timothy, Mary, William, Henry and myself. John has land in Hamilton County in this State, to which he went last fall on business, from there he went to Michigan City in this State, where he was when we last heard from him, but did not know when he should return. George is a blacksmith, and has commenced business at Cambridge sixteen miles west of this. Thomas is in Cincinnati learning the saddling and harness trade ; he went there the latter part of last spring. None of us married.

" Father's general health is excellent, never better than for the last few years ; he is however occasionally afflicted a few days with the rheumatism. Mother's, too, is good, with the exception of frequent headache. . . . .

" Father regretted that thy letter did not designate the employment of several of his relations, who were mentioned as being in situations, and also that it did not state in what part of America his sister Tennant's son* is, but perhaps the latter was unknown to thee. With love to you all, in which the family unites, I am affectionately thy niece,

" E. THISTLETHWAITE."

[Postscript].—We have an account of Uncle Timothy's death taken from the *Monthly Monitor*, which we thought perhaps was the one alluded to by thee. We have copied it for Uncle Isaac."

---

* *i.e.* Thomas Tennant (1373).

John Thistlethwaite (1600), born 14th May, 1817, at Boynton Field House, Boynton, Yorkshire. As an infant he crossed to America with his family, and never returned. On 20th March, 1843, his elder sister writes, " John has land in Hamilton County in this state [Indiana] to which he went last fall on business ; from there he went to Michigan City in this state, where he was when we last heard from him, but did know when he should return." He married 20th March, 1844, Rebecca Symons, by whom he had six children.

    i.   Henry Jefferson Thistlethwaite (1601), whom see.
    ii.   Harriet Thistlethwaite (1612), whom see.
   iii.   Hannah Thistlethwaite (1618), whom see.
   iv.   Charles Thistlethwaite (1624), whom see.
    v.   Edward Thistlethwaite (1637), whom see.
   vi.   Mary Thistlethwaite (1651), whom see.

John Thistlethwaite (1600) married secondly Eliza Bethel on 4th April, 1857. He lived, I believe, at Richmond, Indiana, and died 22nd May, 1888. His widow, Eliza Thistlethwaite, was living at Sheridan, 25th July, 1908. She is a Roman Catholic, as are some of her children, but her step-son Edward Thistlethwaite (1637), writes of his ancestors, " My memory is that they came from Yorkshire and belonged to the Friends' Church, as my father John held to that faith up to the time of his death." By his second wife he had nine children.

   vii.   Johanna Thistlethwaite (1658) has been for many years Sister Maria Theresa in St. Joseph's Convent, Tipton, Indiana.

  viii.   William Thomas Thistlethwaite (1659) died at home, aged about twenty-seven years, unmarried.

   ix.   Carrie Thistlethwaite (1660), married James Murray, and lived on a farm near Hortonville, Indiana. He died without issue in August, 1908, and his widow was living at Sheridan in January, 1909.

    x.   Walter Thistlethwaite (1661), died in the State of Montana, aged about twenty-four years ; unmarried.

xi. Sherman Thistlethwaite (1662), a twin with Grant Thistlethwaite
(1664). In January, 1909, he was living with his mother
at Sheridan, Indiana. He is a widower, with one child.
  i. Harold Thistlethwaite (1663).

xii. Grant Thistlethwaite (1664), a twin with Sherman Thistlethwaite (1662). He died at the age of seven years.

xiii. Oscar Thistlethwaite (1665), "a confirmed old bachelor at the
age of forty; is living with his mother."

xiv. Lillie Thistlethwaite (1666), was married to George Wolfgang.
They live on a farm near Sheridan, and have five children,
  i. Otto Wolfgang (1667).
  ii. Doil Wolfgang (1668).
  iii. Walter Wolfgang (1669).
  iv. Bernice Wolfgang (1670).
  v. Fern Wolfgang (1671).

xv. Grace Thistlethwaite (1672), died aged four years.

Henry Jefferson Thistlethwaite (1601), was three times married,
and had six children. His father was twice married and had fifteen children.
His grandfather was once married and had eight children. His great-
grandfather was three times married, and had nineteen children. To
to some of us who study social science, it is a matter of deep regret that in
England our good yeoman and middle-class stocks are now becoming
relatively sterile. As the prolificy of our lowest stocks is practically
unchecked, degeneration of race will be the obvious result in a very few
generations time. The artificial prevention of Natural Selection, without
the introduction of any substitute, is throwing our social machinery
seriously out of gear, when seen with an eye to the future. Environment
and education cannot, and will never, compensate for hereditary dis-
advantages, and acquirements are not inheritable. The four-generation
series given at the head of this paragraph was, I believe, nothing extraordinary in its own time, although as a proof of my statements *we* are
inclined to express surprise.

Henry Thistlethwaite (1601), died 5th March, 1908. He was born 14th February, 1846, and was a brick and tile manufacturer at Sheridan, Ind. He married first, Vesta Sims, who died April 1886, aged 37, and had issue,

    i.   Hannah Thistlethwaite (1602), married James W. McClain, and lives at 610, West 7th Street, Sedalia, Missouri, U.S.A. He is Passenger Agent for the Missouri Pacific Railway Company, and has issue,

        i.   Vesta Thistlethwaite McClain (1603), born 24th Sept. 1895.

        ii.   Lucille Shortridge McClain (1604), born 12th Dec., 1897.

        iii.   Dorothy Sims McClain (1605), born 15th Sept., 1899.

    ii.   John Alphonzo Thistlethwaite (1606), is married, and lives at Parsons, Kansas. Born 19th March, 1879. Locomotive Machinist.

    iii.   Myrtle Thistlethwaite (1607), married Isaac Lane, farmer, and lives at Sheridan, Indiana. Born 6th April, 1875. Isaac Lane, born June, 1873.

        i.   Paul Lane (1608).

    iv.   Irvin Thistlethwaite (1609), is married and lived at Summitsville, but in 1910 was at Sedalia, Mo. Born 29th Aug., 1884. A locomotive fireman.

        i.   Cecil Thistlethwaite (1610), a daughter.

Henry Thistlethwaite (1601), married, secondly, Burnie Smith by whom he had one child which died an infant. He married a third time, and his widow was living at Sheridan, in April, 1908. She had issue,

    vi.   Maurice Thistlethwaite (1611), living at Kirklin, Hamilton County, Indiana, unmarried.

Harriet Thistlethwaite (1612), married Ammon Cox. They are both deceased, but had issue,

    i.   Mabel Cox (1613), married Earl Reddick, and lives near Lebanon, Indiana. They have four children.

    ii   Ora Cox (1614), " lives in the West, but do not know where."

    iii.   Carrie Cox (1615), married Wal Horney, and lives near Hortonville, Indiana.

        i.   Harriet Horney (1616).

    iv.   Robert Cox (1617), married Madge McKinzie, and lives near Lebanon, Indiana. *Sine prole.*

 Hannah Thistlethwaite (1618), was born 19th June, 1847, at Richmond, Indiana. She was married to William Henry Plew, of Lebanon, Indiana, but they removed to a large farm the address of which was then " near Sheridan." However, since that time the nearer town of Hortonville has been founded. They were living on the same farm in March 1909.

    i.   John Plew (1619), born 4th November, 1880, near what is now Hortonville, Indiana. He was married to Emma Boxley, of Sheridan, in 1908, and lives on a farm.

    ii.   Ada Plew (1620), born 9th September, 1882, on her parents' farm. She is a teacher in the Primary Department of the schools at Hortonville, unmarried.

    iii.   Josephine Plew (1621), born 26th October, 1884, on her parents' farm. She was married in 1906, to Albert Martin, grain-dealer, of North Manchester, Indiana. *Sine prole.*

    iv.   Nell Plew (1622), born 18th September, 1886, on her parents' farm. She is living at home unmarried.

    v.   Eula Plew (1623), born 12th December, 1888, on her parents' farm. She is living at home, unmarried.

 Charles Thistlethwaite (1624), was born 29th September, 1848, probably at Richmond, Indiana. On 1st January, 1901, he was Vice-President of the Thistlethwaite Bank, Sheridan, Indiana. In September,

1908, he was living at Sheridan. He was married, 11th April, 1872, to
Josephine Underwood, who was born 16th April, 1852.

  i.   Elizabeth Thistlethwaite (1625), born 20th March, 1873,
       married 4th March, 1890, to Nelson Parr, and died 5th
       January, 1897, having issue two sons,
         i.   Lester Parr (1626).
         ii. Lowell Parr (1627).
  ii. John Marvin Thistlethwaite (1628), born 17th December, 1876,
       married 17th November, 1902, to Daisy Richey, *Sine prole.*
  iii. Flora C. Thistlethwaite (1629), born 18th December, 1878 ;
       married 28th October, 1896, to Clinton Haughey. She
       died 11th August, 1899, leaving one son,
         i.   Dean L. Haughey (1630).
  iv. Chalmers Z. Thistlethwaite (1631), born 29th July, 1880 ;
       married 20th December, 1894*, to Minnie W. Dowell, and
       has issue,
         i.   Paul Thistlethwaite (1632).
         ii. Josephine Thistlethwaite (1633).
  v.   Lola May Thistlethwaite (1634), born 8th August, 1882, died
       19th February, 1896.
  vi. Frederick Thistlethwaite (1635), born 31st March, 1884, died
       1st June, 1885.
  vii. Ray Thistlethwaite (1636), born 1st September, 1888, died 4th
       August, 1890.

Edward Thistlethwaite (1637), born 13th March, 1850, at
Richmond, Indiana. On 1st January, 1901, he was President of the
Thistlethwaite Bank, and his home is at Sheridan, Indiana. On 14th
January, 1908, he writes me, " I have bought five thousand acres of land
down near the Gulf of Mexico, and aim to start there next Tuesday, and

* Thus in Charles Thistlethwaite's letter to me, but does he intend to write " 1904 " ?

stay the whole of the winter. I have three sons there now. I aim to build a Plantation House, . . . Where I am going the Orange grows, also the Sugar Cane, and Rice. This tract of land is mostly timber of a very fine quality, oak, ash, hickory, and satin-walnut. My boys are building a large mill ready to run now : we will export this lumber." This property is at Washington, Louisiana, near the mouth of the Mississippi.

Edward Thistlethwaite is also vice-president of the Farmers' National Bank, Indiana. He was married 25th September, 1872, to Ludema Waller, who was born 7th May, 1854. By her he had seven children,

    i.   Cora Geneva Thistlethwaite (1638), born 24th December, 1873, married Frank P. Williams, and was living at Sheridan, Indiana, 25th July, 1908.

          i. Paul Williams (1639), born 1894.

         ii. Wannitah Williams (1640), born 1896.

   ii.   Allotes Thistlethwaite (1641), born 19th February, 1876, and called after an Indian Chief. He married India Hadley, and was at Washington, Louisiana, 25th July, 1908.

          i. Dwight Thistlethwaite (1642), born 1897.

         ii. Lawrence Thistlethwaite (1643), born 1905.

        iii. Lu Dema Thistlethwaite (1643a), born 25th October, 1909.

  iii.   Eliza Sadoni Thistlethwaite (1644), born 13th August, 1878, married Harry H. Griffin, and was living at Sheridan, Indiana, 25th July, 1908.

  iv.   Fairy May Thistlethwaite (1645), born 10th January, 1881, married Everett E. Newby, and was living at Sheridan, Indiana, 25th July, 1908.

   v.   John Richmond Thistlethwaite (1646), born 21st August, 1883, " Richmond " being his maternal grandmother's maiden name. He was at Washington, La., 25th July, 1908, unmarried.

  vi.   Jesse Thistlethwaite (1647), born 27th December, 1885, and was at Sheridan, Indiana, 25th July, 1908, unmarried.

vii. Roy Thistlethwaite (1648), born 2nd November, 1888, died
      14th December, 1888.

Edward Thistlethwaite (1637), married secondly Etta Brinegar, 12th
November, 1890. She was born 20th July, 1860, and was living at
Sheridan, Indiana, with her two children, 25th July, 1908.

viii. Edward Duane Thistlethwaite (1649), born 1st April, 1892.

ix. Lamar Thistlethwaite (1650), born 24th July, 1893.

Mary Thistlethwaite (1651), was married to George Drake.
She was living at Sheridan, in March, 1909. Some of her family do not
live in that district, but no further particulars are yet to hand.

   i. Edward Drake (1652), married.
  ii. Annis Drake (1653), married.
 iii. Bertha Drake (1654).
  iv. Beatrice Drake (1655).
   v. Robert Drake (1656), who in March, 1909, had " just arrived
       in New York from a trip around the earth, with the American
       fleet."
  vi. Mary Drake (1657).

Mary Thistlethwaite (1679), the younger daughter of the emigrant,
was a woman of much individuality and intellect, a supporter of the
equality and rights of woman. She married a farmer, named Thomas
Birdsall, who was unlike her in many respects. As I have not yet succeeded in persuading any of her descendants to correspond with me, my
particulars regarding them are few. I believe that she had at least three
sons, two of whom, perhaps, died young. The third was named,

 iii. William W. Birdsall (1680), whom see.

William W. Birdsall (1680), " was a native of Richmond,
Indiana, and a student in Richmond High School, and at Earlham,

graduating from Earlham, in 1873, at the age of nineteen. Later he became a teacher in the Richmond High School, where he taught until he accepted a position as principal of the Boy's High School at Wilmington. Later he was principal and teacher in Friends' Central School, in Philadelphia, then president of Swarthmore College, and at the time of his death was filling a large and influential place as principal of the Philadelphia High School for Girls.

" Honored and loved everywhere by all who knew him, and held in the highest esteem by educators of his time, his was truly a life full of inspiration.

" A memorial service was held in the Earlham Chapel on March 31st, and fitting tribute paid to his life and work. Among those who did him honor were Professor W. N. Trueblood, and Professor D. W. Dennis, both members of his class at Earlham.

" The following was said of him by Mrs. Margaret Dennis Vail :

" ' In Richmond, Wilmington, Swarthmore, or Philadelphia, in his home and social life, or in the discharge of professional duties, among successes or disappointments, he was always the same, true to the highest ideals of manhood, never at any instant or at any point failing to live or to act according to the best possible standards of life.

" ' No one in the range of my acquaintance and observation has ever seemed to me to make a finer or greater success of this life.' " *

William W. Birdsall (1680), was born about 1854, and died in March, 1909. He left a widow and one or two children. He was a well-known member of the Society of Friends in America ; and the City of Philadelphia " took as honorable notice of the passing of Professor Birdsall as it is possible to take."

Henry Thistlethwaite (1684), was born 14th March, 1833, at Richmond, Indiana, and was in 1909 the only one yet living of the emigrants' eight children. He married Emiline Moore in 1863, and had issue,

* Extracted from *The Earlhamite*, April 10th, 1909.

  i. Cyrus D. Thistlethwaite (1685), whom see.

  ii. Grace Thistlethwaite (1693), whom see.

  iii. George Thistlethwaite (1697), whom see.

Emiline Thistlethwaite died 28th December, 1869, on the birth of her youngest child, and Henry Thistlethwaite (1684), married secondly, in 1872, Gemima Singleton, with whom he is now living near Sheridan, Indiana. She had issue one child,

  iv. Burgess Thistlethwaite (1701), whom see.

  Cyrus D. Thistlethwaite (1685), born 4th April, 1864, at Sheridan ; married 6th December, 1883, Laura Ramsey, and is a farmer near Sheridan, Indiana.

  i. Glenn F. Thistlethwaite (1686), born 18th March, 1885, at Sheridan, Indiana. He received his bachelor's degree from Earlham College, Indiana, in 1908, and was in February, 1909, Athletic Director and Instructor in Mathematics at Illinois College, Jacksonville, Illinois, being the youngest College Director in the State. In September, 1909, he became Athletic Director and assistant in Civil Engineering at Earlham College, which is under the auspices of the Society of Friends. This immediate branch of the family still retain their membership as Orthodox Quakers. He is unmarried.

  ii. Raleigh Thistlethwaite (1687), born 26th May, 1888, at Sheridan, Indiana, unmarried.

  iii. Earl Thistlethwaite (1688), born 16th December, 1890, at Sheridan, Indiana ; died 22nd September, 1892.

  iv. Ardra Thistlethwaite (1689), born 28th November, 1893, at Sheridan, Indiana, a boy.

  v. C. Orville Thistlethwaite (1690), born 3rd November, 1895, at Sheridan, Indiana.

  vi. Meveral H. Thistlethwaite (1691), born 17th March, 1898, at Sheridan, Indiana.

vii. Lowell Thistlethwaite (1692), born 27th September, 1902, at Sheridan, Indiana.

Grace Thistlethwaite (1693), born 22nd April, 1867, at Sheridan, Indiana; married 2nd February, 1885, to John Timmons, a farmer, near Sheridan.

    i. Maud Timmons (1694), born 18th February, 1886, died 5th April, 1905; unmarried.

    ii. Claude Timmons (1695), born 20th April, 1888; unmarried.

    iii. Opal Timmons (1696), born 6th May, 1891,; unmarried.

George Thistlethwaite (1697), born 28th December, 1869, at Sheridan, Indiana; married 3rd March, 1892, to Florence Louks, and is a farmer near Sheridan.

    i. Vinton Thistlethwaite (1698), born 16th January, 1893; died 19th October, 1901.

    ii. Monroe Thistlethwaite (1699), born 6th October, 1898.

    iii. Lacy Thistlethwaite (1700), born 27th October, 1900.

Burgess Thistlethwaite (1701), born 2nd August, 1875, at Sheridan, Indiana; married 3rd October, 1894, to Belle Goodner. He is a mechanic at Peoria, Illinois.

    i. Lola E. Thistlethwaite (1702), born 23rd June, 1896, at Sheridan, Indiana.

Eleanor Thistlethwaite (1705), born 13th March, 1798, at Counterside, Wensleydale, Yorkshire. While living at Wakefield, Yorkshire, she was married, 19th September, 1822, at Wakefield Meeting House, to George Webster, of Halifax, in the county of York, grocer, son of George Webster, late of Storthwaite, near the City of York, farmer,

deceased, and Ann his wife, then surviving.   The following witnesses
signed the Marriage Certificate :

John Thistlethwaite (1347)   Joseph Wetherald
Ann Webster   Molly Wetherald.
Hannah Thistlethwaite   James Wetherald
Mary Thistlethwaite (1703)   Rachel Wetherald
Simeon Webster   David Walton
John Webster   William Pickard, Jr.
William Webster   Mary Ann Brearey
Timothy Thistlethwaite (1545)   Deborah Spence
John Thistlethwaite, Jr. (1555)   John Spence
Betty Thistlethwaite   Mary Birkbeck
Elizabeth Webster   Ann Pace
Margaret Thistlethwaite (1782)   Isabella Bradney
Christopher Walker   James Harrison
John J. Nevins   Lucy Lamb
Edward Peck   Elizabeth Guest
Isabella Swan   Ann Hall
Harriet Lambe   Hannah Nevins
Jane Haworth   Caleb Haworth
Timothy Pickard   George Bennington
James Willan   Mary Lee
Susannah Harris   Ann Brooke
Eliza Clemesha   Elizabeth Bleckly
Sarah Lee   Eliza Lee.

Eleanor Webster (1705) for many years carried on a confectionery
business next to her husband's grocery shop.   She died 25th May, 1867,
at Halifax, aged sixty-nine, and her husband died there 3rd December,
1873, aged seventy-eight.

    i.   Joseph Webster (1706), whom see.
    ii. Ann Webster (1725), whom see.
    iii. Charles Webster (1747), whom see.

iv.   Mary Webster (1756), whom see.
v.   George Webster (1759), whom see.
vi.   John William Webster (1775), whom see.

Joseph Webster (1706), born 14th September, 1824, at Halifax.
He was married 11th August, 1853, at Dewsbury Meeting House, to
Elizabeth Brady, daughter of William Brady, of Dewsbury, by his wife
Mary Ann Breary.   Joseph Webster was a high-class tailor at Darlington,
Co. Durham, where he died 17th January, 1893.   His wife died at
Darlington, 28th March, 1891.

i.   Mary Ann Webster (1707), born 3rd or 19th July, 1854, at
    Darlington, died there 28th September, 1854.
ii.   Joseph Brady Webster (1708), whom see.
iii.   Eleanor Elizabeth Webster (1714), whom see.
iv.   William Brady Webster (1718), whom see.
v.   Charles Edward Webster (1721), born February 15th, 1863, at
    Darlington ; died there 26th April, 1870.
vi.   Annie Webster (1722), born 11th March, 1865, at Darlington,
    now a trained nurse ; unmarried.
vii.   Edith Mary Webster (1723), born 23rd July, 1867, at Darling-
    ton ; married, 6th February, 1890, at Darlington, to
    William Edward Brady, of Barnsley, who was her sister's
    brother-in-law, and, I believe, her second cousin ; *s.p.*

Joseph Brady Webster (1708), born 6th March, 1856, at Darlington,
educated at Bootham School, York, 8 mo. 1871 to 12 mo., 1872.   He was
married, 1882, to Sarah Jane Adamson, and died 24th December, 1890,
at Darlington, where he had been a tailor with his father.

i.   Joseph William Webster (1709), born 4th September, 1883, at
    Darlington ; unmarried 1908.
ii.   Frances Brady Webster, (1710), born 5th May, 1885, at Croft
    Spa, near Darlington ; unmarried, 1908.

   iii. Edith Mary Webster (1711), born 20th November, 1886, at
        Darlington; unmarried 1908.
   iv. Grace Elizabeth Webster (1712), born 30th June, 1888, at
        Darlington; unmarried 1908.
    v. Dorothy Webster (1713), born June, 1890, at Darlington;
        unmarried 1908.

Eleanor Elizabeth Webster (1714), born 19th July, 1858, at
Darlington; educated at the Mount School, York, 8 mo., 1872 to 6 mo.
1875. She was married 17th June, 1886, at Darlington, to her second
cousin, Foster E. Brady, of Barnsley, Yorkshire, who is now (1909),
engaged in lecturing and mission-work for the Society of Friends.

    i. Harold Norman Brady (1715), born 19th July, 1887, at
        Barnsley; unmarried 1908.
   ii. Catherine Elizabeth Brady (1716), born 13th May, 1894, at
        Barnsley; unmarried 1908.
   iii. Edward Richards Brady (1717), born 23rd August, 1896, at
        Barnsley.

William Brady Webster (1718), born 17th July, 1860, at
Darlington; educated at Bootham School, York, 8 mo., 1875 to 12 mo.
1876. He was married, 14th April, 1885, at Wakefield, to Eliza Millar
Grace, and is a grocer at Barnsley, Yorkshire.

    i. Arthur Brady Webster (1719), born 15th October, 1892, at
        Barnsley.
   ii. Elsie Margaret Webster (1720), born 16th October, 1895, at
        Barnsley.

Ann Webster (1725), born 25th November, 1828, at Halifax,
Yorkshire. She was married, 8th June, 1853, to John Rowntree, grocer

of Scarborough, who was born 1st December, 1821, son of William Rowntree, of Newcastle (16th March, 1786, to 14th October, 1849, son of John Rowntree, of Scarborough, 1757-1827, by his wife, Elizabeth Lotherington) by his wife Rachel Watson (15th September, 1788, to 6th February, 1845).

Ann Rowntree (1725), died 4th November, 1864, and her husband married secondly Eliza Brady, widow of William Brady, Junr., whose sister married Joseph Webster, Ann Rowntree's brother.

John Rowntree died 1st October, 1894. His second wife is still living with her only child, Alfred Rowntree, J.P., of Kirkby Overblow, near Harrogate, who married Ethel Marguerite Willis, first cousin once removed to Elizabeth Longmire Willis, who married William Timothy Bradley (415), of Wensleydale. By his first wife, Ann Webster (1725), John Rowntree had issue,

    i.   John Watson Rowntree (1726), whom see.
    ii.   George Rowntree (1730), whom see.
    iii.   William Henry Rowntree (1732), born 8th March, 1857, at Scarborough; died 18th February, 1858.
    iv.   Ellen Rowntree (1733), whom see.
    v.   Frederick Rowntree (1739), whom see.
    vi.   Arthur Rowntree (1743), whom see.
    vii.   Emily Rowntree (1746), born 28th April, 1863, at Scarborough, educated at the Mount School, York, 8 mo. 1876, to 6 mo. 1880. She is now proprietor of a boarding house in York; unmarried.

John Watson Rowntree (1726), born 3rd April, 1854, at Scarborough; educated at Bootham School, York, 1 mo., 1869, to 6 mo. 1870. He was married 23rd April, 1885, at Wellingborough, Co. Northampton, to Eliza Stansfield Gravely, of that place, who was born 1st December, 1857. He and his brother George carry on their father's grocery business, and a café, at Scarborough. He resides at "The Rowans," Scarborough, is a Justice of the Peace, and was mayor of the town in 1907. He is also a prominent member of the Society of Friends in the North of England.

During the Anglo-Boer War in 1900, Scarborough was the scene of a considerable riot, which was chiefly directed against John Watson Rowntree and his relatives.* The Rowntree family, as Quakers, were opposed to all war, and were called "Pro-Boers," on account of their attempts to reduce the British national hatred against the Dutch South Africans which the war had produced.

The immediate cause of the Scarborough riot was the invitation of Schreiner, a Boer, to speak at a public meeting in Scarborough. During the evening a mob collected, and threw stones and other missiles, but Schreiner and the Rowntrees escaped unnoticed at the back. The mob proceeded up the main street of Scarborough, smashing the plate glass windows of John Rowntree and Son's grocer's shop, William Rowntree and Son's draper's shop (the largest shop in Scarborough), and also the windows of the private residences of Joshua Rowntree, ex-M.P. for Scarborough, Allan Rowntree, William Stickney Rowntree, and John Watson Rowntree.

John Watson Rowntree remained to protect those of his *employés* who slept at his business premises. His wife, three children, and three maids were at "The Rowans," absolutely unprotected, but fortunately the mob were contented with the destruction of as much of the furniture as could be reached by missiles thrown through the broken windows. The rioters broke down a wall in order to obtain bricks as missiles.

The mob lost the scent of Schreiner, who slept at the house of E. R. Cross, a Scarborough solicitor, and member of the Society of Friends. Schreiner left the house in a cab, and was driven to Ganton Station, thus escaping the hostile crowds gathered at Scarborough Station. It was reported in the town that he had escaped in one of W. Rowntree and Sons' furniture vans.

John Watson Rowntree (1726) had three children, as follows :

    i. Harold Rowntree (1727), born 15th April, 1886, at Scarborough, educated at Bootham School, York, 9 mo., 1900 to 7 mo.

* Edna Lyall mentions the riot in her story "The Hinderers."

1903. Now (1909) unmarried, and in his father's grocery business.

ii. Gravely Rowntree (1728), born 15th July, 1888, at Scarborough, died 22nd July, 1903, at Wellingborough, Northamptonshire.

iii. Kathleen Rowntree (1729), born 10th January, 1891, at Scarborough ; unmarried 1909.

George Rowntree (1730), born 20th December, 1855, at Scarborough ; educated at Bootham School, York, 8 mo., 1869, to 12 mo. 1871 ; married 24th June, 1885, at Scarborough, to Priscilla Gray Wallis, who was born 7th July, 1855, daughter of Francis Wallis, of Scarborough, and sister of Edward Wallis, of Scarborough, who married Annie Johnson (1557), George Rowntree's second cousin. George Rowntree is a grocer at Scarborough, in partnership with his eldest brother. He is a Justice of the Peace.

i. Malcolm Rowntree (1731), born 17th April, 1890, at Scarborough ; educated at Bootham School, York, and at Cambridge University.

Ellen Rowntree (1733), born 29th April, 1858, at Scarborough ; educated at the Mount School, York, 8 mo. 1871 to 6 mo. 1875. She was married, 12th March, 1884, at Scarborough, to her distant cousin, Alfred Henry Taylor, grocer, of Malton, son of Henry Taylor, of Malton, by his wife, Elizabeth, daughter of Richardson Rowntree.

Henry Taylor, grocer, of Malton, was son of Joseph Taylor, of Malton, by his wife Sarah, daughter of George Baker, of Danbydale, and Askham Fields,* by his wife Sarah Hedley, whose sister, Mary Hedley, married Anthony Thistlethwaite (1164), of Darlington. Sarah and Mary Hedley's mother, Sarah Hartas, was great-aunt to Rachel Peacock, who married Jeremiah Thistlethwaite (1218), of Great Ayton.

* "Unhistoric Acts " by George Baker (Headley Bros., London).

   i.   Charles John Taylor (1734), born 8th September, 1885, at
        Malton. He is now (1909) in the grocery business of his
        maternal uncles, at Scarborough, unmarried.

  ii. Maud Taylor (1735), born 9th September, 1888, at Malton,
        Yorkshire ; now living at home ; unmarried.

 iii. Muriel Taylor (1736), born 6th January, 1890, at Malton, and
        died there 24th January, 1890.

 iv. Dorothy May Taylor (1737), born 9th May, 1893.

  v. Joyce Rowntree Taylor (1738), born 20th October, 1898, at
        Malton.

Frederick Rowntree (1739), born 19th April, 1860, at Scarborough ; educated at Bootham School, York, 8 mo., 1871, to 6 mo., 1876. He was married, 6th October, 1886, at Glasgow, N.B., to Mary Anna Gray, who was born 10th June, 1862. He is an architect.

   i.   Douglas Rowntree (1740), born 6th May, 1888, at Brompton,
        Yorkshire ; unmarried.

  ii. Colin Rowntree (1741), born 9th August, 1891, at Glasgow.

 iii. Judith Mary Rowntree (1742), born 21st July, 1893, at Glasgow.

Arthur Rowntree (1743), born 19th October, 1861, at Scarborough ; educated at Bootham School, York, 9 mo., 1872 to 6 mo., 1878. He was a teacher at the same school 1879 to 1882, became Bachelor of Arts, and returned as teacher from 1884 to 1885, and again from 1892 to 1899, when he became Headmaster, a position which he still holds. He was married, 29th October, 1891, to Ellen Hurndall, at Birmingham.

   i.   Joan Hurndall Rowntree (1744), born 23rd April, 1895, at
        York.

  ii. Alyson Hurndall Rowntree (1745), born 26th September, 1897,
        at York.

Charles Webster (1747), born 9th October, 1830, at Halifax. He was for some years apprenticed with David Baker,* grocer, of Guisborough, Yorkshire, and when there became acquainted with Esther Peacock, of Castleton. On 11th September, 1856, in Guisborough Meeting house, Charles Webster, grocer of Halifax, was married to Esther Peacock, " of Castleton near Whitby, daughter of the late George Peacock, of the said town, yeoman, and Elizabeth his wife, now surviving." Their marriage certificate is signed by the following witnesses, *viz.* :—

Elizabeth Peacock
Eleanor Webster (1705)
George Esthill Peacock
Rachel Peacock
Mary Webster (1756)
George Webster, Jr. (1759)
Thomas Hartas Peacock
Benjamin Peacock
Joseph Webster (1706)
William Thistlethwaite (1598)
David Binns
Mary Peacock
Elizabeth Peacock
Eleanor Bowse
William Rickaby
Jane Rickaby
William Hartas
Sarah Mary Hartas
John R. Procter
Lydia R. Procter
Hannah Richardson
Hannah Hall
Hannah M. Thomson
M. Ord

Sarah Stevenson
Thomas Dixon
John Hall, Sr.
John Baker
John Richardson
William Anderson (1158)
Joseph Pease
Emma Pease
John Pease
Sophia Pease
Jane Gurney Pease
Emma Gurney Pease
Eliz. Lucy Pease
Sophia Pease, Jr.
Mary A. Pease
Eliza Barclay
Thos. Jowett
Mary Ann Jowett
Hannah Dale
Mary Stonehouse
Mgt. Ann Coning
Eliza Sweeting
Jane Nightingale
Emma Bulmer

* See " Unhistoric Acts," by George Baker (Headley Bros., London, 1906).

Eliza Jane Ord

Mary Ann Howcroft

John Duck (?)

George Duck (?)

George Morley

George Fletcher

Mary Fletcher

John Hall Baker

David Baker

Sarah Dorothy Baker.

Catherine A. Christian

Wm. Wilson Nellist

Chas. Lowe

John Heselton Kingston

Mary Jane Hodgson

Sarah J. Baker

Annie Orton

Eliz[th] M. Orton

Robt Stevenson

Charles Webster (1747), is a café owner and grocer at Halifax, Yorkshire; now (1910) residing with his elder son, at Poynton, Saville Park Road, Halifax. His wife, Esther Webster, died 23rd July, 1906, at Halifax. Her parents lived at Wooddale House, about half-way between the villages of Ugthorpe and Lealholm, Yorkshire. Her mother was born Elizabeth Hartas, first cousin thrice removed to the husband of Ellen Rowntree (1733), who was niece by marriage to Esther Webster. Her sister, Rachel Peacock, married Jeremiah Thistlethwaite (1218), of Ayton, Charles Webster's third cousin.

    i.   Charles Edward Webster (1748), whom see.

    ii.   George Arnold Webster (1752), whom see.

    iii. Thomas Webster (1755), born 4th July, 1871, at Halifax; died there 14th November, 1872.

Charles Edward Webster (1748), born 27th March, 1868, at Halifax. He was married 1st September, 1897, at Great Ayton Meeting House, to Mabel Tilzey, born 1875, daughter of the late Frederick Tilzey, of Bolton, Lancashire, by his wife, Rachel Darbyshire, now (1909), of Great Ayton, Yorkshire. He is in the grocery business at Halifax, and has issue,

    i.   Clarice Mabel Webster (1749), born 13th August, 1898, at Halifax.

    ii. Marion Webster (1750), born 8th July, 1900, at Halifax.

iii. Nance Tilzey Webster (1751), born 16th August, 1907, at Halifax

---

George Arnold Webster (1752), born 15th November, 1869, at Halifax. He was married 26th June, 1901, at St. George's Church, London, to Nora Harris, of Kingston-on-Thames, who was born 20th May, 1876, daughter of the late Dr. Harris. He was at one time a stockbroker in London, but is now in the grocery business at Halifax. For some years after his marriage he lived at Harrogate, Yorkshire, but in 1909 removed to Heath Villas, Halifax.

    i. Trevor Hartas Webster (1753), born 29th November, 1902, in London.

    ii. Laurence Justin Webster (1754), born 12th December, 1904, in London.

Mary Webster (1756), born 4th October, 1832, at Halifax. She was married, 2nd January, 1867, at Halifax, to William Brook, Liberal Agent, of Halifax, who is still surviving there. She died there, 21st May, 1873, having issue,

    i. Ellen Brook (1757), born 20th November, 1867, at Halifax; now (1909) living there, unmarried.

    ii. Lucy Brook (1758), born 10th April, 1869, at Halifax, now (1909) living there, unmarried.

George Webster (1759), born 1837, at Halifax. He was married 3rd February, 1864, to Elizabeth Benson, formerly a teacher at Ackworth School, who is now deceased. He is a grocer in Wakefield, for which City he is a Justice of the Peace.

    i. Edith Mary Webster (1760), born 16th February, 1865; died 12th September, 1865, and buried in Friends' Burial Ground, Thornhill Street, Wakefield.

ii. George Ernest Webster (1761), whom see.

iii. Alfred Webster (1767), whom see.

iv. Arthur Henry Webster (1770), whom see.

v.   Margaret Webster (1773), born 23rd June, 1875, at Wake-field, now (1909) living, unmarried.

vi. Mary Webster (1774), born 23rd January, 1877, at Wakefield, now (1909) living, unmarried.

George Ernest Webster (1761), born 6th October, 1867, at Wakefield. He was married at Westborough Chapel, Scarborough, 23rd April, 1895, to Florence Eliza Walton, only child of James T. Walton, artist, of York. He is a grocer at Wakefield.

i.   George William Webster (1762), born 29th May, 1896.

ii. Edith Mary Webster (1763), born 27th April, 1899.

iii. Henry Benson Webster (1764), born 13th October, 1900.

iv. John Walton Webster (1765), born 6th May, 1902.

v.   Colin Ernest Webster (1766), born 3rd April, 1907.

Alfred Webster (1767), born 17th January, 1871, at Wakefield. He was married 26th April, 1898, at Westgate Chapel, Wakefield, to Edith Annie Sutcliffe, daughter of Thomas Sutcliffe, Norbury Mills, Cheshire. He is a printer at Leeds.

i.   Marjorie Elizabeth Webster (1768), born 21st April, 1901.

ii. Thomas Alfred Webster (1769), born 27th May, 1903.

Arthur Henry Webster (1770), born 30th November, 1872, at Wakefield. He was married 19th September, 1900, at Westgate Chapel, Wakefield, to Mary Ellen Wood, eldest daughter of Sam Wood, wool stapler, of Wakefield. He is a grocer at Wakefield.

i.   Arthur Guy Webster (1771), born 28th November, 1905.

ii. Eric Webster (1772), born 13th February, 1908.

John William Webster (1775), born 23rd January, 1840, at Halifax. He was married 6th September, 1866, at Manchester, to Lucy Ann Freman, who was born 25th June, 1843, in London, daughter of Henry and Elizabeth Freman. He was a grocer in Birmingham, and died there 21st December, 1904. His widow now (1909) resides at 44, Holmewood Gardens, Brixton Hill, London, S.W.

    i. Henry Freman Webster (1776), whom see.

    ii. Ellen Mary Webster (1777), born 19th June, 1869, at Birmingham ; now (1909) living, unmarried.

    iii. Alice Webster (1778), born 1st April, 1871, at Birmingham ; now living unmarried.

    iv. Frederick Webster (1779), whom see.

    v. Frank Webster (1781), whom see.

    vi. John Webster (1781a), born 23rd June, 1877, at Birmingham ; now (1909), living in London, unmarried.

Henry Freman Webster (1776), born 27th October, 1867, at Halifax ; married 6th August, 1902, at Halifax, to Henrietta Scarborough, daughter of Joseph Scarborough, of Halifax, cotton-spinner. He studied music in Germany, and was a professor of music at Halifax until recently, but is now (1909), studying accountancy in Bradford. *Sine prole.*

Frederick Webster (1779), born 16th July, 1872, at Birmingham ; married 12th September, 1906, at Birmingham, to Esther Herbert, of Penzance. He is a grocer in Birmingham, and has issue,

    i. John Herbert Webster (1780), born 11th July, 1908, at Birmingham.

Frank Webster (1781), born 22nd March, 1874, at Birmingham ; married there 17th March, 1908, to Eliza Williams, of Birmingham. He is a grocer in Birmingham, and was *sine prole* September, 1908.

Isaac Thistlethwaite (1786), born 18th November, 1807, at Over Bentham, Yorkshire. He and his elder brothers William, Thomas and James, had emigrated to the United States some considerable time before 1843. William's grandson, Edward Thistlethwaite (1637), thinks that William settled in Indiana, James in Virginia, and Isaac in New York State. However, in 1843, Isaac was living at Marietta, on the river Ohio, in the State of Ohio, the State of West Virginia being immediately across the river. He was then in difficulty for money, and his sister, Eleanor Webster, of Halifax, England, appears to have written to her brother William Thistlethwaite (1598), of Richmond, Indiana, suggesting that Isaac should return to England. In reply to this, William's daughter, Eleanor Thistlethwaite (1599), writes from Richmond, 20th March, 1843, to her aunt Eleanor Webster, as follows,

"Dear Aunt, Father received thy letter of the 26th of 12 mo. last, and immediately made known to Uncle Isaac the proposition you had made relative to his return to England, although under the necessity of apprising him at the same time that he was unable to render the assistance requisite for such a journey, and more than this he thought that after so long an absence he would be dissatisfied should he return. Father had written to him a few weeks previous to the arrival of thy letter, desiring to know what he would think of removing to Indiana,* but had not received an answer. He again informed him that if near him, he could, without inconvenience, supply him with the necessaries of life in all probability until he could meet with employment ; offering, if he was willing to come, to endeavour to make arrangements to get them here. To the last letter he replied without delay, under date of the 13th of the present month, acknowledging the kindness of his relatives in England for so heartily wishing his welfare, but he adds, " As to my going to that country it is altogether out of the question, if I were ever so disposed, I could not persuade my wife to cross the ocean. It is a hard matter to get her across the Ohio, except in the middle of Summer, in low water." In regard to removing to Richmond, he says, " It would be imprudent at present for

* He was 180 miles distant, in a straight line, from Richmond, Ind.

me to leave Marietta ; neither could I do it honorably, for the following reason : during this winter I have been compelled to run in debt for provision and a little clothing that we could not do without, for which I am pledged to pay for this spring in work. I could not get these things without promising the work whenever they should call for it. After these little jobs are done if there is no prospect of any more work I will then write again to thee " . . . . When uncle Isaac wrote last they were all reasonably well, except the youngest child, which I think is but a few weeks old. He said she had a touch of the croup, but they hoped she would soon be better."

Since this date I can learn nothing respecting him or his descendants, indeed William is the only one of the four brothers whose progeny I have been able to trace.*

* Possibly Mark Thistlethwaite of Indianapolis, who is a subscriber to this book, is a descendant of James or Isaac. He has not yet replied to my letter of inquiry.

LIST OF SUBSCRIBERS.

[All except seven of the subscribers are either Thistlethwaite descendants or connections by marriage.]

———

Alderson, W. C., Esq., 228, South 3rd Street, Philadelphia, Pennsylvania, U.S.A. *Two copies in vellum.*

Ashworth, Miss Dora A., 452, Berea Road, Durban, Natal, South Africa. *Three copies.*

Ashworth, John A., Esq., c/o Wm. Cotts & Co., Point, Durban, Natal, South Africa.

Axford, Herbert, Esq., 801, Electric Street, Scranton, Pennsylvania, U.S.A.

Baker, George, Esq., Acomb Green, York.

Baker, Mrs. T. Hedley, Tonganoxie, Kansas, U.S.A.

Baynes, Ernest Harold, Esq., Meriden, New Hampshire, U.S.A.

Baynes, Oswald B., Esq., B.A., 1, Woodside Terrace, Darlington.

Bentham, Mrs. 5, Clevedon Buildings, Liverpool, S.

Bird, Mrs. R., Whinfell, Bridge-of-Weir, Renfrewshire, N.B.

Booth, Ernest A., Esq., The Laurels, Highworth, Wiltshire.

Booth, Rev. Joseph, Zion Manse, Ossett, S.O., Yorkshire.

Booth, J. Alexander, Esq., 112, Town Street, Armley, Leeds.

Bradley, Miss Bessie, Hillside, Aysgarth, Yorks.

Bradley, Thomas, Esq., Bear Park, Carperby, S.O., Yorks.

Bradley, Wm. T., Esq., Hillside, Aysgarth, S.O., Yorks.

Bradley, W. T., Jun., Esq., B.A., 17, Duchy Avenue, Harrogate.

Brook, Miss, 4, Avondale Place, Halifax.

Brown, Charles, Esq., Rushley Walls, Bollington, Cheshire.

Brown, Mrs. Chas., Rushley Walls, Bollington, Cheshire.

Brown, C. Richardson, Esq., M.B., 79, Hyde Road, Manchester.

Brown, Samuel E., Esq., M.A., Collegiate Institution, Liverpool. *In vellum.*

Brown, Mrs. Wilks, 62, Broughton Road, Banbury. *Two copies.*

Busselle, S. Marshall, Esq., 26, Broadway, New York, U.S.A. *In vellum.*

Carter, Rev. C. A., B.A., St. Titus Vicarage, 29, St. Domingo Grove, Liverpool. *In vellum.*

Carter, Chas. C., Esq., B.A., 9, Northgate Road, Stoneycroft, Liverpool.

Carter, Thomas, Esq., 71, Montague Road, Chesterton, Cambs.

Clark, Mrs. Ed., 40, Woodlands Terrace, Darlington.

Clark, Ed. V., Esq., Litchford House, Monton Road, Eccles, Lancashire.

Clark, Lionel B., Esq., 40, Woodlands Terrace, Darlington.

Clarke, Miss Bertha, Hope Vale, Comrie, N.C.R., *via* Maritzburg, Natal.

Clarke, Miss Evelyn Fothergill, Adam's Mission Station, Amanzimtote, *via* Durban, Natal.

Clarke, J. Fothergill, Esq., Ogada Mission Station, Lake Victoria Nyanza, Central Africa.

Clarke, Miss Minnie, Mount Silinda Mission Station, Melsetter, Rhodesia.

Cookson, Mrs., 20, Merton Street, Queen's Park, Manchester. *Three Copies.*

Crosfield, Mrs. Albert J., 5, Madingley Road, Cambridge.

Cudworth, Mrs., Butts Close, York.

Doeg, George W., Esq., Reading, Berkshire.

Dyhr, Mrs. Peter, West Branch, Cedar Co., Iowa, U.S.A. *In vellum.*

Eccles, Mrs. Alfred E., White Coppice, Chorley. *In vellum.*

Edmondson, Mrs., Woodburn, Ilkley.

Edmundson, Mrs., 1109, Des Moines Street, Des Moines, Iowa, U.S.A.

Edwards, Mrs. F. P., 6, Park Road, Monton, Eccles.

Ellershaw, Arthur G., Esq.,·108, Great Western Street, Moss Side, Manchester.

Ellershaw, Mrs., 142, New Cross Street, Bradford. *Two copies.*

Ellershaw, Thos., Esq., 26, Victoria Road, Stechford, Birmingham.

Fix, Samuel Edward, Esq., Kapowsin, Washington State, U.S.A.

Fothergill, Alexr. Poinsett, Esq., 1144, West 3rd Street, Cleveland, Ohio, U.S.A. *Two copies, one in vellum.*

Fothergill, Miss Ann, 319½, Arctic Avenue, Atlantic City, New Jersey, U.S.A.

Fothergill, C. J., Esq., 548, Harris Street, Vancouver, Canada. *Three copies.*

Fothergill, Gerald, Esq., 11, Brussels Road, New Wandsworth, London.

Fothergill, Henry Chorley, Esq., 21, Grove Lane, Kingston-on-Thames. *Two copies.*

Fothergill, Henry R., Esq., Girard, Ohio, U.S.A. *Two copies.*

Fothergill, Mrs. J. J., Whitby, Ontario, Canada.

Fothergill, John Rimington, Esq., M.D., Chorley Cottage, Darlington.

Fothergill, Miss Margaret, 319½, Arctic Avenue, Atlantic City, New Jersey, U.S.A.

Fothergill, Miss, Richmond Hill, Bowdon, Cheshire.

Fothergill, Watson, Esq., George Street, Nottingham. *Two copies.*
Fothergill, W. E., Esq., M.A., M.D., 337, Oxford Road, Manchester. *In vellum.*
Fothergill, W. S., Esq., 9, Nelson Terrace, Redcar.
Fotheringham, J. T., Esq., M.D., Airlie House, 20, Wellesley Street, Toronto.
Fox, Chas. E., Esq., Beech Grove, Stanhope Road, Darlington.
Fraser, Mrs., Hoylake, Cheshire.
Fry, John Pease, Esq., M.A., J.P., Cleveland Lodge, Great Ayton.
Fryer, George B., Esq., 35, Main Street, Council Bluffs, Iowa, U.S.A. *In vellum.*

Gardner, Mrs. Warren, Union Springs, Cayuga County, N.Y., U.S.A.
George, Mrs., Tawelfan, Llanidloes.
Gill, J. J., Esq., 4, North Terrace, Newcastle-on-Tyne.
Gill, Wm., Esq., Low Row, Swaledale, Yorkshire. *Three copies.*
Goundry, Mrs., 53, Severn Avenue, Weston-super-Mare. *Six copies.*
Green, J. J., Esq., 182, Upper Grosvenor Road, Tunbridge Wells.
Greenbank, Mrs., Harbergill, Dent.
Greenfield, Mrs. David, Morley, Ontario, Canada.
Greenwood, Mrs. E., 25, Earlsthorpe Road, Sydenham, London, S.E.
Griffin, Mrs. 3, Turner Street, Redcar.
Guy, C. H., Esq., Holme Leigh, Menston-in-Wharfedale. *Two copies.*
Guy, John A., Esq., Ellenthorpe, Eccleshill, Bradford.
Guy, T. W., Esq., 166, Cambridge Street, London, S.W.

Hadfield, Mrs. Alan, 8, Station Road, Finsbury Park, London, N.
Hadfield, Mrs. S. F., Lochmaben, N.B. *Three copies.*
Hadfield, S. R., Esq., 105, Broxholm Road, West Norwood, London.
Harris, Edwin, Esq., Wavertree Farm, St. Catherines, Ontario, Canada.
Harris, Mrs. James, Meaford, Ontario, Canada.
Harris, Lewis J., Esq., Taber, Alberta, Canada. *Three copies, one in vellum.*
Harris, Samuel, Esq., Rockwood, Ontario, Canada. *Three copies.*
Harris, Thomas, Esq., Moresby Island, Gulf of Georgia, British Columbia.
Harrison, Mrs., Elmhurst, South Woodford, Essex. *Two copies.*
Harrison, Cuthbert, Esq., Chapel House, Crathorne, Yarm. *Two copies.*
Harrison, Mrs. Edwin, 74, Rocky Lane, Monton, Eccles.
Harrison, Miss Lucy, Cupples Field, Bainbridge, Askrigg, Yorkshire.
Hartley, Joseph, Esq., Dee View, Dent.
Hillary, G. M., Esq., ¶4, Paseo Bolivar, Chihuahua, Mexico. *In vellum.*
Hopkins, Mrs. J. C., Tonganoxie, Leavenworth County, Kansas, U.S.A.
Hustler, Mrs. Benjamin, Wesley P.O., Dufferin County, Ontario, Canada. *Two copies.*

Hustler, John Wetherald, Esq., Lisgar P.O., Peel County, Ontario, Canada. *Two copies.*
Jefferys, Mrs., Castle Green, Kendal.
Jefferys, The Misses, Upperthorpe, Darlington.
Jenkins, H. Stanley, Esq., M.D., Sianfu, Shensi, North China.
Jesper, Alfred, Esq., 19, Micklegate, York.
Jesper, Miss Eleanor, 19, Micklegate, York.
Jesper, Joseph M., Esq., 42, Crocketts Road, Handsworth, Birmingham. *Two copies.*
Jesper, William A., Esq., Claremont, Marygate, York.
Johnson, Henry, Esq., 345, Magee Avenue, Rochester, N.Y., U.S.A.
Johnson, Mrs. H. D., 795, Roosevelt Avenue, Detroit, Michigan, U.S.A.
Johnson, Robt., Esq., 109, Wellmeadow Road, Catford, London, S.E.
Johnson, William, Esq., J.P., Castle Rawe, Toowong, Brisbane, Queensland.
Johnson, W. Samuel, Esq., Municipal Markets, Brisbane, Queensland. *Two copies.*

Kitching, Henry, Esq., J.P., The Grange, Great Ayton. *In vellum.*
Knight, Mrs., 7, Manchester Road, Chorlton-cum-Hardy, Manchester.

Lancashire, J. H., Esq., Deeplish Hill, Rochdale. *Two copies.*
Leach, F. Austin, Esq., Woodbury, 1, Broomfield Road, Tolworth, Surbiton, Surrey. *Two copies, one in vellum.*
Legg, A. H., Esq., Atherfield, Argyle Road, Barnet, N.
Lewis, Mrs., c/o Rev. E. T. Lewis, Grantwood, New Jersey, U.S.A.
Loveridge, Rev. S. M., Culebra, Panama, Central America.
Loveridge, Mrs. Thomas, Kilternan, Llandaff, Glamorganshire. *Five copies.*

Mason, Miss Mary, 69, Hartington Road, West Derby, Liverpool.
Mason, William, Esq., 10, Willow Grove, Beverley.
McClain, Mrs. J. W., 610, West 7th Street, Sedalia, Missouri, U.S.A. *Two copies.*
McGillivray, George, Esq., Spring Valley, Minnesota, U.S.A. *In vellum.*
McGillivray, Rev. N. H., St. John's Manse, 2nd Street, Cornwall, Ontario. Canada.
McGillivray, T. A., Esq., Whitby, Ontario, Canada. *In vellum.*
McGillivray, Mrs. Wm., Pipestone, Minnesota, U.S.A.
McMurtry, Roy F., Esq., King, Ontario, Canada.
McMurtry, W. J., Esq., Temple Building, Toronto, Canada. *In vellum.*
Millott, Mrs., 17, Leyton Avenue, Mansfield, Notts.
Morland, Mrs. H. J., Khoja, Harewood Road, Croydon.
Moss, Miss E., B.A., Edgbaston College, 198, Bristol Road, Birmingham.
Munn, W. W., Esq., 800, Yonge Street, Toronto, Canada. *In vellum.*

Naughton, Mrs., Ellesmere School, Harrogate. *Two copies, one in vellum.*
Newton, Mrs., Lealholm, Great Ayton.
Nightingale, John, Esq., 22, Galloway Road, Waterloo, Liverpool.

Oldroyd, Lady, Hyrstlands, Dewsbury.

Park, Mrs. Hunton, St. Margarets', Beverley.
Pearson, Professor Karl, M.A., F.R.S., University College, London. *In vellum.*
Pease, Sir A. E., Bart., Pinchinthorpe House, Guisborough, Yorkshire.
Penney, Norman, Esq., F.S.A., Devonshire House, Bishopsgate, London, E.C.
Pickard, Miss Eliza, 3, Hatfield Street, Wakefield. *Two copies.*
Plew, Miss Ada, Hortonville, Indiana, U.S.A. *Four copies, one in vellum.*

Reckitt, Mrs. F. I., Wood Grange, Holderness Road, Hull. *Two copies, one in vellum.*
Richardson, Mrs., Park Terrace, Horsforth, Leeds.
Robson, Mrs. John, 252, Enfield Terrace, Gateshead-on-Tyne. *Three copies.*
Rotherford, Mrs., Ingledene, Fulford Road, Scarborough.
Rowntree, Allen, Esq., Westwood, Scarborough. *In vellum.*
Rowntree, Arthur, Esq., B.A., Bootham School, York.
Rowntree, John Watson, Esq., J.P., The Rowans, Scarborough.
Rowntree, Mrs. J. Stephen, Leadhall Grange, Harrogate. *In vellum.*

Salthouse, F., Esq., 22, Galloway Road, Waterloo, Liverpool.
Sedgwick, Mrs. T. T., Spicegill, Dent.
Senior, Mrs., Iquique, Peru, South America.
Shackleton, Wm., Esq., Pudsey, Leeds. *In vellum.*
Simpson, Alfred, Esq., J.P., Dunham Woods, Altrincham. *In vellum.*
Simpson, Mrs. Hannah, Coalbrookdale, R S.O. Shropshire. *Two copies.*
Simpson, Mrs. Joseph, Sunnyside, Mayfield, Staffordshire. *Three copies, one in vellum.*
Smeal, Mrs. Thomas, Meadside, Kilbarchan, Renfrewshire. *In vellum.*
Sparks, Mrs. T. R., 15, Lomond Avenue, Fairview, Dublin.
Starr, Charles, Esq., Newmarket, Ontario, Canada. *Two copies.*
Steventon, S. R., Esq., 4, New Parks Crescent, Scarborough.

Taylor, Mrs. A. H., 7, The Mount, Malton.
Taylor, Mrs. Herbert, Holly House, Sibford Ferris, Oxon.
Taylor, Mrs. J. W., c/o J. A. Thistlethwaite, Esq., 17, St. John's Terrace, Middlesbrough.
Taylor, Stephenson, Esq., The Oaks, Chew Stoke, near Bristol. *Three copies.*

Tennant, Christopher, Esq., Fairfield House, Fairfield Road, Chesterfield. *Two copies.*

Tennant, Henry, Esq. (the late), Holgate Hill House, York. *Ten copies, four in vellum.*

Tennant, Jas. T., Esq., North Street, Abergavenny, Mon.

Tennant, Wm. S., Esq., 40, Belgrave Street, Liscard, Cheshire. *Two copies.*

Thistlethwaite, Alfred, Esq., R.R. No. 1, Tonganoxie, Leavenworth County, Kansas, U.S.A.

Thistlethwaite, Allotes, Esq., Washington, Louisiana, U.S.A.

Thistlethwaite, Anthony, Esq., Stanley Street, Stanley Road, Wakefield. *In vellum.*

Thistlethwaite, Anthony M., Esq., 1423, Charlotte Street, Kansas City, Mo. U.S.A. *In vellum.*

Thistlethwaite, A. H., Esq, Tauranga, New Zealand.

Thistlethwaite, Arthur S., Esq., 45, Rossett Road, Blundellsands, Liverpool.

Thistlethwaite, Arthur W., Esq., Tonganoxie, Kansas, U.S.A.

Thistlethwaite, Miss Beatrice, 45, Rossett Road, Blundellsands, Liverpool.

Thistlethwaite, Bertie F., Esq., Laurel Bank, Nantwich. *In vellum.*

Thistlethwaite, Carl Bertie, Esq., Manager,   Coal Mines, South Africa.

Thistlethwaite, Charles, Esq., Sheridan, Indiana, U.S.A. *Two copies.*

Thistlethwaite, Chas. J., Esq., Fairport, N.Y., U.S.A. *Two copies, one in vellum.*

Thistlethwaite, Rev. Clifton W., M.A., Hampton Bishop, Hereford. *Two copies, one in vellum.*

Thistlethwaite, Cyrus D., Esq., Hortonville, Indiana, U.S.A.

Thistlethwaite, Duane, Esq., Sheridan, Indiana, U.S.A.

Thistlethwaite, Edward, Esq., Vice-President, Farmers' National Bank, Sheridan, Indiana, U.S.A.

Thistlethwaite, Frank H., Esq., 17, St. John's Terrace, Middlesbrough.

Thistlethwaite, George, Esq., Sheridan, Indiana, U.S.A.

Thistlethwaite, G. F., Esq., 45, Rossett Road, Blundellsands, Liverpool.

Thistlethwaite, George R., Esq., Linton House, Fairweather Green, Bradford. *Two copies.*

Thistlethwaite, Prof. Glenn F., Earlham College, Earlham, Indiana, U.S.A.

Thistlethwaite, Guy Wilfrid, Esq., 45, Rossett Road, Blundellsands, Liverpool.

Thistlethwaite, Harris, Esq., Grantham, Queensland, Australia. *Three copies, one in vellum.*

Thistlethwaite, Miss Helen, Gribdale Cottage, Great Ayton. *In vellum.*

Thistlethwaite, Irvin, Esq., 610, West 7th Street, Sedalia, Missouri, U.S.A.

Thistlethwaite, Jesse, Esq., Washington, Louisiana, U.S.A.

Thistlethwaite, J. Altham, Esq., Aysgarth House, Eccleshill, Bradford. *Two copies, one in vellum.*

Thistlethwaite, J. Anthony, Esq., 17, St. John's Terrace, Middlesbrough. *In vellum.*

Thistlethwaite, J. Barlow, Esq., B.A., Hunter's Close, Dean Row, Wilmslow, Cheshire.

Thistlethwaite, J. D., Esq., Manager, Brisbane Dredging and Engineering Works, Queensland.

Thistlethwaite, J. Marvin, Esq., Sheridan, Indiana, U.S.A.

Thistlethwaite, John R., Esq., Washington, Louisiana, U.S.A.

Thistlethwaite, Joseph, Esq., 21, Putney Road, Handsworth, Birmingham.

Thistlethwaite, J. Leayat, Esq., East Rochester. N.Y., U.S.A., *Two copies.*

Thistlethwaite, Miss Laura, Laurel Bank, Nantwich. *In vellum.*

Thistlethwaite, Miss L. M., Eagle House, Great Ayton. *Two copies.*

Thistlethwaite, Mark, Esq., Governor's Office, Indianapolis, Indiana, U.S.A. *In vellum.*

Thistlethwaite, Miss Mary, Hawes, Wensleydale.

Thistlethwaite, Miss Mary, Macedon, Wayne County, N.Y., U.S.A. *In vellum.*

Thistlethwaite, Maurice, Esq., Kirklin, Hamilton County, Indiana, U.S.A.

Thistlethwaite, Oscar, Esq., Sheridan, Indiana, U.S.A. *In vellum.*

Thistlethwaite, R. H., Esq., Stanley Street, Stanley Road, Wakefield.

Thistlethwaite, Miss Ruby, 45, Rossett Road, Blundellsands, Liverpool.

Thistlethwaite, T. V. C., Esq., Waterloo House, Nantwich, Cheshire. *Four copies.*

Thistlethwaite, T. William, Esq., 3021, Avenue H., Council Bluffs, Iowa, U.S.A.

Thistlethwaite, William, Esq., Newton-in-Bowland, Clitheroe.

Thistlethwaite, William, Esq., Stanley Street, Stanley Road, Wakefield. *Four copies, one in vellum.*

Thistlethwaite, William H., Esq., Gribdale Cottage, Great Ayton. *In vellum.*

Thistlethwaite, William J., Esq., 91, City National Bank, Utica, N.Y., U.S.A. *Two copies, one in vellum.*

Thistlethwaite, William P., Esq., Macedon, Wayne County, N.Y., U.S.A. *Two copies.*

Thompson, Miss Alice, Meadside, Kilbarchan, Renfrewshire, N.B.

Thompson, Charles, Esq., Provision Merchant, Gainsborough.

Thompson, Miss Jane, Meadside, Kilbarchan, Renfrewshire.

Thompson, Richard, Esq., Dringcote, The Mount, York.

Thompson, Miss Sophia, 6, Morton Terrace, Gainsborough.

Thompson, Miss Sophia, Meadside, Kilbarchan, Renfrewshire.

Thompson, Wilson, Esq., Meadside, Kilbarchan, Renfrewshire.

Timmons, Mrs. John, Sheridan, Hamilton County, Indiana.

Walbridge, P. H., Esq., Kapowsin, Washington State, U.S.A.

Wallace, Mrs. Hugh, 56, Northumberland Road, Dublin.

Wallace, H. Ellerslie, Esq., 4, Terenure Park, Dublin.

Wallis, Mrs. Edward, Springfield, Scarborough. *Two copies.*

Wallis, Mrs. H., Crow Hill, Mansfield.

Wallis, W. Clarkson, Esq., Springfield, Withdean, Brighton.

Walton, Miss Ethel, 68, Bootham, York.

Walton, Herbert, Esq., 155, Wakefield Road, Dalton, Huddersfield.

Walton, Miss Hilda, Somerville College, Oxford.

Walton, Miss Isabella, 3, High Tenters Street, Bishop Auckland. *In vellum.*

Walton, J. W., Esq., 3, High Tenters Street, Bishop Auckland. *In vellum.*

Walton, Miss Mabel, Friedensthal, Scalby, Yorkshire.

Walton, Mrs. Thomas, 24, West End Avenue, Harrogate.

Watson, Mrs. Ernest, Lahi, Seoni Malwa, India, C.P.

Webster, Alfred, Esq., 28, Rock Mount, Whalley Road, Altham, near Accrington, Lancashire.

Webster, C. Edward, Esq., Poynton, Halifax.

Webster, G. Arnold, Esq., Heath Villas, Halifax. *Two copies.*

Webster, G. E., Esq., Grocer and Provision Merchant, Wakefield.

West, Miss Anne, 62, Broughton Road, Banbury, Oxon. *Two copies.*

Wetherald, Miss Agnes, Chantler, Welland County, Ontario, Canada. *In vellum.*

Wetherald, Charles, Esq., 369, 2nd Street, Oakland, Cal., U.S.A. *In vellum.*

Wetherald, Edward, La Plata, Maryland, U.S.A. *Two copies.*

Wetherald, Miss Jane, 514, 8th Street, Edmonton, Alberta, Canada.

Wetherald, J. Cobban, Esq., Georgetown, Ontario, Canada. *Two copies.*

Wetherald, Samuel J., Esq., Chantler, Welland County, Ontario. *Six copies.*

Wetherald, Thomas, Esq., Bryantown, Charles County, Maryland, U.S.A.

Williams, Mrs., 123-125, City Road, Liverpool, N.

Williams, Mrs., c/o Ed. Thistlethwaite, Esq., Sheridan, Indiana, U.S.A.

Wood, Albert, Esq., Park View, Bishop Auckland.

Yeardley, Mrs., 9, Wellington Park, Clifton, Bristol.